Renegade Regionalists

Renegade Regionalists

---

*The Modern Independence of
Grant Wood, Thomas Hart Benton,
and John Steuart Curry*

James M. Dennis

The University of Wisconsin Press

The University of Wisconsin Press
1930 Monroe Street, 3rd floor
Madison, Wisconsin 53711-2059
uwpress.wisc.edu

3 Henrietta Street
London WC2E 8LU, England
eurospanbookstore.com

4   6   8   7   5

Library of Congress Cataloging-in-Publication Data
Dennis, James M.
Renegade regionalists: the modern independence of Grant Wood,
Thomas Hart Benton, and John Steuart Curry / James Dennis.
296 pp.   cm.
Includes bibliographical references and index.
ISBN 0-299-15580-3 (cloth: alk. paper).
ISBN 0-299-15584-6 (pbk.: alk. paper)
1. Regionalism in art—United States.   2. Modernism (Art)—United States.
3. Art, American.   4. Art, Modern—20th century—United States.
5. Wood, Grant, 1891–1942—Criticism and interpretation.
6. Benton, Thomas Hart, 1889–1975—Criticism and interpretation.
7. Curry, John Steuart, 1897–1946—Criticism and interpretation.
I. Title.
N6512.5.M63D47   1998
709'.2'273—DC21   97-9184

ISBN-13: 978-0-299-15584-1 (pbk.: alk. paper)

With fond memories of
William Richard Dennis and Ellen Jane Dennis

Contents

Illustrations

Preface

Regionalism, as associated with Grant Wood, Thomas Hart Benton, and John Steuart Curry, had suffered critical abuse followed by extensive neglect when I began to explore it. The personal visions, intentions, and accomplishments of its artists had enjoyed little in the way of accurate evaluation. Misconceptions about them, initiated by their own rhetoric, were magnified by biased and repetitious criticism. In the early seventies, a handful of art historians, confronted with fragmented, primarily journalistic, accounts replete with ill-founded generalizations, had much to sift through and sort out, but little scholarly literature to revise. Their efforts to improve this situation set a precedent for properly researched, interpretive publications, and as a result opened Regionalism to ongoing revisionist study.

In 1973 Matthew Baigell published his concise monograph on Thomas Hart Benton and a year later his book-length essay, *American Scene Painting*. Despite these first steps, dubious criticism perpetuated many clichés. That these endured was no fault of two monographs on Grant Wood. In the first, appearing in late 1975 and revised twelve years later, I emphasized the mythic agrarian content of his culturally determined imagery. In the second, a catalogue for her retrospective exhibition of 1983–1984, Wanda Corn concentrated on the immediate regional traditions reflected in Wood's art and career. Meanwhile, Karal Ann Marling, in a singular 1981 article, probed the popular, movie-inspired mindset of Benton's 1927/28 painting *Boomtown*. In her book, *Wall to Wall America,* Marling traced the interrelationships of local legends in New Deal Post Office murals. M. Sue Kendall then published *Rethinking Regionalism: John Steuart Curry and the Kansas Mural Controversy,* a revealing look into the artist's major mural project. Curry's progressive political involvement is the subject of an essay Kendall has contributed to a catalogue for a Curry exhibition opening in the spring of 1998 at the Elvehjem Museum of Art in Madison, Wisconsin.

In the late eighties, Benton continued to attract more published attention than the other two of Regionalism's "triumvirate." Marling produced

Preface

a biographical account of his drawings and Henry Adams accompanied a major retrospective exhibition (1989–1990) with a generously illustrated chronicle of Benton's career. In addition to spirited accounts of the artist, family members, friends, associates, patrons, and enemies, Adams assumed a healthy skepticism about the profusion of contentious polemic that boosted Regionalism's Midwest alliance. At the same time, Erica Doss approached Benton along an American Studies front in her *Benton, Pollock, and the Politics of Modernism: From Regionalism to Abstract Expressionism.* In it, she aligns Regionalism with Benton's "New Deal-linked" murals while defining his politics as a "producer" republicanism inherited from his great-uncle, Senator Thomas Hart Benton.

An historicist approach aims to understand how a work of art is, in effect, a special event in a culture's history. The plurality of art created by Wood, Curry, and Benton was not strictly regional, was certainly not provincial, and in fact was quite capable of modernist expression. Face to face with their major works, a strict designation of "Regionalism" becomes a label as questionable as "Impressionism," "Fauvism," or "Cubism."

In getting this book to the finish line I have had the support of helpful family, friends, and colleagues. For their tolerant reading of early drafts, I wish to thank Jackie Captain, David B. Dennis, and Franklin M. Ludden. For their useful evaluations of later versions I am indebted to Henry Adams, Erika Doss, and David Sokol. I owe a large debt of gratitude to Barbara Melosh for her highly constructive critique of the penultimate draft. To Karal Ann Marling a nod of good will for intensifying my incentive and determination to round the far turn. I am grateful to Sam Diman and Director Allen Fitchen of the University of Wisconsin Press for their loyal support and to Jane Barry for her alert copy editing. Thanks to John M. Dennis for helping me come up with an acute title. Many of the photographs, a key element of a book like this, originated through the photo and slide division of the University of Wisconsin Art History Department under the supervision of Tom Gombar and his able graduate assistant Paul Bacon. I thank them both. I am also indebted to our office staff and to the staff of the Kohler Art Library. The University of Wisconsin Graduate School Research Committee awarded two summer research grants to this project.

Renegade Regionalists

Introduction

Plurality in interpretation is a sign of strength. One should not desire to deprive the world of its disquieting and enigmatical nature.
—Friedrich Nietzsche, *The Will to Power* (Aphorism 600)

In Ad Reinhardt's well-known cartoon of 1946, entitled "HOW TO LOOK AT MODERN ART IN AMERICA," a tree of contemporary art leans to the right from its topmost branches of "pure (abstract) 'paintings'" to its lowest branch of "pure (illustrative) 'pictures,'" pulled down by a weighty cluster of black forms labeled "nudes," "still lifes," "landscapes," and, of all things, "regionalism" (Fig. 1). The thirty leaves of the branch include the names Bishop, Soyer, Sloan, Guston, Gropper, and Kuniyoshi. Below, in a cornfield, guarded by a scarecrow labeled Woolf, fourteen more artists' names appear, including Cadmus, Marsh, and, of course, Wood, Benton, and Curry. In front of the field, signposts indicate the corporate patronage of what Reinhardt, the modernist painter, critic, and theorist, considered corny, undemanding art: *Fortune, Life,* International Business Machines, Pepsi-Cola, Lucky Strike, *Encyclopedia Britannica,* and Associated American Artists. That the three artists he most loved to hate were popular and relatively well supported goes without saying, but the implication that they were totally lacking in independent, modernist qualifications calls for investigation.

Though persistently brandishing their banner of Regionalism, Wood, Benton, and Curry created a generous number of major works whose subject matter and meaning do not bear any unifying regional insignia. Upon close surveillance the battle-worn standard of their tenuous movement diminishes as a stylistic rallying point. Despite their antimodernist rhetoric, they could not escape the inspiration and influence of the assumed enemy, Modernism. They had, in fact, become open and receptive to the great modernist transformation of the teens and had independently adopted characteristics of its advanced styles of pictorial art before banding together in the thirties.

3

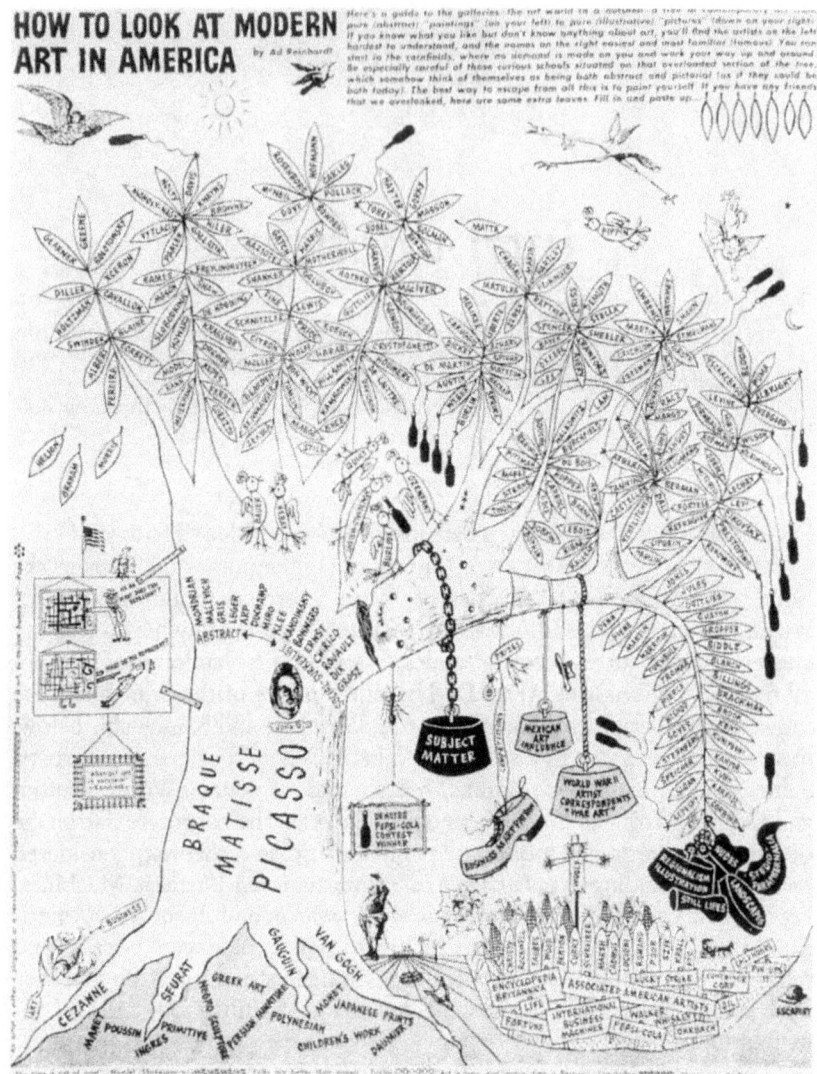

Figure 1. Ad Reinhardt. *How to Look at Modern Art in America.* Pen and ink on paper, published in *P.M.*, June 2, 1946. © 1990 Anna Reinhardt.

Born at the end of the nineteenth century and experiencing the rapid changes of the twentieth through big-city living and international travel, Wood, Benton, and Curry eluded the Victorian beliefs and restraints of their midwestern parents. Innocence as a cultural ideal, the vision of a stable, discord-free society in which one could hide from evil, a "civilized" repression of natural instincts, and total faith in progress for an industrial age, all bases of Victorianism and presumably Regionalism, do not characterize their art, which in total reads as a continuous flux of irregular sensations and recollections. Wood and Benton poked fun at Victorians and caricatured them, while Curry, the sharpest social critic of the three, used images of female innocence to protest against evils of mass male behavior. Although arguably conservative in technique and style, he avoided genteel subject matter in favor of sublimely emotional moments of action capable of delivering moral messages without the didactic pretensions of academic history painting.

All three artists, as panel painters, muralists, and printmakers, shared the democratic urge within Modernism to eliminate the traditional divisions between elite and popular subject matter, the high and the low. They engaged in a form of aesthetic populism called Regionalism. At the same time they were opposed to the closed, deterministic world of nineteenth-century positivism and embraced change and chance, a world of discovery where pluralism counteracted categorization. This was invariably lost on art critics who refused in a modern sense to be open-minded. They insisted on categorizing the three according to what they expected them to produce within a narrowly defined movement. They thereby failed to evaluate them for what they individually pursued up and down the ladder of style and subject matter. By maintaining their independence, the "triumvirate" of Regionalism often proved themselves modernists, in line with the definition of *modern* offered by the culturally grounded sociologist Daniel Bell: "What defines the modern is a sense of openness to change, of detachment from place and time, of social and geographical mobility, and a readiness, if not eagerness, to welcome the new, even at the expense of tradition and the past."[1] To demonstrate this certification through a variety of examples is a primary purpose of this book.

Modernism comprises four elements. While they do not materialize in the same way in all three artists, these are the qualities to look for in the complex intersections of their work during the decade or so with which we are concerned: formal order and aesthetic independence, mimetic reflections of social modernization, critical negations of modernization, and the use of myth as a device for ordering the furor of American history.

In keeping with the first element, Malcolm Bradbury and John Fletcher observe that modernists strive for "that making of pattern and wholeness which makes art into an order standing outside and beyond the human muddle, a transcendent object, a luminous whole."[2] They could have chosen any number of mature works by Wood or Benton from the early to mid-thirties to illustrate this observation. Each in his own way employed qualities of the "machine aesthetic" in an effort to abstract the mythic eternal from fleeting sensations of rural or urban activities.

To Bell this process provided the only cultural context for American modernists: "The one place where there was a modernist culture in the United States was in form and this was the machine aesthetic. . . . The machine aesthetic excluded the self and the person; it was abstract and functional and it was fused with industrial design."[3] In Benton's case, one might argue that the patterned energies of his most vital paintings are primarily urban in origin rather than rural. Even those depicting rural subject matter have the ring of city-centered modernization. They also prove that reality cannot be rendered into a work of art without being mediated, and both Benton and Wood mediated modern reality through the mechanics of modernist composition.

Negation, according to Octavio Paz, is essential to modernism: "Modern art is modern because it is critical." Wood negated the city and the technological advance associated with the city while ironically developing a sophisticated mode of mechanical design for farmland fantasies that appealed to a cosmopolitan patronage in need of momentary escape from New York, Chicago, or Los Angeles. Curry, on the other hand, provided no escape, aiming protest paintings at the fundamentalist religion, racism, and mechanized war inherited from the nineteenth century. In these confrontations he further distinguished himself from Wood in his willingness to abandon myth for immediate reality. Upon returning from three "bohemian" ventures in Paris during the twenties, the Iowan resorted to the primary myth of the United States, agrarianism, through which he lent shape and symbolic significance to the complexities and contradictions of the American experience. The control of the experience moved from the spectator to the artist, wrote Bell, who sees overwhelming the viewer as the intention of Modernism—for example, by manipulations of perspective that eclipse distance. This was a common component of works by the three artists in question.[4]

The critical reception (too often rejection) of the works of Wood, Benton, and Curry is the concern of Part I, whose four chapters examine a comprehensive selection of writings by professional critics, art historians, gallery owners, and museum curators in chronological order. As Chapters 1 and 2 reveal, their various motivations and purposes tend toward an agreement about what the art should depict and how it should do it, regardless of the particular intentions and achievements of the three artists involved. Paradoxically, a central cause of this conflict was the misleading rhetoric of the Regionalist movement itself, originating primarily from Wood and Benton. It helped generate demand for a "direct realism" in stereotyped detail, focused especially on life on a midwestern farm. This, in theory, would ban any emphasis on abstract form or personal fantasies that might offend an urban art market yearning for anecdotal scenes of a rapidly disappearing way of life. Initially intensified by the disheartening years of the Great Depression and the down-home sentiments accompanying World War II, the conservatively biased reception of the Regionalists reappeared, as if by conditioned response, during the Reagan-Bush eighties in reaction to retrospective exhibitions of Wood and Benton. Sacrosanct rural properties belonging to the fleeting American past still had to be posted against the trespasses of such fantastic abstractions as Wood's "jello-mold" trees or Benton's "comic-strip" figures.

Accusations of nationalism, another major category of critical concern and the focus of Chapter 3, were aimed at the "triumvirate" from the beginning of their group identity as Regionalists. Their isolationist inclinations exposed them to attacks from critics wary of "patrioteering." These came, at first, from the *Art Front* left, which accused the three of self-serving propagandistic motives. In the service of their business-centered patrons, it was alleged, the artists encouraged popular identification of free enterprise with frontier individualism in order to steer the public away from the temptations of a socialized economy. Against all charges, their main line of defense was a benign nativism. As Wood's 1935 manifesto, *Revolt Against the City,* proclaimed, a home-grown, nativist artist instinctively relied upon local subject matter and its natural forms of expression in contributing to a national art.

The credibility of this premise was compromised by the often indiscreet, sometimes ethnically prejudiced, defensiveness of Benton and his friend and promoter Thomas Craven. Their intolerant outbursts eventually encouraged accusations that Regionalism was in essence aligned with fascism. The disastrous ramifications of this charge occupy the final chapter of Part I. While the Popular Front of the mid-to-late thirties helped launch the initial insinuations, the climactic indictment came from Horst Woldemar Janson immediately after World War II. Based on flimsy comparisons of two cultures, German and American, this battering shared the flaws of much criticism: biased overgeneralization coupled with careless observation of the visual facts.

In the most aspiring and consequential works by Wood, Benton, and Curry, a modernist pluralism extends thematically from national myths to mimetic imaging of urban modernization, to critical social commentary and protest. As is discussed and evaluated in Part II, they accomplish this span through a colorful cast of characters within which female figures play prominent and often central roles. The divergence of imagery among the three distinctly different personalities far exceeds any definition imposed upon their movement by either self-promotion or stereotyped expectations resulting from it. Whether emerging from the past or the present, from the popular or primarily private, the multiplicity of their iconography may be

7

read as a discourse between individualistic expressions and cultural representations. Within a modern context, they released their feelings, their notions of how things were and should be, their fears and frustrations.

Wood, Benton, and Curry were entirely capable of hitting upon visual ideas of immediate social-political relevance and, in at least one instance, inadvertently scored with a universal American icon. Beginning with *American Gothic,* Wood's depictions of robust farm wives and country schoolteachers were reinforced by a matriarchal guardian image. It was used in five paintings of satiric social commentary that earned the approval of Gertrude Stein. They vary in theme from revolt against the city to ridicule of reactionary Victorianism to protest against superpatriotism.

Negation of modern developments may also be an aspect of Benton's energetic mimicking of industrialization. While men and their machines maintain command of the compositions, in keeping with his self-conscious masculinity and celebration of production, a counterforce of sensuality evokes itself through obsessive eruptions of black smoke and the female body. As fully exposed in his mural panels, *City Activities,* for the New School of Social Research in 1930–31, the latter assumed a prurient form comparable with that exploited by the movie and advertising industries in the guise of a liberating "new morality."

In pronounced contrast, Curry's female figures indicate a growing sensitivity to social conflict, as his early mythic images of heroic frontier motherhood are transformed into updated girl-woman types. Through these innocents he warned against dangers to justice and individual freedom, and in the end against entry into war. Thus, with his ultimately tendentious woman imagery, the third man of midwestern Regionalism moved outside the restrictive boundaries of the "rural idyll" with which Regionalism was and still is commonly identified.

Rhetorical identification of Regionalism as antimodern realism did not prevent its three leading artists from permitting figures and objects to flatten out as relatively abstract shapes on the surfaces of their paintings, the most self-defining factor of pictorial modernism in the opinion of Clement Greenberg. The opening chapter of Part III, focusing on Grant Wood, deals with their investment in abstraction. Wood's interest in modern means of composition originated in the Arts and Crafts emphasis on ornamental patterning. He had become familiar with it in his late teens through a correspondence course in Gustav Stickley's *Craftsman* magazine. By the time he painted *American Gothic* and *Stone City* in 1930, he had abandoned his "impressionistic" style through an assortment of increasingly decorative floral still lifes and landscape studies. At approximately the same time, Benton wrote a series of *Arts* magazine articles titled "Mechanics of Form Organization in Painting." They indicate that his interest in form for form's sake did not cease with his earlier nonfigural brand of Synchromism, a style of color Cubism that he learned in New York before World War I from one of its originators, Stanton Macdonald-Wright. Curry's tendencies toward abstraction, weaker than those of his two colleagues, found expression primarily in the triadic harmonies of the widely marketed Maratta Color System, which he originally applied to his first highly acclaimed painting, *Baptism in Kansas,* in 1928.

American painters found their own source of Modernism in New York, an alternative to the Cézanne-Cubist-Futurist or the Fauves-Matisse "School of Paris." Arthur Wesley Dow's manual *Composition: A Series of Exercises in Art Structure for the Use of Students and Teachers,* first published in 1899, dominated American art education for decades. Not surprising, Japanese *Ukiyo-e* paintings and woodcut prints inspired Dow's understanding of pictorial design as "visual music," a metaphor he gained from Ernest Fenollosa, curator of the Japanese collections at the Boston Museum of Fine Arts. As a junior-high art instructor in Cedar Rapids, Wood was undoubtedly aware of the manual and probably taught from it. Although less explicitly than paintings by Georgia O'Keeffe and Arthur Dove, certain of the more progressive landscapes predating Wood's first trip to Paris in 1921 already show indications of Dow's design principles.

Within close range of Dow's *Composition,* and also counter to increasingly formalized Cubist-Futurist styles, were concepts of "pictorial seeing," as described in 1927 by Leo Stein. Stein's *A-B-C of Aesthetics* may further aid us in appreciating the major changes that occurred in such works as Wood's small but highly significant *Black Barn* of the same year. Stein's preference for "rhythmically related intervals" corresponds to a "curve sense" taught by Wood's only design teacher, Ernest Batchelder, and also coincides with Art Deco adaptations of aerodynamics (witness the streamlined contours of Wood's fantasy farmscapes of the early thirties). Thus, confronting and defeating the inertia of strictly descriptive realism, Wood came closer to the Stieglitz circle of first-generation American modernists than a confirmed antimodernist Regionalist would have considered.

The constant diversification of subject matter in modernist painting, as propelled by increasingly individualistic expression, was accompanied by fluctuating levels of abstraction. These determined the status of the human figure and affected the recognition of its setting and locale. In the case of Wood, Benton, and Curry, in spite of their fondness for distant horizons suggestive of the trans-Mississippi plains, figures and settings in many of their most provocative and profound paintings are not identifiable as belonging to a specific locale. In search of universal meanings, they could easily drift away from the simplistic claims of Regionalism. It is, in fact, symptomatic of the flux and change in Modernism that the claims of one set of artists might well appear to be more consistently practiced in the works of a contemporaneous set of artists presumably opposed to those claims.

As Chapters 9, 10, and 11 demonstrate, such a paradox becomes evident when one contrasts object-oriented, nonfigurative works by three leading East Coast abstract-realists to prominent examples by the three midwesterners. Symbiotically related to the objectivist theories of their friend, the poet William Carlos Williams, Charles Demuth's Lancaster, Pennsylvania, mill and warehouse compositions, Charles Sheeler's photo-paintings of Bucks County interiors and the River Rouge Ford Motor factory, and Marsden Hartley's interpretations of his native Maine may be seen to be more persistently attached to their respective locales than are the paintings of the three celebrated Regionalists to theirs. Wood's principle of "the Imagination Isles" allowed for internal wanderings. Williams, on the other hand, exhorted his fellow modernists to stay put and fix their eyes on the solid things of external reality—the "true American way," he might say.

PART I

Conflicts of Reception

To demand of the artist that he should have the point of view of the spectator (of the critic) is equivalent to asking him to impoverish his creative power.

Friedrich Nietzsche, *The Will to Power*
(The Principles of a New Valuation, no. 811)

1

"Direct Realism" Versus Modern Abstractions

Prominent critics, all of them by necessity urban in their trade, associated Regionalism with the rural Midwest of Grant Wood, Thomas Hart Benton, and John Steuart Curry—that is, the area just beyond the Mississippi River, bounded by Iowa, Missouri, and eastern Kansas. Since a city, no matter how enormous, was not considered a region, urban localists (such as Edward Hopper, Reginald Marsh, Isabel Bishop, and the Soyer brothers) could never qualify. By and large, neither did painters loyal to regions other than that of "the triumvirate." The southern regionalists Robert Gwathmey, John McCrady, Peter Hurd, and Alexander Hogue were relegated to the margins of capital-letter Regionalism, if allowed in at all. The New England painters Stephen Etnier of Maine and Lauren Ford of Connecticut, and even such painters of the near Midwest as Clarence Carter of southern Ohio, failed to be included. Wood, Benton, and Curry came to be ranked as the uncontested national champions of Regionalism basically because they coincidently shared in setting a precedent during the crucial two-year period (from the fall of 1928 to the end of 1930) when the term "American Scene" gained its official status.

Curry led the way when he quite spontaneously painted *Baptism in Kansas* (see Fig. 92) in August 1928 and sent it to the Corcoran Gallery in Washington, D.C., where it was immediately exhibited. *New York Times* critic Edward Alden Jewell praised it to high heaven, and Mrs. Gertrude Vanderbilt Whitney subsidized the Connecticut-based painter for the next two years before buying the painting for the brand-new Whitney Museum.[1] Under this patronage, Curry painted *Tornado Over Kansas* (see Fig. 80), whose glamorized, muscle-bound farmer faces an approaching tornado while he and his beautiful wife hurry their family of four, plus the cat, the dog, and an armful of puppies, into the cyclone cellar. Painted and unveiled just before the stock market crash at the end of October 1929, its melodramatic sublimity on the distant plains of Kansas provided an exciting distraction from the financial crisis. Totally dependent on impersonal agencies to see them through, city dwellers were understandably attracted to the romance of independence, to the sight of a young, self-reliant frontier family fending for itself in a sudden confrontation with nature. Perhaps more consistently than any other narrative painting by the Regionalists, this picture of rural heroics, though resented in Kansas as a poor advertisement for the state, retained its appeal to the expanding urban audience of the Depression from the moment it was exhibited and reproduced. It first appeared in the rotogravure section of the *Herald Tribune* in 1931 and could easily be associated with the opening episode of the 1939 movie *The Wizard of Oz*.

The Wall Street failure also coincided with Benton's breakthrough as an all-American artist. In October and November 1929, the Delphic Galleries on 57th Street exhibited 109 of his most recent works, primarily watercolors and drawings. Typical of much of Benton's work, these were not based on life in his old home state, but derived from a 1928 swing through the deep South, from Appalachia to Texas. Rave reviews by big-name critics like Lloyd Goodrich promptly hit upon the attraction these pictures had for the hard-pressed. Like Curry's initial successes, they showed the rough but rugged independence of life in the hills and hollers, or out in the open spaces. Moreover, caricatured into bent and syncopated forms, the cartoony images of working-poor folks, black or white, seemed eager to mime holy rolling, moonshining, liftin' bales of cotton, or herding cattle in their picturesque settings. Such carefree fantasies of a stereotyped rural life were bound to distract traumatized urbanites from their economically generated anxieties. Thus *Boomtown* (see Fig. 136), the hit of the show, speaks to the jackpot mentality of the American Dream: strike it rich and watch the money roll in.

Grant Wood's *Stone City, Iowa* (Fig. 2) appeared a year after Curry's and Benton's perfectly timed entrances into lasting fame. Fancy in place of reality best characterizes the billowy farmscape that would have looked like paradise to either a financially strapped farmer or a destitute office worker. Its decorative forms and ornamental details guaranteed escapist appeal and widespread popularity among the uninitiated. Such unreal flourishes would be considered improper for Regionalism by critics of various political as well as aesthetic persuasions (as is discussed in Chapter 2). Exhibited at the Chicago Art Institute's annual exhibition of American art, *Stone City* was accompanied by the most referred to American painting ever, *American Gothic*. The latter's modest purchase prize (three hundred dollars) fell far short of the mysterious power its guardian couple would have over the collective imagination of the American people or the perpetual defining and redefining of Regionalism.

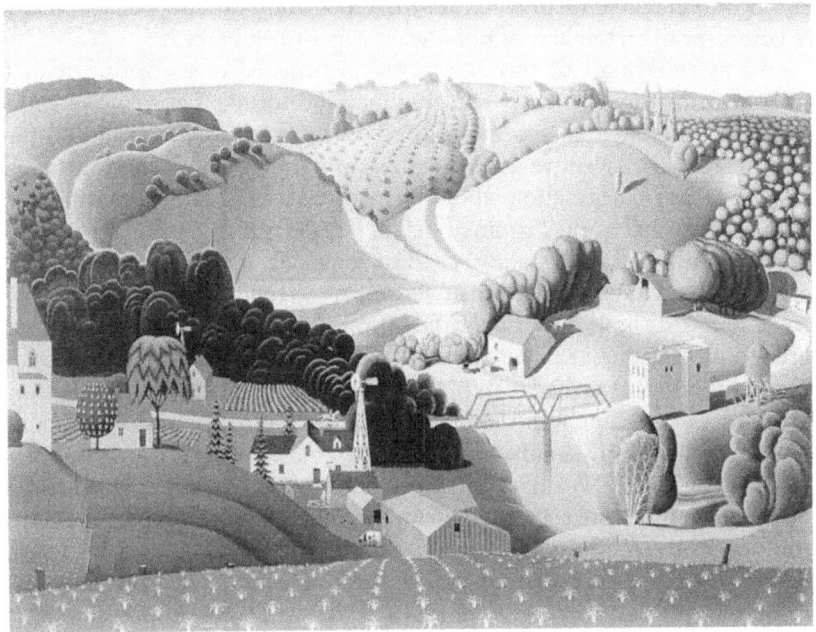

Figure 2. Grant Wood. *Stone City, Iowa.* 1930. Oil on wood panel, 30¼ × 40 in. Joslyn Art Museum, Omaha, Nebraska, 1930.35; Art Institute of Omaha Collection. © Estate of Grant Wood/Licensed by VAGA, New York, NY.

Critical reception of the works of Wood, Benton, and Curry throughout the 1930s and into the 1940s was in one respect modern. Critics generally approved of the popular subject matter in their Regionalist works, as opposed to the hierarchy of "polite" subjects associated with genteel taste by the late nineteenth century. A low genre of rural Americana, at times allegorical in its individual figures, could replace the high but dry classicism of the academy. By glossing over the harshest realities of farming, farm-life imagery provided a mythic sensation of social stability. Here was the comforting innocence of agrarianism, a pictorial release from the turmoil of industrial growth and urban congestion.

A partial compliance with this need for escape ironically caused the three artists to be categorized as conservative or even reactionary. Such blanket criticism denied their thematic and compositional pluralism, their participation in an increasingly positive extension of modernism. An art movement suggests integration, but it is at best an ambivalent merging of mutually exclusive traits, lacking tightly demarcated categories. Wood, Benton, and Curry, though never "stream of consciousness" artists, drew upon a continuous flux of experiences. No restrictive program of themes

15

or motifs dictated to them. Each confronted a world of rapid change, ready to comment upon the new, if not always eager to embrace it.

An essential part of this commentary consisted of mediating reality through individually conceived techniques and forms of abstractive composition. This essential process of Modernism aesthetically distanced the three from their respective subject matters and from each other. How much distortion and exaggeration would be involved was of central significance to their reception as the "triumvirate" of Regionalism.

The conflict of reception was and to some degree remains one of obvious paradox. On one hand, urban viewers of art, and especially those who write about it, look down upon farm folk, people working the land, as little more than quaint. Their appeal is picturesque. On the other hand, the city, in good times or bad, can become disturbing and oppressive, causing a yearning for escape into the open countryside of the middle landscape. As Lewis Mumford summed it up: "In a greater or lesser degree, every city in the Western World was stamped with the archetypal characteristics of Dickens' Coketown. Industrialism, the main creative force of the nineteenth century, produced the most degraded urban environment the world had yet seen; for even the quarters of the ruling class were befouled and overcrowded."[2] At least at a pictorial distance, the barnyard looked better to the city dweller than either the traffic-jammed thoroughfare or the back alley. Thus, in spite of disdain for "hicks," a market for anecdotal farm themes in all media intensified.

Regardless of categorical demands for factual depictions or the artists' accommodations to them, it would be deceptive to deny that at least two of the three leading Regionalists promoted composition for its own sake. To one degree or another, Wood, Benton, and Curry as well encouraged illusionistic forms to surface as distinct shapes on their canvases. As modern artists, they clearly wished their patterned energies to be noticed and appreciated as a pronounced element of their pictures, at least momentarily distinguishable from the description of figures and objects, highlights and shadows. Partitioned by abrupt contrasts of value and hue, the composition of *Engineer's Dream* (1930, Fig. 3) is characteristic of Benton's "mechanics of form organization."[3] The silhouette of a hell-bent locomotive streaming black smoke offsets the free-form shapes of the reclining figure. Bedposts, a telephone pole, and a headlight beam angle into a semi-Cubist formation worthy of Max Beckmann. The curvilinear patterns of Wood's smoothly contoured hillsides, linear plow furrows, patterned corn rows, and ornamental trees, deliberately designed and color-graded, disperse across open space from elevated foregrounds to high horizons (Fig. 4). For Curry, interlocking shapes, cut by the contours of animals, plants, earth, and sky, declare themselves as forceful by-products of his figural animation. Lights and darks, complementary colors, and surface textures activate his canvas

16

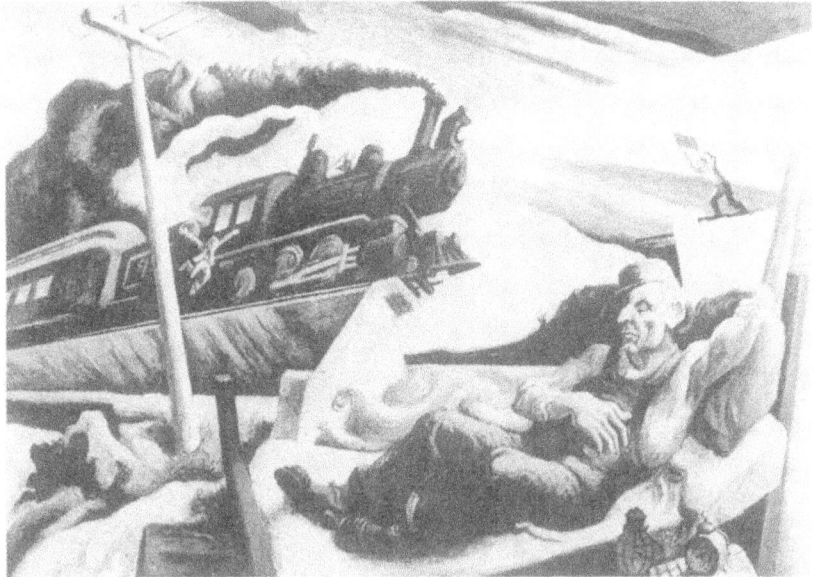

Figure 3. Thomas Hart Benton. *Engineer's Dream.* 1930. Egg tempera and oil on canvas, 30 × 42 in. The Memphis Brooks Museum of Art, Memphis, Tennessee, 75.1; Eugenia Buxton Whitnel Fund. © T. H. Benton and R. P. Benton Testamentary Trusts/Licensed by VAGA, New York, NY.

(Fig. 5). Whether observed actualities or products of the imagination, the subject matter of each artist transmutes into dynamic abstraction.

In discussing a similar trend within "the realist coalition" of New Deal muralists associated with the Section of Fine Arts, the art historians Marlene Park and Gerald Markowitz view it as a democratizing simplification:

Though in the 1930s realism was more abstract in both form and conception of life—whether heroic or homey—than it had been in the nineteenth century, its simplification of form conveyed the ideal of feeling. . . . In keeping with its treatment of form, it simplified the handling of paint, trying for a forceful but rather generalized surface. The greater technical simplicity allowed the artist to speak more directly to the audience.[4]

Emotionally perceived and deliberately composed interactions of line, shape, texture, and color, termed "significant forms" by the English art theorist Clive Bell, scarcely registered with the critics of Wood, Benton, and Curry, conservative or progressive. No matter what their stylistic convictions were, they expected the trio to be loyal to the rural dominance of their home states and maintain an unswerving dedication to reporting it in

17

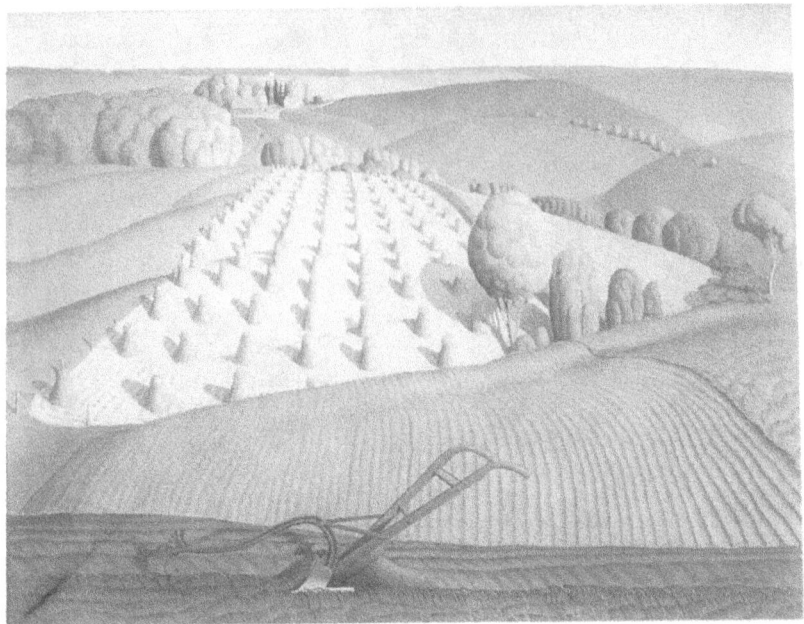

Figure 4. Grant Wood. *Fall Plowing*. 1931. Oil on canvas, 30 × 40¾ in. John Deere Art Collection, Moline, Illinois. © Estate of Grant Wood/Licensed by VAGA, New York, NY.

detail to a distraught urban public yearning for the bucolic. This unheeded demand for what critics termed "direct realism" increased through the Depression and World War II and lingered thereafter.

For an isolated moment, the senior art critic of the *New York Times*, Edward Alden Jewell, acknowledged the importance of abstract composition in Benton's paintings. Commenting on the 1935 debate carried out in print between Benton and the leading American modernist, Stuart Davis (Fig. 6), Jewell wrote that he saw the two as stylistically comparable: "Both artists, in so far as their work really counts, appear to be interested fundamentally in the esthetic side. Both men are fundamentally interested in the creation of works of art rather than in the mere exploitation of subject."[5]

While admitting that Benton had a tendency to become "too illustrational," Jewell risked a major contradiction in claiming that his work was never "representational." Anxious to prove his point, he invited readers to "take into account those powerfully organized form-and-space relationships" which, in his estimation of Benton's style, added up to "something much closer to abstraction" than to something "the Cubists" would dismiss as "illusionistic."[6]

Two and a half years later, an art historian, Wallace Spenser Baldinger,

18

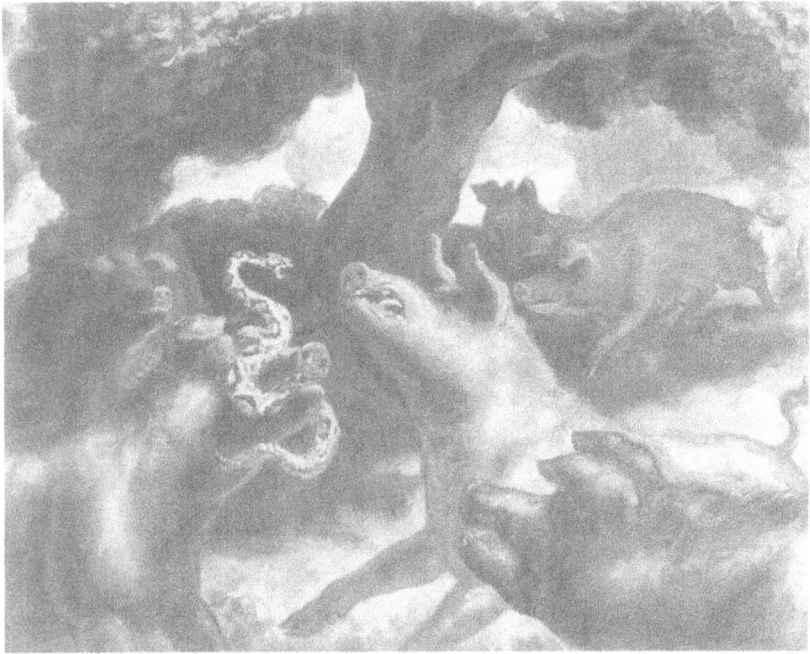

Figure 5. John Steuart Curry. *Hogs Killing a Rattlesnake*. 1930. Oil on canvas, 30⅜ × 38⁵⁄₁₆ in. Art Institute of Chicago, Chicago, Illinois, 1947.392; gift of an anonymous donor. Photograph © 1996, The Art Institute of Chicago. All rights reserved.

under the influence of the German formalist Heinrich Wölfflin, also alluded to Benton's "abstract elements" as part of a "plastic tradition" shared with Kenneth Hayes Miller. "Space, modeling, delineation, lighting, coloring, all are used abstractly." He saw this stress upon visual form in figurative paintings as "the new wind . . . towards abstraction."[7]

Despite these two modernist considerations of Benton's mature methods of composition, "direct realism" prevailed as the primary criterion for judging the works of the Regionalist "triumvirate." In the major review of the forty-third Annual Exhibition of American Painting and Sculpture at the Art Institute of Chicago, published on October 31, 1930, the *Chicago Evening Post* critic Charles J. Bulliet strove to balance his evaluation of Grant Wood, whose work he had just encountered for the first time. First he noted the prevalence of paintings inspired by Cézanne, who had replaced the Impressionist and Cubist influences that had dominated the exhibition a few years earlier. Then he turned to the "biggest kick of the show," a new work by Wood. *American Gothic* (Fig. 7) featured a "pitchfork of pattern" echoed by the farmer's overall bib and inverted by the window of the Carpenter's Gothic house. It also included an "apron with pattern" re-

19

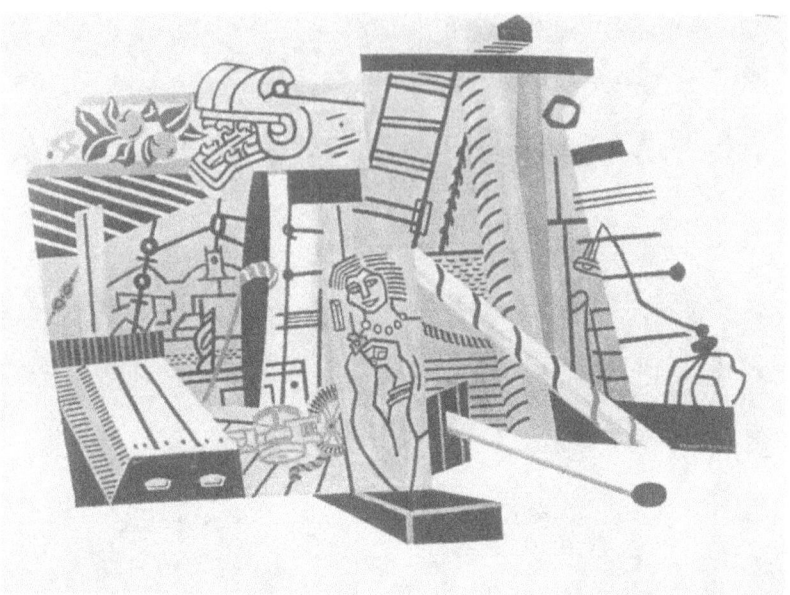

Figure 6. Stuart Davis. *American Waterfront Analogical Emblem.* 1934. Oil on canvas, 32 × 50 in. Private collection. © Estate of Stuart Davis/Licensed by VAGA, New York, NY.

peated in the curtains. While Bulliet accurately responded to Wood's visual puns, he missed the mark in calling him an American Henri "Le Douanier" Rousseau. By that he meant to imply not that Wood imitated any work by the celebrated French amateur painter, but that his composition was comparable to a Rousseau in its naively abstracted motifs. This implication of what was then called "primitivism" contradicted his praise for Wood's sophisticated ability to manipulate surface shapes in a modernist manner.

In contrast to Bulliet's efforts at formalist analysis were the strictly subject-oriented comments of Marguerite B. Williams, art critic of the *Chicago Daily News.* Williams tightened the direct-realist boundaries for appreciating and judging Wood's recent paintings by means of Early Renaissance comparisons. She praised *American Gothic*'s "meticulous kind of realism," its "uncompromising exposition of solid detail," similar to that of a van Eyck or a Ghirlandaio. Then she brought "the prim, suspicious eyed, small town couple" back home as "one of the finest records of Americana that has ever been painted."[8] Contrary to Bell's contention that criticism springs from an emotional appreciation of pure form, Williams's enthusiasm in this case tapped into the urban nostalgia for the rural and simultaneously introduced the paired figures as stereotyped expressions of a middle-American attitude, the crux of their lasting popularity.

The reception of Wood's primarily slow-paced pictures was gener-

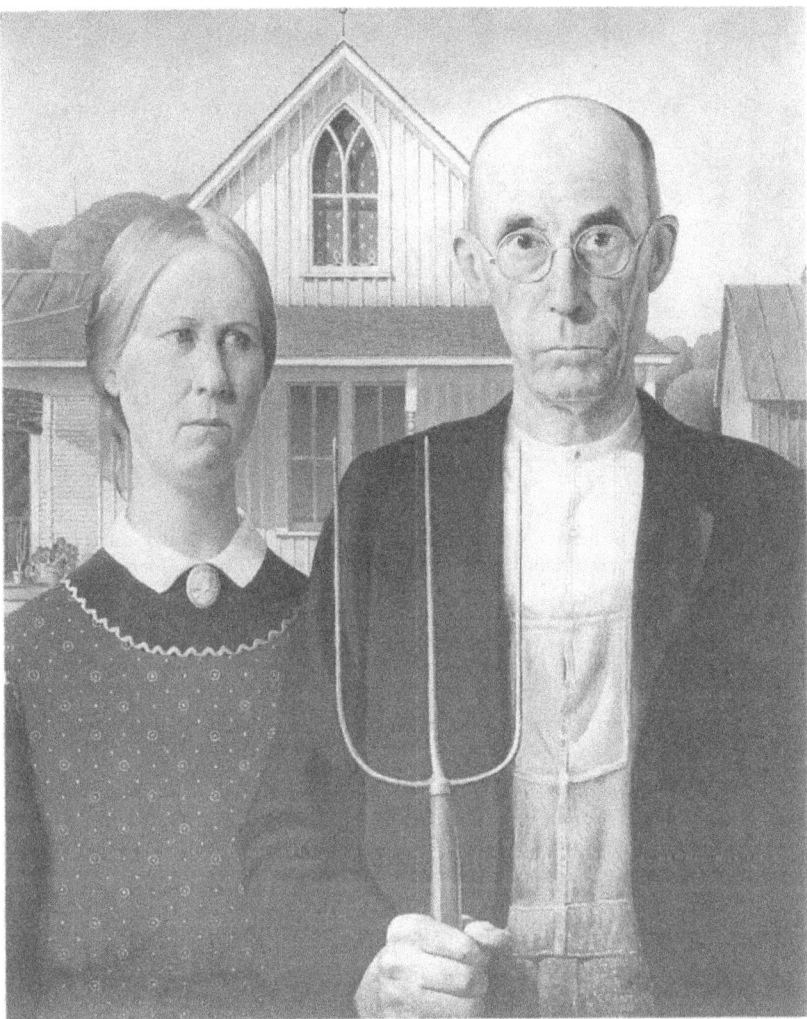

Figure 7. Grant Wood. *American Gothic.* 1930. Oil on beaver board. 29⅞ × 24⅞ in. Art Institute of Chicago, Chicago, Illinois, 1930.934; Friends of American Art Collection. Photograph © 1996, The Art Institute of Chicago. All rights reserved. © Estate of Grant Wood/Licensed by VAGA, New York, NY.

ally calm. Benton's early murals, however, provoked emotional responses to their high-powered compositions or low-brow subject matter. In mid-December 1932, Jewell reviewed Benton's recently completed walls for the Whitney Museum reading room (Fig. 8, and see Figs. 58–59), with special praise for their decorative design. He thought the room "possessed an in-

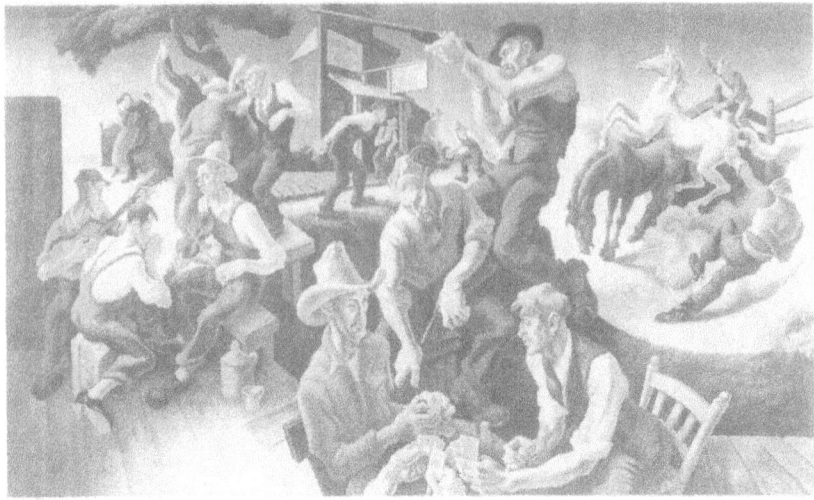

Figure 8. Thomas Hart Benton. *Arts of the West*. 1932. Egg tempera and oil on canvas mounted on panel, 8 × 13 ft. New Britain Museum of American Art, New Britain, Connecticut; Harriet Russell Stanley Fund. © T. H. Benton and R. P. Benton Testamentary Trusts/Licensed by VAGA, New York, NY.

stantly felt unity" of "dynamic bigness and boldness." He even considered the whole effect as "somehow akin" to chamber music, without specifying which composer he had in mind.[9]

Henry McBride of the *New York Sun* disagreed, demonstrating how subjective modern criticism had become. Writing five days earlier, he saw the reading room as "pure tabloid," a work that, to the horror of the refined, would please the "restless illiterates" with its "atmosphere of rebellion." Suited only for the "working classes," the murals' "caricaturish insistence upon everything that is hectic and rowdyish" allows no reference to "the rewards of virtue or the charm in ordered living." Benton's America is "all discord, temporary excitement, roughness and vulgarity."[10]

Social intolerance and class bias joined aesthetic revulsion in two other prominent reactions to the Benton murals, written at the beginning and end of the first phase of Roosevelt's New Deal reforms. In "Ex Reading Room," from mid-April 1933, Paul Rosenfeld attacked the reading room murals as shattering intrusions upon what originally had been "a fairly quiet little place." They were at fault in following a formula of "gyrating, squirming motions" generated by their immediate predecessors on the board room walls of the New School for Social Research (Figs. 9–10). Although "simpler," this new cycle still suffered from a "pseudo plasticity." Its colors did not "function" together and showed no awareness of "contrasting textures."

22

A two-pronged attack on Benton's mistreatment of his ill-chosen subject matter followed. The conflict over whether form or mimesis should be the focus of evaluating the Regionalists' paintings unfolded in a single review. Rosenfeld saw Benton's most recent murals as "but another tiresome expression of the childish lack of respect for the identity of things." As if it were not bad enough that the *Arts of Life in America,* "crude, gross and ungracious," had to be drawn from a "primitive fringe of Indians, city racketeers, burlesque-show entertainers, hill-billies and cornfield Negroes," the artist employed an "unfriendly exaggeration" that was altogether unjust to his representative types. "He has cheerfully turned his ignorant and miserable originals into objects of contempt, aversion and dread." [11] In short, no matter how marginal and repulsive the people were to this disdainful critic, their accurate description should have been Benton's primary purpose, free of caricaturing and abuse as abstract, compositional devices.

Lewis Mumford, writing two years later as the art critic for *The New Yorker,* agreed with McBride and Rosenfeld that Benton's wall paintings too often exploited a poorly chosen subject matter in a highly affected style. Though he would one day accuse capitalism of dismantling "the whole structure of urban life" for "money and profit," [12] he now cringed at Benton's mural interpretations of the laboring poor. Elevating a "seedy" side of American existence to a national symbol, [13] they were much worse in spirit than the most objectionable paintings by Charles Burchfield and Edward Hopper. Perhaps Mumford believed that the American worker should be idealized into a mid-Depression emblem of patriotic pride instead of being shown in a sweaty state of labor or engaged in off-time distractions like music making, dancing, drinking, gambling, and holiness revivals. Their "childishness" was symptomatic of Benton's attempt not to be highbrow and simply left a bad impression of America "in the fashion of the Hearsts." Mumford preferred the artist's small works, which he felt expressed "his direct sense of life" (Fig. 11). They contained "no fake hardness, no fake anti-intellectualism, no silly jingoism; they are Benton at his best." [14]

Benton himself seemed to favor the directness of his smaller works. He showed up to fifty drawings in pen and ink, sepia, watercolor, and pencil at his first one-artist exhibition west of New York. On display in the John Herron Art Institute in Indianapolis in March 1933, these were done directly from Indiana people and places in preparation for the Indiana murals commissioned for the Century of Progress Exposition, then under construction in Chicago. Of their significance to the large finished project Benton said, "If my murals come to have an enduring life, it will be wholly because their form was directed by little drawings like these made in the heat of direct experience." [15]

Thrilled by the high degree of caricature and compositional commotion that bothered the elite band of urbane critics, Benton's most enthusiastic

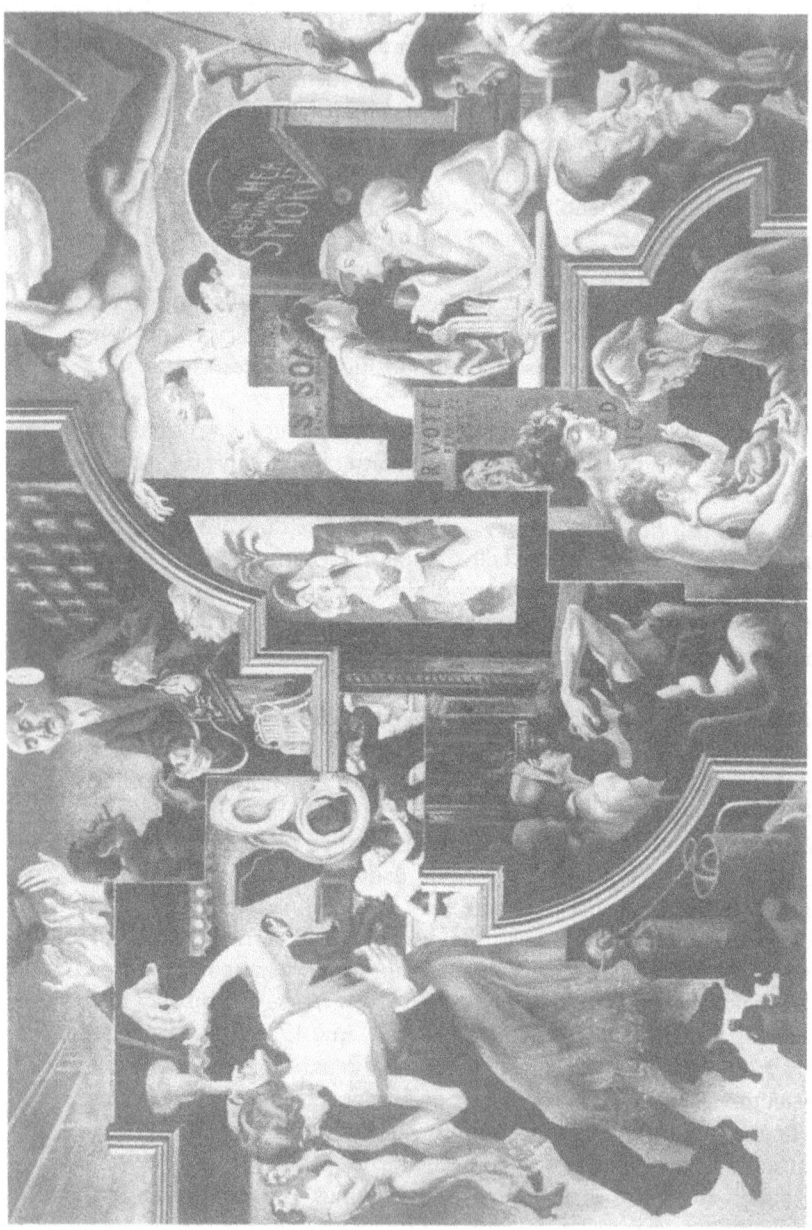

Figure 9. Thomas Hart Benton. *City Activities with Dance Hall* (from *America Today*). 1930. Distemper and egg tempera on gessoed linen with oil glaze, 92 × 134½ in. Mural for New School for Social Research, New York City; Collection, The Equitable Life Assurance Society of the U.S. Copyright © The Equitable Life Assurance Society of the U.S., T. H. Benton and R. P. Benton Testamentary Trusts/Licensed by VAGA, New York, NY.

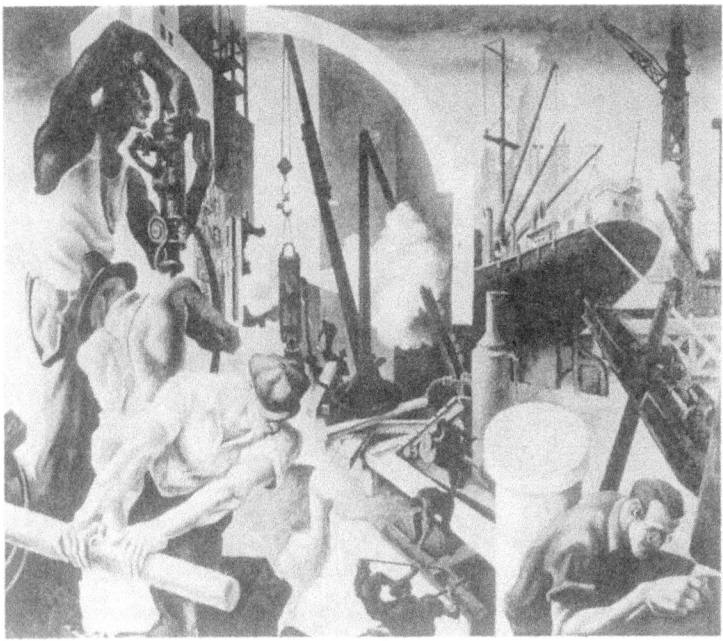

Figure 10. Thomas Hart Benton. *City Building* (from *America Today*). 1930. Distemper and egg tempera on gessoed linen with oil glaze, 92 × 117 in. Mural for New School for Social Research, New York City; Collection, The Equitable Life Assurance Society of the U.S. Copyright © The Equitable Life Insurance Society of the U.S., T. H. Benton and R. P. Benton Testamentary Trusts/Licensed by VAGA, New York, NY.

promoter, Thomas Craven, persistently demanded that American paintings, whatever their figural style, defeat a "parvenu" adoration of European abstraction. In 1927 he had hailed his friend's current works as "the beginning of an epoch in American painting." They were emancipated from slavish imitation of both academic and avant-garde styles by their "genuine, first hand view of life." At the same time, they were created by an artist who was a "specialist in construction, . . . a precise theorist on the principles of abstract design." [16] As Benton completed his second series of murals, Craven concentrated his highest praise on their subject matter, rawbone American life, past and present. The series' indigenous themes and inherent forms preached a "frontier spirit." In furthering the cause of directly perceived realism, it stood in opposition to what Craven regularly condemned as the "snob spirit" of elitist abstractions, "nurtured in the Bohemian slums of Europe." [17] In December 1932, while McBride railed against the Whitney murals as working-class vulgarity, Craven reproved the Rockefellers and Rockefeller Center, "the capitalist's nightmare," for awarding its mural

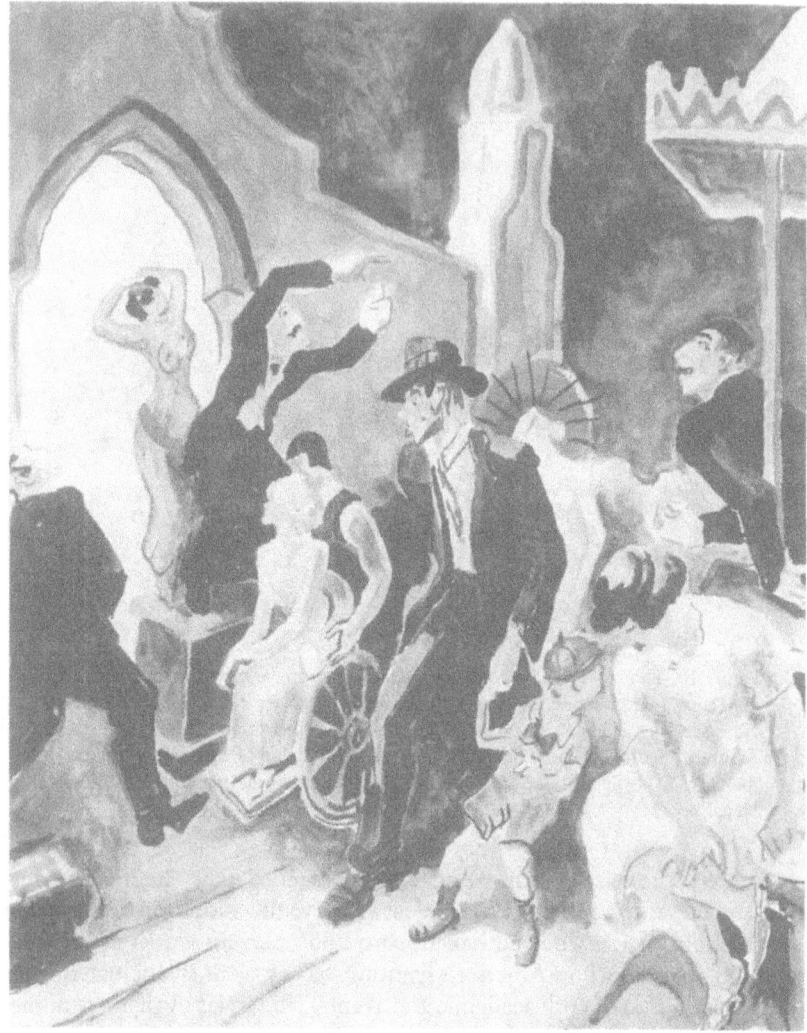

Figure 11. Thomas Hart Benton. *Boardwalk, Chicago World's Fair*. 1933. Watercolor, 20 × 16 in. Private collection. © T. H. Benton and R. P. Benton Testamentary Trusts/Licensed by VAGA, New York, NY.

commissions "to the trained seals of the Academy." He then lauded Benton, "one formidable American," for his "brutally realistic organization of American life" in a mural form free from "Bohemian corruption." [18]

In his widely read *Modern Art* (1934), Craven conceded that Americans might benefit from the many French examples of a self-reliant "cultural expression," though he cited none by name. They proved that creative individualism cannot escape the endemic traits and values that nurture it. This was the point to be hammered home: the most meritorious painters of the United States expressed "the tumultuous forces of America, its manifold dissonances, and its social anarchy."[19] Benton, a "pioneering example," led this trend in American painting "toward strong representation and clearly defined meanings which may be shared and verified by large groups of people."[20] A democratic art, an art for all Americans, it had no tolerance for technical experiments in abstraction as a substitute for easily comprehended experience.[21] Modernism's progressive return to "first principles" from Cézanne to Cubism to Neo-Plasticism had merely "cleared the way for a new order."[22]

Craven's advocacy of a sublime realism as the best style for American painting found support. Princeton University art historian Frank Jewett Mather, an outspoken critic of Modernism, paraphrased point by point what he termed "Mr. Craven's intelligent ferocity" in a rave review of *Modern Art* for the *New York Herald-Tribune:* "The remedy is for the artist to seek a wider experience of his own place, time, and fellow mortals . . . to consider methods less, and more what methods may express; to reach out for a public and disregard the closed clique, as well as the asphyxiating gas of esoteric criticism."[23]

By the summer of 1934, favorable criticism of Benton, Curry, or Wood had, in the wake of Craven's parading of Benton, acquired a hyperbolic edge of Regionalist rhetoric.[24] Promotional articles praised them for keeping in close touch with American life, or, more accurately, for representing what art journalists considered "Regionalist" attributes of American life, namely rural midwestern ones. Needless to say, such reviews paid little attention to abstract form as a stylistic consideration. Evaluations in a period of intense material concern, economically determined, remained subject-prone.

A year before he compared Stuart Davis and Benton as artists similarly involved with composition as abstraction, Jewell celebrated Wood's ultimate utilization of clear design in the service of direct realism. That he saw this occurring in one of the Iowan's most emblematic idylls, *Dinner for Threshers* (Fig. 12), may be explained by the urban-oriented enthusiasm for midwestern farm themes that he shared with both institutional and individual patrons in New York City. In an article on mural painting, he featured a pair of drawings for the end sections of *Dinner for Threshers,* acquired by the Whitney Museum, plus a highly finished rendering of the entire picture sold to collector Stanley R. Resor by Ferargil Galleries.[25] Thanks to the successful efforts of Benton and the Mexican muralists José Orozco, David Siquieros, and Diego Rivera, murals enjoyed an increased

27

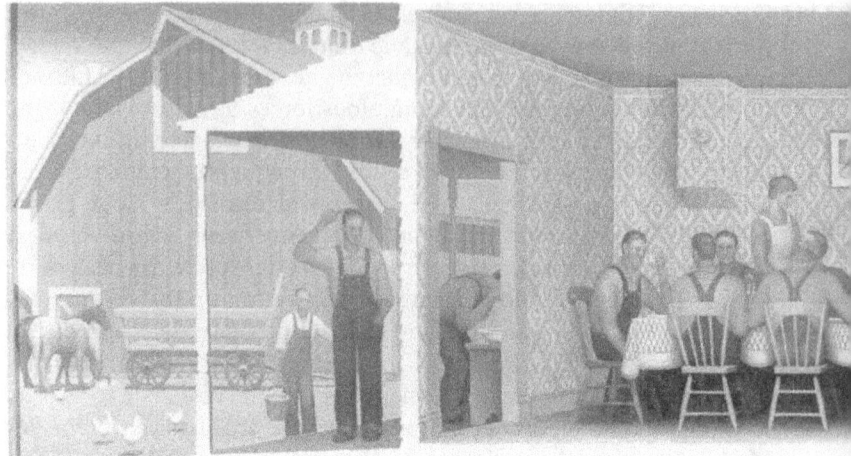

Figure 12. Grant Wood. *Dinner for Threshers*. 1934. Oil on board, 20 × 80 in. The Fine Arts Museums of San Francisco, San Francisco, California, 1979.7.105; Gift

popularity. Wood, a participant in the New Deal's newly inaugurated Public Works of Art Project, declared that *Dinner for Threshers,* though still on his easel, could be successfully enlarged for a wall.

That this proposed final step would never occur was no fault of the farm-hungry Jewell. With a smothering barrage of adjectives, he proclaimed the penultimate version of the painting a perfect portrait of rural America, an insightful synthesis of particularization and monumentality, comparable, no less, to the premier mural cycles of the Early Italian Renaissance:

The spirit of honest labor, close to the soil, unblemished by the least suggestion of sentimentality or by intrusion of naught that could be called extraneous, is communicated to us with a directness that nothing short of passionate sincerity could achieve. The panel is alive throughout, depending at no point upon recourse to mere "picturesqueness" or to a facile stressing of the particular. Its sensitive gravitation toward under rather than over statement assists in the establishment of a mood of monumental simplicity to parallel which we might have to go back to Giotto.[26]

Though hardly a match for Jewell's ebullience, *Time* magazine's account of "U.S. Scene" painting, written by Allen Jackson, art editor, provided a cover-story package of Cravenesque attitudes in Timese wrappings for Christmas Eve, 1934. By calling Wood's *Dinner for Threshers* "simple and direct," it succinctly seconded Jewell's opinion. It then added a nationalistic touch by comparing the painting's "genuine U.S. stamp" to a hot dog stand and a baseball park. True to the Craven scenario, *Time*'s trio of native painters from the Midwest were said to have led the opposi-

28

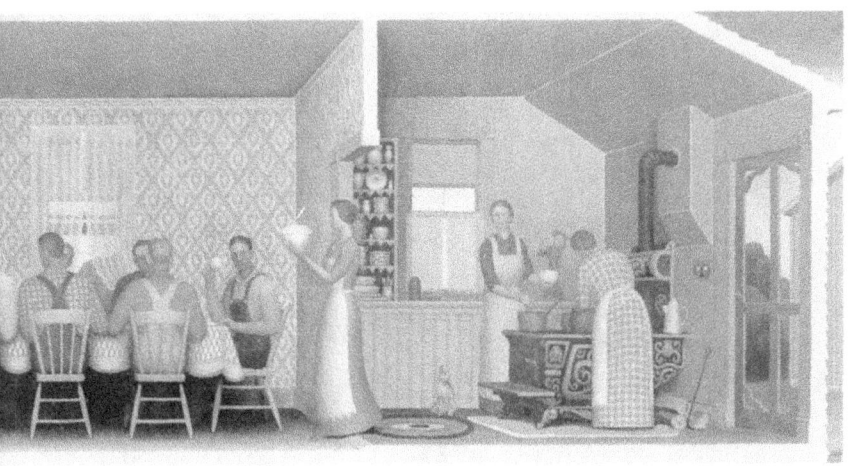

of Mr. and Mrs. John D. Rockefeller III. © Estate of Grant Wood/Licensed by VAGA, New York, NY.

tion to "the crazy parade of Cubism, Futurism, Dadaism and Surrealism," having replaced "introspective abstractions" with "direct representation." By now called a school, these "earthy midwesterners," plus Charles Burchfield from northeastern Ohio, headed the "main stream of U.S. representationalism." Regardless of the "nervous electric quality" in his "Americana" murals or his love affair with the backwoods culture of his native southwest Missouri, Benton, in *Time*'s reasoning, persistently denied sentimentality and was the most objective realist of the trio. "Recognizable observations," after all, originated in his scores of notebooks filled with sketches of real people (Fig. 13). A similar "authenticity" resulted from Curry's habit of drawing from life in preparation for his "simple and dramatic" paintings of Kansas or the 1932 circus season with Ringling Brothers, Barnum and Bailey (Fig. 14).[27]

Observers far to the left of *Time,* aroused by its cover article, severely reproached Wood, Benton, and Curry, not for inaccurately recording tangible details, but for disregarding the realities of economic conflict. Stuart Davis, writing for the Artists' Union's short-lived tabloid *Art Front,* promptly registered his complaint against the claim that the Regionalists offered "direct representation in place of introspective abstractions." He weighed the relative emphases on subject matter and form in their works, and found that the scale tilted toward unfortunate forms of abstraction. Without reference to specific examples, he suggested that Wood's figural style, when applied to a "well-fed farm hand," was actually more of an "introspective abstraction" than a direct representation of what Depression and drought-stricken

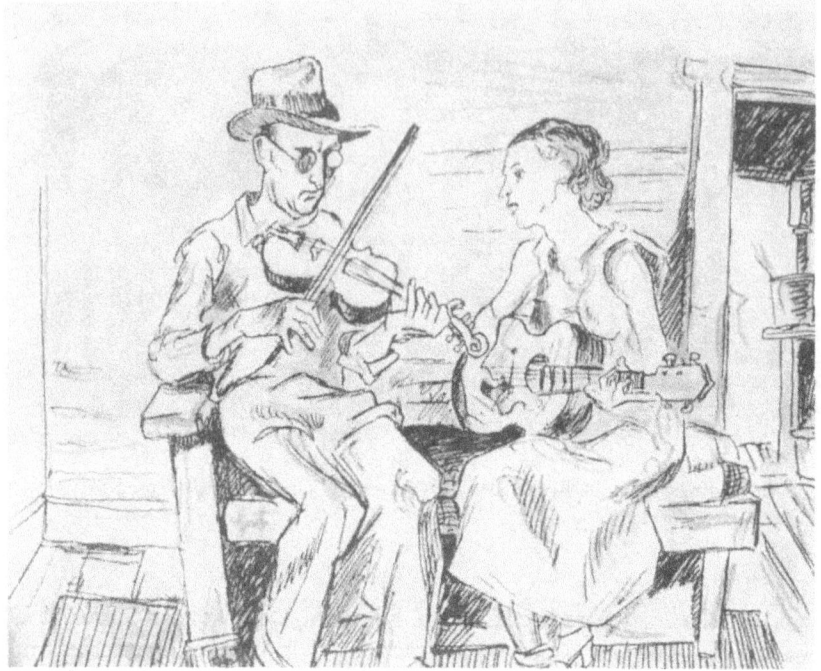

Figure 13. Thomas Hart Benton. *Father and Daughter*. 1937. India ink, pencil, and wash drawing for an illustration in first edition of the artist's autobiographical book, *An Artist in America*, New York: Robert M. McBride & Company. © T. H. Benton and R. P. Benton Testamentary Trusts/Licensed by VAGA, New York, NY.

farm workers must actually look like (Fig. 15). As for Benton's caricatures of black Americans, they were too gross to qualify as realistic: "The only thing they directly represent is a third-rate, vaudeville character cliche with the humor omitted." [28]

Davis also believed that Benton's treatment of black Americans verged on the racist "propaganda" consistently used to disenfranchise them politically, socially, and economically. In ironic contrast to this accusation, the freelance critic Ruth Pickering portrayed Benton as a liberal bent on reforming the living conditions of all the people he depicted. "There glows a tenderness for the dispossessed Negroes throughout the South, for the farmer on the prairies, for the workman on the docks or in the factory, for the seekers after empty pleasures in the cities of the East." To her, Benton's caricaturing of black Americans seemed no more severe than his caricaturing of white people; in fact, he showed a consistent compassion for and empathy with working people in general. [29]

Davis's distrust of Benton's stereotyping stemmed from their political

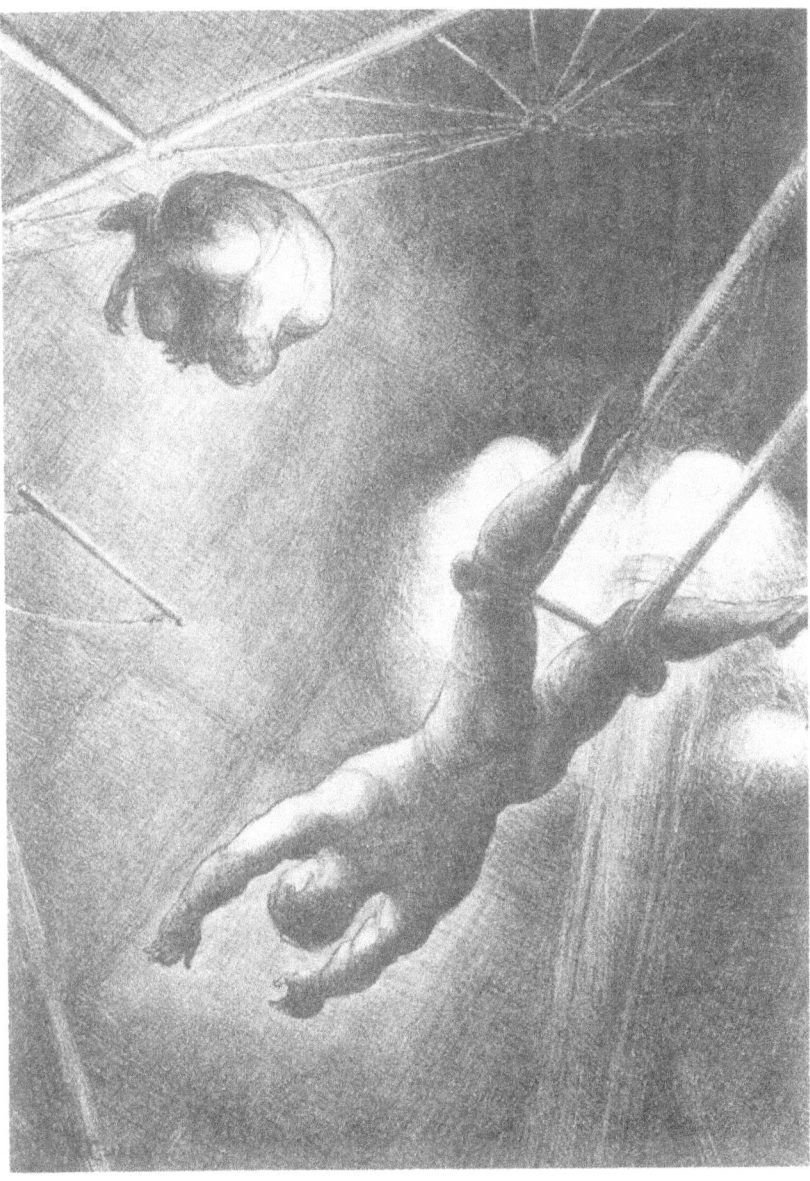

Figure 14. John Steuart Curry. *The Flying Cadonas*. 1933. Lithograph, 15¾ × 9¾ in. Private Collection.

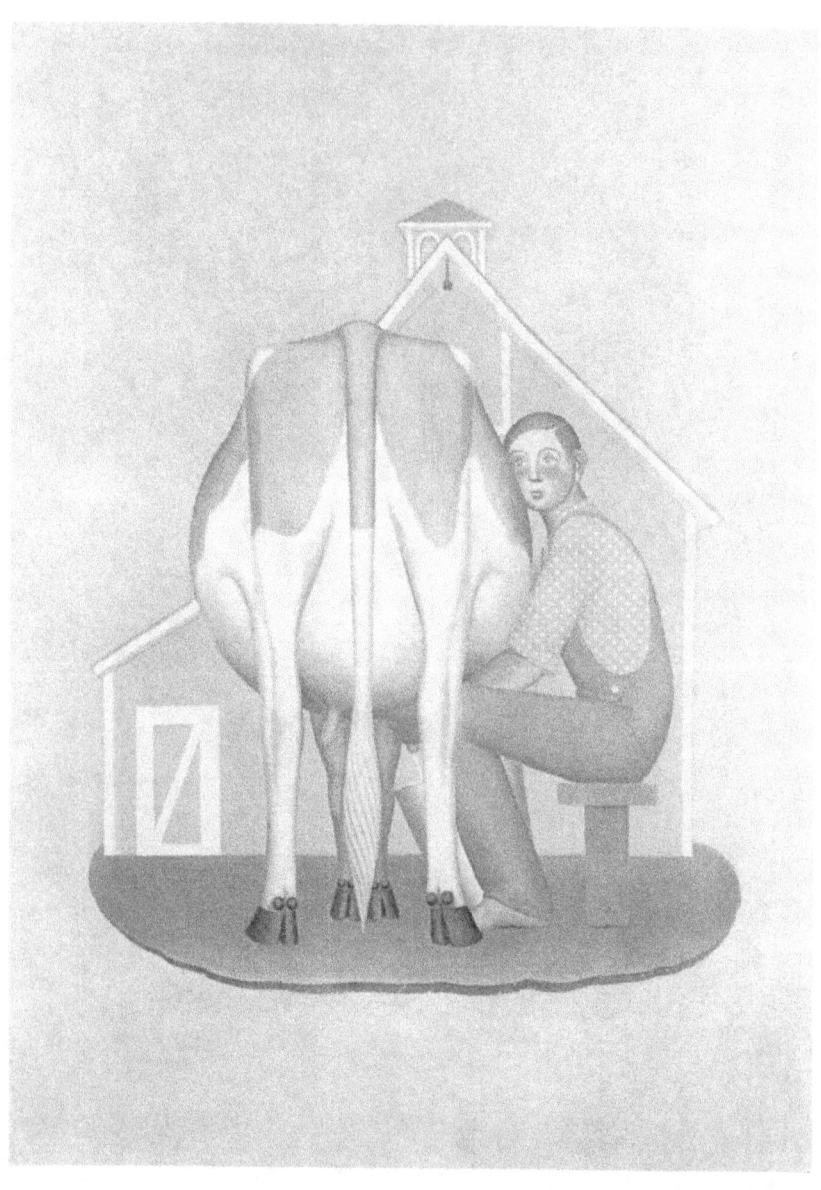

Figure 15. Grant Wood. *Fruits of Iowa: Farmhand Milking Cow*. 1932. Oil on canvas attached to panel, 71¼ × 63¼ in. Coe College Collection, Cedar Rapids, Iowa; gift of the Eugene C. Eppley Foundation. © Estate of Grant Wood/Licensed by VAGA, New York, NY.

differences. As a Marxist, Davis would necessarily stress class conflicts and the inevitability of a proletarian revolution against the power elite of capitalism. Although his article focuses on Benton's imaging of black workers, he must have been offended by all of Benton's working-class figures (see Fig. 10). Their gnarled, malproportioned bodies, bent into angular contortions, were a far cry from the classic, heroic-worker ideal of socialist realism. On the other hand, they possibly signify Benton's inherited populist politics of hope. As emphasized by the social historian Erika Doss, this envisioned a republic of autonomous "producers," a worker-determined economy. It was supposed to reappear from its mythic, early nineteenth-century beginnings to end corporate domination and evolve organically into predetermined areas of manufacturing.[30] Such a dream would explain Benton's disdain for the Comintern, but it also, by the same token, seems somewhat at odds with the ensuing plans for a centrally controlled, federally regulated New Deal economy that he enthusiastically supported.

Curry received an even harsher overall rating from Davis than did Benton. He was said to have turned out "cheaply dramatic" paintings that lacked both cohesive compositions and convincing realism. Therefore, Kansans had revealed wise discrimination in not buying pictures based on the remembrances of a self-exiled native son living in Westport, Connecticut. His works were "negative," both technically and thematically. With regard to the former, he was either ignorant of the "laboratory work" of abstraction carried out by Monet, Seurat, Cézanne, and Picasso, or he chose to ignore it. As for the latter, his depictions of life in rural Kansas shared the "provincial, melodramatic and sentimental" attitudes of all American Scene paintings, including those of New York street life by George Bellows, John Sloan, Glenn Coleman, and oddly enough, John Marin's abstract expressions of either Manhattan or Maine. Three urban realists and a Stieglitz-circle modernist whose work bore some resemblance to Davis's own, they at least had the good fortune to have emerged before "the vicious and windy, chauvinistic ballyhoo" of Craven gained currency through the Hearst press.[31]

As if expanding on Davis's quick stab at Wood, Stephen Alexander of the *New Masses* also found fault with the Iowan for disregarding the harsh economic realities or the "social truth" faced by his state's farmers. The paintings he saw at Wood's first one-artist exhibition in New York, held at the Ferargil Galleries in June 1935, contained "only rich, prosperous farms, with spic-and-span new buildings, fat cattle, fine, fertile crops and peaceful, contented farmers." They paid no attention to current hardships. Without saying so, Alexander strongly implied that an artist whose credo was one of drawing upon immediate experience should go out and depict "the burning of wheat, shooting of cattle and plowing under of crops by the A.A.A. destruction program." By eliminating them, he complained, the Regionalist shirks his duty and "gives people what they want to buy—nice, pleasant pictures: very charming, decorative paintings." [32] By "people" Alexander presumably meant the minute gallery-going public concentrated in New York City.

Wood actually did consider the dire effects of the Depression and the drought on midwestern farmers as a proper subject for a Regionalist artist.[33] He had, however, opted for an escape from painful reality through the "introspective abstractions" of his farmscapes and their occupants. Press photography and film could report distress, catastrophes, and violence more immediately, thereby liberating the painter either to interpret the facts expressionistically as a social realist or indulge in ornamental devices and figural stylizations far removed from the turmoil.

In his *New Yorker* review of Wood's first New York exhibition, Mumford showed little tolerance for the deceits of decorative abstraction on view. Beginning on a compassionate note, he declared it a misfortune that the Iowan had become a national symbol to "patrioteers." He then compared Wood's "innocence of what is vital and original in American painting" with the naivete of the late Vachel Lindsay, who had failed to grasp the social significance of Walt Whitman's best poetry or the critical meaning of his prose pamphlet, *Democratic Vistas.* Briefly reviewing Wood's career to date, Mumford superficially stressed his technical development: he had turned from an early, widely practiced, impressionist style to a highly deliberate technique inspired by fifteenth-century Northern masters. Corresponding to this change, his portraits after 1929 best exemplified his talent for conveying local life: "He has caught the grave, angular faces of the people he knows and loves best." [34] Representative of this facet of his art, *American Gothic* deserved mention as his finest effort to date, while "the famous" *Dinner for Threshers,* weak in design and vacuous as "portraiture," failed to capture the true spirit of the seasonal event it depicted. "It looks like a color photograph of a model of Life in Iowa done for a historical museum." Even less real, and therefore open to ridicule, were Wood's make-believe farmscapes:

Wood's recent landscapes are almost unmitigatedly bad. The soil is modelled so as to resemble carved plaster, and the trees are made of tissue paper, absorbent cotton, and sponge rubber. If that is what the vegetation of Iowa is like, the farmers ought to be able to sell this corn for chewing gum and automobile tires.[35]

Just short of a month later, Mumford reviewed paintings exhibited at the A.C.A. Galleries by the twenty-seven-year-old Joe Jones. "The season's most promising young artist," Jones, of St. Louis, earned Mumford's accolades for the verisimilitude, action, and dynamic composition in such "proletarian" paintings as *We Demand* and *Demonstration.* In *The New*

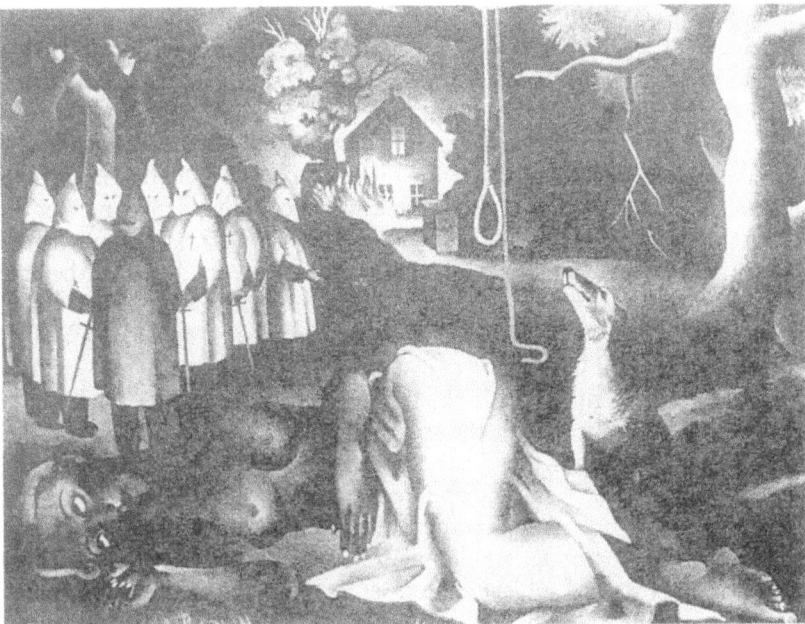

Figure 16. Joe Jones. *American Justice*. 1933. Oil on canvas. Location unknown; no measurements available.

Deal and *American Justice* (Fig. 16), however, the backgrounds were too unconvincingly overpatterned for Mumford's eye, the forms, even those of Klansmen, too much like "paper cutouts." That brought them dangerously close to Wood's "problem." "Carried a little further, this would lead Jones into the same sort of weak simplification as Grant Wood's landscapes."[36] In short, Mumford joined the critical consensus that midwestern Regionalism should deal directly with the realities of rural life and avoid modernist experiments with pictorial design.

James Johnson Sweeney, writing for the *New Republic,* did not even share Mumford's initial sympathy for Wood's exploited innocence of taste. He reacted to the Ferargil Galleries exhibition as a formalist critic, totally intolerant of Wood's subject matter, his technique, and his "slack compositional sense." To him the Iowan's popularity was of interest primarily as an "economic symptom" of a troubled "popular psychology," the projection of a hard-pressed public's need for reminiscences, associations, anecdotes, and "sentimental symbolism." A context of social disturbance, however, provided no rationalization for mediocrity to a critic ever in search of "plastic quality," "plastic organization," and "plastic grounds." With "no sensibility to color," "a feeble sense of modeling," and "insensitively

35

stylized forms," Wood had absolutely no chance of achieving the "unfamiliar idiom" of a nonassociative but "personalized plastic expression" that
must, Sweeney insisted, provoke "an intuitive resentment in the observer"
in order to succeed as a work of art.[37]

Thus, at the pinnacle of his career, Wood suffered an adverse critique
emphasizing form analysis. Whether the Iowan had presented the real-life
experiences of his locale in a straightforward, communicative manner or,
as Mumford thought, had drifted too far into fantasy was of no consequence to Sweeney. For the pure-plastic modernist, the less of either the
better, and his phobia toward any degree of direct realism remained in
diametric opposition to the large majority of published demands made on
Wood, Benton, and Curry.

In his catalogue introduction to the Museum of Modern Art exhibition
of cubist and abstract art in the spring of 1936, Alfred H. Barr, Jr., was
more ambivalent about the elimination of external references in what he
termed "pure abstractions" as opposed to "near abstractions." Somewhat
apologetically he wrote: "Such an attitude, of course, involves a great impoverishment of painting, an elimination of a wide range of values, such
as the connotations of subject matter, sentimental, documentary, political,
sexual, religious; the pleasures of easy recognition; and the enjoyment of
technical dexterity in the imitation of material forms and surfaces. But in
his art the abstract artist prefers impoverishment to adulteration."[38]

Judging Wood, Benton, and Curry according to narrow, single-theme
expectations, a majority of their critics (admirers as well as detractors)
neglected or censured their "near abstractions" of caricatured figures and
exaggerated settings in favor of accurately detailed description. Moreover,
without thoroughly investigating and recognizing the variety of subjects
broached by the three, ranging from personal fantasies to cultural myths,
much criticism begrudged them their independence, a core characteristic
of Modernism. It was decreed that the leading Regionalists should produce designated Regionalist themes in a direct-realist manner. It is with
this conflict of reception that Chapter 2 deals.

2

"Direct Realism" Versus
Mimetic Fantasies

The adaptations of modernist abstraction by the three major Regionalists eluded most of their critics. At the same time, their wide range of subject matter deviated from the expectations of urban viewers who wanted to keep them down on the farm. An array of socially derisive figures, ethnocentric caricatures, satires of American myths, and personal fantasies disturbed the curiously staid critics on the political left up to the end of the Depression. After a long lapse in attention following the Second World War, equally severe reactions accompanied a revival of interest in Regionalism during the ideologically confused post–Vietnam War period.

Acting like art world agents for one constituency or another, a majority of critics found it difficult and at times impossible to accept Wood, Benton, and Curry as modern artists who created pictures determined more by inner perceptions than by the familiar facts of their native region in the midsection of the country. After all, they were supposedly committed to the agenda of a conservative movement. Therefore, a mobile Wood, Benton, or Curry was forsaking an ideological obligation when he abandoned the realities of his birthplace and escaped into a land of make-believe. Fearing for Regionalism as a whole, the Chicago newspaper critic Charles J. Bulliet, the official discoverer of *American Gothic*, detected a highly contagious ailment in Wood's subsequent paintings. "A veritable flock of little Grant Woodses" had shown up in early 1935 at the Art Institute's Annual Exhibition of American Art, for which Wood served as a juror.[1]

Although city dwellers' desire to be momentarily transplanted into a rustic setting intensified, the Regionalist leaders often failed to accommodate them, even if they said they would. Hollywood, on the contrary, was answering the call quite consistently by the time the Depression bottomed out. Before the perils of the uprooted Joad family were revealed in the movie version of the *Grapes of Wrath*, filmmaking had ended the decade on a rural-homecoming note as Dorothy returned from her adventures in the Land of Oz to the family farm in Kansas. She had gone full circle from a Curry-like barnyard, over a yellow-brick road through a Grant Wood landscape, to the waiting arms of Aunt Em, a virtual double for Curry's mother. The American audience could feel secure once again, one year after Iowa's Henry Wallace, secretary of agriculture, introduced a new security plan of parity price supports and government-owned storage bins that would protect grain farmers from the fluctuations of crop yields and the erratic international market.[2]

"Populist romances of agrarian bounty," as the film historians Peter Roffman and Jim Purdy identify the majority of Depression farm films, were launched in 1933 with the classic of the genre: *State Fair*.[3] It was a favorite of movie-lover Grant Wood, although its intimate realism came too late to have any effect on his streamlined style of abstracting the fields and formalizing the people who worked them into smooth-surfaced automata. The film starred Will Rogers, Louise Dresser, Janet Gaynor, and Lew Ayres, and was based on a popular novel by Phil Stong. It accompanies a happy farm family named Frake to the Iowa State Fair. The archetypal Mom (Dresser) mysteriously sweeps all three pickle contests and then wins the bake-off with her secret mincemeat recipe. Meanwhile Dad (Rogers), a prosperous farmer in the guise of a stereotypical country bumpkin with a down-home Oklahoma accent, wins a blue ribbon in the pig-judging contest with his giant boar, "Blue Boy." Their daughter (Gaynor), unbelievably innocent, falls in love with a cosmopolitan newspaper reporter (Ayres), who quotes Schopenhauer and promises to take her off to Chicago and maybe even New York. No allusion is made to the extremely hard times Iowa farmers were sharing with their peers throughout the Mississippi basin. The only poor people in the movie are black roustabouts, seen for a few seconds as they sing a melancholy labor song while putting up the large carnival tents. Otherwise, to borrow from Roffman and Purdy, it is all "gingham whimsies."[4]

Even such rural-based social-problem films as *Cabin in the Cotton* (1932), *Our Daily Bread* (1934), and *Grapes of Wrath* (1940) "show a reluctance to break with the reassuring myths, carefully balancing their discussion of social factors to prepare for an optimistic finale." In the movie *Grapes of Wrath*, Ma's determination to preserve the traditions of life on the land undermines Steinbeck's message (as expressed through her son Tom) of a radical need to revolt against the economic system that is destroying them. Instead, "the final long shot sees their car rambling down a sunny highway framed by neat rows of California orchard trees in full bloom."[5]

Curry's melodramatic depictions of malevolent nature, climatic, animal, or human, Benton's manic thrusts of sinew and smoke, and Wood's finely burnished farm folk in their compulsively fantasized settings hardly project the movies' easily absorbed illusions of rural life, for better more than for worse. By the decade of their rather accidental movement, the three midwestern Regionalists, all well over thirty, had gone off to live in the city and had distanced themselves from whatever they had known of a farmer's existence. This made it a challenge to maintain a convincing rustic facade.

They could barely measure up to the enthusiasm for the latest "Renaissance in American Art" that the liberal art commentator and New Deal art advisor Ralph M. Pearson displayed in a 1935 article. Regionalism was at its peak. Pearson favored accurate depictions of immediate reality and, wished to protect interpretations of American subject matter from extremes of fantasy. Paradoxically, however, he also advocated "creative" composition of forms for form's sake against "noncreative, fact-recording." In a broad reference to the recently legislated New Deal art projects, he stated that federal programs were "the last and only hope" of improving "the aesthetic potentialities of the average citizen . . . enslaved by habit to the copying-nature school." To help deliver a cultural renaissance, Treasury Department murals and pictures sponsored by the Works Progress Administration (WPA) must dramatize contemporary events, good or bad. By the same token, they must organize the figures and objects belonging to this subject matter into "visual music," fusing them into "a color-and-form symphony." "The ideal program," however, "will avoid *all* escapes from reality into the idyllic daydream of innocuous romance."[6] So, from the point of view of tastemaking lyricism, Pearson was attracted to the curvilinear farmscapes of Wood; but as a fact-seeking reformer, he found their fantasy element difficult to accept.

Escapist idylls, or what Wood once termed the "Imagination Isles,"[7] aroused critic Lincoln Kirstein's Marxist positivism in a 1935 *Art Front* diatribe. The Iowan's fantasy farmscapes were too full of "simple-minded mannerism" in place of "intensity of seeing." Numbed by a formula inspired by Flemish Old Masters, this "Iowa Memling" could "neither directly feel, nor wholly observe, nor even completely organize" the facts before him.

Trees in Iowa must have the same generic elements of trunk and leaf as trees in New Jersey or even trees in Burgundy, but not as trees on blue-plate specials. Wood observes the ranks of corn sprouting freshly in his landscape *Stone City,* with charm and quaintness, but the rest of the picture looms up into a fat toy territory, a bulbous "decorative" treatment, about as American as the scenery for the *Chauve Souris* was Russian.[8]

Easily understood visual reports on the current predicaments of midwestern farming, not evasive flights, were Wood's only option if he was to lend "truthful order in his vision." With the same radical class-consciousness assumed by Stephen Alexander in the *New Masses* a month earlier, Kirstein further advised:

> He will have to cauterize that charm which, no matter how accurately he paints, clouds truth. And more than any mere technical mastery, he will have to gain some trace of insight into the real weather of his Middle West—dust storms and drought, slaughtered pigs, unsown crops or crops ploughed under. An element of tragedy would make his cleanly farmers less quaint, but closer to the spirit of the Gothic, which is no less beautiful because it is so grim.[9]

Wood's abstract visions of farms as paradise were propagated in the eighteenth century from ancient pastoral tradition and cultivated through several generations of westward settlement into an agrarian myth. Despite their credentials, in the middle of the "recession" year 1937 they suffered a surprise attack that bore a striking resemblance to that delivered by Kirstein. As Wood completed one of his most realistic works, the mural *Breaking the Prairie* (see Fig. 48) for the Iowa State University Library in Ames, none other than Thomas Craven, prototype booster of Regionalism via Benton, struck hard. Not as interested in the plight of the farmers as the left-wing Kirstein, the erstwhile Kansan nevertheless thought Wood should paint "a closely studied, realistic job without frills or fantasy, a picture in which the trees and farms are as sharply characterized as the faces of his portraits."[10] Like Mumford, Craven considered Wood's portraiture the epitome of his attainments, surpassing even that of John Singleton Copley. But the "decorative machinery" of his post–*American Gothic* landscapes was too elaborate and imaginative for Craven to tolerate.

> In short, the design half consumes the subjects, and the trees and natural forms, arbitrarily forced into a fixed pattern, lose their specific character and become implements in a scheme of self-conscious "stylization." His work in this vein, with its spongy trees, curlique roadways, and miniature houses, has the charm of novelty and makes appropriate overmantel decorations for quaint drawing rooms, but it expresses little. What saves it from frivolity, and from being little more than the indulgence of a fantastic inventiveness usually exemplified by the makers of pictures of the never-never land, is the basic planning.[11]

Thus, the self-styled populist Craven, ironically in league with the cosmopolitan fellow traveler Kirstein, diagnosed Wood's mythic-America fantasies as frivolous self-indulgences, and prescribed a heavy dose of direct realism as a remedy.

Curry, conversely, remained immune to the decorative disease, in spite of his contact with Wood, who helped arrange his return to the Midwest in 1937 as the country's first artist-in-residence at the University of Wisconsin. So implied Craven the following year, heedless of any symptoms of make-believe in the dramatic depictions of sublime nature painted by his fellow Kansan-in-exile. In his view Curry, whom he dubbed "a poet steeped in realities," had formed "no settled method of design, no structural mannerisms in which the pattern basis is emphasized at the sacrifice of meaning." [12] Moreover, his vivid reports of fearful weather, disastrous blizzards, and tornados, or the "frenzied behavior of his people," indulged in no "romantic visions" or "murky symbols." He dealt "directly with objective facts and natural phenomena." [13] A year later Craven summed up his opinion of Curry's paintings of farm life on the Middle Border: "no fantasy builder: he works directly from realities and natural phenomena." [14]

Critical aversion to personal fantasies amounted to a campaign to force Regionalism into a reputed American tradition of "objective" realism. This prescribed restriction denied all three artists any right to modernist exaggeration, distortion, caricature, conceits, or imaginary inventions. Upon appearance, any of these features would either be criticized as flaws or, as Craven did on Curry's behalf, rationalized as true reality. Indeed, a critic for the *London Studio* viewed the "brittle" style and the "precise and meticulous" drawing in Grant Wood's *Midnight Ride of Paul Revere* (Fig. 17) and *Death on the Ridge Road* (Fig. 18), for example, as a "decorative realism." While skeptical of the frills and curves and bizarre foliage of the landscapes, this same anonymous writer nonetheless suggested that *Young Corn* (see Fig. 142) was "a more realistic interpretation than is generally supposed by those unfamiliar with the Iowa countryside." [15] Whether he was painting landscapes, portraits, or allegorical figures, Wood's "naive directness of vision" expressed his inner being, "a calm, self-contained person who looks at life with a clear serenity that even the cataclysm of the worst violence could not long upset." [16]

Wood himself paid lip service to realist restraints before freely expressing enthusiasm for Curry's personal melodrama. After testifying to the "objective styles" of the Regionalists, "in the American realistic tradition of Homer and Eakins, of George Bellows and John Sloan," he praised Curry's "extraordinary vividness and emotional intensity" to the point of implying fantasy. About the Kansan's paintings of boyhood memories he wrote: "It was action he loved most to interpret: the lunge through space, the split second before the kill, the suspended moment before the storm strikes. He remembered the facts accurately, but in his delineations he got beyond factual accuracy into the realm of perception and esthetic intuition." [17]

As the nation settled into waging war, Curry's biographer at the University of Wisconsin agreed with Wood's conclusion that his Regionalist ally delighted in imaginative interpretations of violence. In his final chapter, entitled "A Critic's Opinion," the Progressive-minded Laurence Schmeckebier analyzed two works: the Kansas Capitol Building mural of

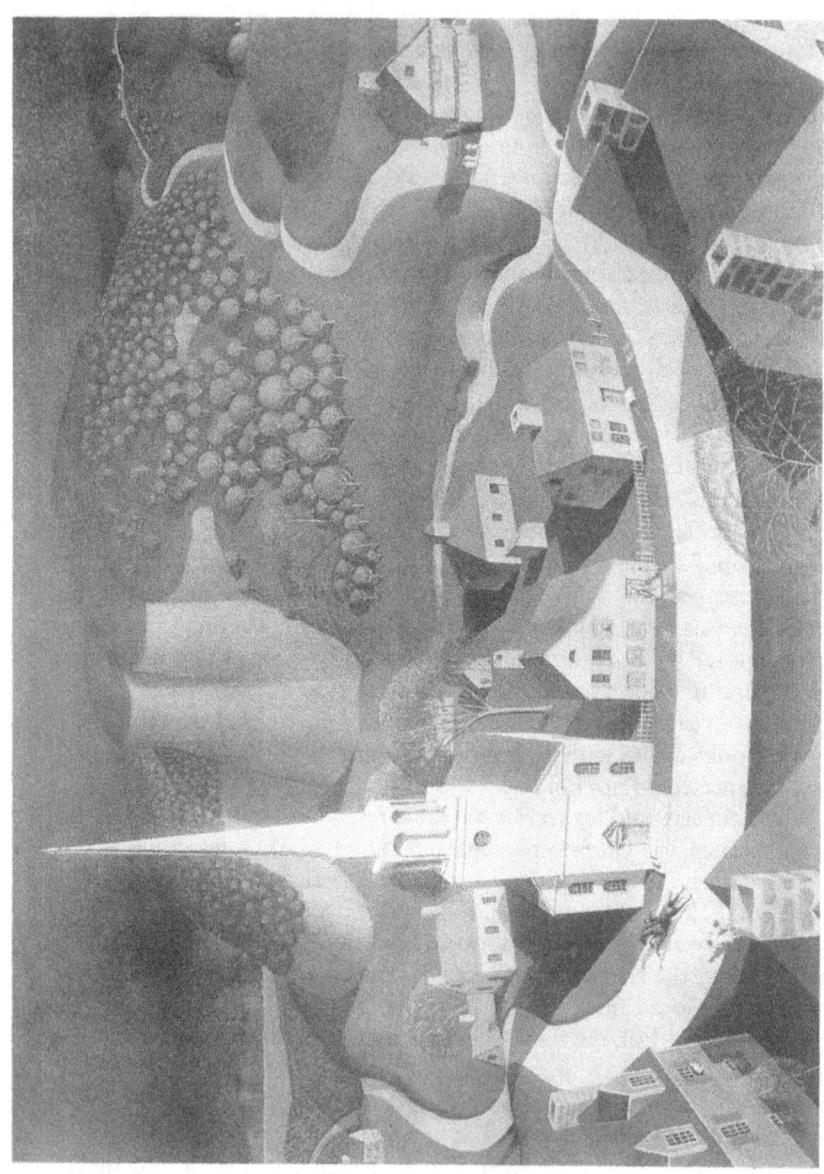

Figure 17. Grant Wood. *Midnight Ride of Paul Revere*. 1931. Oil on composition board, 30 × 40 in. Metropolitan Museum of Art, New York City, 50.117. © Estate of Grant Wood/Licensed by VAGA, New York, NY.

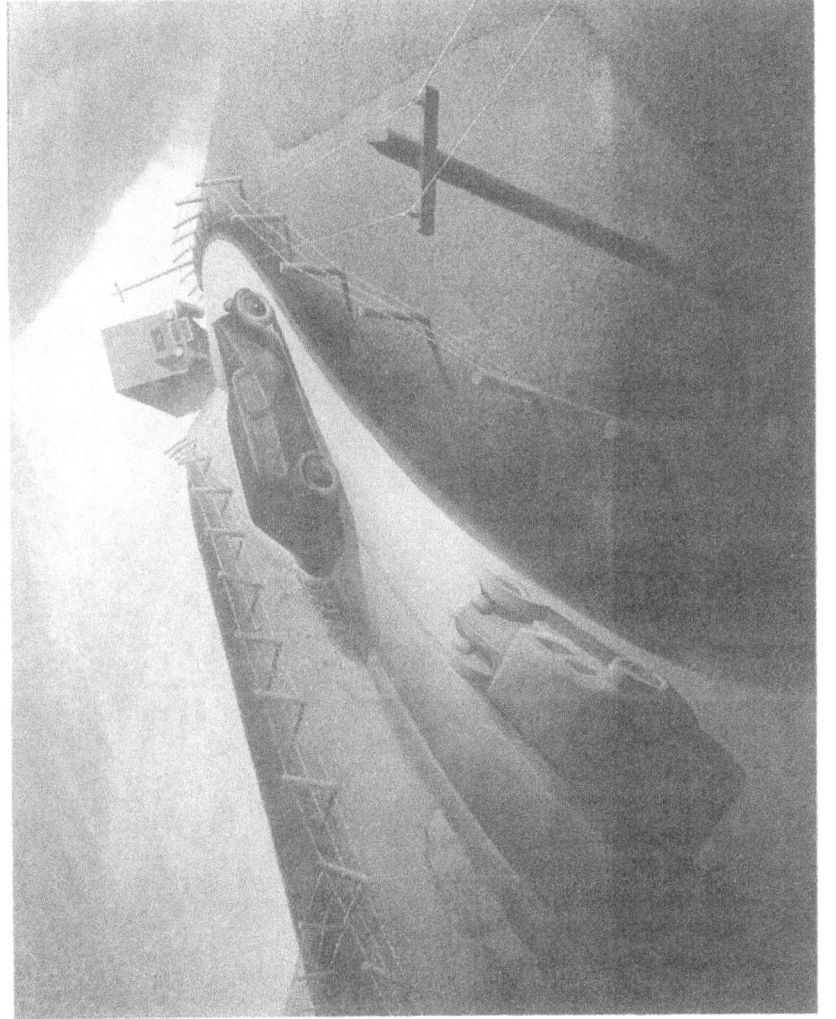

Figure 18. Grant Wood. *Death on the Ridge Road.* 1935. Oil on masonite, 32 × 39 in. Williams College Museum of Art, Williamstown, Massachusetts; gift of Cole Porter. © Estate of Grant Wood/Licensed by VAGA, New York, NY.

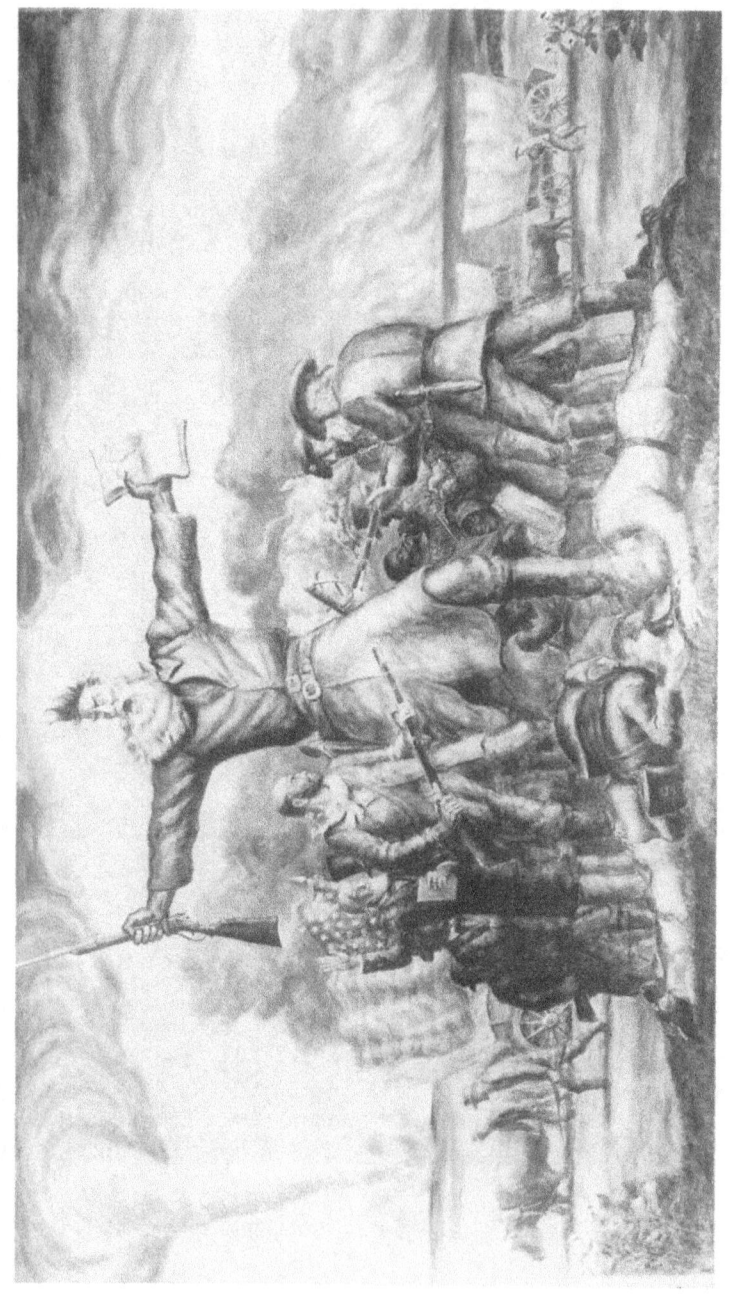

Figure 19. John Steuart Curry. *The Tragic Prelude.* 1937–42. Oil and tempera on canvas, 11 ft. 6 in. × 22 ft. Kansas State Capitol Building, Topeka, Kansas.

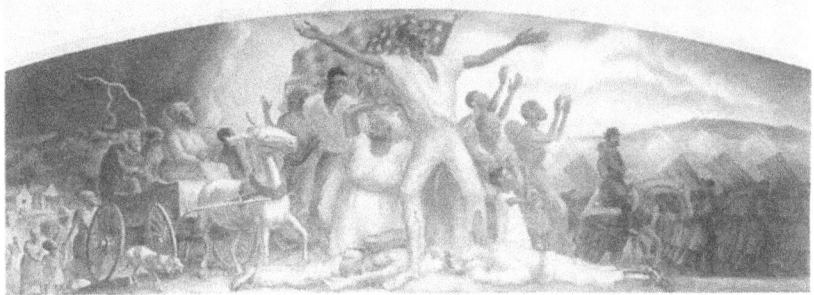

Figure 20. John Steuart Curry. *The Freeing of the Slaves*. 1942. Oil and tempera on canvas, 14 × 37 ft. Mural in the Library of the Law School, University of Wisconsin–Madison, Madison, Wisconsin.

John Brown, *The Tragic Prelude* (Fig. 19), and the recently installed University of Wisconsin Law Library mural, *The Freeing of the Slaves* (Fig. 20). He could hardly deny that their interconnected themes of abolitionist frenzy appealed to Curry's love of exaggeration. Both fantasize "an emotional state wherein unlimited flights of imagination could be set off by realistic fact and controlled by an artistic form."[18] First came visions of fanaticism and jubilation, then composition. Realistic facts amount to props for dramatizing history. Both murals flout the directly witnessed "realities and natural phenomena" that Craven claimed were typical of Curry.

Into the late thirties and beyond, criticism of Benton's fanciful indulgences continued. Caricature was the most politically vulnerable aspect of his indirect approach. In 1938, focusing on the Missouri Capitol Building murals of two years earlier (Fig. 21), the *New York Herald* critic Malcolm Vaughan confounded the political-aesthetic debate of direct realism versus fantasy with contradictory arguments. On one hand, he scorned Benton's impulse to paint "plebeian America, the rude scenes and subjects associated with what we used to call our 'lower classes,'" as placing too much "stress on grossness,"[19] that is, too real, too uncultivated. On the other, he accused the painter of cynical "cartoonery," of "poking fun at the simple and the lowly."[20] With "no desire to uplift the down-trodden by focusing attention on them," Benton's unreal figural style remained flawed by "lack of compassion."[21] Not to be excused as fantasy, "this satiro-grotesque characteristic becomes insidious burlesque; indeed, a note, a look, a distinct air of smart alec caricature hangs over his work as a whole."[22]

Aside from these and other attacks on the vulgarity of his subjects, writhing in a "grotesquerie" of distorted forms, certainly the condemnation most searing for Benton must have been Vaughan's rejection of his murals as compositions totally unrelated—indeed, alien—to their subject matter. Though intended to express the restlessness and confusion, the vio-

45

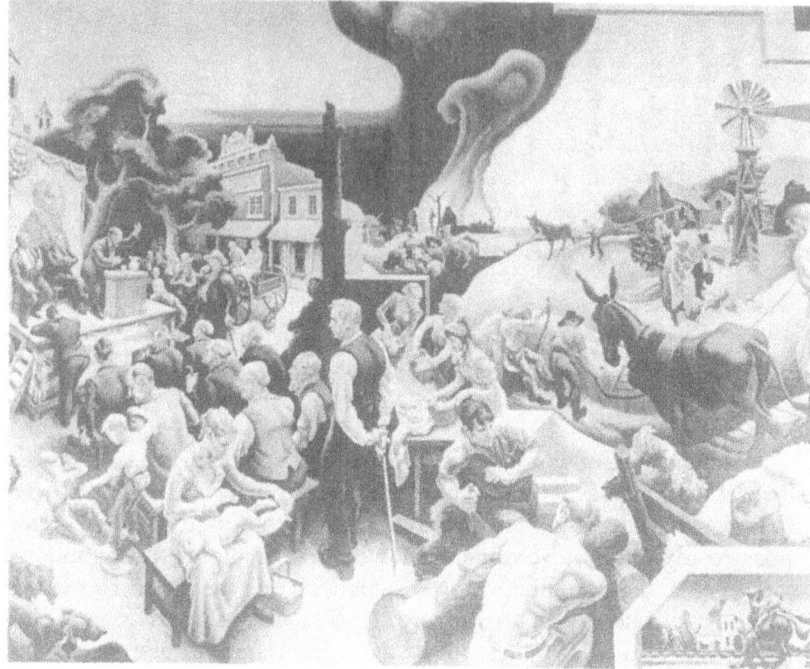

Figure 21. Thomas Hart Benton. *Politics and Agriculture*. 1936. Egg tempera and oil on canvas mounted on panel, 14 × 23 ft. Missouri State Capitol Building, Jefferson City, Missouri. © T. H. Benton and R. P. Benton Testamentary Trusts/Licensed by VAGA, New York, NY.

lence and chaos of the United States, they smacked of stylistic convention, a Baroque mode that the artist unsuccessfully struggled to reconcile to his visions of Americana. "His form is thus no creative outgrowth of his material, no natural, harmonious fusing of spirit and body." [23]

Vaughan would, on this basis, have questioned an open letter Benton posted on his scaffolding while working on the House Lounge walls. In it the painter announced to all visitors that his choices of Missouri subject matter were determined by their "similarity and near relationship" to his own direct experiences. Futhermore, the "realness" of his mural depended "on a lot of abstract adjustments of lines and planes and gradations of color." [24]

Meyer Schapiro, a highly esteemed Columbia University art historian and politically radical critic, reviewed Benton's autobiography, *An Artist in America,* for the *Partisan Review.* Schapiro did not question the morality of habitual caricaturing, nor did he dwell upon the alienation between content and stylized composition that Vaughan perceived in Benton's murals. Of more crucial concern, from his Marxist point of view, were the built-in fantasies, the "illusion of mystical rapport" with those things that the romantically liberal Benton conceived of as the essence of an American world: the anecdotal nativism of railroad trains, farmers, "Negroes," local history, bits of local genre, and ingratiating domestic customs, all detached as so much "fiction" from the "tense historical reality of our time."[25]

In agreement with the liberal conservatism of the lower middle class, Benton, according to Schapiro's astute leftist analysis, simply felt that the American people would in the long run coalesce in a community without classes. The wealthy, "an accidentally privileged, immoral minority," must somehow vanish as the country returned to a legendary stage of popular rule, liberated from the failing capitalism of the big cities. Erika Doss has recently alleged that such persuasions, far from being naive, were actually a sophisticated derivation of the views of Benton's great-uncle, Senator Thomas Hart Benton. Senator Benton had preached faith in a republic of virtuous workers, or "producers," who could both independently and collectively advance the American economy without corrupting either it or themselves.[26] In this view, the artist filled his best-known murals of the early thirties with numerous working scenes to illustrate this nineteenth-century utopian premise. Instead of class struggle, the New School for Social Research murals (1930), the Whitney Museum Reading Room murals, and the Indiana mural for the 1933 Chicago World's Fair emphasize labor's generous contribution to industrial growth.[27] In this manner they anticipated a major theme of New Deal art, to which even the fellow traveler William Gropper would conform in his Department of the Interior mural celebrating dam building (1938). Woody Guthrie also participated, hired by the Bonneville Power Administration to write his famous songs about the construction of the Bonneville and Grand Coulee dams in the Columbia River Valley.

The dream of America as a land of perfectly harmonious classes provided the basis for the enormous popularity of the so-called screwball comedies that poured out of Hollywood during the thirties. The most memorable of these were directed by Frank Capra. If such movies as *Mr. Deeds Goes to Town* (1936) did not directly contribute to Benton's blindly optimistic ideology, they certainly paralleled it.[28] Guided by gullible optimism, Benton, in Schapiro's opinion, concocted an "escape from the demands of the crisis" and provided a "pitiful and inept" alternative to a "realism guided by radical values."[29] The picturesque, "unpolitical," everyday world that he popularized divided the United States into regions instead of recognizing the division of its classes. From Schapiro's revolutionary standpoint, "Regionalism" obscured the crucial forces of history, as defined by Marx, and provided entertaining distractions from the realities facing oppressed people.[30]

Schapiro may also have been reacting to the painter's three-part "Confessions of an American," published in the July, August, and September 1937 issues of *Common Sense*. "Why I Don't Like Marxism," "Marx and the Jefferson Ideal," and "Class Rule vs. Democracy" progressively introduce Benton's well-meaning but extremely utopian political position. It seems that he wanted to synthesize socialism and capitalism through a nonprofit entrepreneurship, an "ownership" of antienterprise managers, whose decisions would be determined by a majority vote of customer-constituents in a huge cooperative:

With the vast majority of those in the middle class I do not object to ownership in itself. I would not close the door on that sense of individual responsibility which goes with ownership. But I would make ownership responsible to all the people that it affects rather than to a profit system in which the satisfaction of human need is but a byproduct. This kind of ownership borders on collectivism. It is ownership not so much by absolute legal right as by majority suffrage.[31]

Two and a half years after Benton's *Common Sense* essay, the art historian Milton Brown approached the artist's achievements disapprovingly (though much less ideologically than Schapiro) through a basically determinist frame of reference. The stock market crash followed by the Great Depression had obviously intensified dissatisfaction with capitalism's inability to solve its inherent shortcomings. Regionalism, whether in economics, culture, politics, literature, or art, was essentially a revolt against at least one major evil of the industrial revolution: mass centralization. It was hoped that recognition of distinct locales would accommodate a nationwide return to "basic principles" and "traditionalism"; these, in turn, would encourage "anti-urbanism" and "anti-cosmopolitanism." Forgetting or intentionally ignoring Benton's romance with high-speed locomotives, smoke-belching threshing machines, oil derricks, and the like, Brown summed up the content of his paintings as "those forms of contemporary life least touched by twentieth-century industrialization."[32] By such generalizing, Brown (like critics of various convictions before and after) reduced a career of highly varied subject matter, of modernist pluralism, to "nothing more than a retreat to ruralism."[33]

While preoccupied with masculinity and proving himself equal to "any member of a Kiwanis Club or saloon patron," Benton had also overindulged in childish whimsies: figures that resembled "small animated toys," distorted surroundings made up of "props for the homely and the cute," and spatial manipulations that looked to Brown like "artificial constructions or stage sets."[34] Such personal fantasizing proved too farfetched for an essentially apolitical observer who could understand why a hardtimes art might revolt against, or retreat from, contemporary reality into a "sectional mythology," but distrusted Regionalism as "an exploitation of the nostalgic and sentimental."[35] With no mention of Benton's beloved steam engines, Brown dismissed his work as coming little closer to "a thorough-going examination of regional life under modern industrial conditions" than did Wood's ornamental, streamlined farmscapes or Curry's melodramas of boyhood experiences on a midwestern farm heightened by exaggerated encounters with wild nature. While intending to expose their lack of relevant realism, Brown underlined the diversity of imaginative themes among the three midwestern Regionalists. In so doing, he inadvertently hit upon the fantasy factor that had eluded or upset critics of Regionalism from the outset.

A year and a half after Benton died in 1975, as interest in the Regionalists revived amid the back-to-the-land sentiments of the late sixties and early seventies, *Art in America* critic Lawrence Alloway somewhat vaguely, but unmistakably, reverted to the original consensus that a Regionalist could successfully draw and paint only the most immediate barnyard episodes. Everything else—particularly mythic American figures and historical events—was subject to too much invention; such items were, in a word, fantasized. In the case of Curry's John Brown and "Wild Bill Cody" (i.e., Wild Bill Hickok), the imaginary imagery was so "devastatingly mannered" that it lived on borrowed "cultural time," as opposed to the "family time" in pictures based on direct personal knowledge. The latter could include Curry's 1932 circus paintings, (see Fig. 14) which earlier critics had disregarded as non-Regionalist.[36] Alloway, allowing his own imagination to come into play, saw the circus as "an exotic extension of farming: aerialists, lion tamers, animals, all echo the physicality of life on the farm."[37]

However farfetched this interpretation might be, it recalls how necessary it was to the critics in the thirties that midwestern Regionalism maintain a home base on a farm in order to meet the needs of its frustrated urban viewers for a rural distraction. Within the "double time-perspective" shared by all the Regionalists, Curry's "command of reality" remained on target in the barnyard, and there alone. Unlike Benton, Alloway held, Curry should never have delved into nineteenth-century history: "The past was real insofar as it was personal memory, but aberrant and distant to the extent Curry had to invent it."[38]

The perennial demand of the thirties for direct realism versus make-believe unreality refused to die. In fact, it gained new life with a major retrospective of Regionalism forty-some years after Pearl Harbor. Reviewing the 1983–84 Grant Wood exhibition and curator Wanda Corn's catalogue, the modernist critic Hilton Kramer, editor of the conservative *New Criterion,* exceeded all of his predecessors in attacking the creator of *American Gothic* for his fantasy-farm paintings. Echoing Brown's historical appreciation of why these "cultural anodynes" appeared in years of economic distress, he concluded that Wood

told the country exactly what it wanted to hear about a way of life and a vein of experience it preferred not to look into too closely. It was perfectly appropriate, then, that it was in the Thirties—when the real life of the midwestern farming communities suffered the worst crisis in their history—that this fantasy version of their existence enjoyed its greatest popularity the country over.[39]

In reaching that conclusion, however, Kramer registered his intolerance of Wood's distance from "the real thing."

Disregarding the possible connections between imaginary bliss and the traditional tendency among American farmers-in-crisis to appeal to the agrarian myth, Kramer launched into a rather unprofessional sequence of insults. It climaxed in a devastating condemnation of Regionalism for its lack of direct realism. Not only was Grant Wood's imagery "a calculated lie from start to finish—the fantasy of an emotionally retarded, adolescent sensibility desperately seeking refuge from the realities of life in a dreamworld of his own invention"; it was "abysmally phony," "pervasive fakery," "shallow," "trashy," and "Camp." As a "psychological deformation," Wood's "compulsive need to invent an idealized childhood dreamworld" typified the whole school of Regionalist painting, which, "while wholly dependent upon the techniques of representation, has absolutely nothing to do with the aesthetics of realism."[40]

This emotional tirade thus ends, as if by rote, with a familiar refrain. Bypassing his own allusion to the social significance of Regionalist fantasy as an escape from reality, and thereby reflective of it, Kramer followed his predecessors in a straight line of monotonous repetition. He then accused Wood and his fellow midwestern Regionalists of ultranationalism. He judged them guilty of unadulterated chauvinism, a "shameless" extolling of native self-righteousness, and a "ruthless" rejection of alien influences.[41]

These accusations were already in circulation during Regionalism's peak year of 1935, and would stay around for another decade or so. By then, Benton was the only member of the "triumvirate" left standing. Abstract Expressionism became the new national school and Regionalism lost its credibility.

3

Nationalism!

During their decade in the limelight, Wood, Benton, and Curry were expected to provide a positive, sanitized, rural image of the nation. The Great Depression was a period of protective isolationism, and, since technology had compressed time and space, the distinction of place gained significance. Observing modern resistance to an increasingly homogeneous world, the social geographer David Harvey identifies an anxious form of localism: "Modernism, seen as a whole, explored the dialectic of place versus space, of present versus past, in a variety of ways. While celebrating universality and the collapse of spatial barriers, it also explored new meanings for space and place in ways that tacitly reinforced local identity." [1]

Wood and Curry indicated an initial tendency to explore the heartland sites of their birth and upbringing in major paintings of 1929 and 1930. But they soon paralleled Benton in considering diverse subject matter in a way that combined a modern universality of personal expression with revelations of contemporary life in the United States.

Early in the Depression decade, the Regionalist label began to signify opposition to Social Realism and vice versa. By 1935 both had gained equal status as the leading subcategories of the movement popularly known as the American Scene. Regionalism was stereotypically associated with nostalgia for rural life and its conservative values, while Social Realism was identified as harshly urban and class-consciously critical in emphasis. Regardless of their differences, the two were ostensibly allied against a common enemy that had first invaded New York from Europe well over twenty years earlier under the banner of Abstract Art.

Opinions differed within this quasi-alliance as to what the official painting of the United States should be. Hard lines of controversy were drawn between artists and critics alike by 1930, the year of *American Gothic* in Chicago and the *America Today* murals in New York City (see Figs. 9–10). Benton's upbeat, large-scale montages of life in the big city countered the often desolate and forlorn urban realism of Edward Hopper and

51

Charles Burchfield. This difference in outlook reflected a debate generated by the persistent advance of machine-age industrialization. Were its material benefits worth the social and psychological stresses caused by rampant urbanization? If not, some sort of release from the city was warranted.

A lost sense of community, with dwindling financial security, intensified the need for a renewed national identity. Whether the country's artists should concentrate on filling that need became an issue. Artists and their critics voiced a rare and short-lived affirmative consensus during the peak American Scene season of 1931–32. The Philadelphia critic Dorothy Grafly, reviewing the American section of the Carnegie Institute International, perceived "a deep national significance" in the mere inclusion of ordinary objects. "Everything from a stove pipe to an automobile tire" represented a "rich discovery of the American Scene," as well as an outward turning, an objective vigor, contrary to the mysterious subjectivity of a Picasso, Kandinsky, Ernst, or Miró, for example.[2]

Confronting this foreign menace, Edward Alden Jewell of the *New York Times,* writing in the April 1932 issue of *Parnassus,* rather pretentiously awarded American painting its "toga virilis" for having reversed an unreasonable "adulation of modern French art." While warning against "a patrioteering debauch," he not only announced the "coming of age of American art," but also claimed that some of us "are quite prepared to assert that contemporary American art is second to no other contemporary art in the world."[3] Thus the American Scene was officially launched from the depths of the Depression with a distinct thrust of national pride.

With no explanation of how they might relate to his assertions, Jewell illustrated his article with four recent paintings. The first is a ludicrous *Liebespaar* by John Carroll, whose popularity as a semimodernist was apparently based on his banal subject matter and his superficial abstractions of the figure. It is followed by a painterly caricature of the humorous printmaker Peggy Bacon by her husband, Alexander Brook. Then come a Precisionist-Cubist composition, *The Bridge,* by Peter Blume, and Edward Hopper's *Early Sunday Morning* (Fig. 22), the most overtly American of them all. Perhaps Jewell, in accordance with his nationalist theme, intended to display the range of American painting, with Carroll's dismal misappropriation of the figural style of Picasso, Matisse, or some feeble follower at the bottom. Whatever the context, Hopper's empty street can be read as a pleasantly sunlit scene on a sleep-in morning or as a social-realist cry against an estranged existence in an impersonal city environment.

The extreme nationalist point of view held that subject matter drawn directly from a particular locale and the innate forms it assumed should excise any European style, academic or avant-garde. Toward this unlikely end, Grant Wood, as early as March 1931, offered one of his earliest and most rhetorical Regionalist pronouncements. The "new movement" of painting,

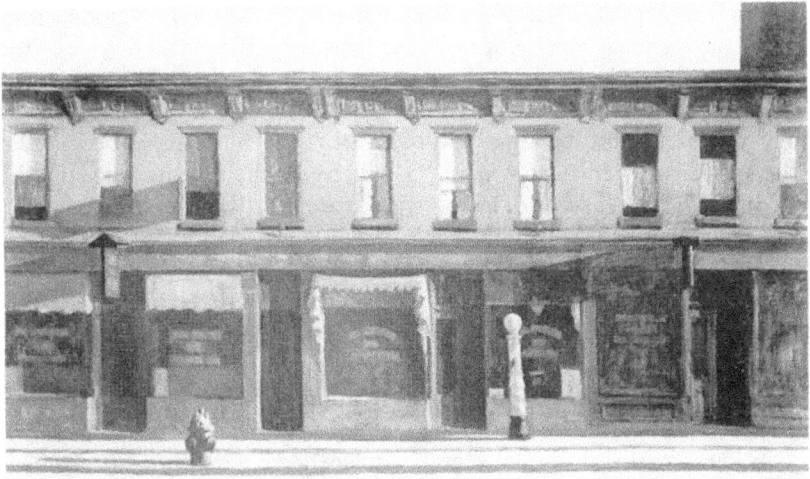

Figure 22. Edward Hopper. *Early Sunday Morning*. 1930. Oil on canvas, 35 × 60 in. Whitney Museum of American Art, New York City, 31.426, Purchase, with funds from Gertrude Vanderbilt Whitney. Photograph © 1997 Whitney Museum of Art.

in order to be truly American, had to be "anti-colonial" — that is, liberated from imported traditions and trends. Addressing the Fourth Annual Regional Conference of the American Federation of Arts, held in Kansas City, he called for "Regionalism" to rebel against any "colonial" dependence on European sources.[4] Benton and Curry, newly established and not yet acquainted with each other or with Wood, had already sounded their refrain that the truest art must be indigenous. Free from institutional dictation or authoritative expertise, artists and viewers could instinctively set aesthetic standards suitable for the community they shared. In total, regional art works would emit a national stylistic identity through a democratic diversity of techniques, compositions, subject matter, and content. The quest to package a distinctive American art may well have momentarily obscured the possibility that such unavoidable pluralism would challenge any restrictive label, including Regionalism.

As Benton began work on his mural series, *The Arts and Life of America,* for its reading room (see Figs. 8, 58–59), the newly opened Whitney Museum of American Art staged a timely debate on February 23, 1932, addressing the question "Nationalism in Art — Is It an Advantage?" Forbes Watson, editor of *The Arts,* presided. The affirmative was taken by the sculptor William Zorach and Richard Lahey, a printmaker; the negative by painter-sculptor Maurice Sterne and Joseph Pollet, a painter who had been trained by Robert Henri. The judges were museum officials, led by Juliana Force, director of the Whitney, and Alfred H. Barr, director of the

Museum of Modern Art.[5] Zorach and Sterne, by far the most loquacious of the participants, complemented each other's opinions and received little assistance from their respective partners. Zorach repeatedly referred to the artists' need to plant firm roots in the "soil of national life" from which art draws its inspiration regardless of subject or form. Then, he concluded, if a work is of "sufficient stature," it will eventually take its place in "the universal art of the world." This would occur without conscious effort now that American art had outgrown its adolescence and no longer needed guidance from abroad.[6]

Sterne, although arguing that the language of art was universal—its basic vocabulary, even when remotely initiated, understood by all—paradoxically leaned more toward nationalism than the other debaters. As a country matures, its art will respond to a self-conscious solidarity of nationalism and patriotism. At the same time, it would remain a discrete branch of its "international, parent trunk." Independent growth or attachment would be affected by a major military victory or a disastrous defeat. In the former case, its artists would benefit from a prosperous nationalism— a provocative comment during the darkest year of a worldwide depression.

To learn the bases of nationalism, American art students should go abroad and experience the works of old and modern masters in their native locales. By avoiding provincial isolation, "a great American art" would evolve. It would blend "our ancient racial instincts" with an internationally acquired art language. Whatever he meant by the former, they should not preclude national newness. Sterne concluded, "Through sensitive reaction and complete absorption we shall express something new simply because America is new and different from any other place in the world. . . . We will create work which will have a true American flavor."[7]

Whether the attainment of universality ranked first or last, a nation's art work, all seemed to agree, would by inheritance and/or group instinct express characteristics of its culture. Since neither Zorach nor Sterne specified exactly what he meant by "the soil of national life" or "a true American flavor" and emphasized international values instead, Benton more than likely would have identified both with what he chastised as the trans-Atlantic cult of "special sensibilities."

The aloofness Benton sensed in "aesthetic internationalism"—or, worse yet, "international art appreciation"—was the primary target of his speech to the annual convention of the American Federation of Arts, held in Chicago in June 1933. Any point of view that placed art above the "common ideologies of life", or indeed separated it from "the vulgarities of common life," vexed him. The "scholastic seclusion" of the literature surrounding an overly refined, Cubist-derived abstract art coincided in his mind with the didacticism of Communist ideology and its "proletarian propaganda."

Both were as doctrinaire as Christian theology and as oblivious to the present-day concerns of the American majority.[8]

In his wonderfully peculiar lunette mural of 1932, *Political Business and Intellectual Ballyhoo* (Fig. 23), Benton not only ignored the officially announced rural limits of Regionalism but turned around, as both Curry and Wood did in a number of their major works, and questioned extreme patriotism. A spread eagle, symbol of republic and empire, perches on top of a megaphone attached to a pedestal inscribed "FROM THE WRITINGS OF THE FOUNDERS." The megaphone emits a monumental sound wave that ends on a stanza of a raucous song ridiculing the great bird, thus bringing it down to earth. To the right the business of politics is represented as a broomstick scarecrow in a top hat and a hair shirt, covered over by a tieless white shirt front. A decadent "representative of the people" blurts out a kind of verbal halitosis, to which a jingle on a rectangular base alludes. "We nominate for . . ." signals the politician's obsession and Benton's distrust.

Underneath the eagle, Benton shifted into a lower gear of ideological attack. His failed flirtation with the intellectual left wing is introduced by the "LITERARY PLAYBOYS LEAGUE OF SOCIAL CONSCIOUSNESS." In the guise of the comic strip characters Mutt and Jeff, the Captain from the "Katzenjammer Kids," Andy Gump, and Mickey Mouse, the "LEAGUE" stands behind the tabloid *New York Post*. Below, representatives of radical to liberal positions move appropriately from left to right. Accompanied by arched announcements of a "Greenwich Village Proletarian Costume Dance" and "American Class Solidarity," a curly-haired, bewhiskered, hook-nosed, and chinless radical bearing the Communist Party's *New Masses* says: "THE HOUR [for revolution] IS AT HAND." In the middle, a pink, effete-looking, professorial type in horn-rim glasses emerges from *The Nation* to say: "YOU DON'T KNOW THE HALF OF IT DEARIE." Finally, chin up, nose in the air, eyes closed, the third figure concludes: "REALLY, MERELY QUANTITATIVE," as he holds the *New Republic* above his bare legs, the left one sporting a pink garter. As if to ridicule Walter Lippmann's recent qualitative evaluation of America's loss of "ancient habits," that is, codes of good behavior, in his book *A Preface to Morals,* Benton located the head of this high-brow against a crowd-pleasing *New York Post* banner, "LOVE NEST MURDER."

In the face of the mural's left-bashing negativism, Erika Doss assures us that Benton, the patriotic idealist, "clearly trusted in the historical promise of collectivism" and saw America's history as "that of assembly and fellowship," that he wished to return to a fabled republican past of totally democratic "producerism."[9] His Jacksonian great-uncle, Senator Thomas Hart Benton, clearly recognized the increasing conflict between the productive middle to laboring classes and the nonproducing profiteers in con-

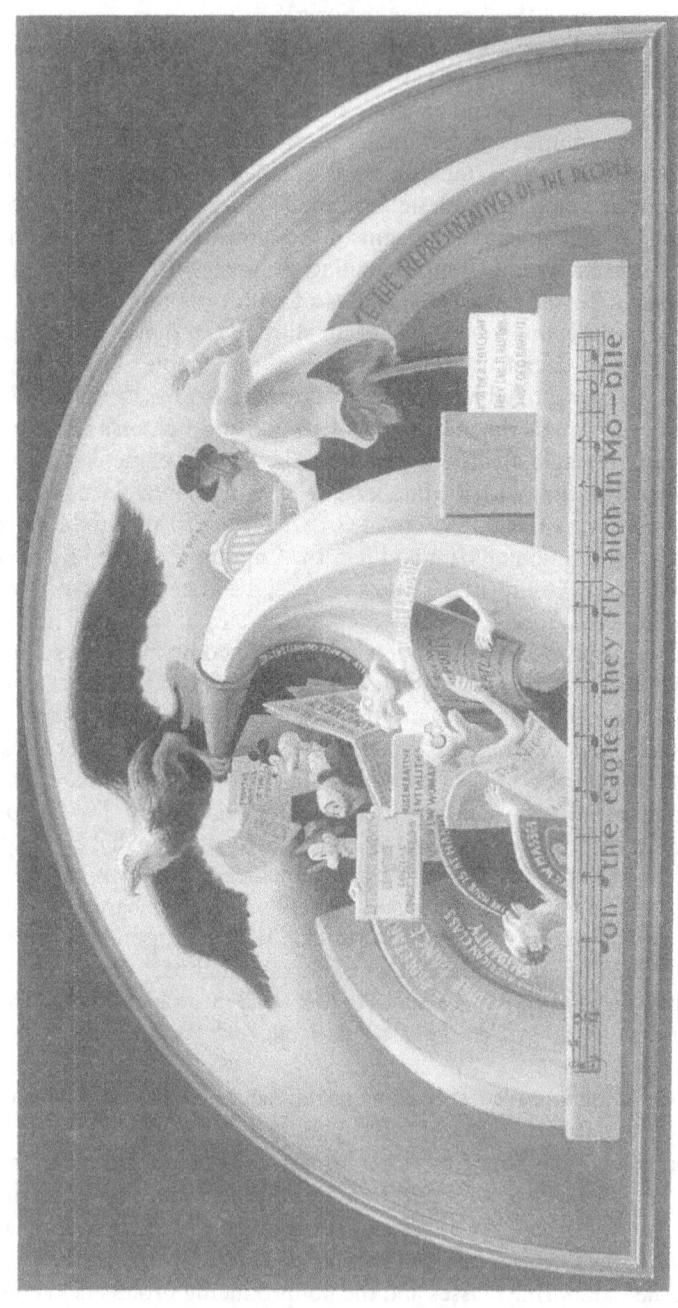

Figure 23. Thomas Hart Benton. *Political Business and Intellectual Ballyhoo*. 1932. Egg tempera and oil on canvas mounted on panel, 4 ft. 8½ in. × 9 ft. 5 in. New Britain Museum of American Art, New Britain, Connecticut; Alix W. Stanley Foundation Fund. © T. H. Benton and R. P. Benton Testamentary Trusts/Licensed by VAGA, New York, NY. Photo: Arthur Evans.

trol of government agencies, particularly the banks. Continued resistance to the concentration of wealth and power in a single, speculative class may well have been a preoccupation in 1932. Certainly this background helps explain Benton's symbiotic relationship with the political left and his distrust of exploitative elitism of all kinds.

However much concern for working people and independent enterprisers Benton had inherited, as a modernist attracted to the mythology of place, he was obviously worried about the possible collapse of his nation's reputation as a bountiful land. For him, place identity could not be isolated to a region but had to include the grand assortment of work and entertainment from coast to coast. To properly absorb all this, one must be born and raised to American mobility. "It follows that no American art can come from those who do not live an American life, who do not have an American psychology and who cannot find in America justification for their life." [10] If by American "life" and "psychology" Benton meant renewed opportunities to work and pursue happiness, he may have been hailing the efforts of the newly inaugurated Roosevelt administration to revive the nation's economy through a pragmatic mixture of monetary manipulation, federal budget balancing, relief spending, business–government planning, and agricultural supports. Without a consistent economic philosophy or a grand plan, the New Deal evolved as a coalition of diverse experiments intended from beginning to end to rebuild capitalism as a system of profit-motivated production in the face of alien threats of revolution.

As a dynamic record of the American Scene, Benton's broad-based pictorial nationalism was also characterized by multiformity. Regardless of his populist-sounding localist rhetoric in the name of Regionalism, Benton's early thirties pictures, from drawings to murals, range with reckless abandon through an entertainingly pluralistic crowd of industrial and agricultural workers, heavy-duty machinery, people at urban play, music makers, legendary historical episodes, folklore, and voyeurism. In total, his art defies any particular label within its broad frame of national reference.

Following Benton's insistence on an American art by Americans for Americans, a young Maynard Walker proclaimed "real American art" an accomplished fact. (Two years later he would become the "triumvirate's" exclusive New York dealer.) In late August 1933, Walker was back home in Kansas City with an exhibition he had organized for the Ferargil Galleries in New York. He called it "American Painting Since Whistler" and promoted the event with an article for the Kansas City *Journal-Post,* his former employer. In it he set out to merchandize the "big three" in totally nationalistic terms. "Coming out of our long-backward Middle West," Benton, Curry, and Wood were creating "an art which really springs from American soil and seeks to interpret American life." It represented "much of the most vital modern art in America," and had already replaced "shiploads of

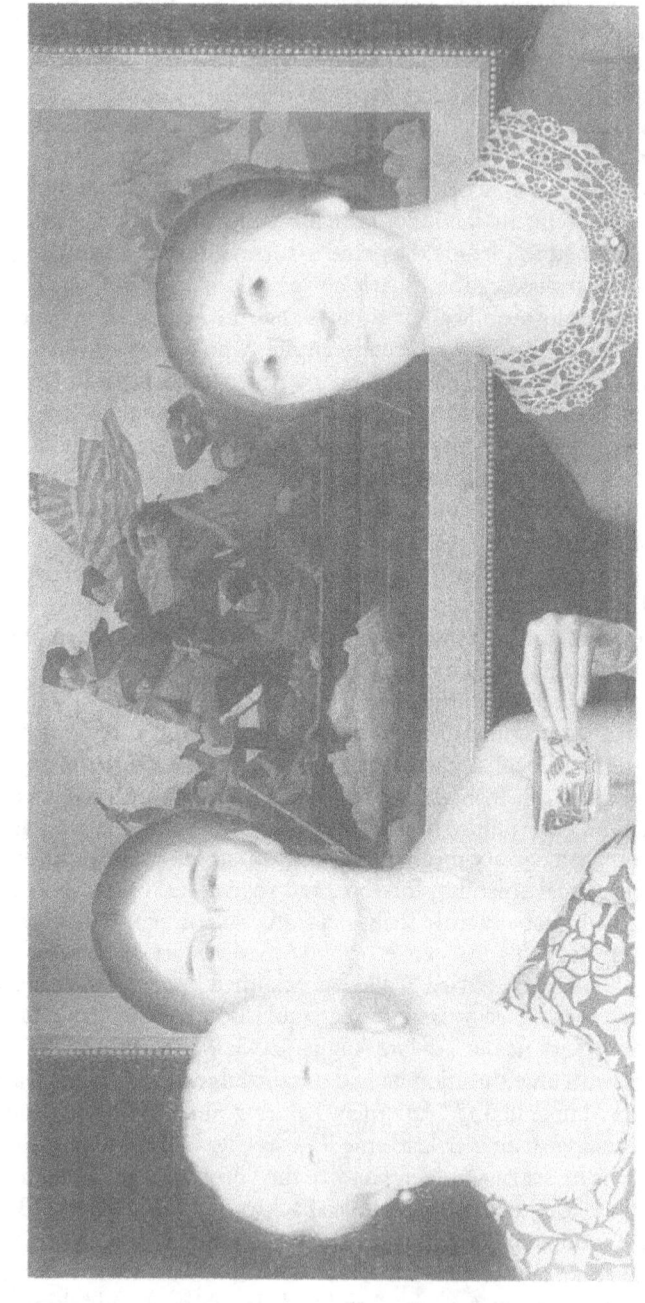

Figure 24. Grant Wood. *Daughters of Revolution*. 1932. Oil on masonite, 20 × 40 in. Cincinnati Art Museum, Cincinnati, Ohio, 1959.46; The Edwin and Virginia Irwin Memorial. © Estate of Grant Wood/Licensed by VAGA, New York, NY.

rubbish that had been imported from the School of Paris." All the country needed was more museums like the Whitney Museum of American Art to support this "indigenous art expression." [11]

With none of Walker's Cravenesque fervor and form, and none of the dealer's market-bound ulterior motives, Hazel Crow Ewell also sought to nationalize Regionalism by releasing it from strict identification with any one section of the country, in particular the Midwest. Ewell was a participant in Grant Wood's short-lived summer art colony at Stone City, Iowa in 1933 and a contributor to the *Christian Science Monitor*. While the Regionalist should turn to his own experiences in his own environment for his subject matter, he should also, if so inclined, be free to drift far afield. Without mentioning the American love of the road, she allowed the artist-as-Regionalist to roam like Benton through various geographic areas, provided he demonstrated "penetration." This she defined open-endedly as the ability to emphasize and analyze what was of personal significance to him. Whatever that might be, it separated the wandering Regionalist from the local colorist whose superficial work lacked "the authenticity and conviction which results from real knowledge and strong emotional reaction." Since they were simply reporting the typical, "American Scene" painters employed by the Public Works of Art Project in 1934 failed to qualify. Many were merely provincial, and "the less provincial a painter is the better regionalist he will make." The true painter's reality is, after all, conditioned by his own emotions, experiences, and ability to analyze. These will relate his work to contemporary times and places as long as he avoids a "top lofty" idea of his art, as long as he refuses to become too aesthetic—that is, too abstract and therefore alien to the nation's best cultural interests.[12]

The need to distinguish provincials and local colorists from the artist who could penetrate the stereotyped facades of a given region with emotional depth and analytic, even critical, interpretation prompted the nativist emphasis of Grant Wood's 1935 manifesto, *Revolt Against the City*.[13] As implied by its title, the essay's nationalism rested on a populist stand against the cultural colonialism of eastern cities. As seaboard metropoles had looked to Europe, especially Paris for guidance, midwesterners had, in turn, looked to the East Coast for cultural leads. Now, a nationwide introspection prompted by the Great Depression revealed itself in a growing aesthetic appreciation of local experiences. Symptomatic of a self-contained America, that appreciation ostensibly evoked the old frontier virtue of individual self-reliance, while a major reaction against economic and political entanglements in European affairs sanctioned isolationism.[14] Although *American Gothic* (its humor aside) could have served as an allegorical illustration of this policy, the only other painting by Wood that alludes to it ridicules it. The patriotic ladies caricatured two years later in *Daughters of Revolution* (Fig. 24) accompany the nation's favorite depiction of the American Revolution, *Washington Crossing the Delaware*, painted on the Rhine River in Düsseldorf during the Revolution of 1848 by the German-American Emanuel Leutze. Contrary to Wood's manifesto, the *Daughters*, purchased by the movie star Edward G. Robinson, a son of eastern European immigrants, was intended to underline the absurdity of intolerance toward outsiders in a nation uniquely populated from around the world.

An interregional conflict of taste and values, a cultural defensiveness, would appear to be at the root of Wood's populism if it were not for his cosmopolitan ability to satirize the people he lived among and to fantasize their countryside beyond strict local identity. What seems an ironic contradiction must be viewed as a matter of vested interest. By 1935, after all, identification with Regionalism as a precisely defined movement was of commercial significance to its "triumvirate." They enjoyed name recognition with a marketable product bearing a popular label. Far be it from Wood to ruin a good thing when secession from Europe, involving music, theater, and literature as well as painting, was to be heralded as a complete reversal of "the revolt against the village" spurred by the critical satire of Edgar Lee Masters, Sinclair Lewis, and H. L. Mencken.[15] Their cynicism toward rural life and the provincial parvenu was another facet of an urban imitativeness of European fashions.

In place of these imitations, distinctly indigenous art forms would arise, as Benton might have put it, from "an American way of looking at things, and a utilization of the materials of our own American scene," versus "the French mental attitude and the use of French subject matter," whatever either of these phrases might denote.[16] Wood qualified the "American way" as a "feeling for one's milieu" and (with a less ironic choice of words) a recognition of "the validity of one's own life and its surroundings."[17] While this might be called a patriotic attitude, it should never be considered "mere chauvinism," a rebuff exploited by critics and dealers with a vested interest in imported art goods. In fact Wood preferred not to think of it in terms of sentiment at all but as "common-sense utilization for art of native materials—an honest reliance by the artist upon subject matter which he can best interpret because he knows it best."[18] This was the classic definition of Regionalism, and in his works Wood came closer to its consistent application than did either Benton or Curry.

To use material that was truly a part of himself, Wood's model Regionalist as nativist, while possibly traveling abroad in order to develop new perspectives, centered his efforts in his home region. He did not tour other regions or countries in search of the picturesque or the quaint. The midwestern artist sought and creatively captured local material, as did the New Yorker, the New Englander, or the Southwesterner. In Wood's admittedly biased opinion, the Middle West, especially Iowa, contained more sincere and honest painting material than existed anywhere else, and it "gains in depth for having to be hunted for." [19] Emerging from such "analysis," it was "less obscured by 'picturesque' surface quality"—it did not suffer from "the thinness of things viewed from outside." [20] At the same time his particular inside view could claim no preeminence over that of any other artist in command of native material: "I shall not quarrel with the painter from New Mexico, from further West, or from quaint New England, if he differs with me; for if he does so honestly, he doubtless has the same basic feeling for his material that I have for mine—he believes in its genuineness." [21]

As a central motive of the midwestern scene, the farmer inhabited Wood's thoughts, writings, and pictures throughout the 1930s. The farmer stands as the exclamation point of his art in the lithograph *Sultry Night* (see Fig. 149), and approximately a quarter of *Revolt Against the City* is occupied with this mythical being. Contemporaneous farm strikes proved to the East that the midwestern farmer was not just a stereotyped oaf to be ridiculed for his isolation and inarticulateness, but a thinking, feeling, individual human being. The farmer offered intensely dramatic material for midwestern artists to interpret. While choosing not to do so in his fantasy farmscapes or allegorized farm figures, Wood did encourage midwestern artists to pay attention to the struggles farmers waged seasonally against natural and economic forces intensified by the Depression. He and a poet friend from Cedar Rapids, Jay Sigmund, regularly visited farmers in Waubeek, Iowa. With a trace of cultural racism Wood attributed their survival to their descent from New England fishermen and their "old Anglo-Saxon reserve." [22]

Ethnic partiality aside, Wood visualized the growth of a national culture through competition among regions. Like French Gothic architecture, it would arise town by town, or out of a network of regional schools and mural programs sponsored by the central government. Allied with state universities, federal support should provide student painters opportunities to learn what they needed to know about natural science, "the general liberal arts culture," and just plain thinking and feeling. [23] Annual exhibitions of their work would serve two vital purposes: to excite local pride, and to alert an enlarged American art public to a long-awaited American art.

Much less verbal than either the garrulous Benton or the judicious Wood, Curry held steadfastly to his conviction that an indigenous art of any originality must arise from within the person of the artist. Innate faculties and capacities, although obviously conditioned from without, count for much more in a work of art than any prescribed subject matter of a given region, let alone any nationalist aspirations. Addressing the Madison, Wisconsin Art Association in January 1937, he warned against the Tainesian tendency to overvalue the role of a specific place in the formation of art: "Some of us look forward to a great and alive art in the Middle West, but be reminded of this—the great art is within yourself. . . . Your greatness will not be found in Europe or in New York, or in the Middle West, or in Wisconsin, but within yourself."[24]

In Curry's "heart," as he preferred to say, the vital experience, force, and power behind his expression originated in the human struggle with nature for survival. He personalized and localized this confrontation as a family tradition—indeed, "the tradition of a great majority of Kansas people," if not of most Nebraskans to the north and Oklahomans to the south. Consequently, in reference to his Kansas State Capitol Building murals, in particular *The Tragic Prelude* (see Fig. 19), the "vital experience" for him lay not in the controversial John Brown allegory of fanaticism but in "the great backdrop of the phenomenon of nature, and to those who live and depend upon the soil for life and sustenance this phenomenon is God."[25] It was of this spiritual emphasis on the terrible sublime, signified by a tornado and a prairie fire, that he wished to convince the Kansas legislative commission in charge of reviewing his preparatory studies.[26]

Scarcely nationalistic, Curry told a student audience that the way to a distinctly American painting, one "worthy of foreign respect," was now being led by the young artist returning to reality, "the reality of his experience." In keeping with his own works of unmistakable protest against nationwide racism and terror, he foresaw a new kind of painting marked by "an awakened liveliness that embodies the shock of vital subject matter." By this he apparently meant an art of social significance, one that provided "a more exciting and real subject matter than what in former times was provided by the contemplation of abstract nature."[27]

Far outside the rhetorically defined boundaries of an innocuous, homegrown, midwestern Regionalism, Curry painted politically charged pictures meant to protest against deadly unlawfulness. A member of the National Urban League and a civil-rights activist, he depicted an array of crucial African-American experiences from the early thirties to the early forties.[28] In the face of increased Ku Klux Klan activity, lynchings, and expanding discrimination, *Manhunt* of 1931 (Fig. 25) was followed by *The Fugitive* (Fig. 26), painted for an exhibition sponsored by the National Association for the Advancement of Colored People (NAACP), "An Art Commentary on Lynching," originally scheduled to open at the Jacques Seligmann Galleries in New York on February 16, 1935. Because of "an outburst of opposition," Germain Seligmann canceled the exhibition at the last minute, explaining: "I wish to keep the galleries free of political and racial manifestations."[29]

The exhibition did open and run on schedule at the Arthur U. Newton Galleries on East 57th Street. It also included Benton's painting *A Lynching* (Fig. 27), and Isamu Noguchi's polished chromium figure of a black man at

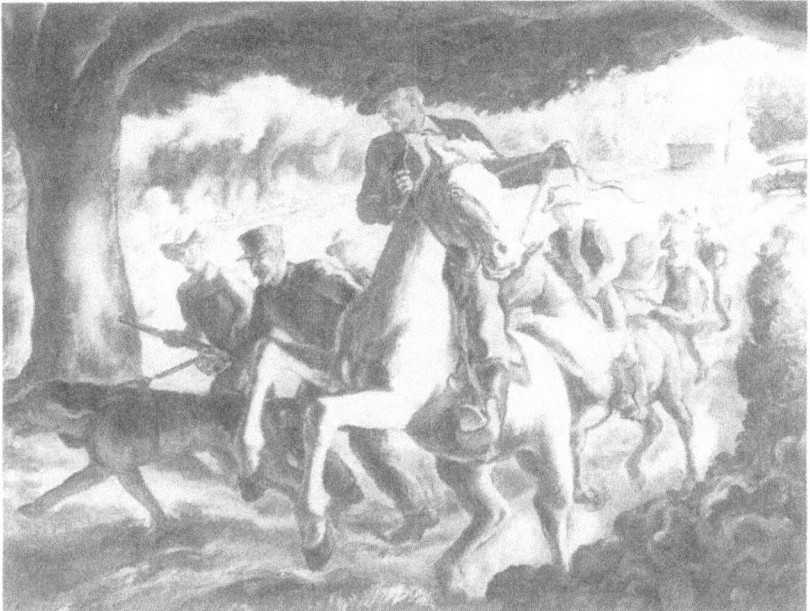

Figure 25. John Steuart Curry. *Manhunt*. 1931. Oil on canvas, 30 × 40¼ in. Joslyn Art Museum, Omaha, Nebraska, 1979.142.

the spasmodic moment when his neck is broken by the rope. Georgia-born and raised Erskine Caldwell wrote an introductory note for the catalogue, whose cover bears a reproduction of *The Fugitive*. He emphasized the increase in lynching in recent years and the need to legislate against it.[30]

That same year saw Curry's flooded black family in the painting *The Mississippi* (see Fig. 81) and, in the lithograph of the same subject, *Mississippi Noah*. Two years later he completed the mural *Justice Defeating Mob Violence* (Fig. 28) for the new Justice Department Building in Washington, D.C., in place of the originally intended *The Freeing of the Slaves* (see Fig. 20). Not to be wasted, this large canvas ended up permanently installed in the library of the University of Wisconsin Law School, thanks to its dean of 1942, Lloyd K. Garrison, great-grandson of the abolitionist William Lloyd Garrison. None of these works relate exclusively to Curry's place of birth, let alone to his experiences there. The time was ripe for such critical art. From 1933 through 1935, sixty-six lynchings were reported. NAACP lawyers drafted an antilynching law that was introduced to the Senate in 1934 as the Wagner–Van Nuys Bill, only to be filibustered away by southern members in 1935. President Roosevelt lent no support to the bill.[31] As for Hollywood's reaction, two *white* lynching movies were made:

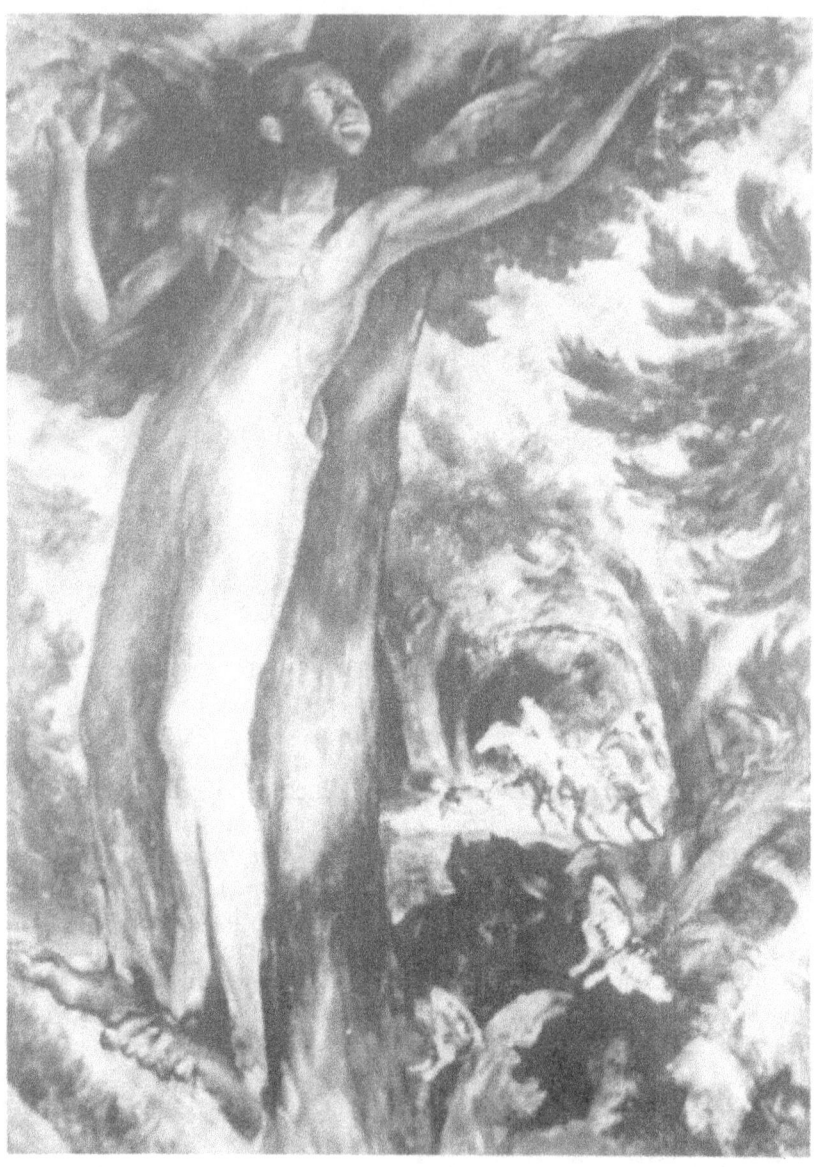

Figure 26. John Steuart Curry. *The Fugitive*. 1933. Oil and tempera on canvas, 38 × 36 in. Kennedy Galleries, Inc., New York City; private collection. Photo courtesy of Kennedy Galleries, Inc.

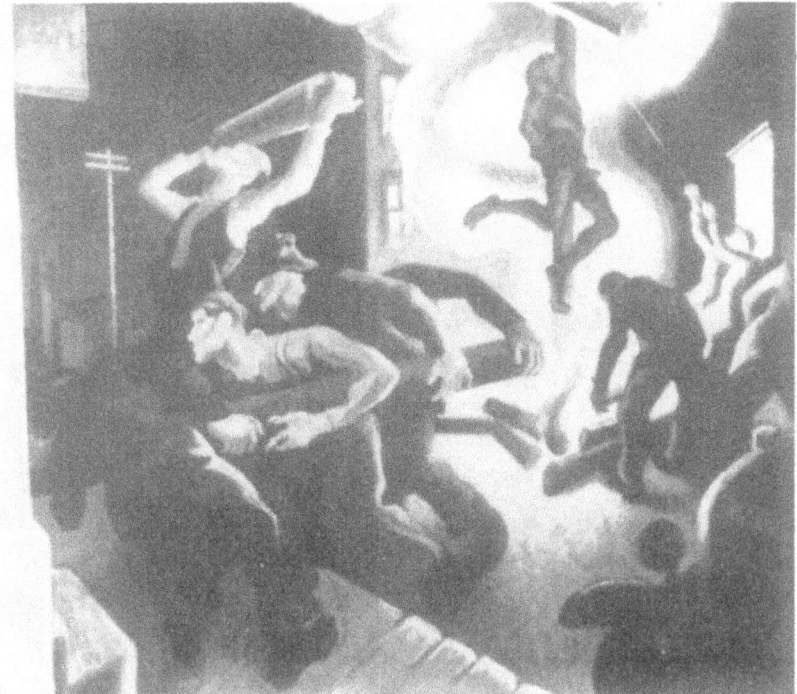

Figure 27. Thomas Hart Benton. *A Lynching*. 1934. Oil on canvas. Water-damaged and lost. Reprinted from *Art Digest*, February 15, 1935. © T. H. Benton and R. P. Benton Testamentary Trusts/Licensed by VAGA, New York, NY.

Fury in 1936, directed by Fritz Lang, and *They Won't Forget* in 1937, directed by Mervyn Leroy. Only one black appears momentarily as a witness in either film, and he is a Stepin Fetchit–like stereotype.

In contrast to this evasive whitewashing, Curry believed American painting should be charged with a historically accurate, stop-action intensity: exciting, vital, and personally real in expression. Settled in Madison, Wisconsin, by the beginning of 1937, he was inspired by the liberal isolationism of the Progressive Party, originated by Robert La Follette. His anti-interventionist, death's-head painting *Parade to War: Allegory* (Fig. 29, discussed in detail in Chapter 7)[32] clearly aimed its denunciation of war at the entire nation as the Nazis blitzkrieged Poland and the Roosevelt administration prepared to enter World War II.

His ultimately failed isolationist point of view never blinded Curry (or his antiauthoritarian Regionalist colleagues) to the dangers of a right-wing threat that had accelerated immediately before his return to the Midwest. The warning signals in movies and over the radio, in books and through

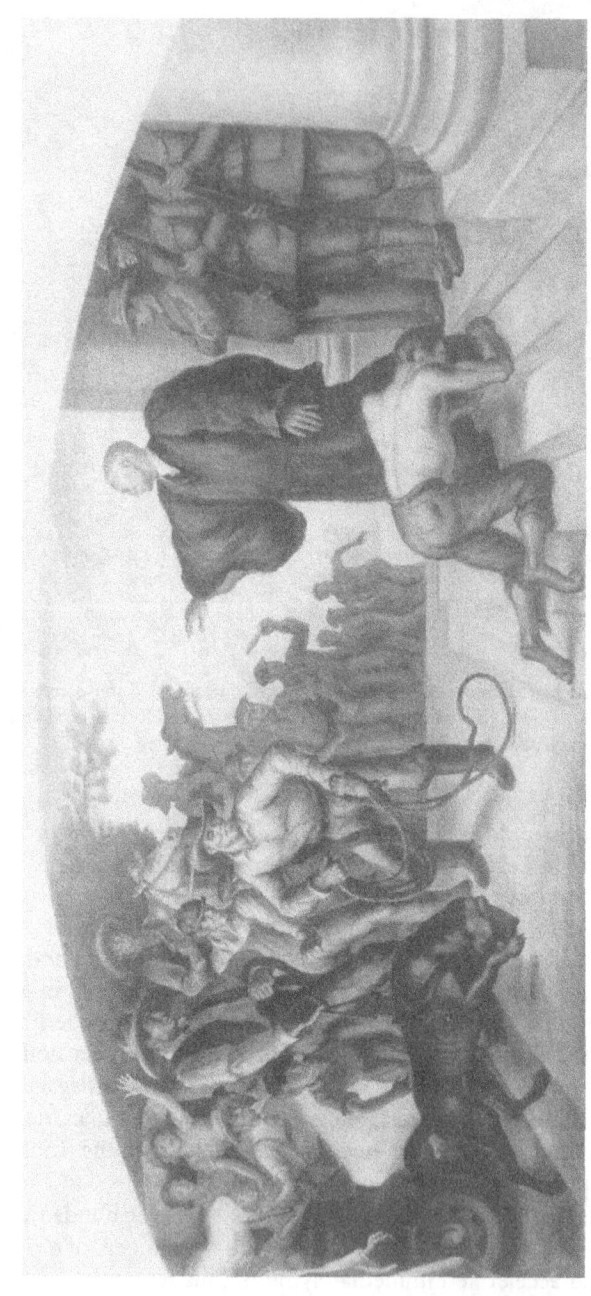

Figure 28. John Steuart Curry. *Justice Defeating Mob Violence.* 1936–37. Oil and tempera on canvas, 8 ft. 6 in. × 20 ft. 6 in. Mural in Department of Justice Building, Washington, D.C.

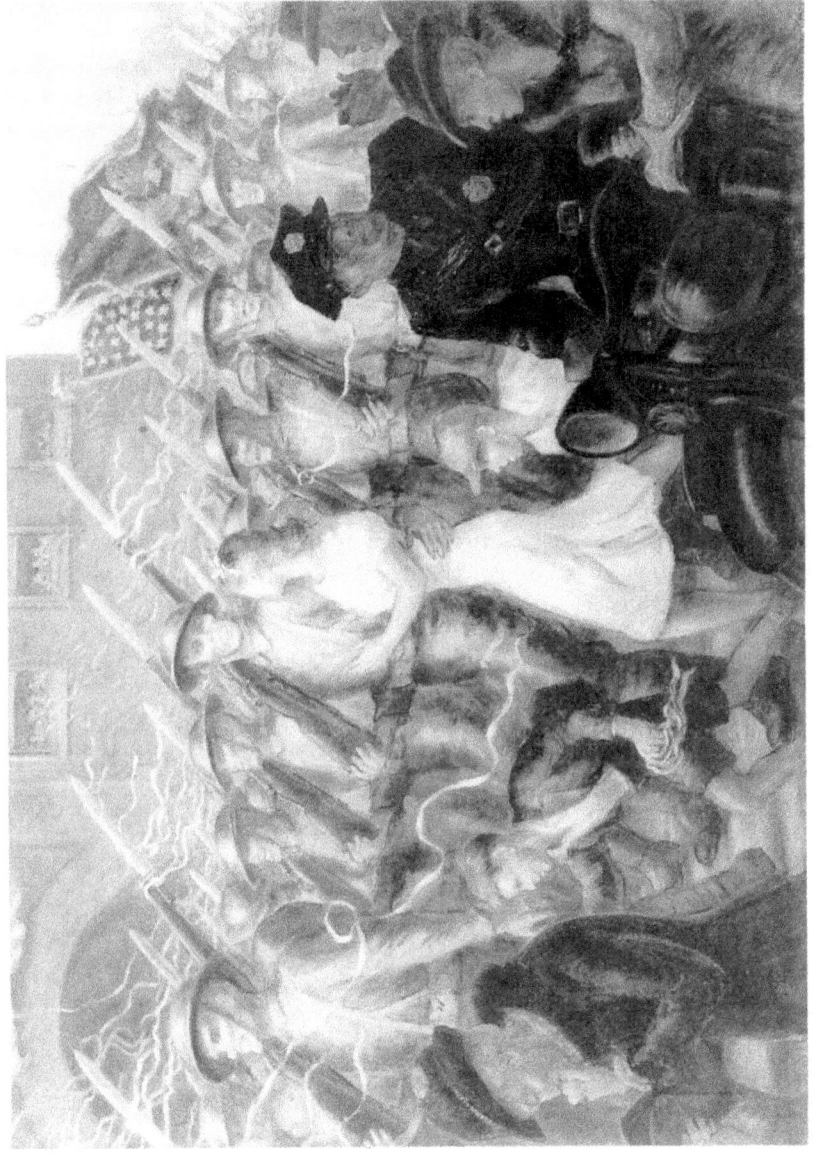

Figure 29. John Steuart Curry. *Parade to War: Allegory*. 1938–39. Oil on canvas, 40½ × 56 in. Cummer Museum of Art & Gardens, Jacksonville, Florida, AG. 91.4.1; gift of Barnett Banks, Inc.

the mail, were loud and clear. A film blatantly advocating an American dictatorship, *Gabriel Over the White House,* was produced by Walter Wanger for William Randolph Hearst's Cosmopolitan Pictures in 1933; it met its counterstatement two years later in Sinclair Lewis's *It Can't Happen Here,* first as a discursive novel and then in a play that ran for five years in coast-to-coast performances by companies of the New Deal Federal Theatre Project.[33] Mailings and broadcasts from the Huey Long "Share Our Wealth Clubs" were followed by Father Charles Coughlin's demagogic "Radio Audience." Native Fascist groups, the Silver Shirts and the Black Legion, organized by William Dudley Pelley and V. F. Effinger, respectively, found theoretical encouragement in *The Coming American Fascism,* written by the Harvard-educated Lawrence Dennis and published in 1936. It is not surprising in this atmosphere that distrust of Regionalism, viewed as a nationalist movement, could go to extremes.

Despite their lapses into promotional localist rhetoric, the words and works of Wood, Benton, and Curry prove them to be anything but ardent nationalists. At the crest of their fame as a virtually contrived three-artist movement, they were individually engaged in a pluralistic pictorial expression that involved the whole country rather than any single region. Included were "common life" experiences of work and play, personal fantasies, political bones to pick, satires aimed at provincial narrowmindedness, protests against social injustice, and withal a self-generated *élan vital* of modern independence.

4

Fascism?

A charge of exploitative nationalism was frequently leveled against Wood, Benton, and Curry, especially from the left and culminated in 1935, Regionalism's peak year. An image of regressiveness, amplified by the *Time* magazine cover article featuring Benton and by Wood's Regionalist polemic, *Revolt Against the City,* impeded any identity the three might have acquired as modern independents. At variance with their proclaimed focus, they had been pursuing increasingly universal aesthetic values and social meanings in their highly varied works. This mattered little to their most ardent opponents.

Writing in the Communist-dominated *New Masses,* the journal's art critic, Stephen Alexander, attempted to dismiss Wood's art as a "frantic patrioteering" that had been rushed to the aid of an endangered capitalist country. Wood, in Alexander's eyes, had shrewdly taken advantage of the rising tide of flag waving during a period of economic disaster by simulating the "archaisms" of the early American limners and the Currier and Ives prints dear to a fearful upper middle class.[1]

Such accusations, in the latter half of the thirties, were provoked less by the Depression and more by foreign affairs as attention shifted to the crises caused by Mussolini, Hitler, Franco, and the warlords of Japan. In response to the initiation of the antifascist Popular Front in 1935, a large majority of the artists and critics convening in New York at the first American Artists' Congress vehemently opposed emphasis on the making of an "American Art" as totally reactionary.[2] A few went so far as to identify Regionalism with the propaganda art of fascism.

Even after World War II, charges of right-wing subject matter, comparable to that favored by the defeated Axis governments, cropped up. The art historian H. W. Janson overextended his "modernist" aversion to the work of Wood and Benton to the point of demonstrating poor historical judgment. As will be seen, his articles on the two not only perpetuated the critical minimization of their richly varied themes but mistakenly equated certain of their values, basic to the modern American experience, with those of Nazi Germany.

Four months before the Popular Front was officially announced, when the Seventh World Congress of the Communist International in Moscow called for all democratic parties of the Western world to join in a common alliance against fascism, Stuart Davis aggressively reproached Benton for demonstrating fascist-racist tendencies. In an article for the April 1, 1935, issue of the *Art Digest,* Davis pointed out what he considered contradictions and evasions in Benton's discursive answers to ten questions submitted to him, (at his own request) by the editors of *Art Front*.[3] For example, while heralding the Middle West as the least provincial area in the United States, he boasted of its aesthetic isolation, or, as Davis would put it, "cultural backwardness." Also, how could Benton maintain that all meaningful art forms of any value resulted from direct contact with community subject matter, when at the same time he rejected "social understanding" as a body of belief that generally hampers an artist's directness of perception?[4] Viewed from Davis's basically Marxist position, this implication of non-commitment seemed not only contradictory but socially irresponsible.

As for the primary point of contention between the two painters, Benton claimed to follow an inherent, "from the gut" attraction to vanishing ways of life still relatively free of advanced, urbanized civilization. Davis, though allowing for a given "weapon of theory," insisted that the imaginative perceptions that weapon released must keep the practical realities of rapid economic and social change in sight. The abstractionist, in this case, drew his iconography directly from the ever-changing urban scene and abhorred what he narrowly viewed as the rural romances of a self-styled Regionalist. In fact, Davis not only repudiated Benton's claim to an instinctive style of expression but questioned his intelligence.

It is now clear that the disorganization, the bad color, the unpleasant surface and the social nihilism of his work are not, as he himself boasts, the crudities of a man of the soil and of the pioneer stock, but rather the logical result of an innate inability to think straight and realistically.[5]

Davis even doubted Benton's ability to understand "the ideological basis" of the "great art of the future" about which he wrote: his Regionalist "jingoism and chauvinism" held him back. Davis was also on alert for examples of "racial chauvinism," and in particular anything resembling current developments in Germany. Benton, at his most cynical level of performance as a muralist, "should have no trouble in selling his wares to any Fascist or semi-Fascist type of government." One work alone certified his "qualifications" for such patronage (see Fig. 23):

Specifically he could point to his lunette in the library of the Whitney Museum of American Art where his opinion of radical and liberal thought is clearly symbolized. It shows a Jew in vicious caricature holding the *New Masses* and saying "the hour is at hand." Hitler would love that.[6]

Following Davis's "exposure" of Benton—which, if accurate, would certainly be an exception to the political moderation and overall sense of social propriety practiced by the Regionalists—the accusations of fascist equivalence subsided until the very end of the movement. In 1943 Samuel Kootz, a dealer-critic trading in paintings of Cubist persuasion, had no vested interest in promoting Regionalists when he called them (including Reginald Marsh) "America's Nationalist School."[7] To him, their only value was to produce "painting reports" full of "unassailable facts" that eased the frustration of economic loss and helped fill an underlying need for security. Familiar affirmations from "chauvinistic brushes," pictures of rich farmlands, mines, water power, vast industries, and "familiar homely scenes," reassured a culturally bereft middle class whose additional social insecurities had fostered a "Decade of Nationalism." Satire and occasional criticism aside, a new confidence was inspired by an "America of insistent actuality, whether it was attacked or affectionately fondled."[8]

As for the "Fascist" elements, Kootz somewhat hesitantly suggested their existence in the nationalist appeal Regionalism held for its vulnerable audience.

Chauvinism of this type requires no civilized or disciplined understanding of esthetics, but insists only upon a bigoted outlook. In its bombastic philosophy Nationalism, at its worst, is too related for comfort to the opinionated Fascism that has itself sponsored just such local, familiar narcotics. It is an innocent approximation of the Fascist attitude, but actual design is not required to show us its unfortunate qualities.[9]

Four years before Kootz's book appeared, a University of Iowa art history instructor completing his Ph.D. dissertation for Harvard developed a personal dislike for Wood. H. W. Janson, born in East Prussia, focused on the Iowan's paintings in hinting at broad-based stylistic resemblances between Regionalist and Nazi art.

Janson taught at Iowa from 1939 to 1942. Any contact he had with Wood most likely occurred during his first year, but that the two saw much of each other is questionable. In the summers of 1940 and 1941, neither was in Iowa City: Wood was painting in his studio (an abandoned train station) on Clear Lake in northern Iowa; Janson was working on his dissertation in Europe or back at Harvard. Wood spent the academic year 1940–41 on sabbatical, and by the fall semester of 1941–42 he was sick and dying from pancreatic cancer. His conflicts with the art department, especially with its chairman, Lester B. Longman, who had a Ph.D. in art history from Princeton, had alienated him from it. He disliked the new "overemphasis" of art history, which he believed stifled "the creative spirit" of the students, and had earlier called for Longman's resignation, to be replaced by himself. Short of this, Studio Art under his direction and Art History under Longman should become two distinct departments.

As Wood's sabbatical year came to an end, the director of the university's School of Fine Arts, Earl E. Harper, agreed to a compromise arrangement. It allowed Wood, essentially an artist-in-residence with the rank and tenure of full professor, to teach his courses in a generous studio space located away from the department. His students would earn independent credits outside the combined studio–art history curriculum, and Wood would be answerable to the director. While this arrangement was being negotiated, Wood was facing accusations that he drew and painted his figures' faces from projected photographs. Disregarding the modern precedents for such a practice, dating from the advent of the camera, Longman made this charge at the Western Arts Conference in Wisconsin in October 1940. A visiting artist, Fletcher Martin, along with a printmaking instructor, Emil Ganso, reiterated it to a *Time* magazine reporter, Eleanor Welch. The charge ignored Wood's habit of caricaturing his models, whether from photographs or direct studies. The artist was finally scheduled to prove his ability to draw by doing an accurate pencil portrait from life of the president of the university, Virgil M. Hancher.[10]

In the face of all this confusion and loss of influence, it would seem highly doubtful that Wood could persuade a dean or a director to make a personnel change. Janson tells us that Wood had him fired for taking a group of students to the Chicago Art Institute in early 1940 to see the Museum of Modern Art's exhibition of forty years of Picasso's work, although Longman soon negotiated his reinstatement. The story, though entertaining, seems at best tenuous.

The first published indication of Janson's extremely critical attitude appeared in a *College Art Journal* article, "The International Aspects of Regionalism," published in May 1943 and occasioned by the Grant Wood memorial exhibition at the Art Institute of Chicago. The essay rightly questioned the popular notion that Wood's paintings belonged exclusively to a particular region and were totally free from European influence. The well-traveled Iowan, even at his most Regionalist, could not have broken ties with his art ancestry abroad, no matter how loudly he protested against academic tradition or the School of Paris.[11] According to Janson's scenario, Wood one day went to the Alte Pinakothek in Munich, where he observed that the Flemish and German Old Masters had incorporated local settings of towns and landscapes into their paintings. He then returned to Iowa determined to do the same. But, indifferent to the "expressive and imaginative values" of Late Gothic paintings, he disregarded their "surface textures" and ignored their "international" character.[12]

Wood's conscious desire to avoid the true qualities of the Northern Masters plus his "fondness of geometric patterns" aroused Janson's art historical suspicion that there was another, unacknowledged influence. This, he discloses, came from a group of paintings circulating throughout Germany by 1928 under the museum exhibition label of *Neue Sachlichkeit*. With no reference to any German painter (for example, Georg Scholz [Fig. 30]) or any mention of possible Italian precedents in *Valori Plastici* or *Nove Cente* works, Janson confined his characterization of *Neue Sachlichkeit* to a "strong nationalistic tinge," acquired as *Neue Sachlichkeit* converts broke from "the abstract 'constructivism' of the Cubists and the undisciplined emotionalism of the Expressionists."[13]

While *Neue Sachlichkeit* painters professed to have rediscovered the national heritage of German painting from the fifteenth and sixteenth centuries, their actual sources of inspiration were German Romantic painters of the early nineteenth century. These artists (presumably he had the Nazarenes in mind) had been "the first to pledge allegiance to the late Gothic in a spirit of nationalism."[14] Analogous tendencies within *Neue Sachlichkeit,* in Janson's opinion, caused the movement to deteriorate into what he called a Neo-Biedermeier style. While admitting that it might be difficult "in terms of comparisons between individual pictures" to prove that Wood derived his Regionalism from this Neo-Biedermeier phase of *Neue Sachlichkeit,* Janson rested his rather tenuous case on what he vaguely referred to as a "similarity."

Wood's mature style, Janson maintained, like that of the *Neue Sachlichkeit* painters as a whole, registered a reaction against spontaneity, especially against that of the German Expressionists. Wood and his German counterparts insisted on being "unsophisticated" and "normal." They were allegedly preoccupied with idyllic aspects of rural and small-town life and shared a habit of paring down forms of this reality into smooth-surfaced, stereometric units, a remnant, Janson says, of Cubist abstraction. Painstakingly calculated compositions, as well as the dry and laborious tempera technique with its emphasis on neatness, precision, and "craftsmanship," were likewise Neo-Biedermeier traits.[15]

Thus, with a curious twist of logic and a complete avoidance of examples, Janson associated *Neue Sachlichkeit* with a national heritage of German painting identified with the Biedermeier period of the Romantic era and, citing a list of partially inaccurate traits ostensibly held in common, labeled and categorized Wood as Neo-Biedermeier. Accordingly, Wood's "amazing popularity" resulted from "a vision of stability and security" untouched by the economic and political crises of the Depression or by the

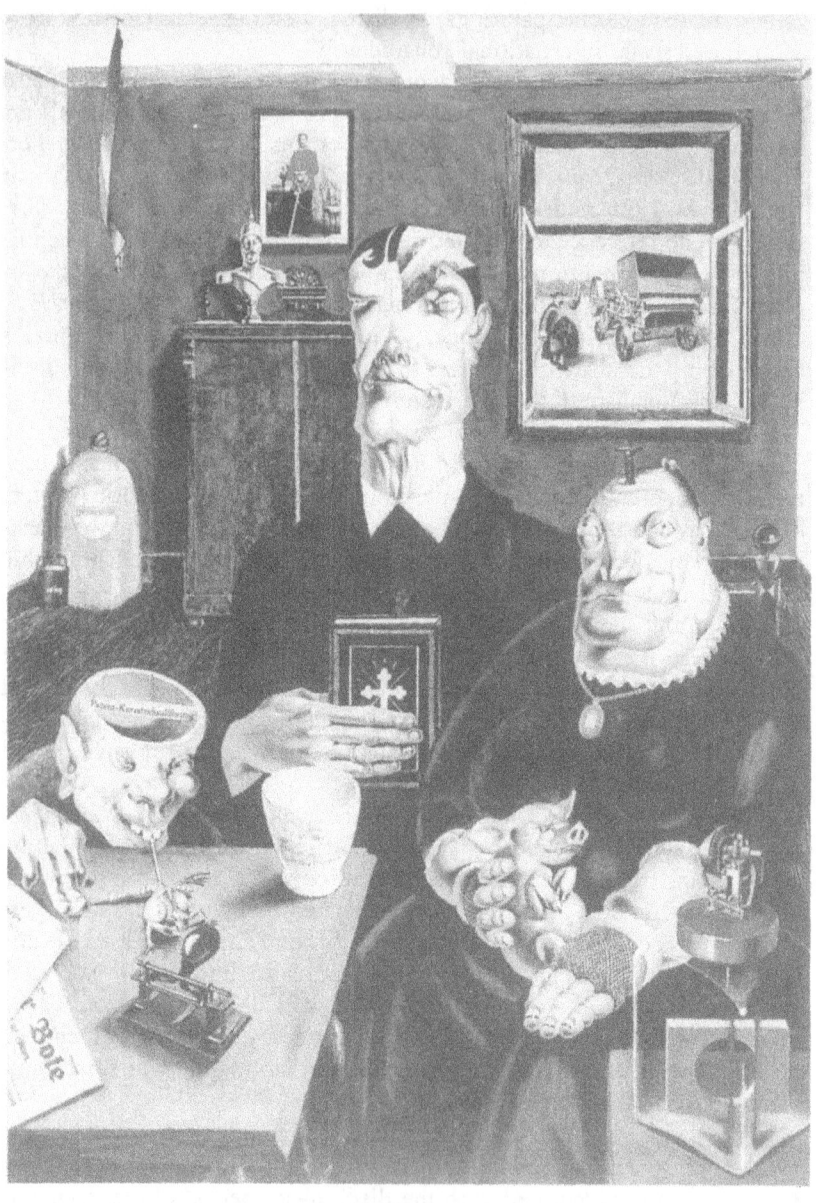

Figure 30. Georg Scholz. *Industrialized Farmers*. 1920. Oil and collage on wood panel, 98 × 70 cm. Von der Heydt Museum, Wupperthal, Germany.

shadows of war abroad. This unreal vision "he placed before the public," providing the urban population in particular with a much needed "substitute reality"—a service Janson found totally objectionable. He further suspected Wood of self-promotion through the use of "demagogic" publicity schemes. His Regionalist doctrine was "put across" in powerful, conservative publications dedicated to nationalist movements.[16] "Little wonder, then, that Grant Wood's style should prove to be so similar to some of the artistic developments accompanying the rise of nationalism in Europe since the late 1920s."[17] Among the developments Janson evidently meant, though he hesitated to say so, were those officially sanctioned in Nazi Germany when Hitler took over the country in 1933.[18]

Three years after this article appeared, a year after World War II ended, and four months before Curry died, Janson published his most obsessive attack on Regionalism.[19] Abandoning nuance and ambiguity, he wrote of a direct relationship, if not a direct causal connection, between the "styles" and attitudes of Wood and Benton and those of Nazi art. Janson felt that the vast majority of the American public would have agreed with the *Reichskulturkammer* in its condemnation of Expressionism. To support this assertion, he cited Jacques Barzun's comment on the "insecure esthetic instincts" of the German lower middle class, confirmed in its acceptance of Nazi policies toward "modern art."[20] It followed that people of the United States would also have been easily persuaded that modernist distortions of the human figure should be considered degenerate; Janson stopped short of saying that Americans would have approved the suppression of artists.

By the mid-forties, New York avant-garde painters (Pollock, Rothko, and Motherwell, for example) had turned against Cubism. Apparently unaware of this, Janson assumed that the "man in the street" prejudice against Picasso-inspired painting resulted from a reactionary conspiracy of "powerful pressure groups of artists, critics and publicists." Of these "the most powerful" were "the so-called regionalist movement" and its "most vehement champions," Grant Wood and Thomas Benton. Though weakened by the war, Regionalism remained "sufficiently dangerous." Its sources, aims, and methods, as well as "the underlying reasons" for its popular success, invited "the closest scrutiny." In his 1943 article Janson had advised "closer scrutiny," but he now more specifically diagnosed the symptoms of Regionalism as those fundamental to American society: "the same ills that in more virulent form produced National Socialism in Germany."[21]

One could be legitimately concerned about a rise of nationalism in a postwar United States armed with the Bomb and faced with a mobilized Soviet Union on its way to the Bomb. Even continued fear of a latent American fascism might have been understandable at the beginning of the

Cold War. But to sound another warning against the moribund Regionalist movement in order to "reduce its influence" would seem anachronous, especially in view of the rise of Abstract Expressionism between 1943 and 1946.[22]

Dislike for Wood and Benton—indeed, outspoken prejudice against them and their respective "styles"—rendered objective art historical analysis impossible. Janson repudiated the "Americanism, i.e. nationalism" in their works as a weak substitute for "esthetic values of any kind." To him Regionalism as a whole was "essentially anti-artistic in its aims and character." Whether conservative or progressive, the Regionalists consistently refused to uphold the values of the past or to acknowledge the values of the present, and consequently "most of their work is bad painting" by any standard.[23] As if this were not enough, Janson denied Wood and Benton any interest in compositional form, accused them of opposing imagination, and limited them to antiurban, rural subject matter:

Among their countless public statements one searches in vain for any discussion of such matters as "style," "form," "design," etc.; the term "painting" is always assumed to mean simply the rendering or depiction of a particular scene, so that subject matter becomes the one and only measure of merit. And even that is closely circumscribed; imagination in any form is frowned upon, the subject must be directly taken from everyday life. However, in order to be truly American, a picture must show an American farm scene in plainly recognizable fashion, since the cities are polluted by alien influences.[24]

In overemphasizing a singular subject matter to the neglect of any other consideration, Janson aligned himself with a majority of the short-sighted critics who had evaluated Regionalism through the years. By assuming that the three leading Regionalists "rendered or depicted" only local scenes—or, more narrowly still, "everyday life" on a midwestern farm—he missed the crucial mark. Numerous paintings and prints that might be categorized as allegorical rather than anecdotal-narrative greatly expanded the total complex of works by Wood and Benton. The variety of Curry's subjects, many of them critical of the events depicted, grew to be just as large. Janson's art historical inaccuracy paralleled the inadequacy of his search through "countless public statements" for any discussion of basic stylistic matters. He either missed or bypassed the most obvious example: Benton's series of five articles on "Mechanics of Form Organization," published in separate issues of *Arts Magazine* from 1926 to 1927. As to the remark that "imagination in any form" was negated by an obsession with everyday subjects, it seems rather absurd in view of Grant Wood's 1921 invitation to go on a trip through "Imagination Isles" as an escape from the machine-driven efficiency of a materialistic society. More accessible evidence of imaginative play may be found at the head of Janson's article, where *Stone City* (see Fig. 2), the first of the Iowan's fantasy farmscapes, is illustrated.

By fragmentarily quoting and selectively paraphrasing Wood's *Revolt Against the City,* Janson obviously intended to emphasize its most populist jibes at the Europe-oriented artists, critics, publishers, and dealers in East Coast cities. In so doing he exaggerated the nationalist fringes of Wood's Regionalist rhetoric at the expense of its core content: a nativist-realist appeal for a distinctly indigenous art, "a common sense utilization of native materials—an honest reliance by the artist upon subject matter which he can best interpret because he knows it best." [25] Although it was equally applicable to the art of one of his favorite American painters, Stuart Davis, Janson strained to twist Wood's open-ended credo into an expression of provincial jingoism.

After accurately quoting the most flag-waving phrase of the artist's definition of Regionalism, "an American way of looking at things, and a utilization of the materials of our own American scene," Janson inaccurately wrote, "All this, the author claims, is not mere chauvinism but genuine patriotism." [26] What Wood actually committed to print unequivocally denied the former and cautiously defined the latter as a sentiment or attitude conditioned by an artist's experiences at home in a given locale: "This is no mere chauvinism. *If* it is *patriotic,* it is so because a feeling for one's own milieu and for the validity of one's own life and its surroundings is *patriotic.*" [27] Yet, in keeping with his refusal to acknowledge Wood's distinction between the two degrees of nationalist sentiment, Janson overlooked the fact that chauvinism was one of the main targets of Wood's least Regionalist and most amusing paintings: *Daughters of Revolution* (see Fig. 24), *Midnight Ride of Paul Revere* (see Fig. 17), *The Birthplace of Herbert Hoover,* and *Parson Weems' Fable* (see Fig. 37). (The art historian did single out the earliest of these as "a truly satirical picture," even though "directed against a safe and well-worn target.") [28]

Though perhaps only a coincidence, it was "no less interesting" to Janson "that many of the paintings officially approved by the Nazis recall the works of the regionalists in this country." [29] If stripped of swastikas, flags, and uniforms, the "conservative" paintings acclaimed by the Nazis as *echt Deutsch* "might have been done almost anywhere." The Regionalists, "similarly international in style," likewise revoked "allegiance to humanity as a whole" by incorporating unmistakable, if less obvious, signs of nationalism into their works. [30] In a nationalist spirit, both Wood and Benton had criticized the "stultifying" effects of New York City's "colonial" dependence on influences from abroad. Janson likened what he knew of their antiurban polemics to those of "the Nazi theorists" who condemned the growth of German cities as an international "source of evil"—one that "does not breed 'Kultur' but only 'Asphalt-kultur,' a pseudo-culture rooted to the dead pavements of city streets rather than to the soil, from which all true strength and virtue derive and to which the artist must return if he is to develop 'a German way of looking at things.' " [31]

In need of a point of comparison between Regionalist art and Nazi art, Janson's accusation pivoted on exaggerating the number of country scenes verses city scenes in *Neue Sachlichkeit* subject matter. National Socialist painters and the Regionalists would have to concentrate on farms and farmers to express the underlying character of their respective nationalities and their natural roots, and Wood's "regionalist style" would have to appropriate the *Neue Sachlichkeit* attempt to seek "refuge from the frightening and apparently insoluble problems of the machine age among the idyllic aspects of rural and small-town life." [32]

By audaciously narrowing the subject matter of the three groups of painters to a nationalistic commemoration of life on or near the soil, Janson apparently convinced himself that Wood, Benton, and, by inference, Curry had created a one-dimensional art that paralleled a major segment of Nazi propaganda art (which had, in turn, sprung from a central theme of the *Neue Sachlichkeit*). Although Wood spent several pages of his *Revolt Against the City* advocating farm life, including current farm crises, as preferred subject matter for regional artists,[33] only about one-fifth of his total output in all media can be categorized as such. "Small-town life"—that is, any aspect of it that might be characterized as idyllic—is an even rarer subject. A small percentage of Benton's vast output depicts rural labor on plantations in the South or on ranches in the West rather than a quiet life on a middle-landscape farm. As for Curry, portraits, natural catastrophes, and distraught animals dominated his rural paintings until he became the artist-in-residence for the Agricultural College at the University of Wisconsin and settled down to depicting local, experimental farmland during the last years of his life. Works by the so-called *Neue Sachlichkeit* painters, several of whom, in keeping with Expressionism, indulged in grotesque caricaturing, spanned an even wider variety of subjects. Among these, rural depictions were few and far between.[34]

Pictures of German peasants did in fact increase during the mid- to late thirties in obedience to National Socialist dictates (Fig. 31).[35] The question remains: Did the words and pictures of Wood and Benton communicate nationalistic beliefs or sentiments parallel to Hitler's blood and soil propaganda? Though clearly distinguishable in cultural attributes, accessories, form, and content, did their rural productions of the thirties, or Curry's for that matter, bear sufficient similarities to Nazi idylls to justify a zealous "exposure"? Having fled the catastrophe of his native land, and perhaps overanxious to demonstrate his newly established allegiances, Janson apparently lacked the historical perspective to draw the necessary

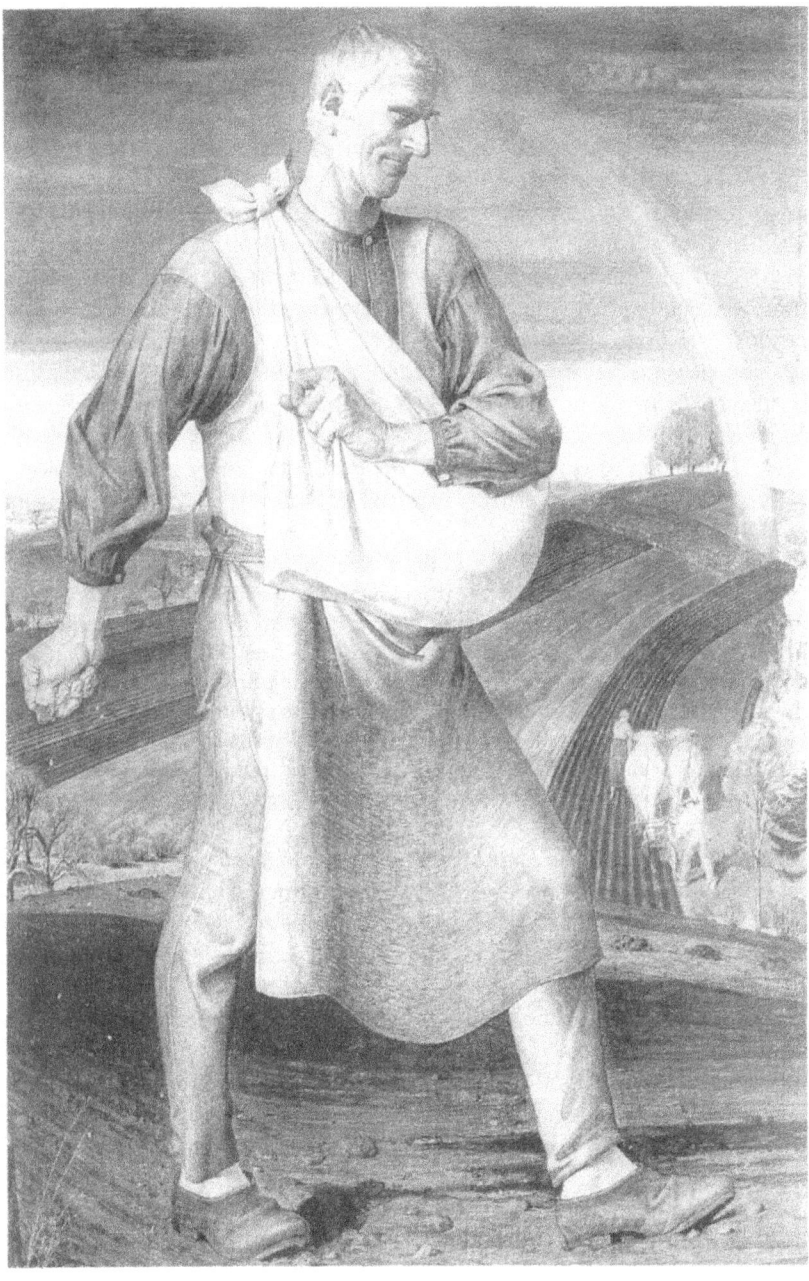

Figure 31. Oskar Martin-Amorbach. *The Sower*. 1937. Oil on canvas, Zentralinstitut fuer Kunstgeschichte, Munich, Germany. (No measurements available.)

distinctions between the *Volk* ideology of Germany and the populist sentiments of the midwestern United States. The former, firmly believed in and politically exploited by Hitler and his "Nazi theorists," was rooted in what historian George L. Mosse has conclusively demonstrated to be a unique obsession with national self-awareness and an antimodernist desire to unite the people through a Germanic "essence."[36] This essence to the romantic mind was located in their native landscape, their *Heimatland*. Members of Volkish youth groups, *die Wandervögel* among others, and utopian, return-to-the-soil settlements such as *Eden* and *Mittgart*, were imbued with a transcendental spirit, whether sublime or pastoral in its outward manifestations.[37]

The peasant became a "primordial image of the Volk" and was so portrayed in many novels as well as paintings approved by the *Reichskulturkammer*.[38] Quoted by Berthold Hinz in his *Art in the Third Reich*, F. A. Kauffmann forcefully conveyed the Nazi attachment to the traditional Volkish image of rural Germans featured in National Socialist paintings:

They set to work where closeness to the native soil, the restorative powers of the landscape, the protection of the race from impurities, the force of deeply rooted tradition, and the blessings of beneficent labor have kept the human substance healthy. It follows from this that our contemporary painting frequently portrays the faces and figures of men who follow the old callings close to nature: farmers, hunters, fishermen, shepherds and woodcutters. . . . It is not surprising that women and girls from the same spheres of life are also represented. Together with their male partners, they form the rugged stock of our people. The sight of them is particularly impressive as we seek to show the immense importance of our folkish substance.[39]

The Marxist art historian Meyer Schapiro, in closing his review of Benton's autobiographical *An Artist in America*, concluded that the Missouri-born artist's "hatred of the foreign, his masculine emphasis, his antagonism to the cities," accompanied "his uncritical and unhistorical elevation of the folk."[40] However, in contrast to the severe countenance and statuary poses shared by peasants, soldiers, children, and nudes in uniformly styled Nazi paintings (Fig. 32), the individually stylized figures of Benton, Wood, and Curry, whether confronting nature sublime, working fantasy fields, or running steam engines, prove to be essentially innocuous (Fig. 33). Belonging to a migratory nation of much less deep-rooted tradition and far removed from a quasi-religious, solar mysticism that endowed its native soil with a transcendent significance intelligible only to pure "Aryans," the "Regionalism" of the midwesterners, in polemic or pictorial form, reflected cultural aberrance and personal eccentricity resistant to control.

Analyzing the American nationalist movements of the Depression era, the sociologist Morris Janowitz concluded in 1951 that the religious and

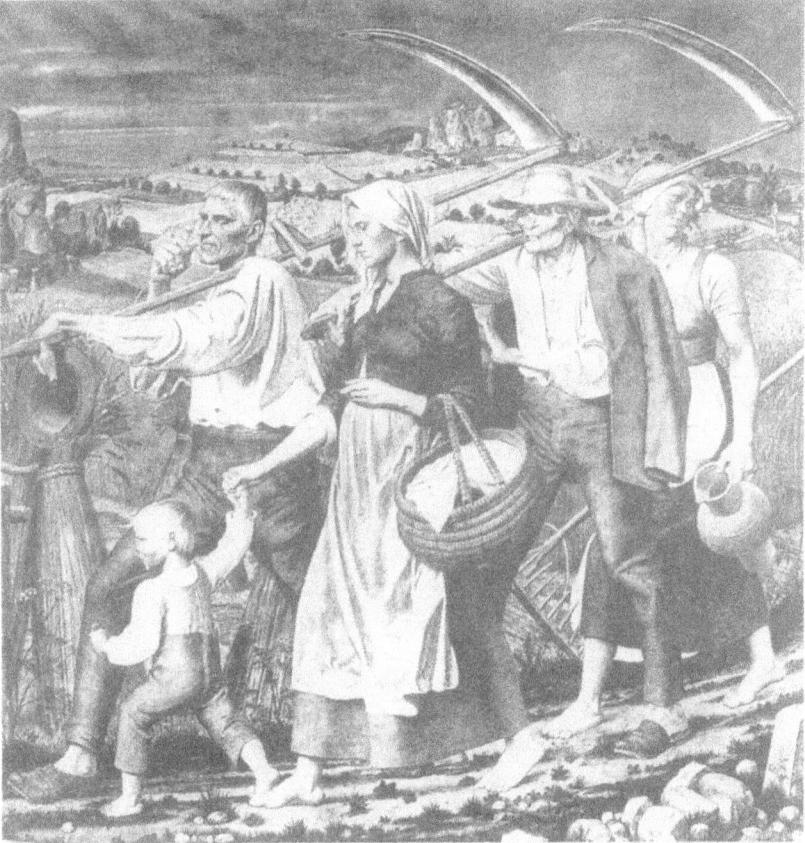

Figure 32. Oskar Martin-Amorbach. *Out to Harvest*. 1938. Oil on canvas, Zentralinstitut fuer Kunstgeschichte, Munich, Germany. (No measurements available.)

ethnic heterogeneity of the United States was too vast, the roots of egalitarianism too deep, and the distrust of authoritarianism too great for fascism to be a threat, let alone the ideology of a threatening majority. In spite of economic insecurities, "the ideology of America as a land of personal mobility was too strong to permit the development of an authoritarian solution and politics of intolerance."[41]

To identify the motivations behind the paintings of Wood and Benton, or the motifs they evoked, with those of National Socialist art is groundless and unhistorical. In the thoroughly informed opinion of the Berlin-born and -raised Mosse, who followed Janson at the University of Iowa, German fascism and American Regionalism were axiomatically incompatible. The former was centered on singular symbols of "nationalism as a civic

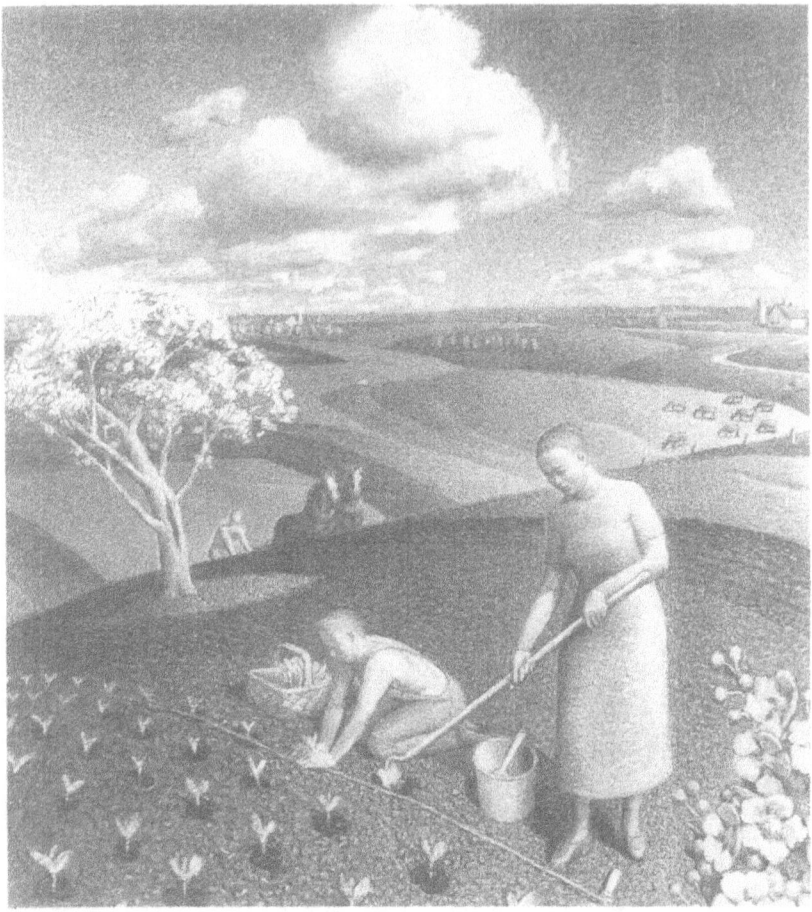

Figure 33. Grant Wood. Cartoon for *Spring in the Country*. 1941. Charcoal, pencil, and chalk on paper, 23½ × 21½ in. Private collection. © Estate of Grant Wood/Licensed by VAGA, New York, NY.

religion." The latter, contrary to simplistic notions that it did nothing more than worship local rural life as an agrarian utopia, was thematically diverse. Mosse's conclusion with regard to the nation as a whole applies to the combined efforts—or, better, the pluralism—of the three artists in question:

> The Great Depression led to a search for the true nation—just as in Europe—but here the search did not end in the confirmation of a national mystique, a civic religion, but instead was informed by the rediscovery of a wide variety of men and women as symbolic of America. . . . This was a search for roots, for the Volk, but not on the European model.[42]

Two basic reasons can be detected for the extreme accusations leveled at Wood and Benton, symptomatic of the overall criticism they and Curry endured. First, critics (friendly or hostile) could not, or simply did not, thoroughly appreciate a triadic pluralism of style and content as they rushed their opinions into print. Careless writing that focused on particular works repeated inaccuracies and oversimplifications. Second, critics too often suffered from a strain of what might be called a post-Craven virus. Favorable reviews and articles too often sound as if they could have been written by Craven himself, absorbed in promotional rhetoric and blind enthusiasm for "the movement." Detractors might assail the art, in reaction to the Cravenesque bombast that helped to initiate it.

Defense of the three leading Regionalist artists against misappropriated promotion or ideologically biased attacks ultimately materialized. In *Antifascism in American Art,* Cecile Whiting contends that by the time the United States entered World War II, "many" critics perceived a dangerous affinity between Regionalism and "Hitler's nationalistic artistic doctrine." [43] With brief reference to accusations by Janson, Charles J. Bulliet, and Peyton Boswell, she sets out to demonstrate that Wood, Benton, and Curry "were actually anything but sympathetic to fascism," that "they had to come to terms with the fascist challenge" by somehow retooling their "home-grown," "folksy" imagery into "an internationally significant art form." [44] Faced with the inevitable methodological problems of trying to impose a singular intention on any group of modern artists, Whiting finally concedes that obligating them to serve some "international imperative" is virtually impossible. [45]

Benton included a few swastikas and German-looking hats in his 1942 series, *The Year of Peril,* which Samuel Kootz recognized as a "Remember Pearl Harbor" statement against the Japanese. [46] In the largest of the paintings, *Exterminate,* an American soldier drives his bayonet into the heart of a fat Asian clutching a rising-sun flag, identified by Whiting as "a greenish fascist brute." [47] In the second largest canvas, *Invasion* (Fig. 34), mountains come down to the bay of the skyscraper city under attack, suggesting Seattle or San Francisco (not, as Whiting interpreted it, New York's harbor). The soldiers, not wearing German or Italian helmets or jackboots, are stereotyped "Japs." One bayonets an American farmer to death while two others rape a full-bodied, basically naked, blonde, one of Benton's favorite images. The body of her lifeless son lies on the ground below her splayed legs. A doll baby in a wagon and a blanket trailing down two high wooden steps lead the viewer's eye from the lower right corner to the central figures, bracketed by eruptions of thick black smoke. By lending his modernist manipulations of perspective and a longstanding iconography of dissolute sexuality to a protest against war, Benton recalled Picasso. But, intent

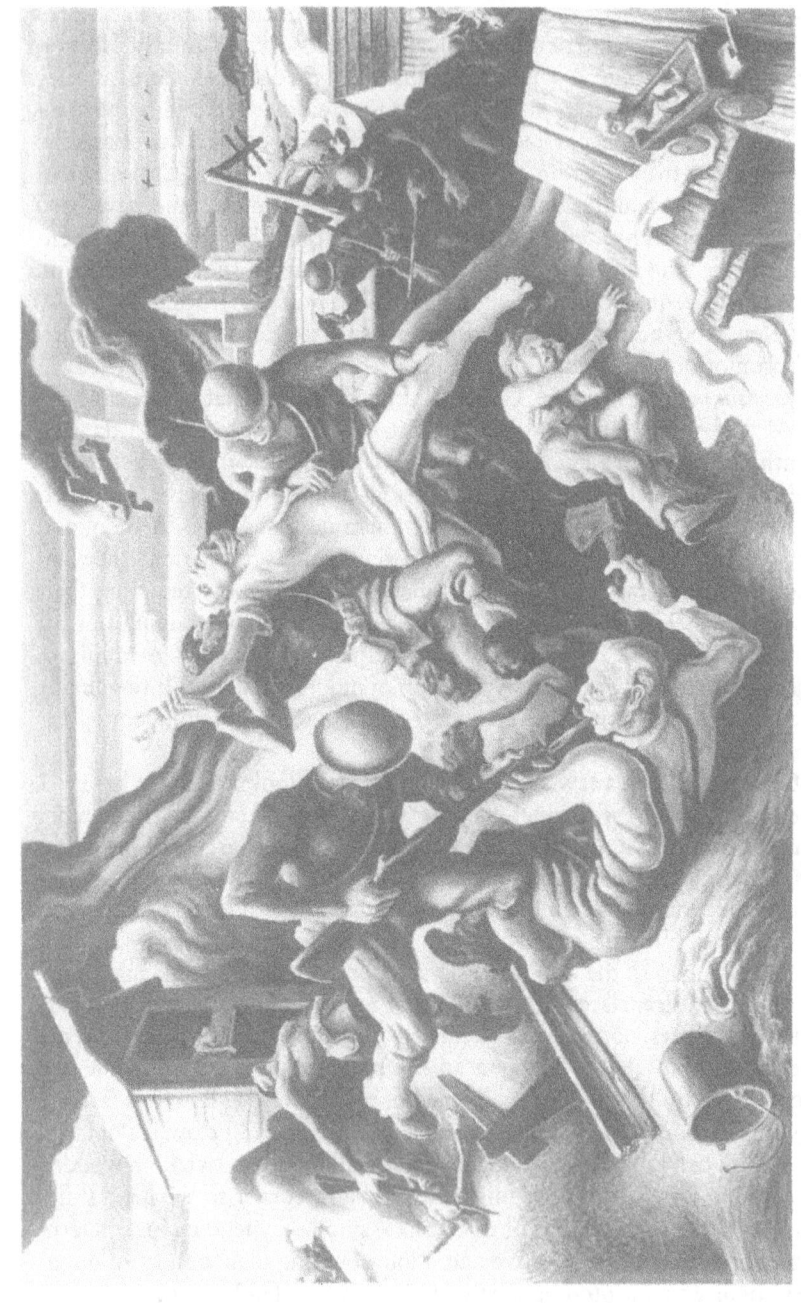

Figure 34. Thomas Hart Benton. *Invasion* from *The Year of Peril* series. 1942. Egg tempera and oil on canvas mounted on panel, 48 × 78 in. State Historical Society of Missouri, Columbia, Missouri. © T. H. Benton and R. P. Benton Testamentary Trusts/Licensed by VAGA, New York, NY.

on propaganda, he failed to moderate the thrill of blatant sensuality and missed an opportunity to elevate his protest toward the height of *Guernica*.

Whiting's search for "a meaningful synthesis between regionalism and war" faced an even greater challenge in Curry's work. His belief in disengagement, as expressed at the end of the thirties in *Parade to War* (see Fig. 29), "tended to err." [48] By this she means it excluded elements popularly understood to be Regionalist. These should have been used allegorically to address "the international situation." [49] In other words, a leading Regionalist should have lived up to his art-market label and fought fascism with recognizable Regionalist elements, presumably rural. Instead, he converted what appears to be a photo-journalist's recording of a Main Street patriotic event into an isolationist's antiwar statement. By adding the shocking detail of death's-heads on his marching soldiers, Curry met modernism halfway. He overwhelmed the viewer and universalized a personal sentiment.

While more in keeping with the Kansas settings of his earliest successful paintings, the war poster Curry produced after the United States entered the war also includes no direct antifascist references. *The Farm Is a Battleground, Too* of 1942 (Fig. 35), places a monumental wheat farmer, pitchfork over his shoulder, in front of two infantrymen charging into battle. They are supported by a tank with blazing guns as a second farmer on a tractor peacefully plows his midwestern field. In avoiding Benton's vociferous allusions to an enemy, Curry's effort resembles the many German paintings and posters of Volkish peasants working their fields to feed an army that is presumably off on another victorious campaign (see Figs. 31–32). Unlike the designers who turned Lucky Strike green into red, white, and blue, Curry seemed to remain reluctant to go to war, at least against a specified foe.

Grant Wood was hardly any more cooperative in enlisting his Regionalism in the war effort or, in a larger, less defined context, establishing "a meeting ground for regionalist and international concerns." [50] He explained his 1941 companion pieces, *Spring in the Country* and *Spring in Town* (see Figs. 33, 52), in what might be considered antifascist terms — that is, as responses to Roosevelt's appeal to defend "the American way of life." [51] Yet Whiting chooses not to discuss them as such. She also passes over the "Blitzkrieg" poster that he donated to the 1940 Bundles for Britain campaign for the same reason she turned down Curry's *Parade to War*: because it lacks the "hallmarks of his regionalist style." [52] In doing so she underlines the multifariousness of the Regionalists' independently modern careers. By the same token, she would undoubtedly dismiss Wood's littleknown pencil-drawn caricatures of Hitler as a snarling wolf and Prime Minister Neville Chamberlain as a weak-kneed lamb (Fig. 36).[53] Reactions to the disastrous compromise at the 1938 Munich Conference, these were as overtly antifascist as Wood would get before his death from cancer less than two months after the attack on Pearl Harbor. Once again, without a

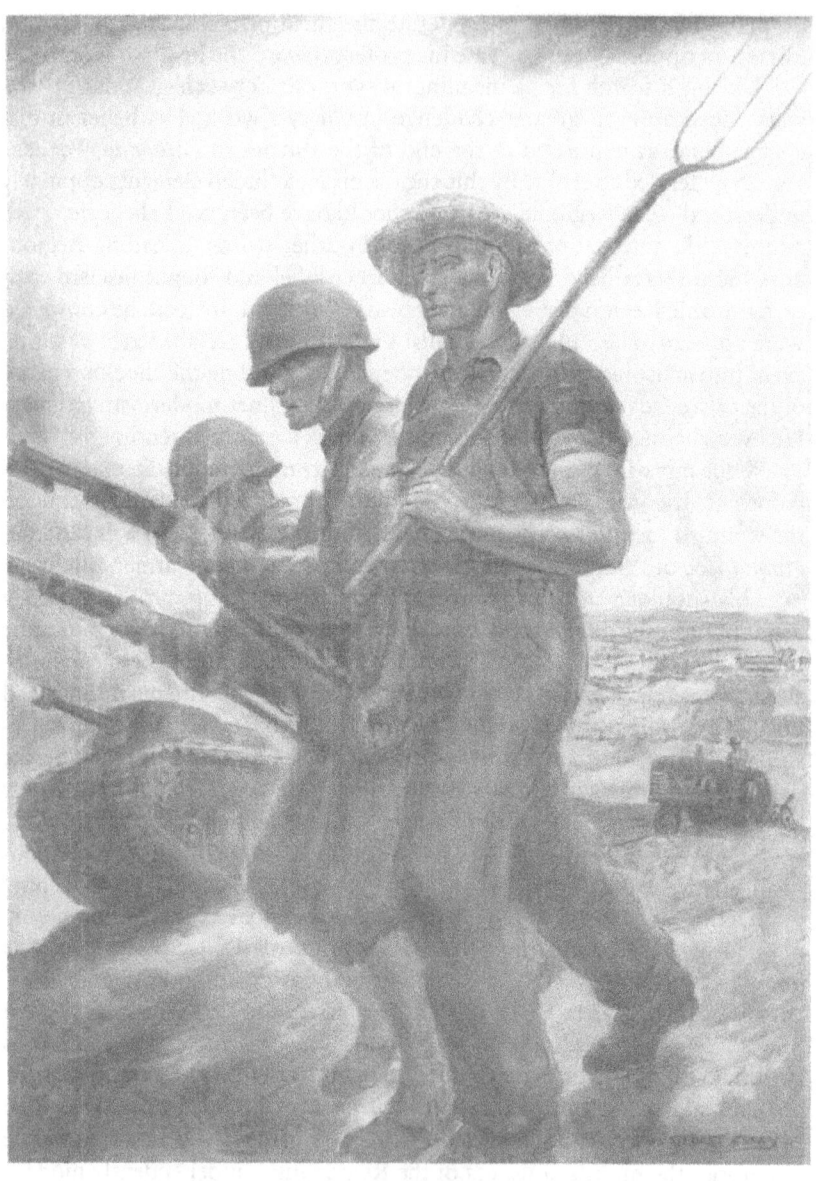

Figure 35. John Steuart Curry. *The Farm Is a Battleground, Too*. 1942. Oil on canvas, 59 × 42½ in. Davenport Museum of Art, Davenport, Iowa.

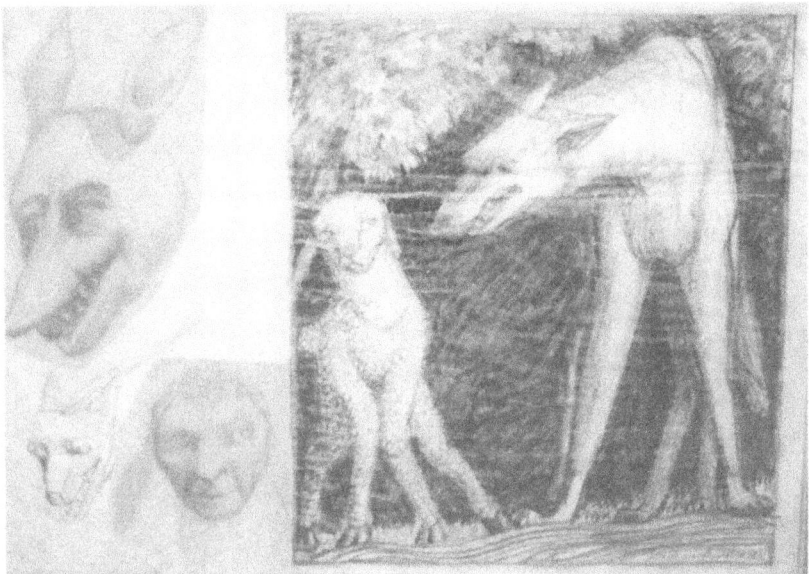

Figure 36. Grant Wood. Drawings of Adolf Hitler and Neville Chamberlain as a Wolf and a Lamb. c. 1938–39. Pencil and charcoal. Private Collection. © Estate of Grant Wood/Licensed by VAGA, New York, NY.

programmatic response, the "triumvirate" addressed current international crises in a pluralistic manner, true to a spirit of modernist detachment and noncommitment.

As the shadows of world war spread to the middle of the land, Regionalist points of view lost ground to Internationalism. In retrospect, this transfer of interest kindles a temptation to fit one of Wood's most endearing parodies of American myth-making into an antifascist context. Whiting's premise that the 1939 painting *Parson Weems' Fable* (Fig. 37) was meant to fortify American patriotism in the face of the fascist threat drew upon a gallery press release that the painter may or may not have written. Quoted in the release, a November 1938 *Atlantic Monthly* article by the literary critic Howard Mumford Jones had advocated using national myths, rooted in authentic historical anecdotes, against the propaganda art of the "dictator nations." By "treating history itself as an artifice" of storytelling, *Parson Weems' Fable*, according to Whiting, did just the opposite. It came "dangerously close" to certain concoctions of the Nazis that fictitiously identified "Aryan" qualities with classical myths.[54] At odds with this deconstructive reading is little George's strange-looking Gilbert Stuart head: the dollar-bill Washington is an American in-joke, hardly comparable to the racist idiocy of a Nazi Venus and Adonis painted by one of Hitler's favorite art-

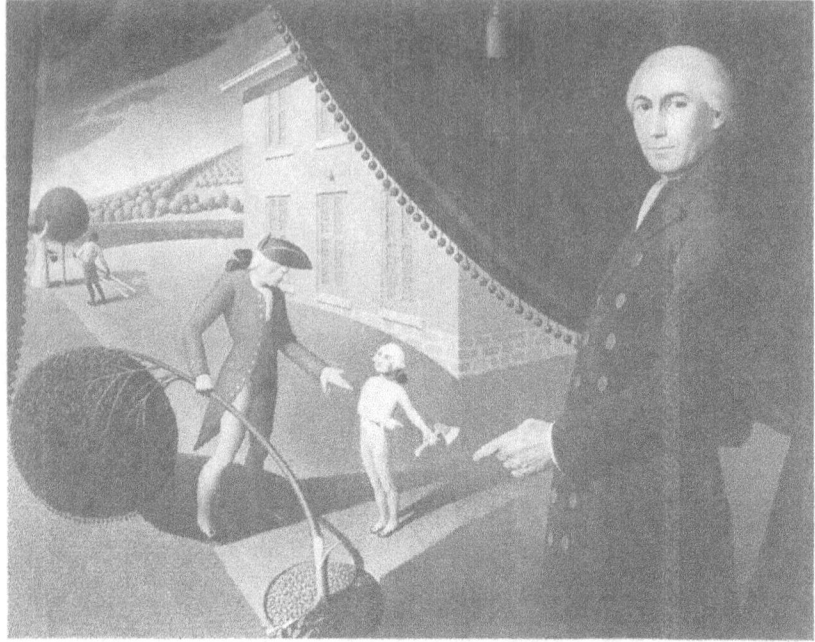

Figure 37. Grant Wood. *Parson Weems' Fable*. 1939. Oil on canvas, 38⅜ × 50⅛ in. Amon Carter Museum, Fort Worth, Texas, 1970.43. © Estate of Grant Wood/Licensed by VAGA, New York, NY.

ists. Wood's playful tinkering with history, overlaying that of Mason Locke Weems, doubtless contributed little if anything to the fight against fascism and comes off in the long run as a harmless deceit.

Six of the two dozen or so major works by Wood after *American Gothic* made light of American myths. One of his primary purposes in playing with the Parson Weems tale was to protect the privilege of doing so from literal-minded debunkers of popular fables.[55] By 1940 and the onslaught of the Axis military forces, an entertaining tribute to Weem's myth-making inventiveness and the comedic impudence of burlesquing it, could be further appreciated and justified as answering to a modernist need. Freedom of expression included the privilege of satirizing the rural-based didactics found in the primers of the nineteenth century. The preacher-teacher, Parson Weems, stands before his classroom, in our space, on the picture plane. He stares at us darkly but smiles knowingly as he holds back the cherry-fringed, deep-red curtain and points to the fatal wound caused by at least eight chops of the brand-new hatchet into the slender main stem of the bent-over cherry tree. It had grown out of a perfect circle of cultivation, and its perfect sphere of foliage and fruit casts the shadow of a driver's head on the flawless golf-green lawn, an American obsession that had its beginning on Washington's bowling green in front of Mount Vernon.

The house in the painting very generally resembles the mid-nineteenth-century brick structure Wood had restored in Iowa City, but he could not include its window arches or large eave brackets. They would have cluttered the central area of action in his design, and, besides that, he needed the unbroken vanishing lines of the facade to draw attention to the only African-Americans he ever depicted. Holding a ladder in line with the main thrust of perspective, a well-behaved young man helps his mother pick cherries from a healthy tree as storm clouds gather to disrupt their momentary contentment. At stage front, in spite of the comedy routine of pointing hands, Wood's social comment on American racism is played out. No matter how destructive little George might be, he is in the glowing white light of privilege and has it in his head to be our pater patriae as he fesses up.

With the remotely possible exception of the house, *Parson Weems' Fable* contains no local Regionalist reference. It is modern in its spatial and temporal detachment as well as in its abstract order. Its fastidious linear composition resulted from Wood's system of mechanical design, known to his students as "the thirds." The points where the sides, top, and bottom are divided into thirds are indicated by such attractions as the two trees, the edge of the opened curtain, the tassel, and the corner of the arbitrarily illuminated rectangle of lawn. The curving diagonals that connect these points create large shapes in the composition, easily read on the surface as the abstract components of its stylization. The making of a whole pattern, the order of an art object mediating reality, and the possible mimicking of technology through its compulsive technique qualify the painting as unmistakably modern.

If Benton may be momentarily excused for being Benton à la Craven in his theoretical intolerance for nonfigurative abstraction, he did, with hindsight, eventually observe that both his personal brand of history painting and the mature style of his most famous student, "Jack" Pollock, would for the most part benefit from ongoing interpretations. Both drip and history would thus gain "evocative properties other than those intended by their creators." [56] No matter how their collective efforts might be categorized, the overall production of Wood, Benton, and Curry was by the forties undeniably varied in terms of individual style and highly diverse in subject matter and theme. That no single art historical label can possibly contain them is nowhere better evidenced than in their images of women, the subject of Part II. As will be witnessed, the modern pluralism of their female figures was motivated largely by instinct. A three-way split of personal identity, therefore, underlies the historical and social identification of their most significant iconography.

PART II

A Modern Pluralism

Eleanor, if you want to be President in 1940, tell me now so I can start getting things ready.

Louis Howe to Eleanor Roosevelt, 1935

5

Grant Wood's Matriarchate

To be designated the "triumvirate" of midwestern Regionalism was, as we have seen, of immediate promotional significance. It implies unity and uniformity, when in actuality Wood, Benton, and Curry remained, as modern artists by definition must be, independent in subject matter and style.

The "movement" got its start more or less by accident when several of their "American Scene" paintings from 1928 through 1930 were seen to bear overlapping rural references. Arising from a wide range of personal themes, Wood's newly evolved, stylized farmscapes (see Figs. 2, 4), Benton's angular farm folk (see Fig. 56), and Curry's richly chromatic Kansas farm remembrances (see Figs. 80, 92) fed into an intensified need for a rural-based national identity during crucial months of economic disaster. Regionalism was most often identified by critics with the farm belt immediately west of the mid-Mississippi—the artists' adjacent native states. It followed, as if scripted, that the three painters would meet and get acquainted during the early thirties. Then, with the encouragement of the patiently enterprising Wood, ensconced in the state university at Iowa City, Benton returned to the Midwest to settle in Kansas City, and Curry followed suit, though he wound up somewhat on the periphery, in Madison, Wisconsin.[1]

By mid-Depression they were presented and received nationwide as a heartland package of cultural uplift despite their transregional multiplicity of pictorial messages. Some of these, especially those by Wood and Curry, were ironically skeptical about basic American traits and practices; others, particularly those by Benton, were ardently cynical about them. Altogether, many of their socially significant images nullify popular presuppositions about what Regionalists could be expected to do. This may be most thoroughly witnessed in the three artists' imaging of women, which spans a modern spectrum, from social satire to mimetic reflections of contemporary work and pleasure, from frontier myth to social protest.

Quite capable of fending for themselves, Wood's premier women deliver far-reaching signals. At least five of his most memorable examples, led by the woman of *American Gothic,* transgress their initial impact as icons of stereotyped domestic tranquility to become widely recognized carica-tures of moral order and control. They play affectionately on the guardian-matron archetype projected by the aging leadership of the women's move-ment during Wood's youth. Once committed to this provocative referent, he departed from it in only one major painting during his most creative period, a contrived portrait of his sister, whose up-to-date glamour-girl ap-pearance he ironically compromised by surrounding her with the trappings of a colonial portrait (Fig. 45). A "New Woman" image was thus restrained on the Middle Border by early American, East Coast conventions, and all signs of midwestern Regionalism vanished.

Benton liked to give his female figures, regardless of their assigned roles, place, or time, physical attractions equal to those of his male figures (see Chapter 6). They might therefore be interpreted, borrowing a phrase from the cultural historian Barbara Melosh, as modern "endorsements of female participation."[2] In urban and rural settings alike, his men and women pro-vide "images of sexual complementarity" to a decade in which the post-suffrage feminist movement foundered and the economic mechanisms of masculine security broke down. A common denominator of potent sexu-ality modifies a strict Regionalist reading, which, if insisted upon, would also have to explain away the agitated abstractions of a Benton compo-sition. The unmistakable dynamics of his style, recently overdefined by Joyce Carol Oates as "'common' populist scenes which acquire a surreal, mock-heroic, frequently caricatured hyper-vividness,"[3] persistently refuse to comply with an effect Melosh determined was the essence of Region-alism. "The soft light of an anticipatory nostalgia"[4] was impossible for an artist who glorified male dominance in practically every way, shape, and form.

During the same years of maturation, as Chapter 7 reveals, Curry's variations on an Americanized version of noble motherhood share his dramatic narratives with a girl-woman figure activated by social protest. Caring for infants and small children during natural and social disasters, none of his maternal women, in company with their men, inhabit a Re-gionalist idyll. They brave tornados, floods, and hunger and hark back to a stereotyped pioneer mother ultimately adopted by Curry for his Washing-ton, D.C., murals during the last half of the Depression (see Figs. 85–86, 88). Their "sunbonnet myth" reflects a traditionally rural helpmeet rela-tionship. The woman and her husband struggle together, side by side in a "configuration" of mutual support, an equalizing, "comradely ideal."[5]

Contemporary or legendary, the nobility of motherhood, especially under critical conditions, lent sanctity to the official New Deal policy call-ing for women to forsake their quest for equal opportunities and stay out of the labor market. They should, as much as possible, remain homemakers.

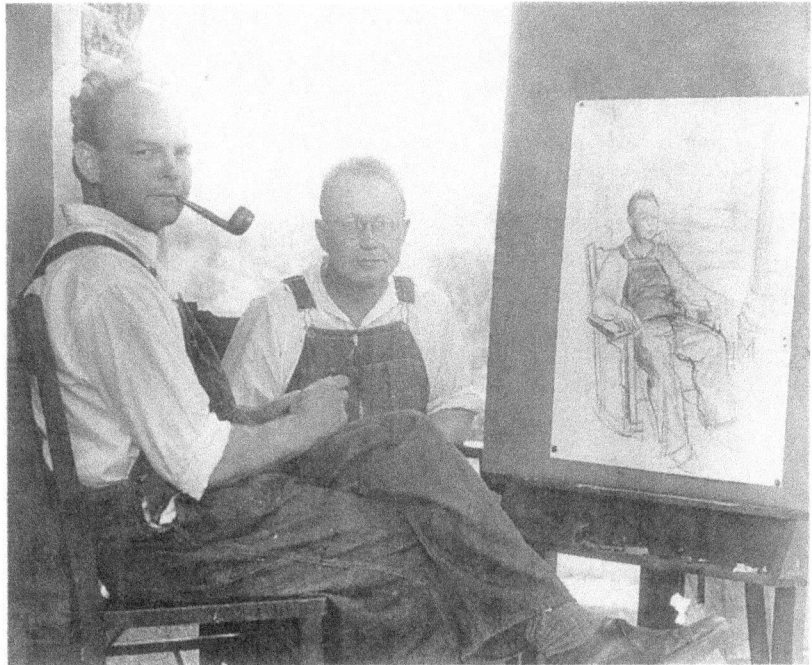

Figure 38. Grant Wood and John Steuart Curry at Stone City, Iowa, summer 1933. Photograph: John W. Barry.

By not competing for the few jobs available to them that could be held by men, women would be doing their part in restoring the lost manly pride of their unemployed mates. A model for this traditional supportive relationship survived in the diminishing farm couple. Monumentalized by Curry in the Kansas State Capitol Rotunda as the Depression drew to a close, it approximated the frontier ideal of steadfast comradeship (Fig. 90). In the meantime, his alternate female image of protective innocence performs in paintings of protest against male-dominated fundamentalist religion, racism, and war (see Fig. 29).

Posing in bib overalls for a Cedar Rapids photographer on the day they met in Stone City, Iowa, in the summer of 1933, Wood and Curry enjoyed sharing and showing off their rural origins (Fig. 38). As artists, however, both had already transcended the subject matter that they, their promoters, and their critics designated "Regionalism." They had both covered a wide range of provocative themes. The content of their works to come would remain much more diverse, and, of course, personal in nature than the American Scene subjects of New Deal post office murals, which soon provided innocuous reminders to widespread communities of their mail ser-

95

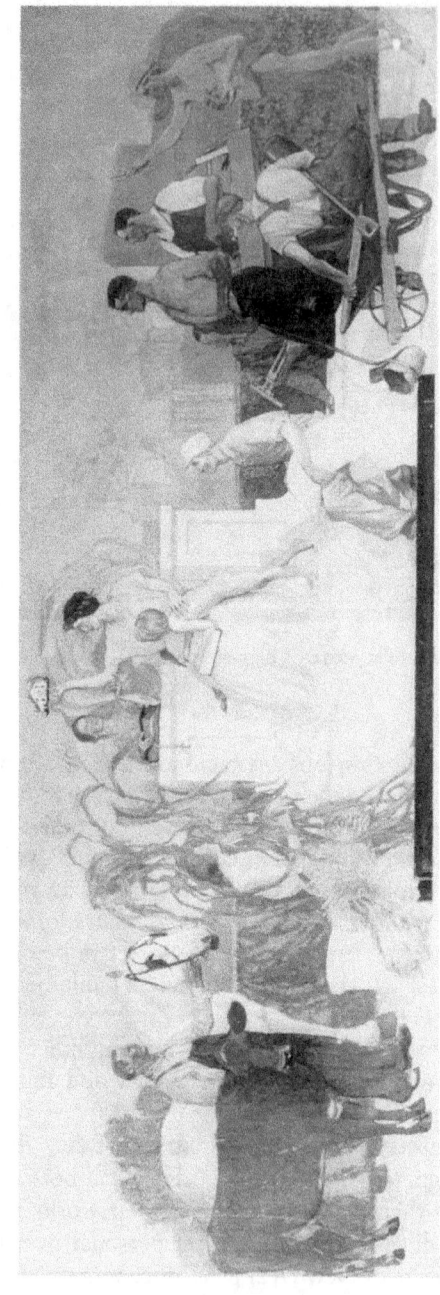

Figure 39. Grant Wood. *The Adoration of the Home.* 1922. Oil on canvas attached to wood panel, 22¾ × 81⅜ in. Cedar Rapids Museum of Art, Cedar Rapids, Iowa; gift of Peter F. Bezanson. © Estate of Grant Wood/Licensed by VAGA, New York, NY.

vice, area industries, folklore, and founders.[6] Strictly forbidden on a post office wall, social and political commentary infiltrated the works of Wood, Curry, and their prolific colleague, Benton.[7] Of central significance to this dimension in their art and to a fuller understanding of its varied content is their imaging of women.

In 1922 Wood focused on home and mothering in a traditional—indeed, academic—painting dedicated to mercantile-industrial growth. Faithful to paternalistic idealization, *The Adoration of the Home* (Fig. 39) displays its maternal woman on a pedestal. By doing so it reflected a developing reactionary attitude promoted in women's magazines, particularly *Ladies' Home Journal*. Since the nineties its editors had occasionally justified a new independence for American women, but by the late twenties they again insisted that the woman's primary option was to be a housewife and mother.[8]

The Adoration of the Home resulted from a commission to create an outdoor sign for the clapboard office of a Cedar Rapids realtor who specialized in postwar suburban development. By painting the figures as portrayals of people in the community, Wood personalized a prescribed style of public art still being used for allegorical murals in governmental and commercial buildings. In the center he elevated a yellow-draped woman on a marble exedra, where she displays a pristine white house in her upraised right hand, thus sanctifying Home. The naked child leaning over a book on her lap signifies Education. A second female figure represents Religion as she looks up from her Bible at the symbolic house and gestures to the central woman. A third, enclosed by corn plants and wheat shocks, symbolizes Demeter, goddess of plenty, of bountiful harvest. In addition to the horse-and cow-flanked farmer, smiling from the left, the male support figures of breadwinning practicality include three craftsmen, an industrial worker, and a surveyor. All adore the home. Against the industrialized skyline, an amusingly individualized Mercury enters from stage right as god of commerce, carrying a purse of profit and waving his caduceus.

Wood's didactic centering of a monumental mother to promote "owning your own home" may be traced back to an Anglo-American cult of motherhood arising at least a hundred years earlier.[9] *The Adoration of the Home* thereby demonstrates the exploitation of unswerving middle-class values that originated in a protoindustrial period when Iowa still belonged to the Indians. With the increased displacement of the father's place of work from the self-sustained household into a shop or office, the home-body mother became increasingly sanctified as the pure source of spiritual beneficence to nineteenth-century society. As Ruth Bloch indicated in her seminal article on moral motherhood, "It was above all as mothers that women were attributed social influence as the chief transmitters of religious and moral values."[10] At odds with what she called the "domestic

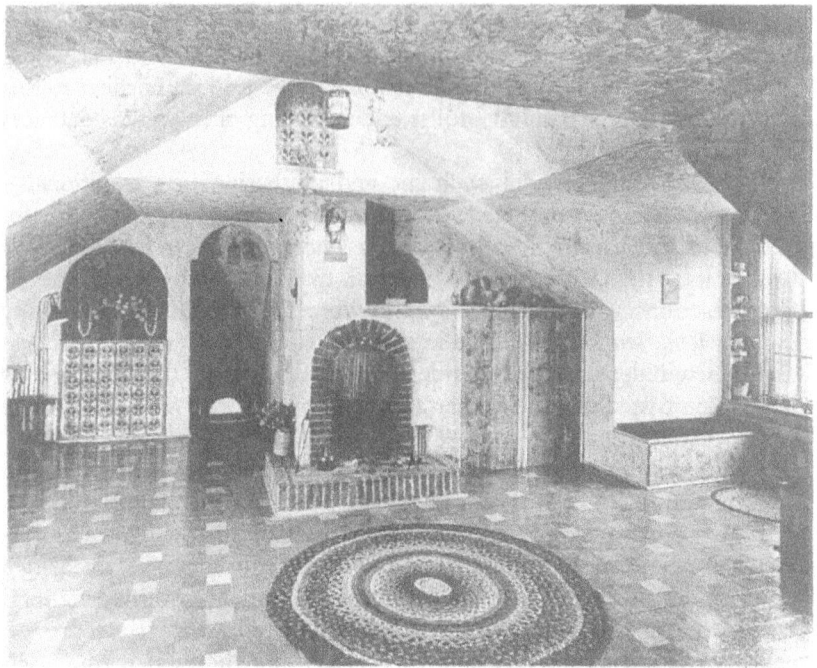

Figure 40. Grant Wood. *No. 5 Turner Alley, Cedar Rapids, Iowa.* c. 1930. © Estate of Grant Wood/Licensed by VAGA, New York, NY.

mythology" or "maternal pieties" adhered to by most feminists, Charlotte Perkins Gilman, the leading radical intellectual of the movement, first challenged their mother-centered position in her now famous *Women and Economics* (1898). As a natural and inevitable result of Industrial Age economic and social evolution, the modern world would no longer be deprived of free and equal women engaged in "Human Work" outside the household. Children would benefit from an increasingly educative, better-trained profession of shared "motherhood." While not equal to Gilman's utopian vision, Wood's rural interpretations of the maternal do see women, in Bloch's phrase, "as the main 'conservators of morals' through their beneficial influence on both men and children." [11]

Until the last few years of his life, Wood was aided by matronly, maternal women who appreciated his quiet charm, creativity, and homecraft. Wherever he lived and worked, he designed and constructed a picturesque setting that he would finish with imaginative touches of warmth and well-being (Fig. 40). Flower boxes and flower gardens played an important part in this domestic transformation. On the other hand, he tended to be impractical, especially about time, schedules, and getting from one place to another. He consistently relied on a guardian mother, either his own or a surrogate, to help keep such aspects of his life in order.

Wood was ten when his father died in 1901. His mother, Hattie D. Weaver Wood, moved her family of three sons and a daughter from the farm near Anamosa, Iowa, into Cedar Rapids. While his brothers and sister married and went their individual ways, Wood repeatedly returned to his Quaker mother: from his early attempts to make it on his own in Chicago, from the army in 1918, and from his four trips to Europe during the twenties. He provided a home for her in the carriage-house studio where he painted his most famous works, anticipated in style and content by his portrait tribute to her in *Woman with Plants* of 1929 (Fig. 41). Placed high on a hill overlooking a farm, she poses between a begonia and a philodendron, holding a sansevieria in an earthen pot. An elderly, pensive woman, she wears a cameo brooch of Diana, an antique symbol of untainted feminine youth, now as blurred as her faded, side-turned eyes. Her elevation against the horizon of a pastoral landscape in autumn pays homage to her life as a farmer's widow and a dedicated mother. The universal association of woman with nature, her correspondence with its life cycles and seasons, unite the painting with the observation of a late eighteenth-century Philadelphia Quaker:

The tender feelings, the cries, the powerful emotions of nature . . . the sentiment, at one sublime and pathetic. . . . These great expressions of nature, these heart-rending emotions, which fill us at once with wonder, compassion and terror, always have belonged and always will belong only to women.[12]

Assertive, independently political women had risen to national prominence by the time of Wood's birth. Their collective image as guardian matrons had advanced through the women's movement, diminished by the deaths of Susan B. Anthony and Elizabeth Cady Stanton soon after the turn of the century. According to the historian William O'Neill, "Maternity was not only a unifying force but the enabling principle which made the entrance of women into public life imperative."[13] O'Neill quotes Elizabeth Boynton Harbart's *History of Woman Suffrage* (1878) on the national need for mothering: "The new truth, electrifying, glorifying American womanhood today, is the discovery that the State is but the larger family, the nation the old homestead, and that in this national home there is a room and a corner and a duty for 'mother.' "[14]

Fortified by this growing status, mature women throughout the country strove to increase their influence in their communities. By the beginning of Wood's lifetime, Bloch concludes, "motherhood often came to be viewed as a powerful vehicle through which women wielded broad social influence. . . . Maternal moral influence permeated throughout society."[15]

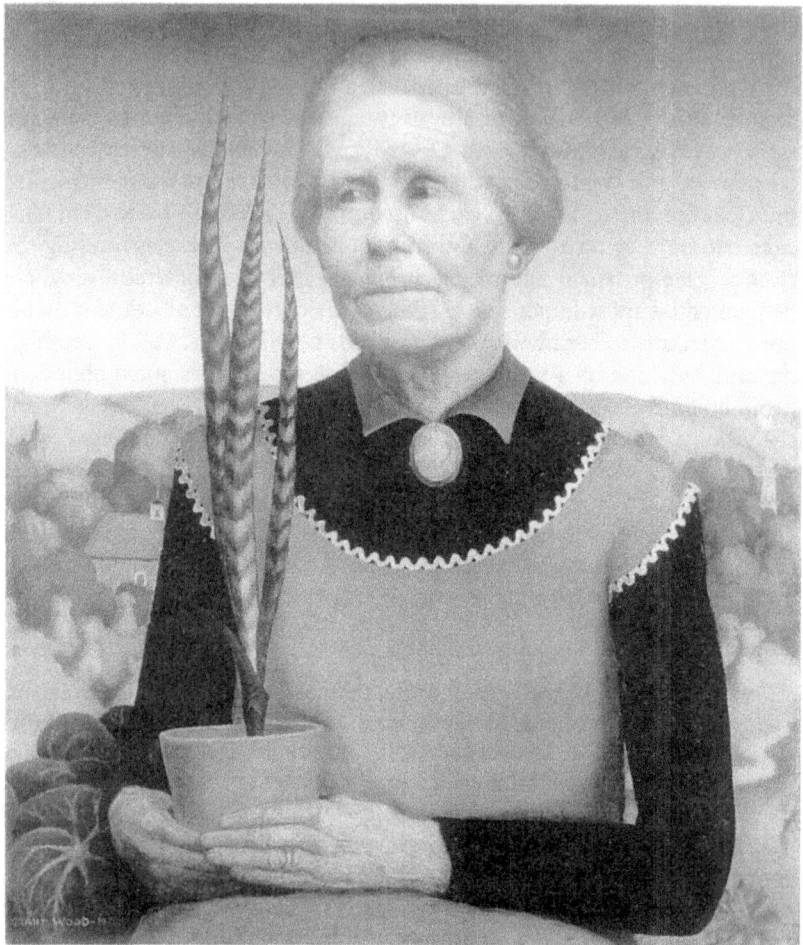

Figure 41. Grant Wood. *Woman with Plants*. 1929. Oil on upsom board, 20½ × 18 in. Cedar Rapids Museum of Art, Cedar Rapids, Iowa; Cedar Rapids Art Association Purchase. © Estate of Grant Wood/Licensed by VAGA, New York, NY.

A woman need not be depicted with a child to identify her as a secular Madonna; maturity alone could project maternal morality. Thomas Eakins had aged his still-youthful female sitters in order to enhance their look of introspective wisdom. Forty years later Wood would age his thirty-year-old sister Nan to fit the role of guardian matron in the iconic centerpiece of modern figural painting in the United States, *American Gothic* (see Fig. 7).

Within a context of prescribed male dominance, this singular figure among Wood's women takes charge of the man in protecting their place in the world. As is characteristic of his most engrossing female imagery,

100

she appears willful, alert, guiding, and on guard. Such steady confidence departed from the age-old gender-dividing tradition of differentiating intuitive, passive female nature from that of the reasoning, active male.

Wood could find historical antecedents for mature maternal strength in turn-of-the-century feminist pronouncements and social reform efforts. Most notably, the Chicago settlement leader Jane Addams motivated the women's movement to extend its moral authority beyond the customary boundaries of the home into the needy community.[16] This domestic advance of maternal-cum-matronly power into the public sphere entered the White House with Franklin Delano Roosevelt's New Deal administration. Eleanor Roosevelt epitomized the "accommodating feminism" that, in accordance with historian Ellen Wiley Todd's findings, characterized the New Woman of the early Depression years. It advocated that the woman serve the public in the name of communal domesticity without abandoning her home duties.[17]

This national "couple-front" message acquired an entertaining, easy-to-remember, easy-to-parody emblem in *American Gothic*. Though never nationalistic in intent, Wood's world-famous small-town pair was, he insisted, above all "American." As the most widely dispersed painting in the history of its nation's art, it could hardly be localized to Iowa, let alone limited by an America First isolationism. In discussing its conception three years after it was painted, Wood made no place reference: "I saw a trim white cottage, with a trim white porch—a cottage built on severe Gothic lines. This gave me an idea. That idea was to find two people who, by their severely strait-laced characters, would fit into such a home. The cottage was to be a farmer's home. I finally induced my own maiden sister to pose and had her comb her hair straight down her ears, with a severely plain part in the middle. The next job was to find a man to represent the *husband*."[18] It is significant that the wife was visualized first.

As their attire and accessories change from one parody to another, their gender relationship varies, often to the loss of original Regionalist associations.[19] The bib-overalled, bespectacled man stands stationary, stolid, and unmovable, eyes fixed in a disconcerting stare. The woman at first seems to obey the historical obligations of female submissiveness. She wears the homely, brown-print, Sears Roebuck apron of her daily chores over her white-collared black dress, the color of formal portrait attire for married women in the United States a century earlier. Her mother's Diana brooch is now in sharp focus, its mythological implications of aggressive pursuit contrasting with the domesticity signified by the houseplants at the far end of her apron's rickrack trim. She turns slightly and peers watchfully over the three tines of a pitchfork. The foremost object of the painting, it was drawn in menacing focus. As a no trespassing sign, it warns strangers against sudden approach. In contrast to the blank severity of her sentrylike mate, hints of apprehension linger about the woman's mouth and eyes. The contour lines of her upper lids may signal some compassion, as her brows, not knitted, tighten. The loosened hair on her forehead, the strand falling behind her right ear, suggest chance, spontaneous movement. Anxious, she appears to be poised for imminent challenge, capable of asserting her underlying concern. If legible at all, the countenance of the *American Gothic* man is one of staid bewilderment. The *American Gothic* woman, in contrast, is more likely to act or, as the decision-maker, to precipitate action. Thus, as moral guide and guardian, armed with her intuitive attentiveness against disruption, she stands slightly to the rear of the husband who poses "at the ready," waiting for an order from her more alert mind.

Maternal power, backed by historical evidence of moral supremacy in a bygone "mother age," must be reutilized for the good of us all. So argued the veteran women's rights leader Elizabeth Cady Stanton in an address to the National Council of Women in 1891, the year of Grant Wood's birth. She encouraged her assembled associates to strengthen their self-respect through awareness of an ancient matriarchate: "It lasted through many centuries when the greatest civilizing power existed as the wisdom and tender sentiments growing out of motherhood. Her varied responsibilities as mother . . . raised her to intellectual and inventive supremacy and made her the teacher and ruler of man."[20]

Monogamous marriage with descent through the male line and the Pauline Doctrine of female inferiority had deprived women of their personal independence, of their former authority in ruling councils and religious bodies, and of absolute control of home, property, and children. The woman's turn would come again, Stanton concluded, if not for supremacy, then certainly for complete equality.[21]

Closer to the rural midwestern location of the imagery and the woman's role in *American Gothic*, a report on women's new prominence in the Farmers' Alliance was delivered to the same meeting of the National Council of Women by Mary Lease of Kansas, a lawyer and mother of four children. Her views were to surface again during the farm depression of the 1920s. Following her Populist attack against "20,000 millionaires," who through their control of government, money, prices, taxation, and tariffs were robbing America of 500 farms a week, she told of how women were helping farmers to clarify their own interests: "The farmers, in their unswerving loyalty and patriotism to party, have been too mentally lazy to do their own thinking. . . . they have voted poverty and degradation not only upon themselves but upon their wives and children." But now the Farmers' Alliance had opened its ranks to upwards of half a million "patient burden-bearers of the home," who had concerned themselves with social and political problems by "studying and investigating the great issues of the day."[22]

The self-reliant farm woman, standing politely firm against intrusion

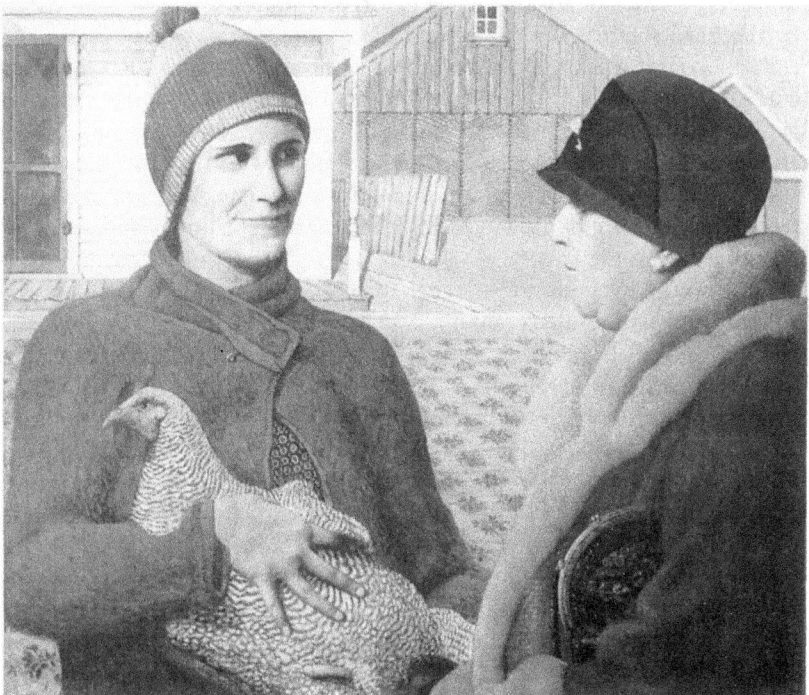

Figure 42. Grant Wood. *Appraisal*. 1931. Oil on composition board, 29½ × 35¼ in. Carnegie-Stout Public Library, Dubuque, Iowa. © Estate of Grant Wood/Licensed by VAGA, New York, NY.

from the city, received Wood's sympathetic treatment in *Appraisal* in 1931 (Fig. 42). As Wanda Corn concluded, the confrontation has to do with the challenge of urban modernity to a dwindling agrarian life.[23] By apparently identifying with the latter and fixing our attention on the deep-eyed expression of silent appraisal, Wood whimsically negates modernization. The fine clothes and accessories of the woman who has driven out from town symbolize the parvenu pretensions of a new, more materialistic, technological age. Such affectations tended to provoke modern artists, otherwise open to change, into class-conscious commentary. This once vertical painting, originally fenced in with a foreground of chickenwire, expresses a mutual skepticism heightened by an extended agricultural depression that widened the breach between rural and urban values. The woman of the land is neighborly, but watchful. She lives close to the soil, at one with animals, in the midst of rural purity: a potato patch and plain wood buildings. She wears a coarse cloth jacket pinned together at the top and a knit cap. On the other side and slightly to the front, the stern-faced city woman projects the cus-

103

tomized elegance of leisure versus labor. She stands shielded from nature by the hard shell of her cloche and the cosmopolitan luxury of her fur-collared coat.[24] Counterpoised to the magnificent Plymouth Rock rooster cradled in the hands of the earthbound provider, a beaded purse gradually gains attention as the loaded weapon of the prospective consumer. Thus armed, the matronly woman, Wood's generic power figure, would appear to command the outcome of a momentary stalemate. But, mounted on a rectangular closure of glowing white clapboards, the down-home composure of her rival prevails.

Back in town, with no reference to rural Regionalism whatsoever, reactionary, self-appointed community guardians, dead set against any modification of social standards or cultural values, prompted Wood's most satiric caricature. The tenacity with which the elderly can cling to the past in the face of another new generation inspired the singular figure of the 1931 *Victorian Survival* (Fig. 43). Wood portrayed his aged Aunt Matilda in yellow-gray tones to simulate a time-stained daguerreotype many times enlarged.[25] The elongation, proportionate size, and positioning of the hands in relation to the cameo pin, the exact location of the black choker on the long neck, and the tightly contoured, small, round head accentuate a paradoxical correspondence between the antiquated, uptight woman and the up-to-date upright telephone. She distrusts its proliferation and stares slightly off to her right through wide-open, glazed eyes, thin lips pursed in silence. The remnant of a waning age of privacy, she sits quietly bewildered on the edge of disruption. A technological intruder from the ensuing electronic era threatens to break through the hush. Which side Wood was on, that of the new dial phone representing modern technology or that of his Victorian model, is hard to say. He worked out the visual pun by revising the appearance of his aunt, as he had revised his sister's appearance for the woman in *American Gothic*. But instead of seeing figure and object as complements in spirit, they were now in generational opposition; and while he satirized his subject as anachronistic, he looked askance at the phone he had aimed at her head.

Aunt Matilda's sisters in temperament, style, and lack of Regionalist reference peer myopically out of the 1932 *Daughters of Revolution* (see Fig. 24), which cleverly derides nationalism through three of its most stolid purveyors. Long-necked, thin-lipped, and snugly coifed, they owe their stereotyped appearance to portrait photos Wood compounded from yearbooks of the Daughters of the American Revolution (DAR). Bemused by the Daughters' chauvinistic ancestor worship, he placed his takeoffs in front of the steel engraving of *Washington Crossing the Delaware* in keeping with the bicentennial of the great father's birth.[26] Though distributed as an embodiment of America First patriotism, the print reproduces a large oil on canvas painted in Düsseldorf on the Rhine by the German-American

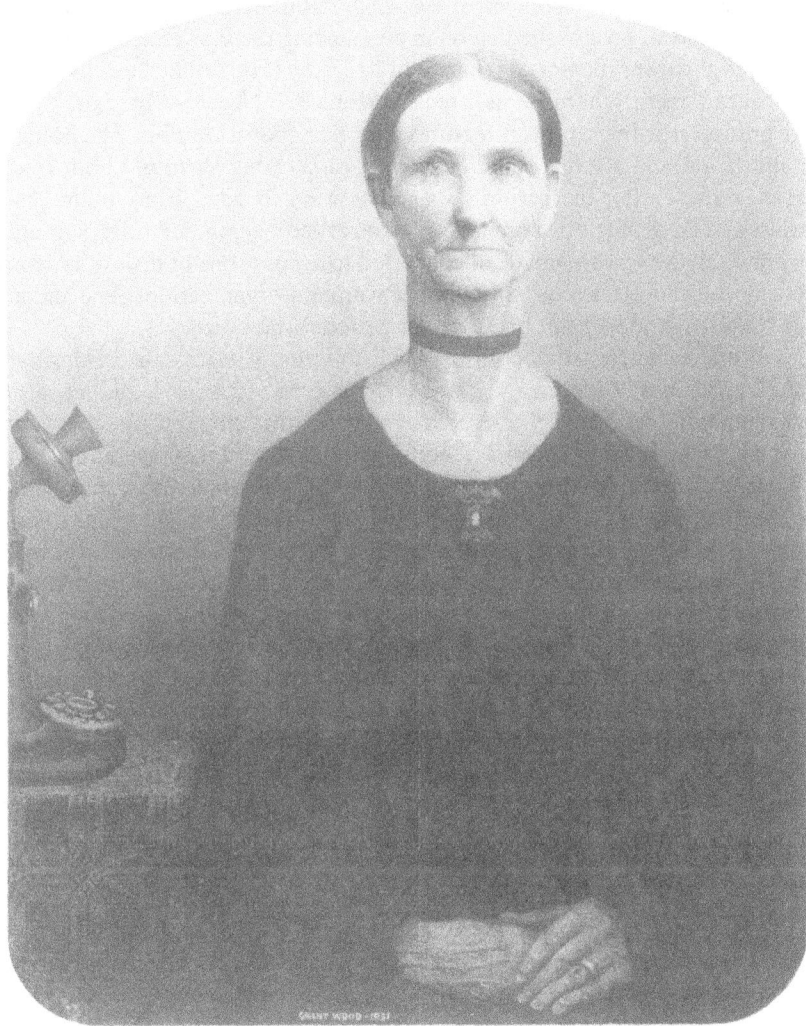

Figure 43. Grant Wood. *Victorian Survival*. 1931. Oil on composition board, 32½ × 26¼ in. Carnegie-Stout Public Library, Dubuque, Iowa. © Estate of Grant Wood/Licensed by VAGA, New York, NY.

Emanuel Leutze to encourage participation in the ill-fated Revolution of 1848.[27]

Founded in 1890, the DAR intensified its original benign nationalism into venomous superpatriotism following World War I. In particular, it allied itself to right-wing veterans' organizations like the American Legion and the Military Order of the World War and even turned to red-baiting

feminists.[28] Several members of the Cedar Rapids chapter publicly seconded the local post of the Legion in denouncing the fabrication of Wood's
stained-glass war memorial window of 1927–29 (Fig. 44) by "enemy" German craftsmen, whom he assisted in Munich.[29] Never so memorable as
its predecessor by Leutze, it features a sixteen-foot Columbia. She holds a
palm frond and a wreath high over the heads of her variously uniformed
sons, representing the nation's six major wars to date. Irony built upon
irony as a large patriotic commission to an artist-veteran, featuring a monumental, all-American female allegory, led to accusations of disloyalty from
one of the country's most nationalistic women's organizations. The affront
provoked Wood to paint his most antinationalistic satire.

While a charter member of the DAR in Cedar Rapids called *Daughters
of Revolution* a "hideous monstrosity," the critic Charles J. Bulliet, after
viewing it in the 1934 Century of Progress art exhibition, praised the painting as an enduring "social lampoon," free from retaliatory bitterness.[30]
Wood explained his interpretation of the DAR as a whimsical but determined exposé of their "great inconsistency" as Americans: "They were
forever searching through great volumes of history and dusty records, trac-
ing down their Revolutionary ancestry. On the one hand, they were trying
to establish themselves as an aristocracy of birth, on the other they were
trying to support democracy."[31] Though starting out as a personal matter
on a local level, Wood's taunting use of an internationally popular myth of
revolutionary fortitude as a backdrop to ethnic elitism assumed a modern
detachment from particular place and time despite its American context.
As does his three-chicken allegory of *Adolescence,* conceived a year later,
this caricatured farce of a painting contributes to the twentieth-century
confusion between high and low art.

Another, somewhat more subtle, parody of ancestral status-seeking,
Wood's 1933 portrait of his sister Nan entails a visual double-entendre
(Fig. 45). Her fashionably marcelled blond hair, the exaggerated arch of
her penciled brows, and the frivolous blouse, sleeveless with black polka
dots and butterfly bows at the shoulders, complement each other as a chic
early-thirties ensemble. The accessories from a colonial setting, while in-
congruous, made perfect sense within the "American Scene" search for
national identity. The heavy drapery swag and Hitchcock chair enhance
the air of early American antiquity. The decorator effect is even more tan-
gibly evoked by the oval frame, a favorite eighteenth-century format often
employed for Puritan divines and their wives. The chick-in-hand contem-
plating a ripe plum recalls the fruit and small animals used in portraits of
children and young women by pre-Revolutionary Boston's John Singleton
Copley. A bird symbolizing free spirit and the plum as a sign of independence[32] coincide with the costume change by which Nan shifted from her
role of maternal alertness in *American Gothic* to an outward show of glam-

106

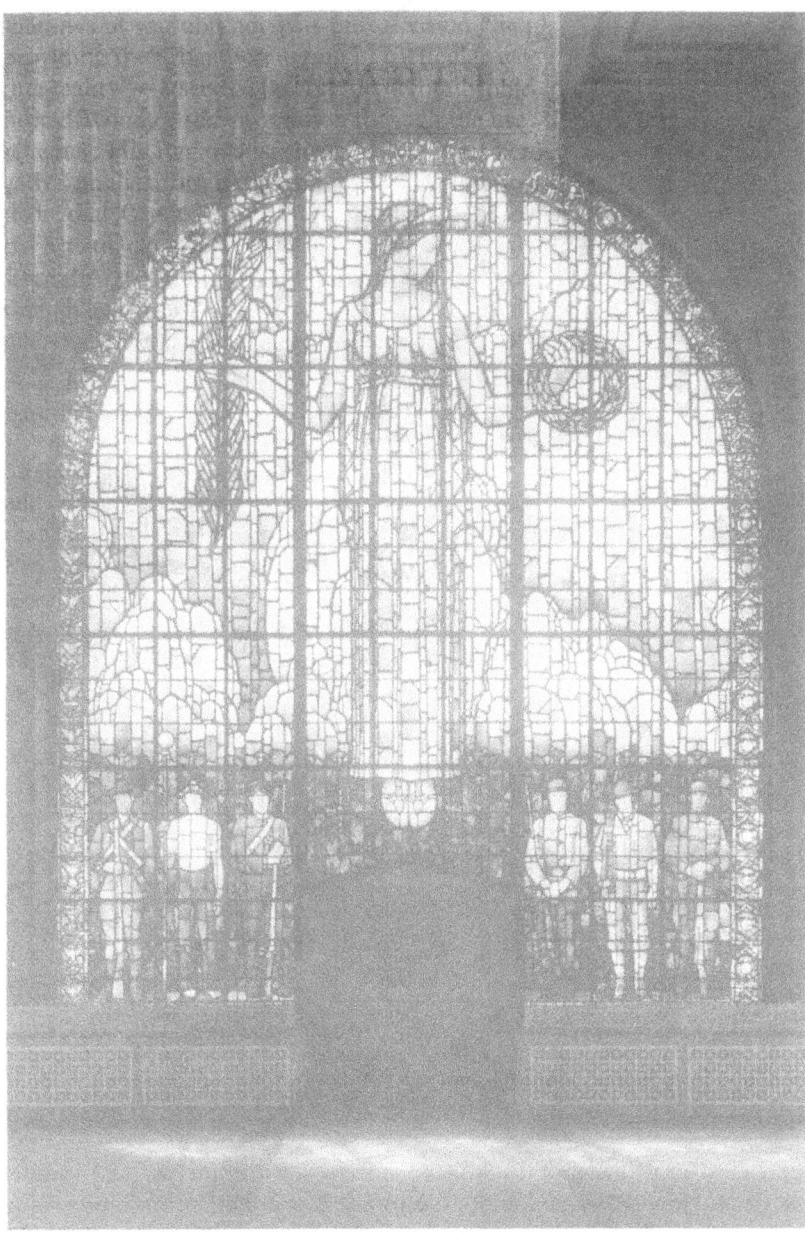

Figure 44. Grant Wood. *Memorial Window*. 1927–29. Leaded stained glass, 24 × 20 ft. Veteran's Memorial Building, Cedar Rapids, Iowa. © Estate of Grant Wood/Licensed by VAGA, New York, NY.

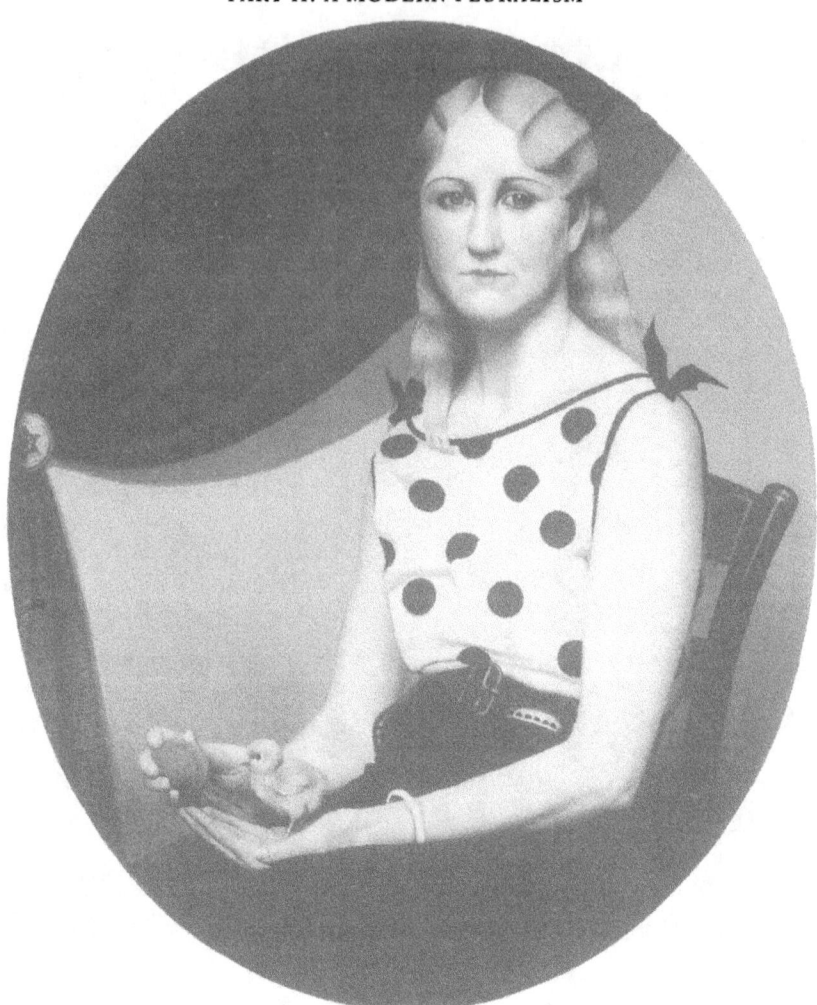

Figure 45. Grant Wood. *Portrait of Nan*. 1933. Oil on masonite, 34½ × 28½ in. On loan to the Elvehjem Museum of Art, University of Wisconsin–Madison, Madison, Wisconsin. © Estate of Grant Wood/Licensed by VAGA, New York, NY.

our. This transformation took place, however, with no change of countenance. She continues to stare out at us like a guardian, at once protective of her "New Woman" liberties and protected by a puritanical setting. As a merging of the mutually exclusive through paradox and ambivalence, the painting achieves one of the ultimate goals of modernism.

With Eleanor Roosevelt occupying the White House, the New Deal provided opportunities for women to inject moral principles into public work.[33] Her friend and co-worker, Molly Dewson, a leader of the National Consumers League, took over the Women's Division of the Democratic Party in 1932. With the aid of thousands of women "Reporters" who went door to door, she worked to broaden its constituency by emphasizing the "security of the home" and the need for a new public welfare program.[34] Frances "Ma" Perkins, secretary of labor, the first woman to hold a cabinet post, maintained a cautious opinion that women should remain domestic. They should "keep their place" in the world of business and government and, if they could afford not to work, concentrate on motherhood.[35] Regardless of the official support for a new assertiveness outside the home, women were still requested to stay put in their traditional role of helpmate.

Two of Wood's early Depression paintings of ever-bountiful farming, sentimental evasions of the droughts and foreclosures of those years, find the farm woman doing her job without a wrinkle. She is confined to the timeless, sanctified tasks associated with serving the men of the fields. In his mural panels called *Fruits of Iowa,* painted in 1932 for the Montrose Hotel dining room in Cedar Rapids, members of the farm family function as iconic, cornucopian figures in votive poses of constant plenty. Or, as Melosh sums up New Deal depictions of family harmony and shared labor by Treasury Section muralists, "The powerful emotional resonance of domesticity conveyed the reassuring ambience of an imagined rural idyll, a prosperous and stable life on the land."[36] The boyish farmer, hair parted and combed for the occasion, displays a bushel basket full of a prize money crop. His pink-nosed, piggy-bank porkers wait for market (Fig. 46). His ample wife feeds a goose that has wandered into her chicken yard (Fig. 47). Her somber blue glance, though shyly avoiding direct contact, is more thoughtfully expressive than the wide-eyed, ingratiating eagerness of her husband. And her daughter, loaded down with a big bowl of string beans in one hand and a huge cabbage-plus-peppers in the other, takes after her.

Dinner for Threshers (see Fig. 12), painted two years later, portrays a ritual celebration of annual cooperation that furnished a transitory social base for midwestern rural culture. Perennial bib-overalls and pioneer dresses join mementos of homestead settlement in a sanctuary of the ever-present past. The magnificent wood stove, the gas lamp, and the hand pump commemorate the virtuous housework that preceded rural electrification. The popular steel engraving of the white mare seeking security beside the black stallion in a thunderstorm doubtless reflects the underlying attitude of those seated at the table, being served with solemn, silent anonymity. The quartet of true womanhood, smoothly rendered in calico, spotless white aprons, and uniform bun-tight hairdos, was obviously not intended to expose the hard life on a Great Plains farm.

In any case, no Regionalist painting dedicated to nationalist uplift would ever tell the story of forty-five-year-old Lydia Stoner of Minnesota.

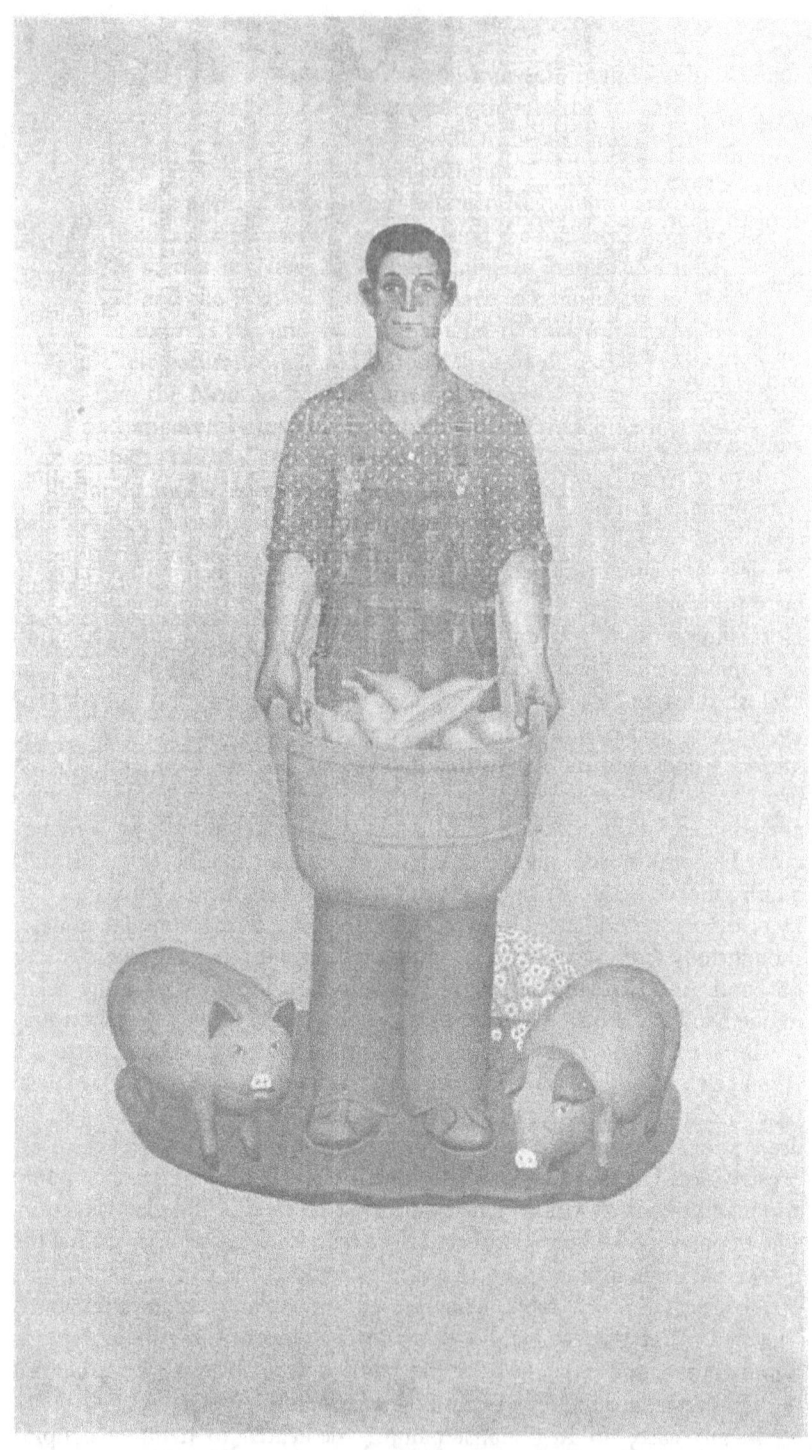

Figure 46. Grant Wood. *Fruits of Iowa: Farmer.* 1932. Oil on canvas attached to panel, 71¼ × 49¼ in. Coe College Collection, Cedar Rapids, Iowa; gift of the Eugene C. Eppley Foundation. © Estate of Grant Wood/Licensed by VAGA, New York, NY.

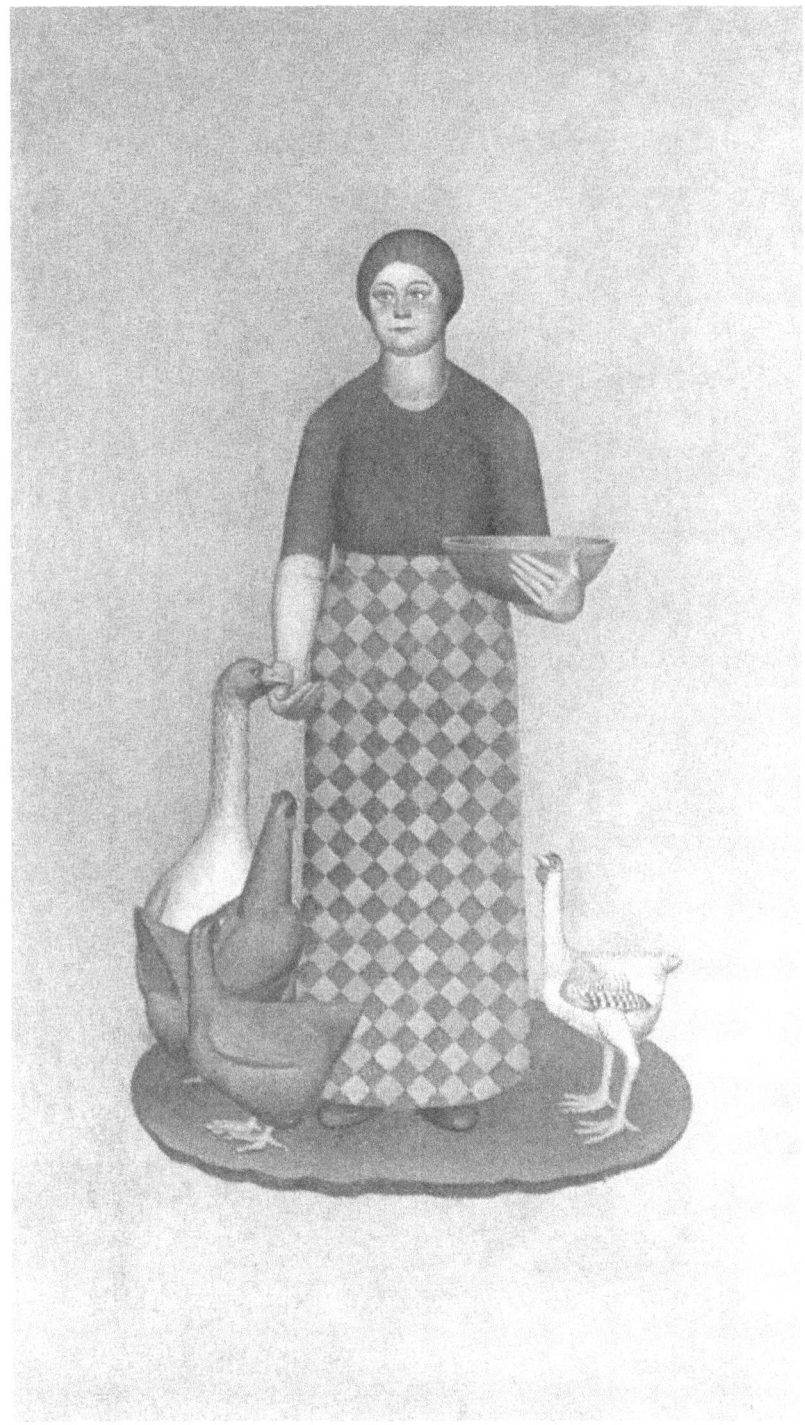

Figure 47. Grant Wood. *Fruits of Iowa: Farmer's Wife*. 1932. Oil on canvas attached to panel, 71¼ × 49 in. Coe College Collection, Cedar Rapids, Iowa; gift of the Eugene C. Eppley Foundation. © Estate of Grant Wood/Licensed by VAGA, New York, NY.

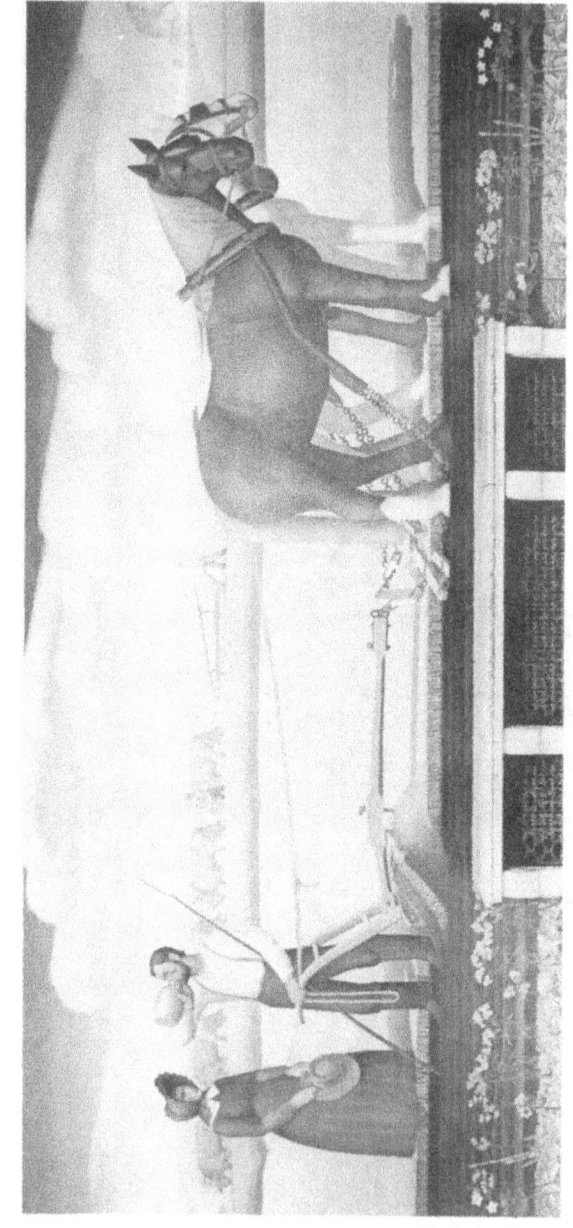

Figure 48. Grant Wood. *Breaking the Prairie*. 1934–37. Oil on canvas, 11 ft. × 23 ft. 3 in. Mural in Iowa State University Library, Ames, Iowa. © Estate of Grant Wood/Licensed by VAGA, New York, NY.

Early on August 6, 1876, she bore her tenth baby as she had done all the others, at home without a doctor or anesthetic, and then sat up in bed to peel potatoes for a threshing crew due to arrive that same day.[37] Conversely, an independent farm woman who had assumed control of a homestead without first becoming a widow also lived outside the inherited categories of Middle Border allegory. Imagine an officially sanctioned narrative painting of Grace Wayne Fairchild riding the range of the South Dakota stock farm she had taken over from an irresponsible husband and expanded to approximately 1,500 acres.[38]

In a 1934 Public Works of Art mural for a first-floor alcove in the Iowa State University Library in Ames, Wood and his student assistants from the University of Iowa in Iowa City depicted a pioneer farm wife who has left her household chores, but only for a moment. Wearing her sunbonnet to the field, she holds her husband's straw hat while watching him pause between the handles of his plow to drink from a jug of cool water she has brought him (Fig. 48). The inscription quotes from a speech by Daniel Webster, champion of industrial development and speculator in western land: "When tillage begins, other arts follow. The farmers therefore are the founders of human civilization." The arts, represented in the murals leading up the staircase to the reading room, leave the nineteenth century far behind. Belonging to a modern time of advanced technology, they include only the practical arts of applied science and engineering, appropriate for boosting a land-grant university of agriculture. As Melosh points out, "Land-grant universities sought to educate future farmers and to replace old methods with techniques aimed at high-volume commercial agriculture." [39] Men experiment in the laboratory and test their findings in the barn, while women sew, dust, cook, and care for the offspring. Accordingly, the civilization founded by farmers unfolds as one of research and development. Housework, in the meantime, is a family resource and consumer science practiced by efficient housewives, the modern descendants of the original sunbonnet support system (Fig. 49).

An arcadian dream world of classical origin would obviously not have been complete without nurturing women bearing, rearing, and teaching children. Its modern sequel, the agrarian myth, of lasting rhetorical significance to the history of family farming in North America, assimilated their multiplying chores in an increasingly mechanized kitchen as well as those in the rest of the house. It still sent them to the poultry yard and occasionally out into the field. Myth, at the risk of oversimplification, lends a sense of order to the growing complexity of modern, machine-age history. Wood's strongest mythic urges culminated in up-to-date abstractions of eastern Iowa into smoothly contoured earth-mother farmscapes (see Figs. 2, 4). In their midst he generated the ideal of a restorative teacher, an ideal based on real-life experience.

113

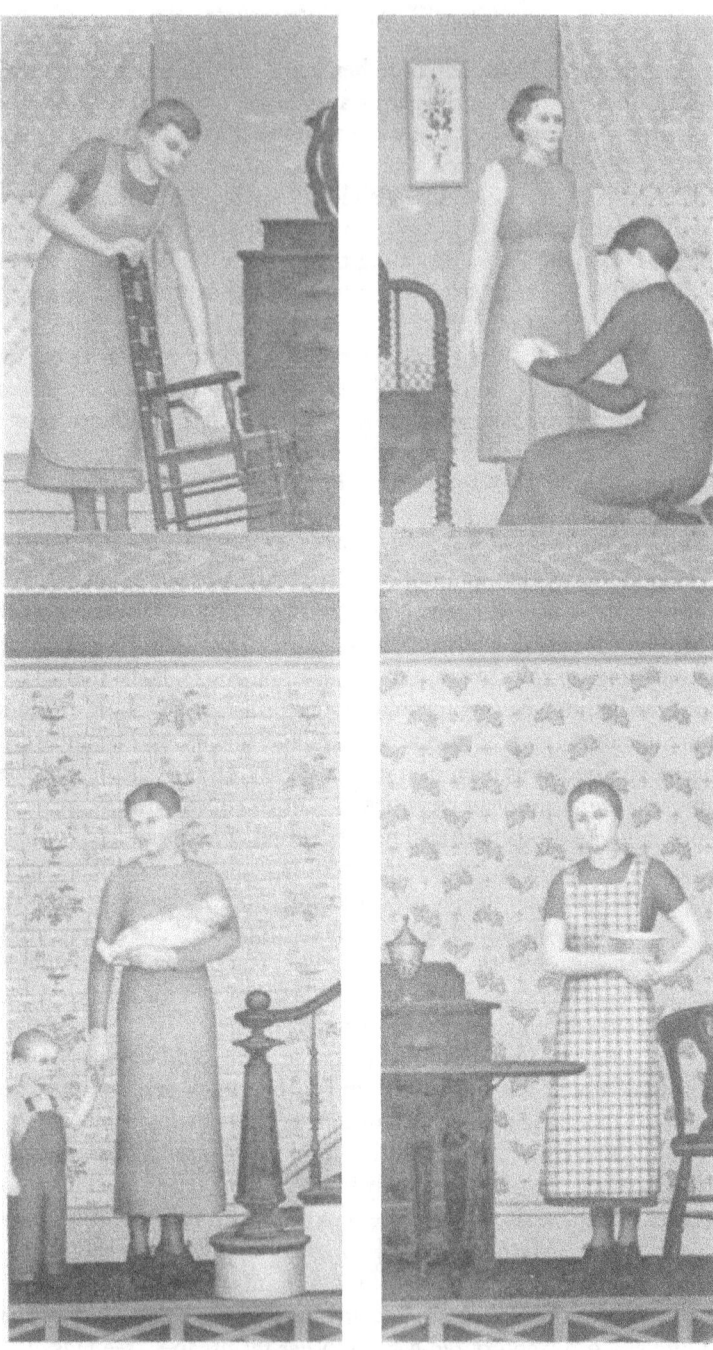

Figure 49. Grant Wood. *Home Economics*. 1934–37. Oil on canvas, 16 ft. 9 in. ×
4 ft. 5 in. (each vertical pair). Mural in Iowa State University Library, Ames, Iowa.
© Estate of Grant Wood/Licensed by VAGA, New York, NY.

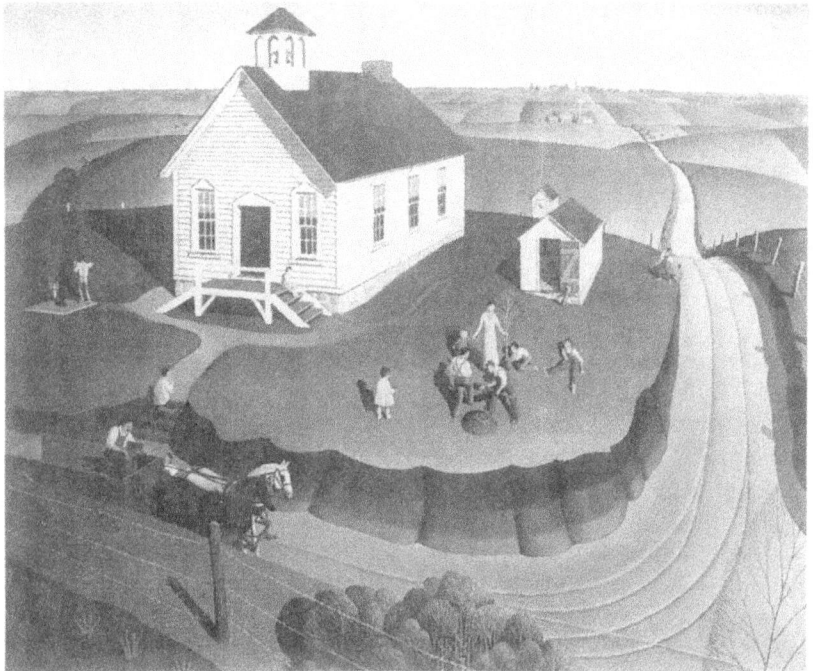

Figure 50. Grant Wood. *Arbor Day.* 1932. Oil on masonite, 24 × 30 in. Commissioned by Cedar Rapids Community Schools; memorial to Catherine Motejl and Rose L. Waterstadt, McKinley School; collection of William I. Koch. © Estate of Grant Wood/Licensed by VAGA, New York, NY.

In two closely related pictures of 1932 and 1933, *Arbor Day* (Fig. 50) and *Tree Planting* (Fig. 51), the country schoolyard constitutes a recognized female domain in the open, male-dominated farmscape. Tenderly holding the hand of a preschooler, the motherly teacher supports a sapling, waiting for the bigger boys to dig a hole for its planting. The girls are on the schoolhouse porch, relegated to the role of idle observer. The most immediate inspiration for the theme of elementary education derived from Wood's own experience in this segment of the woman's sphere. He admired several of his seasoned female colleagues, and had dedicated paintings to them. He was especially inspired and guided by Frances Prescott. She was a charismatic, matriarchal Cedar Rapids educator who had advanced to the position of junior-high principal and approved and defended the unorthodox teaching methods of her uncertified art teacher. A second mother figure, she also chauffeured him around town and advised him on personal concerns.[40]

In the very last examples of Wood's idealized, fantasy Iowascapes, the

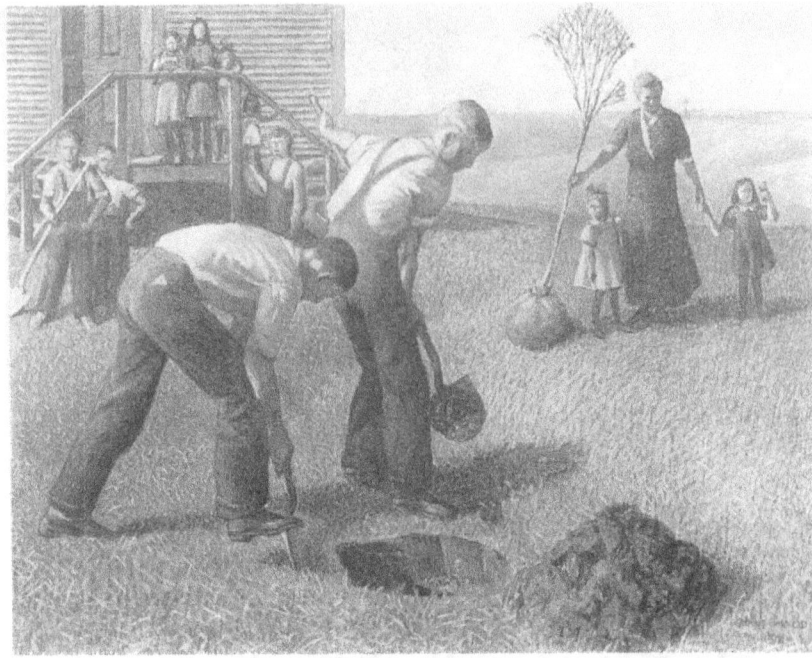

Figure 51. Grant Wood. *Tree Planting* (study for *Arbor Day*). 1937. Charcoal, pencil, and chalk on paper, 21¾ × 28 in. Cedar Rapids Museum of Art, Cedar Rapids, Iowa; Cedar Rapids Community School District Collection. © Estate of Grant Wood/Licensed by VAGA, New York, NY.

earthbound, hardworking women are still there, following their prescribed roles, as he must have remembered his mother fulfilling hers alongside his father. In *Spring in the Country* (see Fig. 33) and *Spring in Town* (Fig. 52), the faithful wife and caring mother, in nondescript housedress, leads her son in planting seedlings and hangs up her quilts to dry. The man hand-plows or spades the soil (no tractor or major mechanization is in sight). Industrialization, with its high smokestacks, is at a safe distance, barely discernible in the right-hand background of *Spring in Town*. A pair of un-contaminated country scenes, these final paintings continue Wood's debate with industrialized progress.

Unlike the factory workers manning their machines in a series of paintings he did for a Cedar Rapids dairy equipment company in 1925,[41] rural people working together, outdoors, were meant to symbolize the best of American life, a life worth fighting for in the World War year of 1941. Industrial power and competitiveness had caused nothing but tragedy six years earlier in *Death on the Ridge Road* (Fig. 18), and Wood, a modern

116

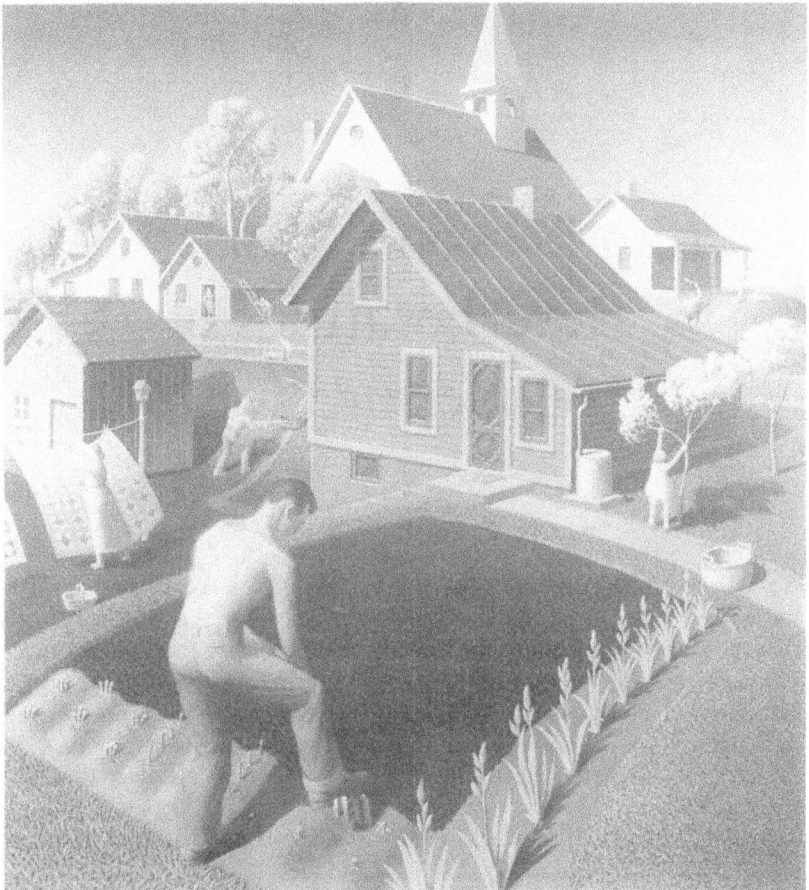

Figure 52. Grant Wood. *Spring in Town*. 1941. Oil on masonite, 26 × 24½ in. The Sheldon Swope Art Museum, Terre Haute, Indiana. © Estate of Grant Wood/Licensed by VAGA, New York, NY.

independent, countered a sudden demand for increased mobility with his striking negations of modernization. He had reached that point of paradox through the imaging of women, from his forceful guardian matron in charge of domestic morality to his farmmother ideal, an emblem of social security in a decade of financial worry and impending warfare.

6

Tom Benton's "Girls" as Reverberations of Modernization

A touch of blond glamour in the midst of Wood's guardian matrons, *Portrait of Nan* (see Fig. 45) gave a polite nod to a new type of female imagery that the Jazz Age had unleashed through popular novels, magazines, advertisements, and the movies.[1] Benton and Curry, in following their respective instincts and intentions, proved to be more attracted to this commercial exploitation of the New Woman, as indicated by its appropriation into some of their most non-Regionalist works. Whatever their motives were, primarily personal in Benton's case and sociopolitical in Curry's, the results appear independently modern: they welcome the new as they comment either positively or negatively on cultural modernization.

The accelerated diversification of women's roles, manners, morals, and styles provided a new territory to explore. From the immediate postwar period to the stock market crash in 1929, the newly enfranchised, erratically emancipated New Woman who captured the public imagination was embodied in a dubious image. The flapper, as caricatured by John Held, Jr., for the cover of the original *Life* magazine, shed her corset, hiked up her skirt, rolled down her stockings, and danced to hot music (Fig. 53). In big cities she could smoke, drink, and swear in public and allegedly practice "free love" with no sexual inhibitions. Women's rights veterans like Charlotte Perkins Gilman saw such liberation as superficial in light of the continued economic inequality between the sexes.[2] She considered the increased display of the female body for purposes of male titillation a major reversal. As historian Ellen Wiley Todd observes, "The flapper's expression of her sexuality could turn against her as her body became another commodity on display in a burgeoning consumer culture."[3]

118

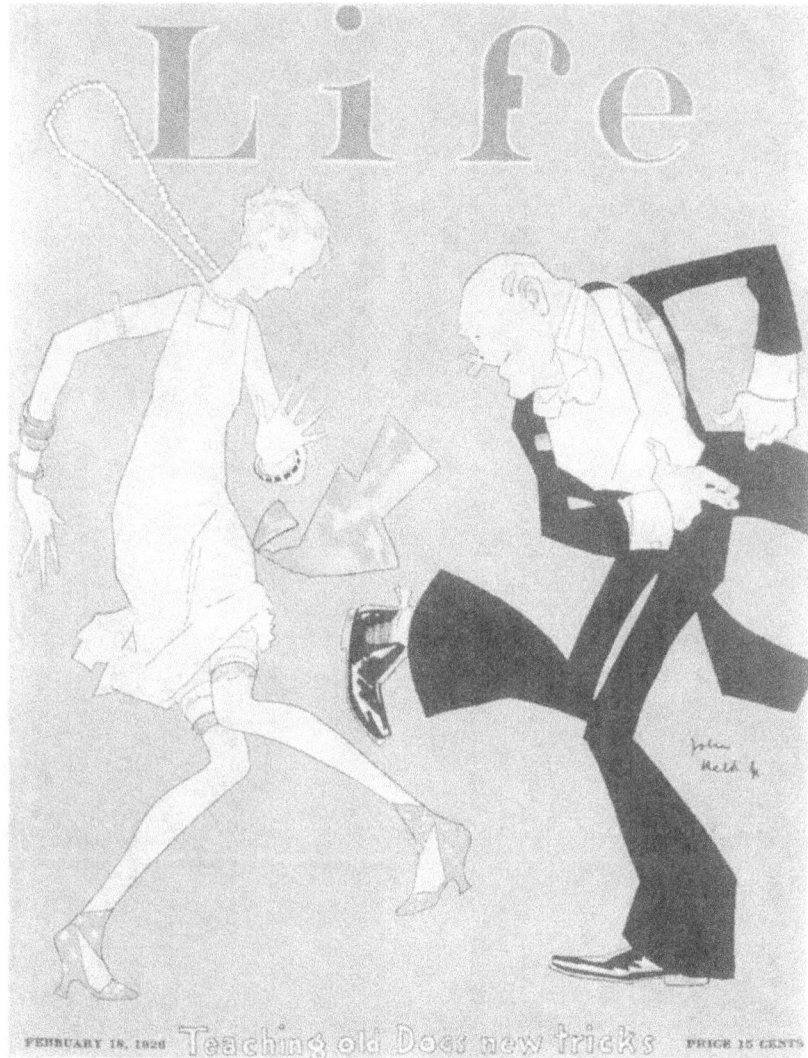

Figure 53. John Held, Jr. Cover of *Life*. February 18, 1926.

During the years Benton was developing his figural style, the adventures of a carefree, working-girl flapper became a profitable movie formula. A 1927 film version of Elinor Glyn's novella *It* clinched stardom for Clara Bow, as the lingerie salesclerk who gets the handsome owner of the department store by taking him to Coney Island, where she could display her cute sensuality (Fig. 54). Anticipating the "It Girl," the first Miss America

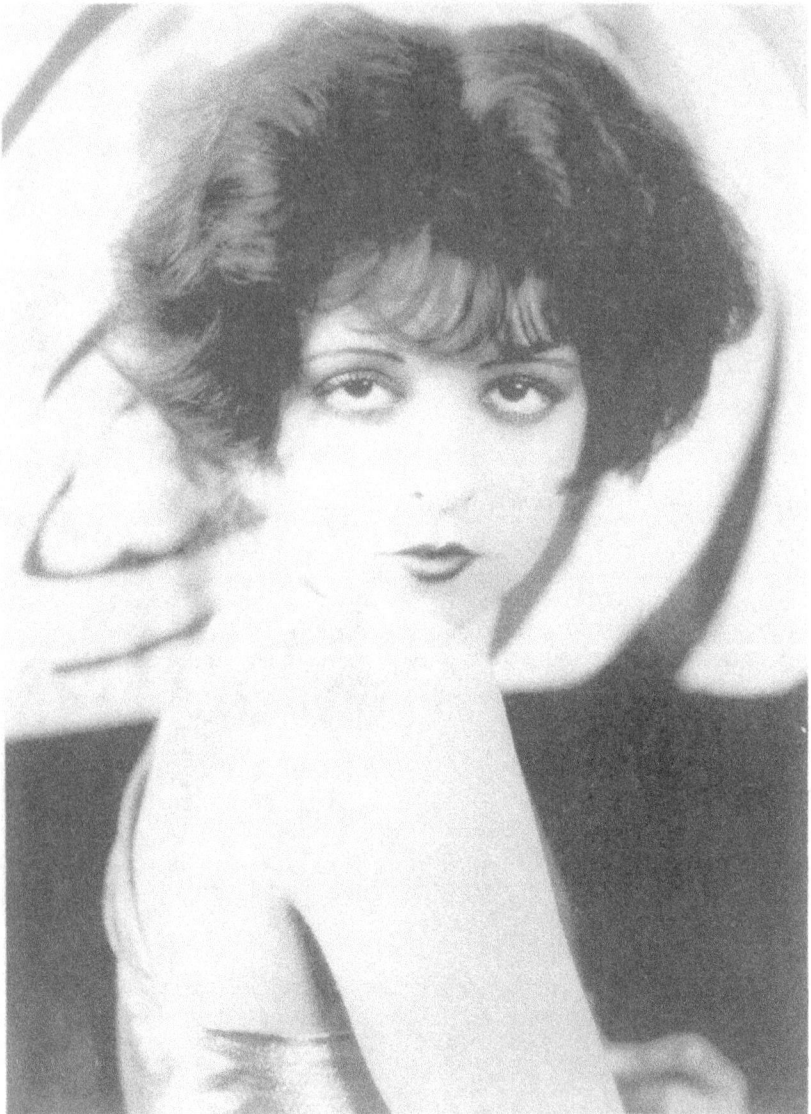

Figure 54. Clara Bow, 1926. Photograph: Eugene Robert Richee.

Pageant, back in 1921, attracted a crowd of at least 100,000 to Atlantic City. Colleen Moore in *Flaming Youth* (1923) made bobbed hair and short skirts popular throughout the country. In the role of Patricia Fentriss, she flirts, teases, wiggles, and dances the Charleston with what appears to be sexual abandon in accordance with the legendary license of the Roaring

Twenties. In the end, however, she jumps off a yacht into the ocean to preserve her virtue from a rich would-be seducer. Marjorie Rosen's *Popcorn
Venus* reminds us that the headstrong jazz baby was a highly moral girl
at heart, still impelled by stringent Victorian standards in her quest for
a suitable husband.[4] Modern advertising, however, successfully persuaded
young married women that they must remain at all costs sexy, as the social
historian Stuart Ewen documents. "Ads of the 1920s were quite explicit
about this narcissistic imperative. They unabashedly used pictures of veiled
nudes and women in auto-erotic stances to encourage self-comparison and
to remind women of the primacy of their sexuality."[5] Ads featured beautiful young women displaying a wide variety of household products in high
and low degrees of dress and undress. Some of the sexiest of these were
created by the illustrators Coles Phillips and Neysa McMein. The "Phillips
Girl" often appeared on the cover of *Good Housekeeping,* while McMein
contributed her sensual new woman to numerous ads in the *Ladies' Home
Journal* and to covers for *McCalls* (Fig. 55).

Such surface display of the "new morality" entranced Thomas Hart
Benton. By the late twenties he consistently accented his expanding array of
paintings with abundant, full-bodied female sensuality, at the risk of totally
eclipsing his occasional images of motherhood and piety (Fig. 56). Benton's self-consciously masculine imagination replaced the stock-in-trade
classicistic goddess figure so persistently employed by the previous generation of academic muralists. The new sex-object formula energetically
picked up on the naughty body of "flapper" fame in both his easel and wall
paintings. Benton's autobiographical *An Artist in America* (1937) invariably and appreciatively describes young women as "girls" in the spirit of
a new sexist sexuality. Gone is the nineteenth-century worship of women
as spiritually superior, pure, and pious. While he discusses his father,
"Colonel" M. E. Benton, extensively, he refers to his mother, Elizabeth
Wise, only once—not by name, but as a young woman from Texas who
had four children.[6] By the word *people* he meant men: "I didn't give a damn
what people thought, how they ate their eggs or approached their females,
how they voted, or what devious business they were involved in."[7]

In writing of New York City, it is his memories of young women that
he describes most vividly. They correspond to the sensual female figures
with which he enlivened the *City Activities* panels of his 1930 *America
Today* murals on the board room walls of the New School for Social Research (Fig. 57, and see Fig. 9) and the *Arts of the City* panel for his 1932
reading room murals in the Whitney Museum (Fig. 58). In the former,
bare-bottomed "shimmy shake" dancers and a dime-a-dance hall of svelte
young women in revealing gowns solemnly tolerate odd-looking men. A
blonde in a red dress succumbs to her seducer on a park bench while at
the opposite end of the same panel burlesque star Peggy Reynolds, dolled

121

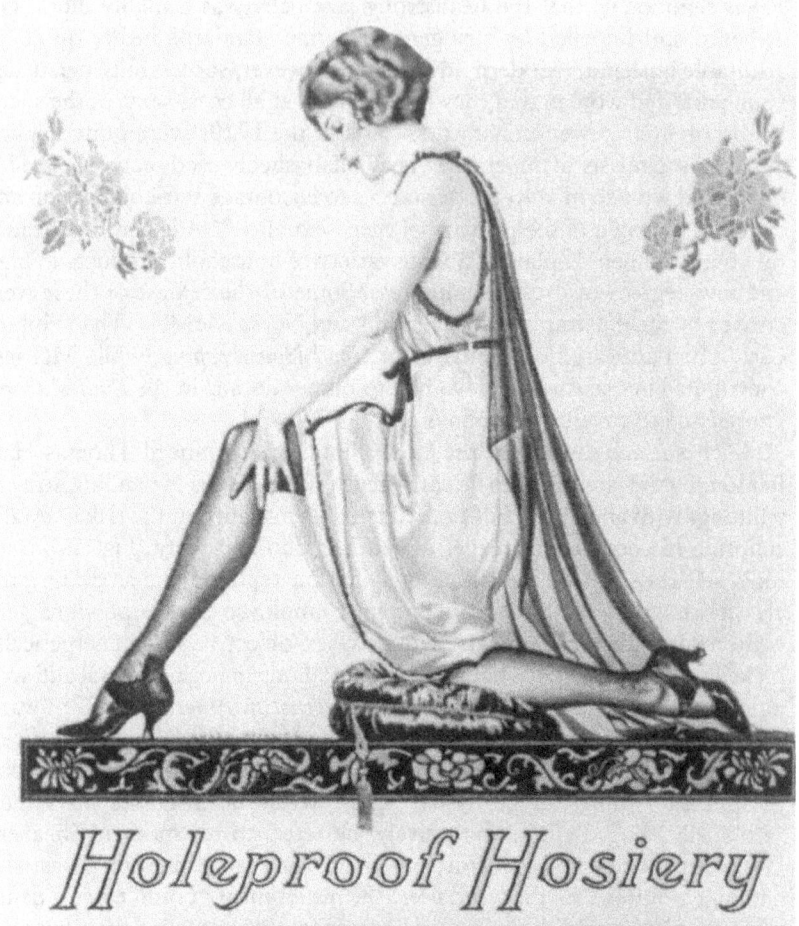

Holeproof Hosiery

HOLEPROOF offers women a sensible combination in hosiery that can be found in no other makes—long wear and beautiful appearance.

Some hose may equal Holeproof in appearance but they lack the phenomenal durability that has made Holeproof famous. Others may approach Holeproof in wearing quality, but at the sacrifice of fine texture and sheerness.

If you are interested in getting hosiery that will give extraordinary wear and at the same time is sheer and beautiful, ask for Holeproof.

At all good stores—in many styles, in all approved colors. Silk, silk-and-wool, wool, silk-faced, and lusterized lisle. Styles also for men and children. If not available locally, write for booklet and prices.

HOLEPROOF HOSIERY COMPANY, MILWAUKEE, WISCONSIN
Holeproof Hosiery Company of Canada, Limited, London, Ontario

© H. H. Co.

Figure 55. Coles Phillips. Holeproof Hosiery Company advertisement. 1922.

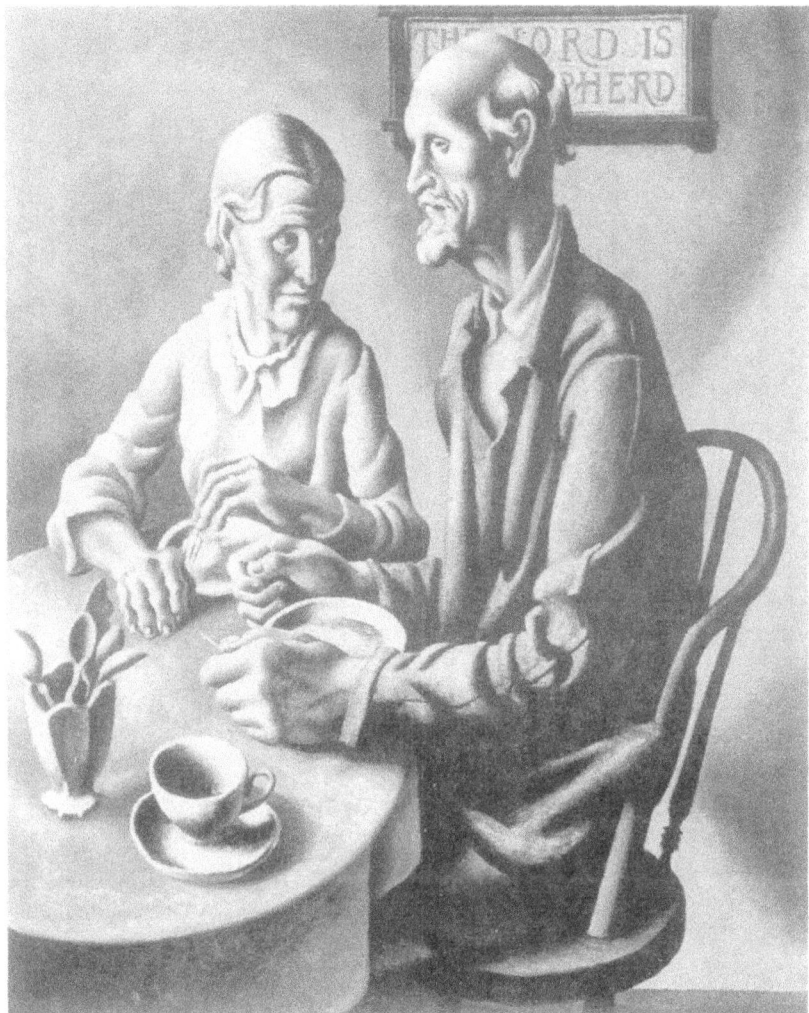

Figure 56. Thomas Hart Benton. *The Lord Is My Shepherd.* 1926. Egg tempera and oil on canvas, 33¼ × 27⅜ in. Whitney Museum of American Art, New York City, 31.100, Purchase. Copyright © T. H. Benton and R. P. Benton Testamentary Trusts/Licensed by VAGA, New York, NY. Photograph © 1997 Whitney Museum of American Art.

up as a flapper and hanging on to a strap in a subway car, gets ogled point blank by a seated Max Eastman. Women in the *Arts of the City* entertain men as bathing beauties, a cocktail waitress, a nightclub singer, a black-stockinged prostitute, and a vanity figure "dolling up" in front of her mirror. "I shall think of the shopgirls with their slim waists and swishing tails who, in the past before I was married, of course, used to be a favorite sub-

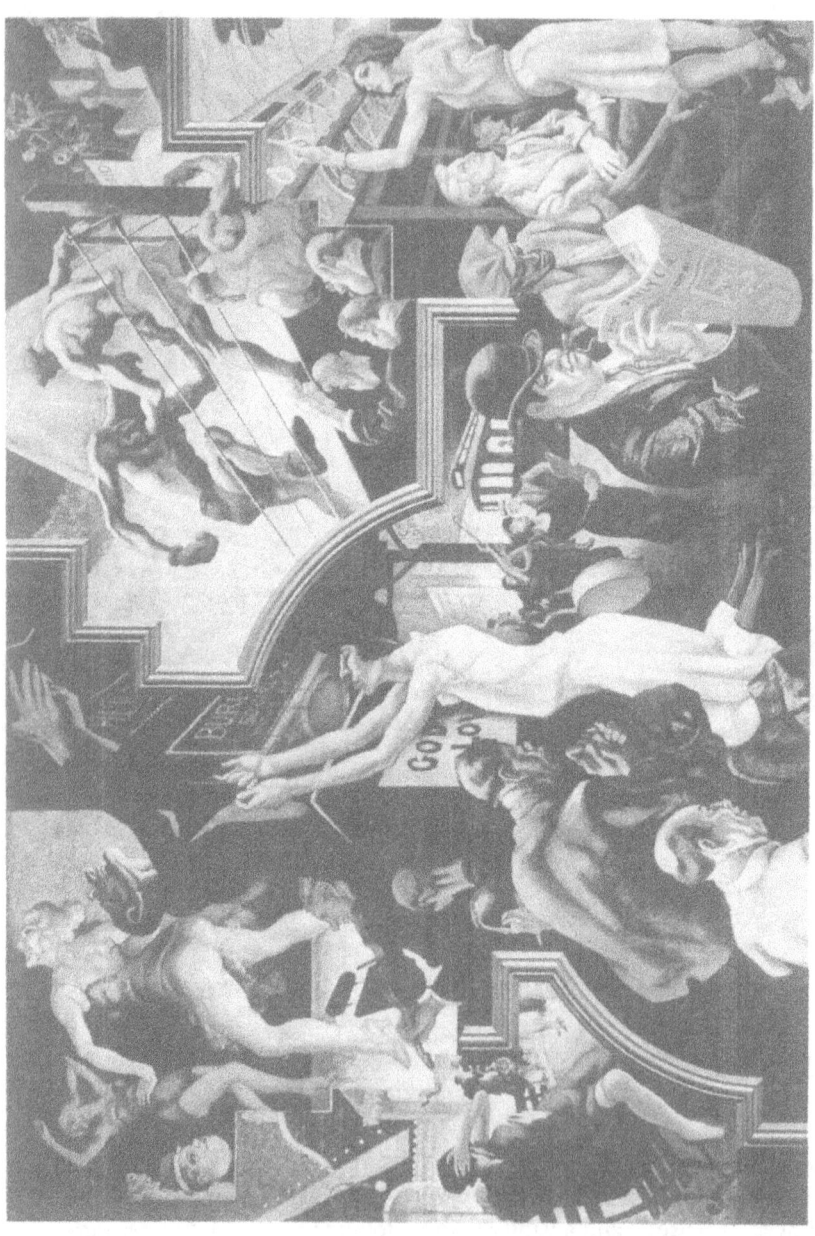

Figure 57. Thomas Hart Benton. *City Activities with Subway* (from *America Today*). 1930. Distemper and egg tempera on gessoed linen with oil glaze, 92 × 134½ in. Mural for New School for Social Research, New York City; Collection, The Equitable Life Assurance Society of the U.S. Copyright © The Equitable Life Insurance Society of the U.S., T. H. Benton and R. P. Benton Testamentary Trusts/Licensed by VAGA, New York, NY.

ject of contemplation," Benton wrote fondly in his autobiography. "I shall think of the burlesque shows, particularly of the one on 14th Street, now gone . . . where the art of "stripping" just began, used to make the old boys drool at the mouth and keep their hands in their pockets." [8]

In the most politically provocative panel of the Whitney Museum reading room murals, *Political Business and Intellectual Ballyhoo* (See Fig. 23), Benton vented his disillusionment with the political left. Its only female reference shows up in its most cluttered area, left of center, where a partially obscured light-blue placard exclaims, "REGENERATIVE POTENTIALITIES . . . THE NEW WOMAN." Given the overall tone of the lunette, as discussed in Chapter 3, this ambiguously broken quotation comes across as a caustic comment on a progressive faction of the women's movement. As such, it would seem to be in agreement with Walter Lippmann's attitude toward the "emancipated woman." The *New Republic* pragmatist, who had rejected moral absolutes in his 1914 book *A Preface to Politics,* now numbered her among the evils of recent, amoral, relativist trends: "The evidences of these greater difficulties lie all about us . . . in the women who have emancipated themselves from the tyranny of fathers, husbands, and homes, and with the intermittent but expensive help of a psychoanalyst, are now enduring liberty as interior decorators." [9]

Benton either ignored or instinctively belittled "THE NEW WOMAN" through his objectifying female imagery. No ideological reason for this is apparent other than a possible rebellion against the Victorian repression of his father and the social ambitions of his mother. He had launched this rebellion in Joplin, Missouri, by the time he was seventeen.[10] His visual improprieties toward women may also mimic the rapid modernization of urban life that had occurred by the time he was forty. While perhaps entertained by increasingly unrestrained modes of behavior, he reveals less respect for contemporary human activity in general than he does for the machinery that accompanies it. Defending his choice of subject matter, Benton explained to a New York *Evening Journal* reporter: "It is true my murals include the synthesis of the color and tempo of the jazz age as represented by racketeers, fast women, gunmen, booze hounds and so on. . . . My subjects portray American life in the 20th century realistically. It may be life that should be criticized; but not my painting of it." [11]

In describing and depicting women of the South, "a great land for riotous whoredom," Benton seemed most enthusiastic about evangelistic ecstasy at backwoods "holiness" gatherings. His most ambitious dramatization of this experience is staged biracially with two juxtaposed clusters of figures in *Arts of the South* (Fig. 59) for the Whitney Museum reading room. Whether black or white, three sensual women in tight-fitting skirts, one clutching her thighs, are looked down upon as they follow the rhythmic lead of the male majority. In the more immediate *Lord, Heal the Child,*

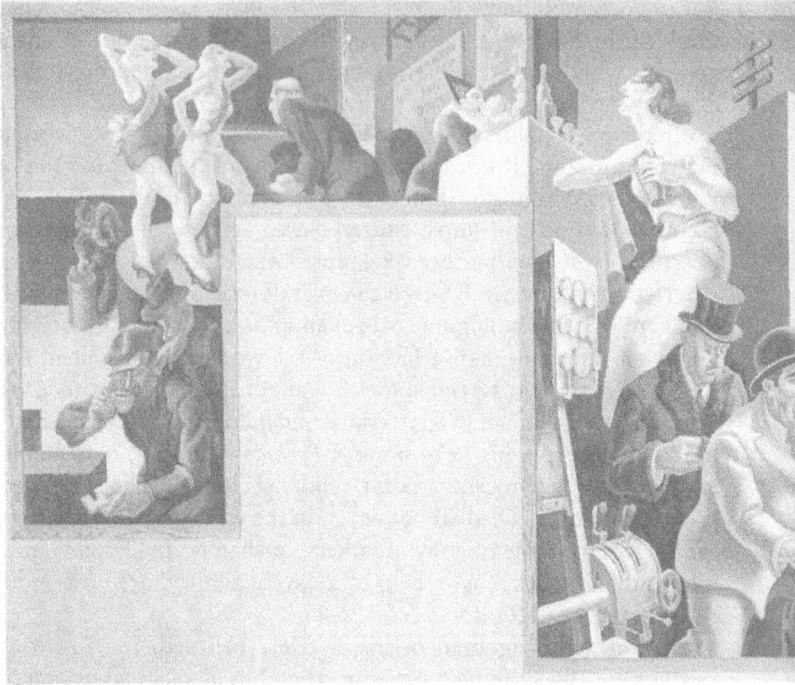

Figure 58. Thomas Hart Benton. *Arts of the City*. 1932. Egg tempera and oil on canvas mounted on panel, 8 × 22 ft. New Britain Museum of American Art, New Britain, Connecticut; Harriet Russell Stanley Fund. © T. H. Benton and R. P.

painted two years later (Fig. 60), a young blond woman with a showgirl figure approximates the current ideal type of Hollywood: the Siren, epitomized by Jean Harlow.[12] But instead of performing in an Art Deco ballroom, she preaches under a kerosene lamp to a small congregation in a rough wooden interior. In keeping with a dance-like stride, her long arms extend gracefully to the accompaniment of a country string band and a female trio. The object of her prayers, a little girl sitting on a stool in the center of a plank floor, wears a nondescript pale-blue dress identical to that of the shapely preacher. Benton had once watched with prurient interest as a young southern Appalachian girl writhed under the spell of holy salvation: "The hymn ended. The girl lay on the ground, her hips rising and falling in the semblance of an orgiastic spasm. She twitched. Her breasts quivered. Her breath came fast."[13]

From religious frenzy to rituals of courtship, Benton remained observant, maybe overly aware, of stimulated young bodies. Watching black youths on the South Carolina Sea Islands near Beaufort, he observed: "At night after work the girls dress and parade about, swishing their tails and

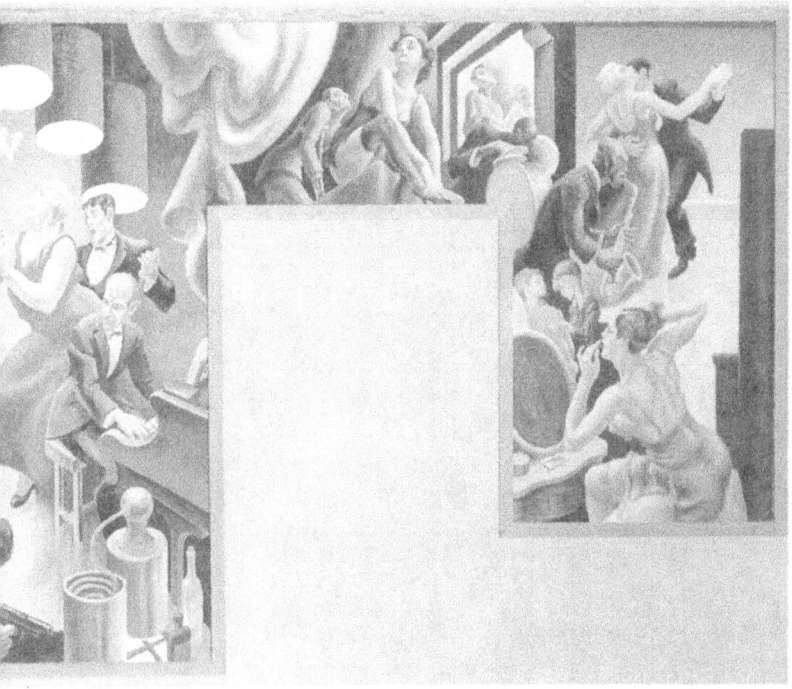

rolling their eyes. The boys close in on them and nudge them and pinch their buttocks while they squeal with pretended anger."[14] Benton's approving attitude toward physical manipulation of women was not unique. The director Josef von Sternberg, in reference to his work with Marlene Dietrich, wrote: "It is the nature of woman to be passive, receptive, dependent on male aggression. . . . In other words, she is not normally outraged at being manipulated; on the contrary, she usually enjoys it."[15]

Benton even managed to exploit the slight potential of the mythic frontierswoman for suggestive handling. The two most active female figures of the "Cultural Progress" sequence in his State of Indiana mural for the 1933 Century of Progress Exposition in Chicago are a maternal abolitionist reaching for black slaves and an early suffragist (Fig. 61). Both are dressed decorously in the full flowing skirts, long sleeves, and bonnets of the midnineteenth century. The "Industrial Progress" sequence of the 230-foot-long mural, however, features two physically exposed pioneer women. One strides alongside her husband at the plow, and the other works a spinning wheel; both wear tight, unbelievably scanty dresses that emphasize their bottoms (Fig. 62).

127

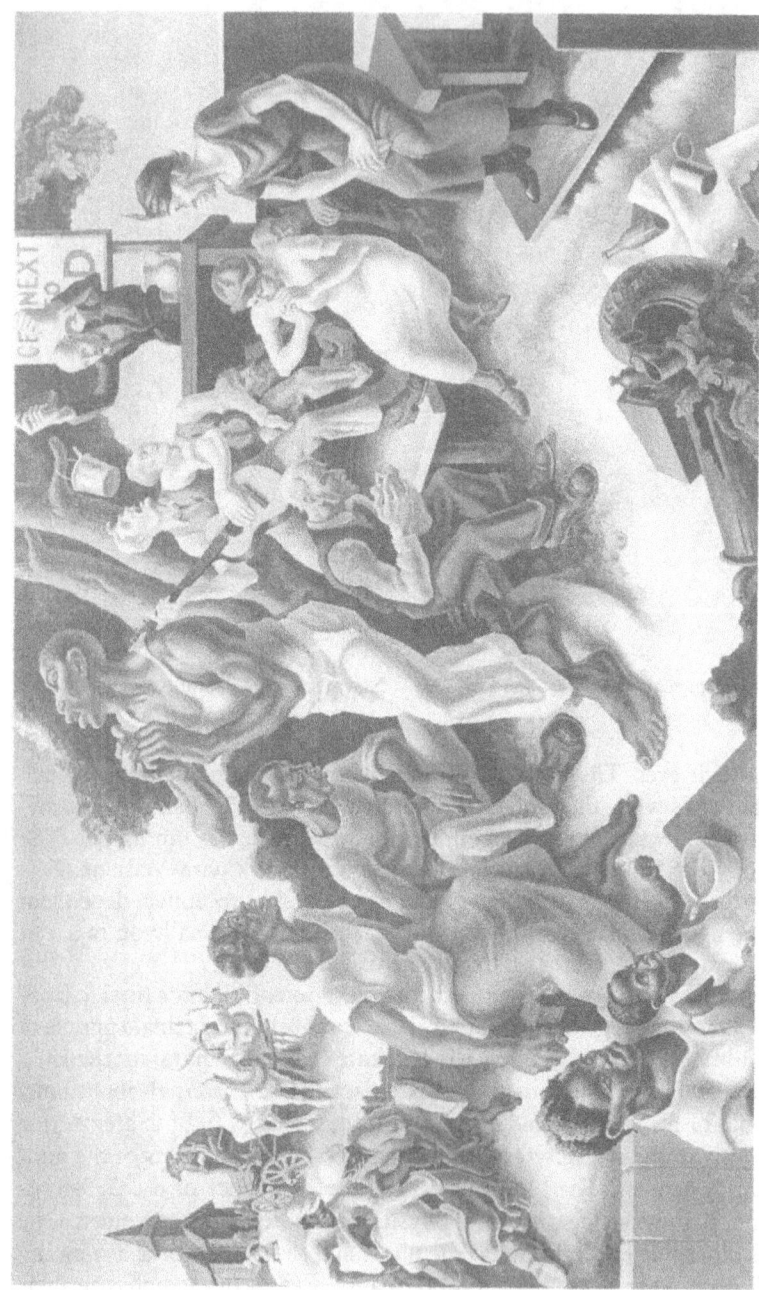

Figure 59. Thomas Hart Benton. *Arts of the South*. 1932. Egg tempera and oil on canvas mounted on panel, 8 × 13 ft. New Britain Museum of American Art, New Britain, Connecticut; Harriet Russell Stanley Fund. © T. H. Benton and R. P. Benton Testamentary Trusts/Licensed by VAGA, New York, NY. Photo: Arthur Evans.

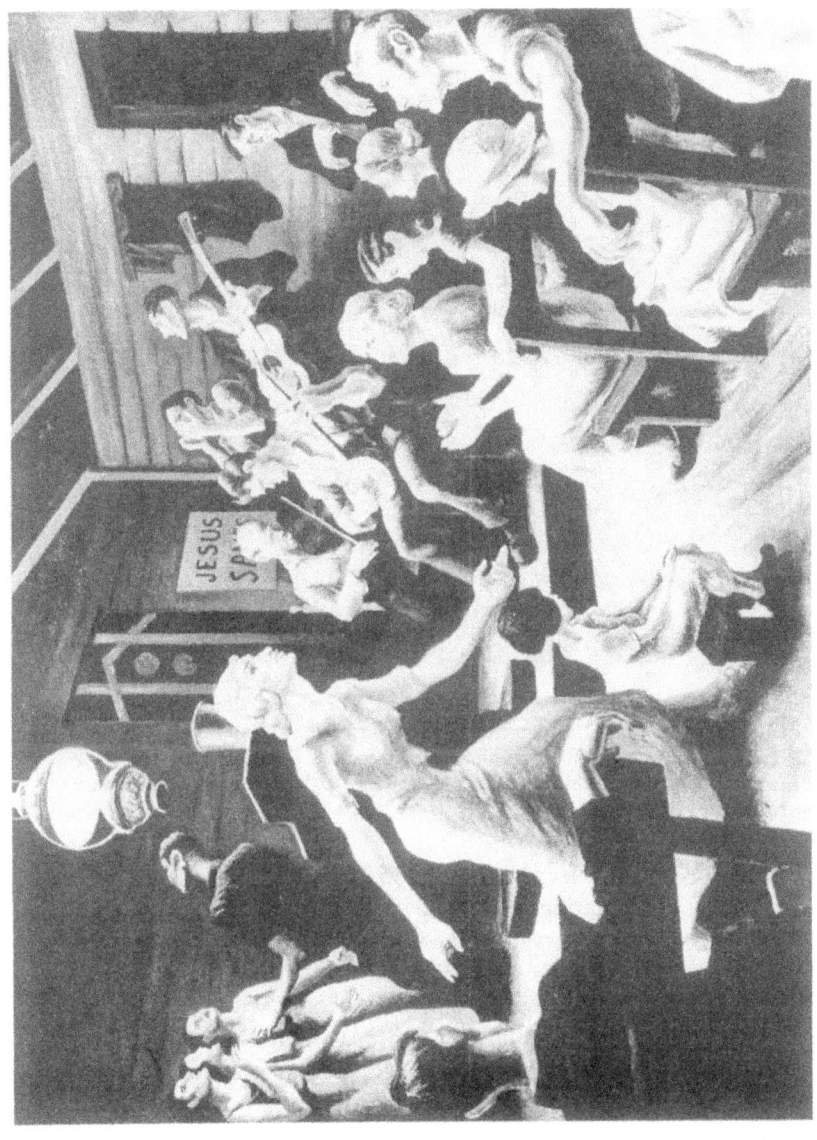

Figure 60. Thomas Hart Benton. *Lord, Heal the Child.* 1934. Egg tempera and oil on canvas, 42¼ × 56¼ in. Private collection. © T. H. Benton and R. P. Benton Testamentary Trusts/Licensed by VAGA, New York, NY.

129

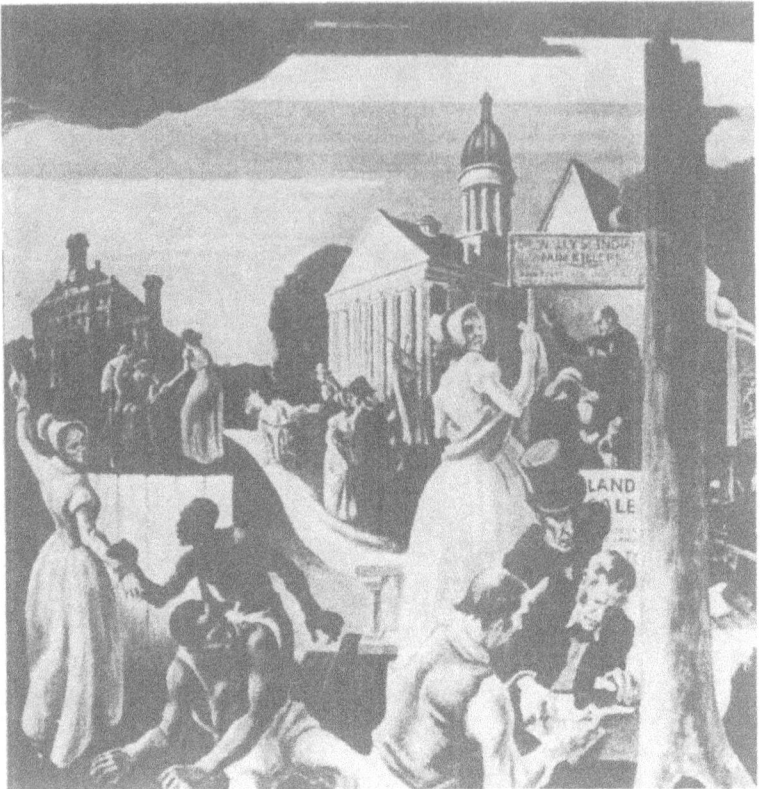

Figure 61. Thomas Hart Benton. *Woman's Place and Reformers*. Cultural Panel 4 from State of Indiana Exhibit at Century of Progress International Exposition, Chicago, 1933. Egg tempera and oil on canvas mounted on panel. 12 × 10 ft. Indiana University Auditorium, Bloomington, Indiana. © T. H. Benton and R. P. Benton Testamentary Trusts/Licensed by VAGA, New York, NY.

By the time he left New York in 1935 to settle in Kansas City, the women in Benton's paintings tended toward a passive loss of individual identity similar to that observed by the film historian Lucy Fischer in such Busby Berkeley musicals as *Dames* (1934). Their famous production numbers transformed women into essentially plastic forms with masklike faces, either wide-eyed or drowsy. Animation shifted to their "knees in action." [16] Though primarily single, not multiple, images, Benton's favorite female figures share both of these characteristics. Holding a pearl-topped scepter, a nearly nude "strawberry blonde" in high heels strikes a standard, hand-on-hip glamour pose in the exact center of his 1937 tribute to movie making: *Hollywood* (Fig. 63). Surrounded by men and their electronic machinery, she is glorified beneath a white arch supported by classical columns. The

130

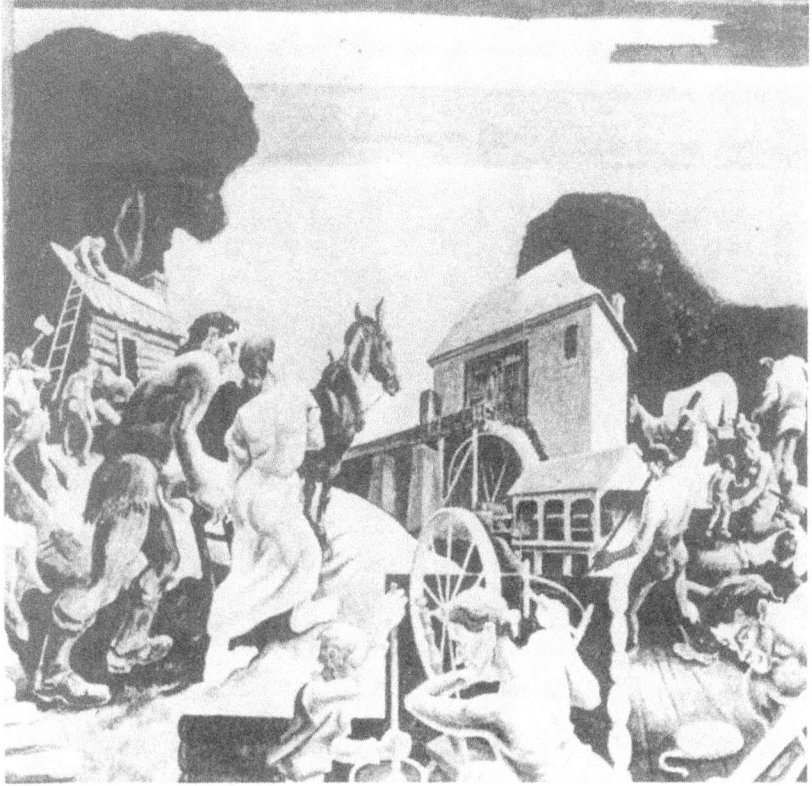

Figure 62. Thomas Hart Benton. *Home Industry*. Industrial Panel 4 from State of Indiana Exhibit at Century of Progress International Exposition, Chicago, 1933. Egg tempera and oil on canvas mounted on panel, 12 × 10 ft. Indiana University Auditorium, Bloomington, Indiana. © T. H. Benton and R. P. Benton Testamentary Trusts/Licensed by VAGA, New York, NY.

male lead, sporting patent-leather hair and a black suit, kneels directly in front of her, belly high. In the immediate foreground, next to the director, her stand-in sits on window display while other blond actresses submit to remodeling in the makeup room. Still another arches over backward in the arms of a hero on the set of a thriller being filmed in the background.

The female victim of lethal male brutality in folk song and theater satisfied Benton's propensity for imaging women as sexual prey. In two thematically related canvases, *The Ballad of the Jealous Lover of Lone Green Valley* (1934, Fig. 64) and *Poker Night, Streetcar Named Desire* (1948, Fig. 65), men play and drink at a table while the women suffer a tragic fate. The barefoot woman of *The Ballad* grasps her stabbed bosom, stares upward in moonlit bewilderment, and parts her exposed knees to her enraged lover. As a grotesquely tragic sex object, Stella Kowalski of Tennessee Wil-

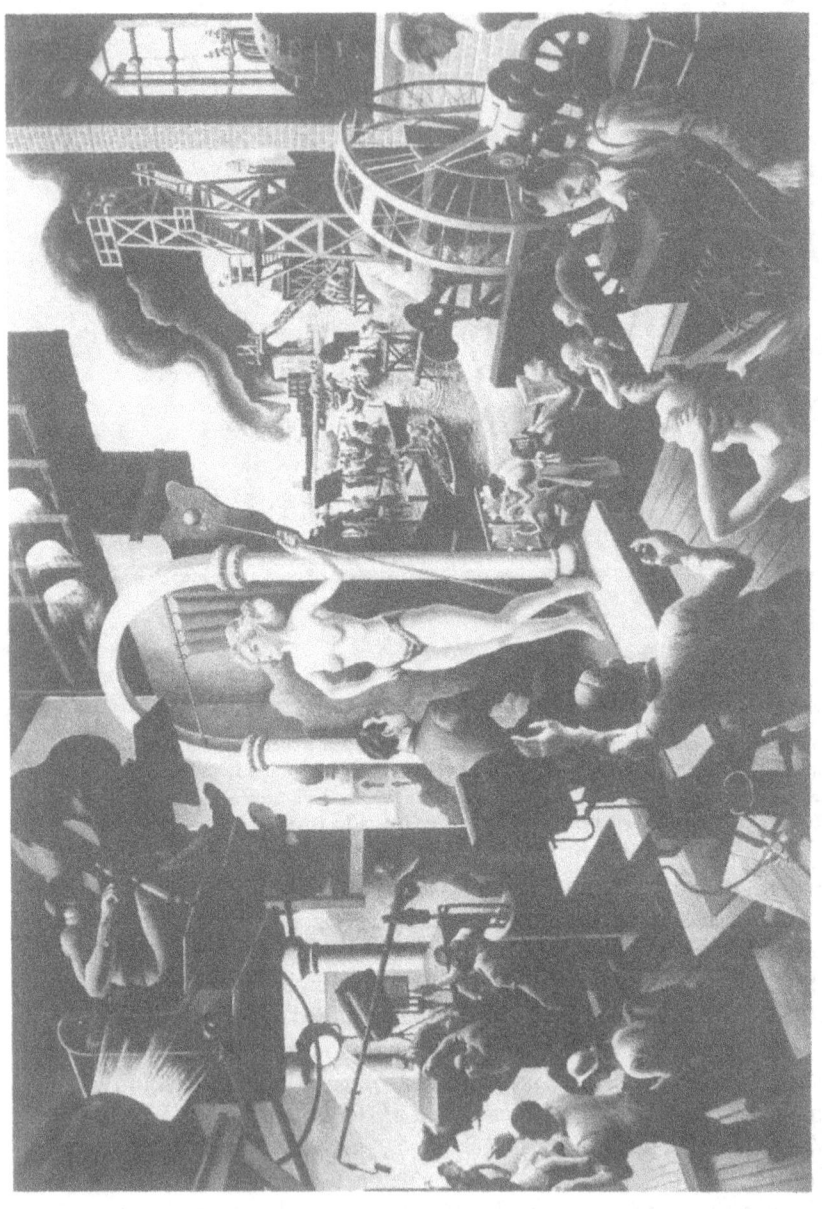

Figure 63. Thomas Hart Benton. *Hollywood.* 1937. Oil on canvas, 56 × 84 in. Nelson-Atkins Museum of Art, Kansas City, Missouri, F75–21/13; bequest of the artist. © T. H. Benton and R. P. Benton Testamentary Trusts/Licensed by VAGA, New York, NY.

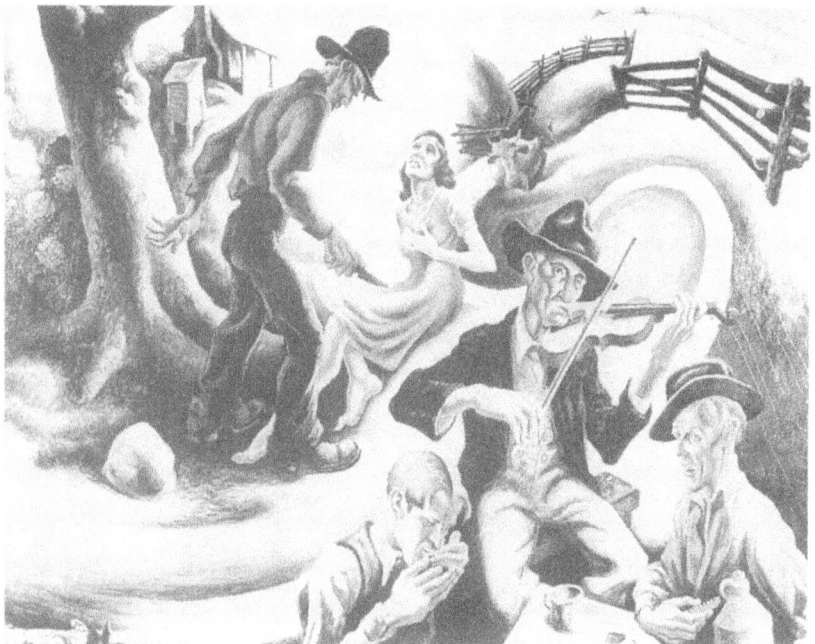

Figure 64. Thomas Hart Benton. *The Ballad of the Jealous Lover of Lone Green Valley.* 1934. Egg tempera and oil on canvas, 42¼ × 53¼ in. Spencer Museum of Art, University of Kansas, Lawrence, Kansas, 58.55; museum purchase, Elizabeth M. Watkins Fund. © T. H. Benton and R. P. Benton Testamentary Trusts/Licensed by VAGA, New York, NY.

liams's *Streetcar* commands the foreground of Benton's interpretation. She stares into a hand-held mirror as a bright light out of nowhere illuminates her face, shoulders, and chest. From protruding breasts to naked knee, her voluptuous body is barely wrapped in a short blue slip. As an accessory of Stanley's brutal chauvinism, her sister Blanche cowers behind the over-stuffed chair that supports both women in their half of the picture. The bitter irony of a beautiful woman flaunting her physical charms for the sake of a villain who destroys her loses some of its dramatic edge when the artist lingers too long over the rendering of bare legs and arms, hips, belly, breasts, and an ecstatic, upturned face.[17]

The monumental glamour girl used in *Poker Night* had appeared as a rape victim in the 1942 *Year of Peril* painting, *Invasion* (see Fig. 34). She had recovered by 1947 to perform as a pair of pinnacle figures in *Achelous and Hercules,* a mural Benton painted for a women's clothing store in Kansas City (Fig. 66). Placed precariously on a cornucopia, the two are accompanied by a seated young man in bib-overalls fondling his provocatively positioned horn. Minus his music, they dance and swoon in body-revealing

133

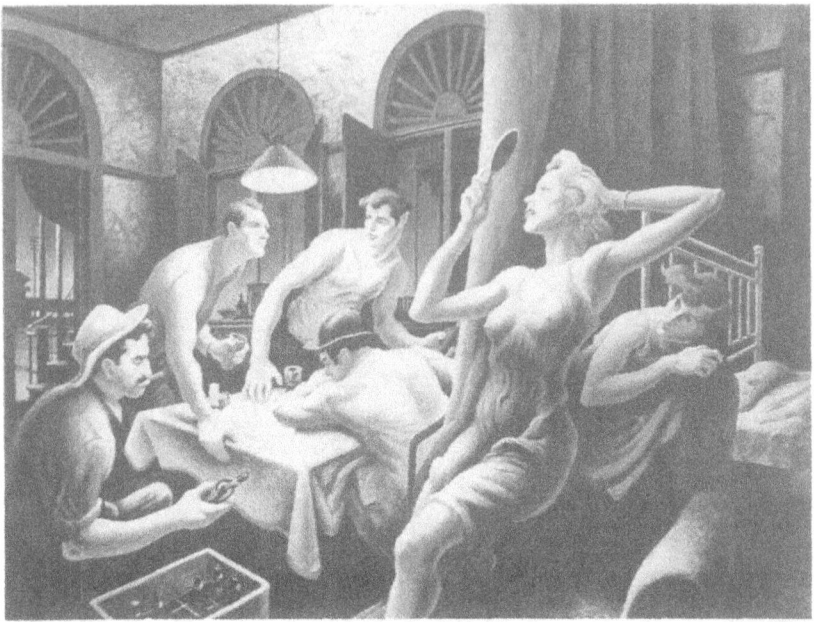

Figure 65. Thomas Hart Benton. *Poker Night* (from *A Streetcar Named Desire*). 1948. Egg tempera and oil on canvas, 36 × 48 in. Whitney Museum of American Art, New York City. 85.49.2, Mrs. Percy Uris Bequest © T. H. Benton and R. P. Benton Testamentary Trusts/Licensed by VAGA, New York, NY. Photograph © 1997 Whitney Museum of American Art.

nightgowns. Eyes closed, their faces turn up to a flood of light that further accents breasts, thighs, and knees. Nine years later Benton's favorite stereotype once again returned, this time in the foreground of *Trading at Westport Landing* (Fig. 67) in the guise of an Indian maiden holding a phallic fur pelt between her thighs. Only a recessive pioneer mother wearing her sunbonnet accompanies the musket-toting, axe-wielding men in Benton's Truman Library mural of the late sixties–early seventies. The erotic woman image waited to make a final appearance as a barefoot, knee-swinging dulcimer player, the foremost figure in his very last work, *The Sources of Country Music* (Fig. 68), a mural for the Country Music Hall of Fame in Nashville.

Benton's incessant voyeurism, freely expressed in words and pictures, might be interpreted socially as irresistible refluence of blatant commercialization. Overt sexuality, exploited by Hollywood in the thirties and embodied by Harlow's "Blonde Bombshell" and Johnny Weissmuller's Tarzan, while alluring, was potentially threatening to the mutual well-being of both genders. His autobiography, as well as his iconography of women, offers evidence that Benton, a short man, experienced personal

134

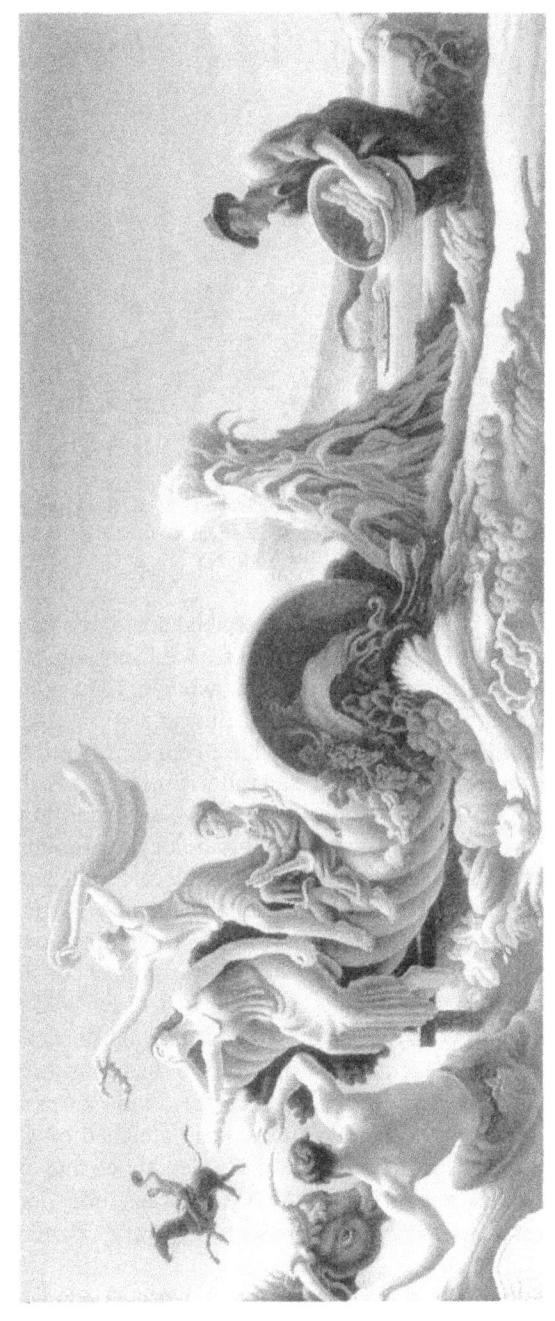

Figure 66. Thomas Hart Benton. *Achelous and Hercules* (detail). 1947. Egg tempera and oil on canvas mounted on plywood, 62⅞ × 264⅛ in. National Museum of American Art, Smithsonian Institution, Washington, D.C., 198522; gift of Allied Stores Corporation, and museum purchase through the Smithsonian Institution Collections Acquisition Program. © T. H. Benton and R. P. Benton Testamentary Trusts/Licensed by VAGA, New York, NY.

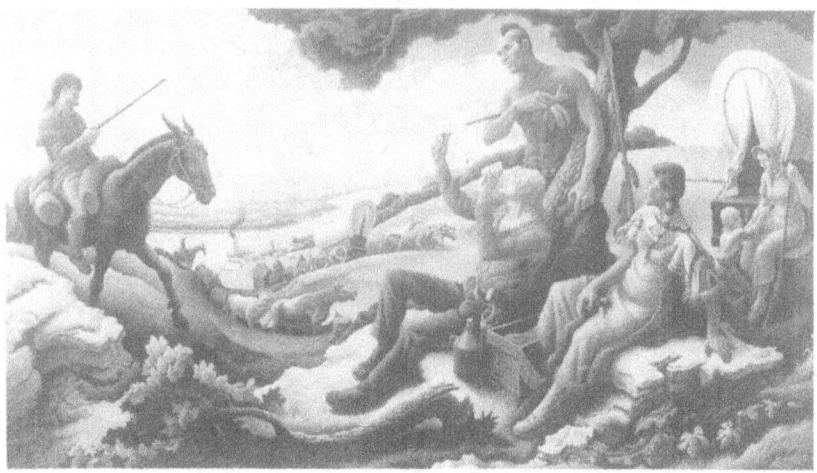

Figure 67. Thomas Hart Benton. *Trading at Westport Landing*. 1956. Egg tempera and oil on canvas mounted on panel, 51½ × 89¾ in. Private collection. © T. H. Benton and R. P. Benton Testamentary Trusts/Licensed by VAGA, New York, NY.

frustrations from not measuring up to prescribed standards of masculine appeal.[18] Unrelated to the Depression-based fear of losing one's manhood to unemployment, his objectification of young women, right up to the end, signifies the insecurity of a widely shared machismo.

This sociopsychological problem may have kept him from abstracting an image of woman into a significant, metaphoric meaning. Perhaps it led him to the reactionary academic device of lingering over the unclothed female body under the pretext of allegory, mythology, or Biblical illustration. In his attempt at such traditional subjects, "local" yokels perform as lecherous elders surrounded by tidbits of Benton's brand of Regionalist setting. But as quaint narrative accessories these hardly compensate for the inability of mundane, life-model studio studies to compete convincingly as *Susannah* (1938, Fig. 69), *Persephone* (1939, Fig. 70), or Eve in *The Apple of Discord* (1948, Fig. 71) with the celebrated goddesses of Botticelli, Titian, Tintoretto, or Rubens. In each of Benton's efforts, bedroom eyes, vulnerably raised arms, naked torsoes, discarded clothes, and "knees in action" advanced a modern formula of male amusement launched by Courbet in bold defiance of Victorian decorum. High-heeled shoes and pubic hair added even more shock appeal, as, to the horror of his more conservative midwestern viewers, Benton outstripped contemporary calendar art and gas-station pinups.[19]

En masse, Benton's "girls" represent what Betty Friedan termed "a strangely joyless national compulsion."[20] That is, they eagerly adopt a sur-

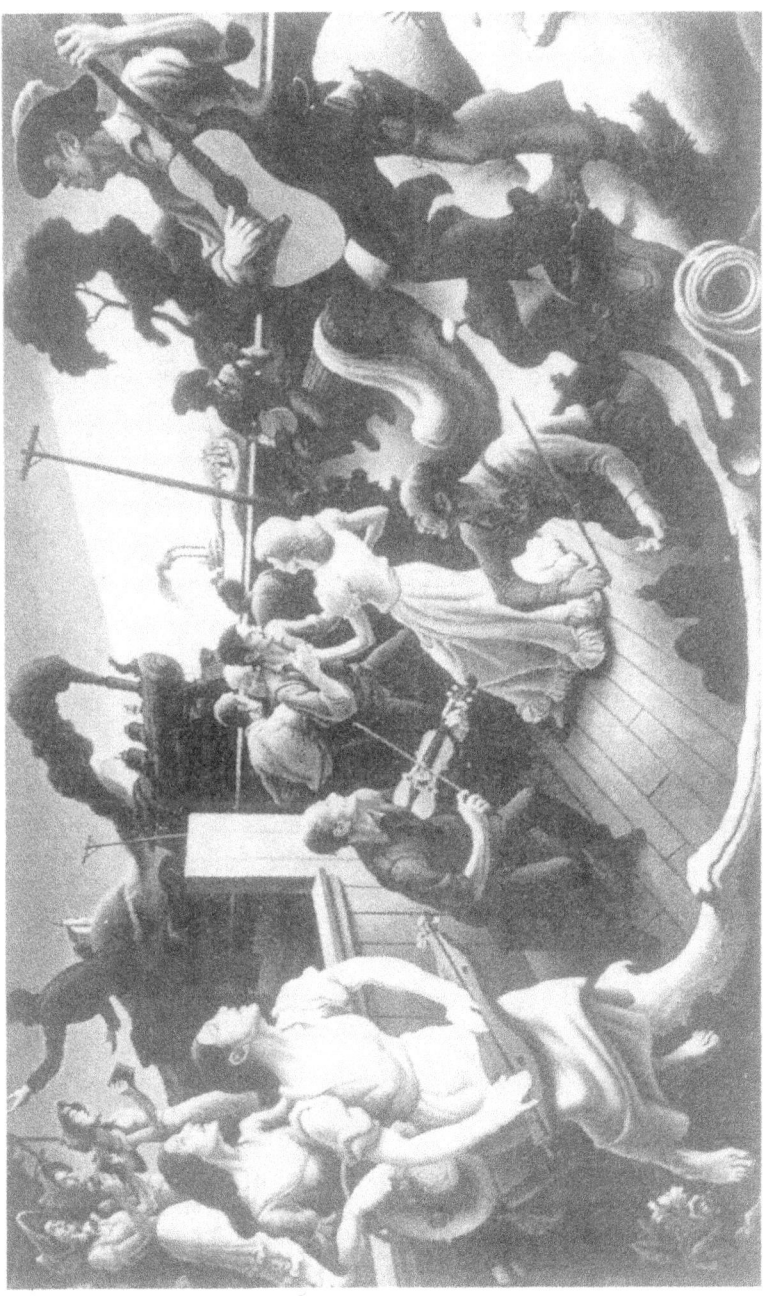

Figure 68. Thomas Hart Benton. *The Sources of Country Music.* 1975. Acrylic on canvas mounted on panel, 72 × 120 in. Collection of the Country Music Foundation, Nashville, Tennessee. Courtesy of Country Music Foundation. © T. H. Benton and R. P. Benton Testamentary Trusts/Licensed by VAGA, New York, NY.

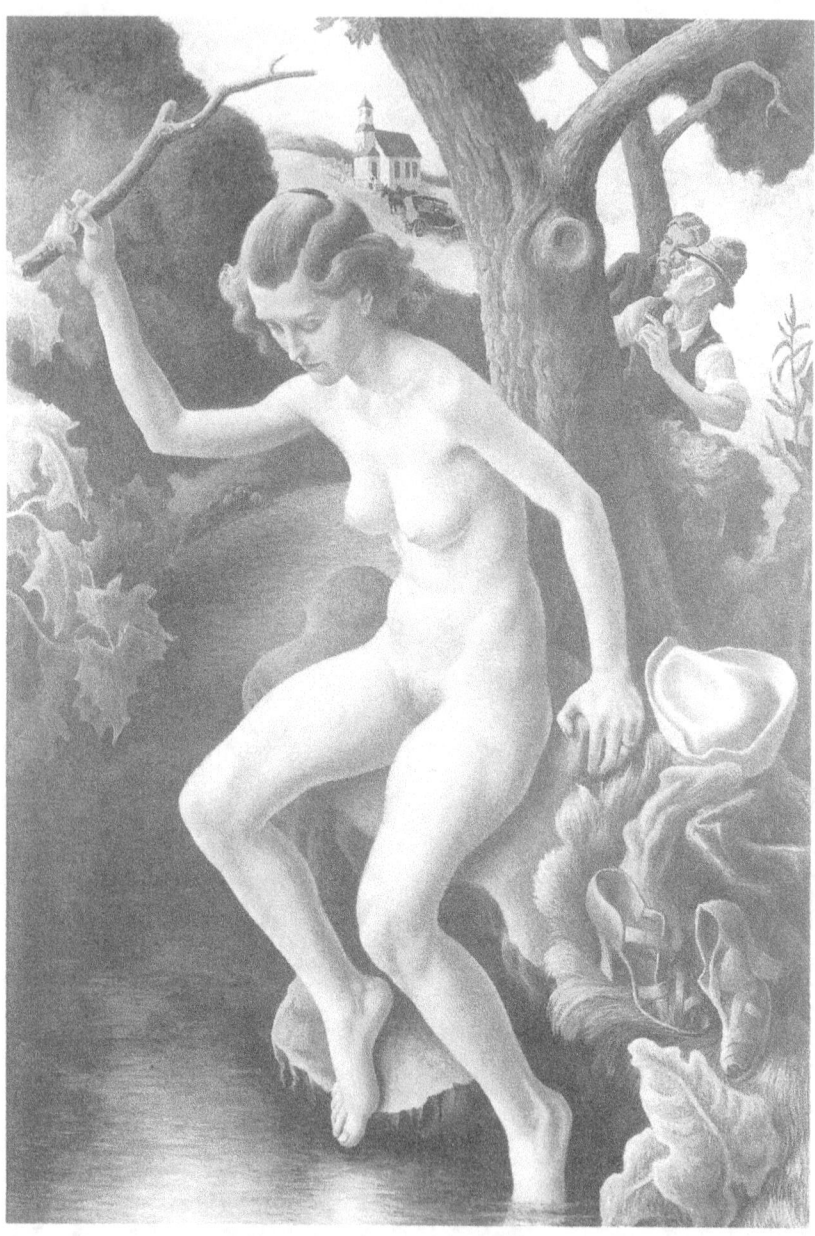

Figure 69. Thomas Hart Benton. *Susannah and the Elders*. 1938. Egg tempera and oil on canvas mounted on panel, 60 × 42 in. The Fine Arts Museums of San Francisco, San Francisco, California, 1940.104; Anonymous gift. © T. H. Benton and R. P. Benton Testamentary Trusts/Licensed by VAGA, New York, NY.

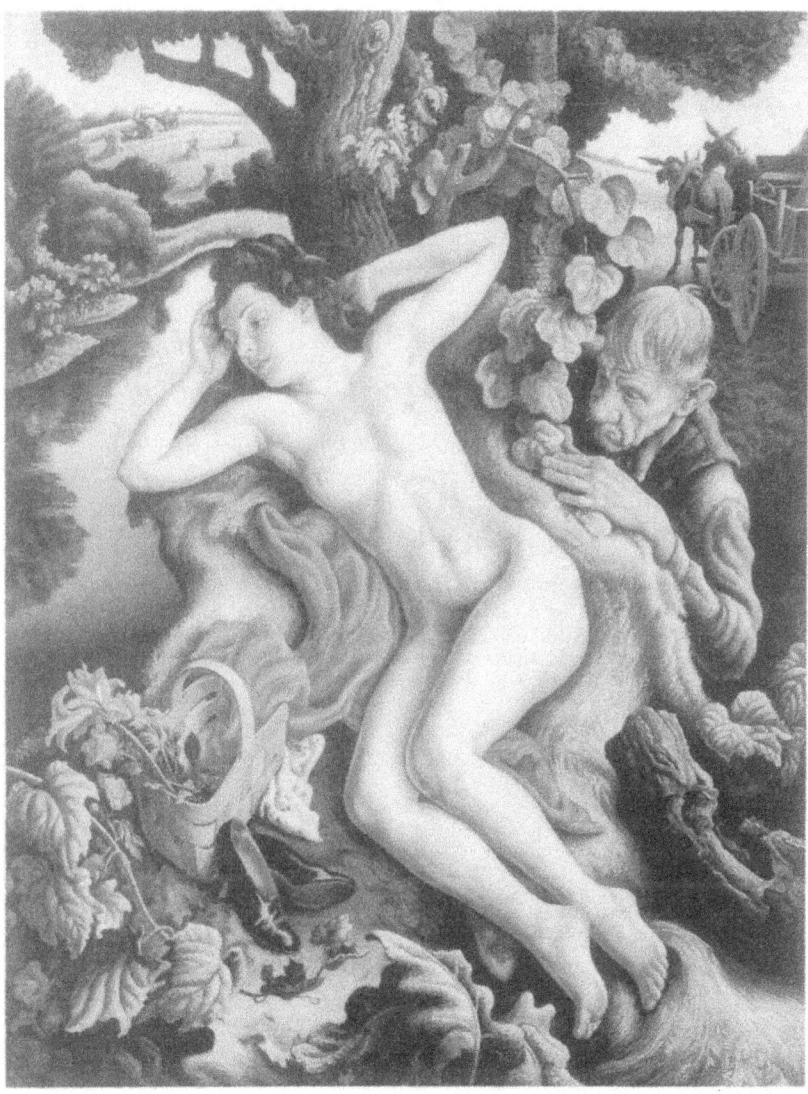

Figure 70. Thomas Hart Benton. *Persephone*. 1937–39. Egg tempera and oil resin over casein on linen mounted on panel, 72 × 56 in. Nelson-Atkins Museum of Art, Kansas City, Missouri, F86–57; Yellow Freight Foundaton Art Acquisition Fund, Mrs. H. O. Peet, Richard J. Stern, the Doris Jones Stein Foundation, the Jacob L. and Ella C. Loose Foundation, Mr. and Mrs. Marvin Rich, and Mr. and Mrs. Richard M. Levin. © T. H. Benton and R. P. Benton Testamentary Trusts/Licensed by VAGA, New York, NY.

139

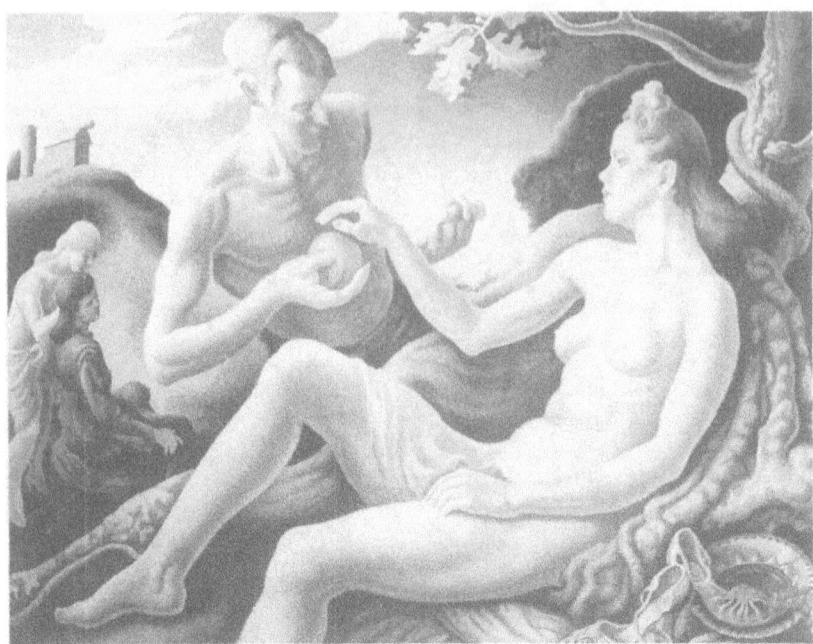

Figure 71. Thomas Hart Benton. *The Apple of Discord*. 1948. Egg tempera and oil on canvas mounted on panel, 37 × 48 in. Private collection. © T. H. Benton and R. P. Benton Testamentary Trusts/Licensed by VAGA, New York, NY.

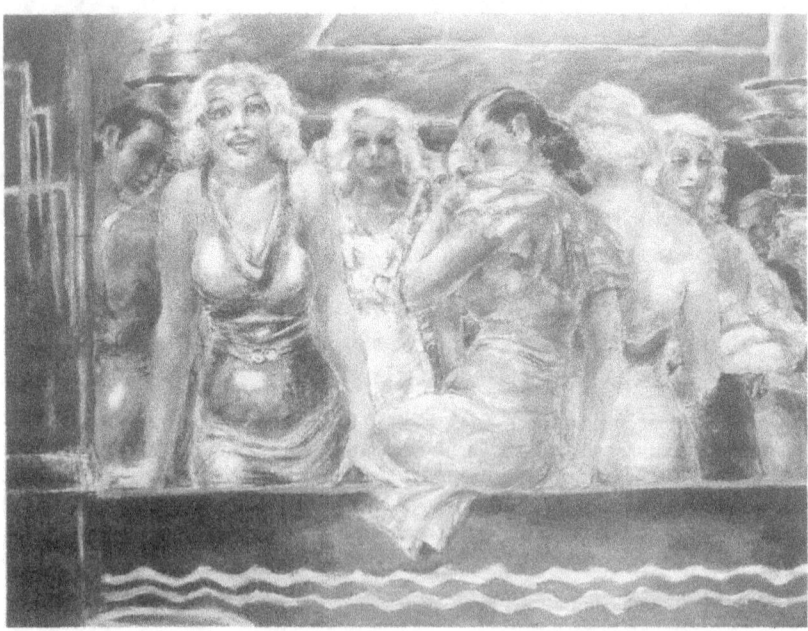

Figure 72. Reginald Marsh. *Ten Cents a Dance*. 1933. Egg tempera on panel, 36 × 48 in. Whitney Museum of American Art, New York City, 80.31.10, Felicia Meyer Marsh Bequest. Photograph © 1997 Whitney Museum of American Art.

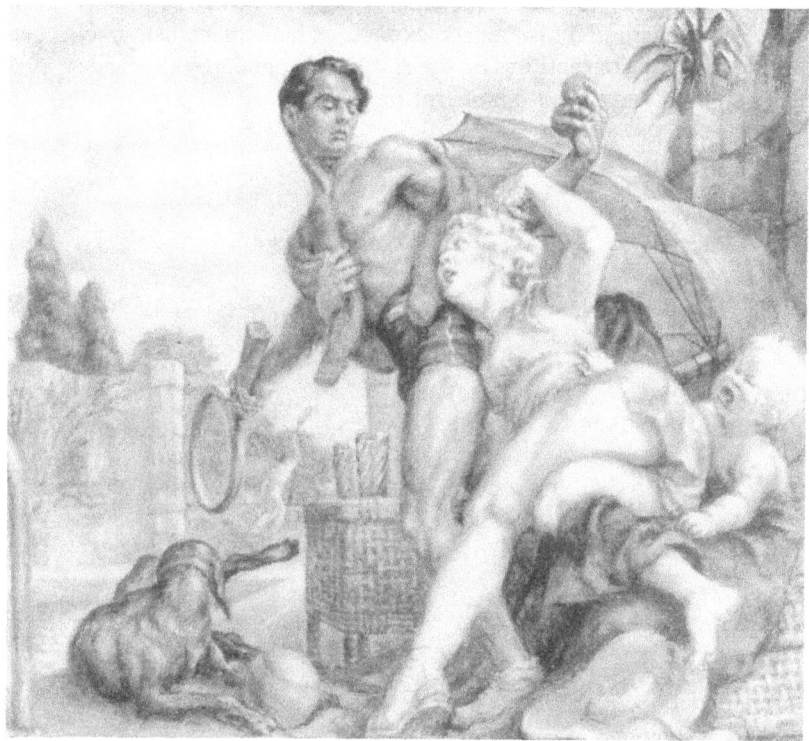

Figure 73. Paul Cadmus. *Venus and Adonis*. 1936. Oil and tempera on canvas mounted on pressed wood panel, 28 × 32 in. The *Forbes* Magazine Collection, New York City, All rights reserved.

face attraction originating most immediately in new modes of male titillation in the 1920s. The exotic fantasy of Theda Bara's short-lived Vamp or the flirtatious vitality of the virtuous flapper led to sexual oversell in a resilient consumer economy. Erotic images of voyeuristic indulgence became symbols of a moral maladjustment, evinced by exaggerated voluptuousness and empty, expressionless faces. Benton's resonate with modernization and inadvertently mimic its commerce of sexuality in a manner approaching the blatancy of the contemporary New York City painters Reginald Marsh and Paul Cadmus (Figs. 72–73). All three defied Victorian visions of a discord-free society in which one could hide from evil and practice "civilized" repressions of natural instincts. They participated in a continuous flux of irregular sensations and helped eliminate distinctions between high and low, elite and popular art at the expense of academic tradition.

Their contemporary, Curry, painting his best-known paintings in Westport, Connecticut, also broke away from the dictates of gentility as an illustrator of Wayside Tales and Wild West stories and as a painter of sublime action, natural disasters, and exposés of fundamentalism, racism, and war. Chapter 7 concentrates on the role his changing female imagery plays in this progression toward modernism.

7

John Curry's
Reactive Women:
From Myth to Protest

Women held the attention of Wood, Benton, and Curry for a large variety of reasons. Many of these reasons were undoubtedly autobiographical and psychological, a pluralistic need for moral and sensual gratification. Their personal categories of imagery unavoidably absorbed some of the modern sociopolitical changes that American women were undergoing from the late nineteenth to the mid-twentieth century: from the maternal suffragist, the New Woman feminist, and film-industry glamour girl to the post-franchise, moderate feminist involved in consumption, family affairs, and economic independence.[1]

No American painter thoroughly documented any of these phases. Attracted to working people, the antibourgeois Robert Henri advocated going into their neighborhoods to paint their real-life experiences directly. But seldom do the paintings of his circle follow women into their workplaces to depict secretaries, salesclerks, seamstresses, or scrub ladies. Henri did closeup portraits of working-class women, along with working-class men and children, idealizing them as the world's innocents. William Glackens married well and away from the streets and lingered over richly hued women of privilege. Everett Shinn dreamed up a pretty theater doll to occupy the spotlight in his paintings of the stage as George Luks searched out female characters in their lower Manhattan haunts for their colorful "edge." Only John Sloan focused on the energetic "working girl," striding joyously through streets and squares sporting bobbed hair and increasingly high hemlines through the teens and into the twenties. Women as shoppers preoccupied Kenneth Hayes Miller; and, in the thirties, the "Fourteenth Street School" painters Reginald Marsh, Raphael Soyer, and Isabel Bishop

143

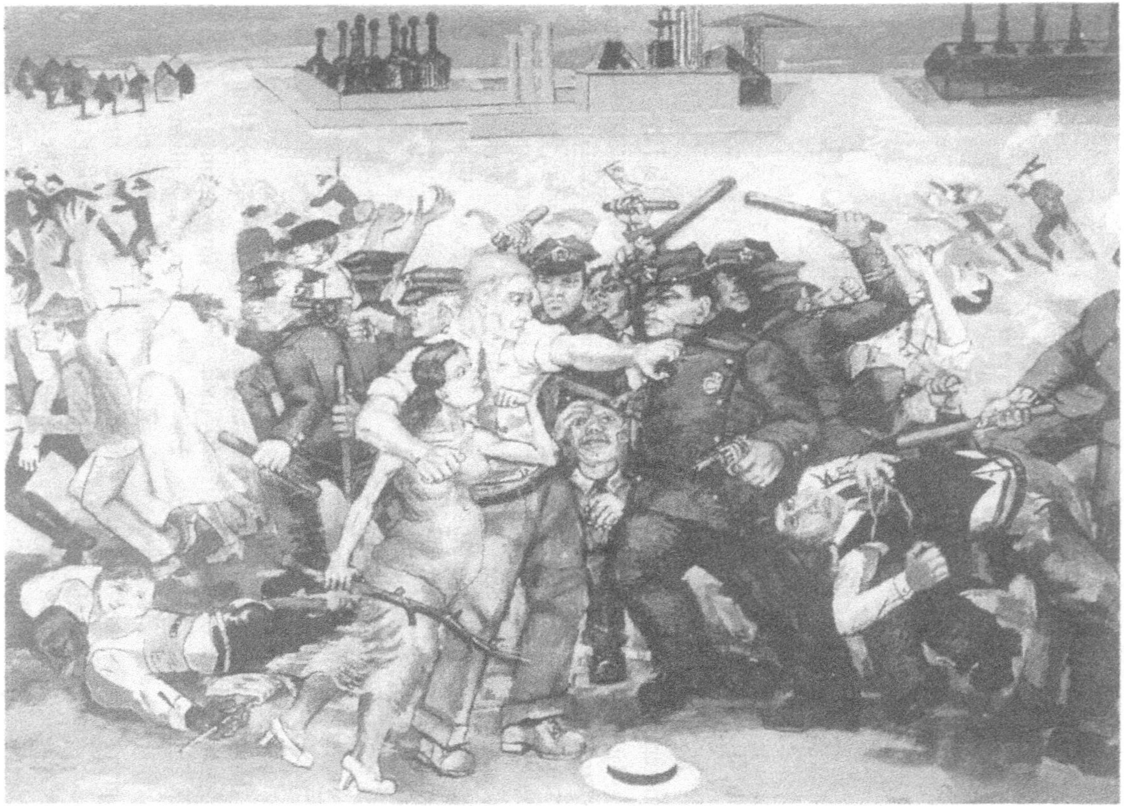

Figure 74. Philip Evergood. *American Tragedy*. 1937. Oil on canvas, 29½ × 39½ in. Private collection.

depicted young working women en route to and from their office jobs. With little or no social concern, the men more often than not "checked them out" with prurient interest. Bishop drew and painted them for their "mobility," an ambiguous concept that she increasingly applied to motion studies of walking rather than to the American dream of improving one's economic status.[2] It took Philip Evergood to activate young women politically in such social-realist paintings of protest as *American Tragedy,* his melodramatic response to the 1937 "Memorial Day Massacre" at the South Chicago plant of Republic Steel (Fig. 74).

Curry would approximate such aggressiveness in his *Parade to War* two years later (see Fig. 29). Before that time the fatalistic courage registered by his most prominent class of female figures, symbols of undaunted motherhood, could very well have reassured viewers suffering from the immediate consequences of economic disaster. By the outbreak of World War II, Curry had chosen to aim his supplementary female figures at universal threats to well-being. His relatively small share of vulnerable girl-woman types had been transformed, as will be seen by the end of this chapter, from helpless victims of patriarchal oppression to activated images of admonition. They warn us of discrimination; of personal, mob, and mass violence; of threats to individual freedom, social justice, and to life itself.

The significance of women in Curry's iconography counteracts the masculine force that dominated his personality. Kansas farmboy, athlete, hunter, and illustrator of adventure stories, he relished boars, seed bulls, and *The Black Stallion* (1937, Fig. 75), all evocative of brute strength. Patriarchal power he celebrated in a portrait of his father as the *Kansas Stockman* (1929, Fig. 76), in his portrait of *Chris L. Christensen,* head of the Agricultural College at the University of Wisconsin (1941, Fig. 77), in *The Plainsman* (1940, Fig. 78), and in his portrait of John Brown (see Fig. 19). Only momentarily, in an athletic capacity, do women achieve an anonymous, indeed tenuous, equality with men: as daredevil aerialists. Predictably the trapeze artist who falls in Curry's circus is a woman (Fig. 79).

While acknowledging Curry's preference for the masculine, it may be seen that for a dozen or so years his paintings also emphasized the noble mother. For example, a narrative succession of women tend to their families in the face of natural disasters. Resigned, the mother quietly struggles to survive against extremes of violent weather in three major paintings: *Tornado Over Kansas* (Fig. 80), *The Mississippi* (Fig. 81), and *Hoover and the Flood* (Fig. 82). In his most famous work, dated 1929, the family gathers in fear and trembling as a young, broad-shouldered, strong-armed farmer anxiously gauges the approaching funnel and urges the children and their pets to follow Mother into the cyclone cellar. She clutches the quilt-wrapped baby and looks back at her house with stalwart resolve to return. In the lower-right corner, her complement, an unruffled hen, stands on the

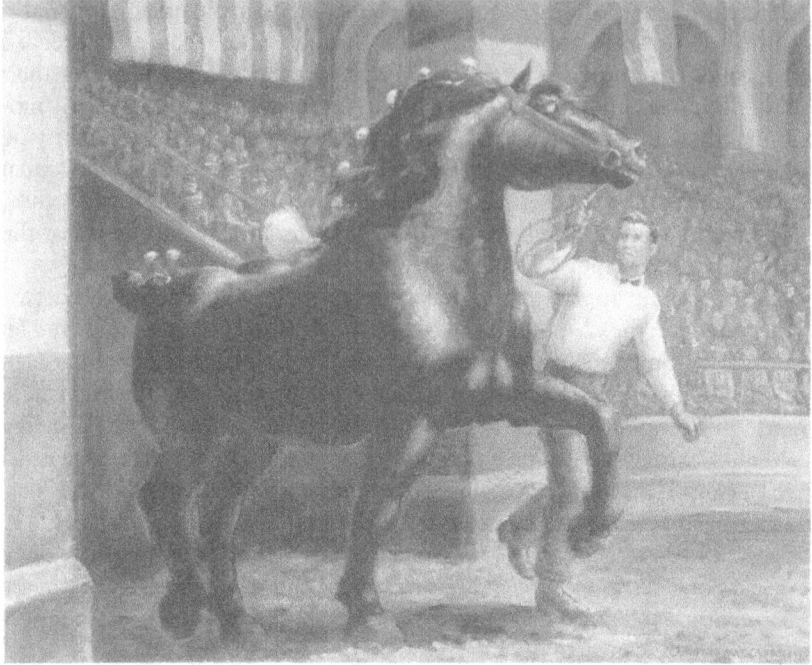

Figure 75. John Steuart Curry. *The Black Stallion*. 1937. Oil on canvas, 24½ × 30½ in. New Britain Museum of American Art, New Britain, Connecticut; gift of Stevan Dohanos. Photo: E. Irving Blomstrann.

plank approach to the porch steps. The white barn creates a nimbus around the woman's head.

As a long-suffering black woman, the noble mother remains calm and controlled in *The Mississippi* (1935). On top of a flood-swept shanty, she bows her head over an infant. Three older children cling to their father, who pleads for deliverance through the heavenly light. While the great relief adviser, Secretary of Commerce Herbert Hoover, an army officer, and a government agent inspect the disastrous results of the Mississippi flood of the spring of 1927 in *Hoover and the Flood* (commissioned by *Life* magazine in 1940), the mother sits stage-front as a contemporary Madonna dei Latte. No husband in sight, she and the baby are tended to by an aging nurse and accompanied by a little daughter with a doll baby. This maternal group shares an axial prominence with the central, paternalistic, male figure: a black elder who raises his hands wide apart as he prays over his people carried by flat boat to high ground for emergency medical care.[3]

Producing melodramatic paintings and heroic murals made Curry sus-

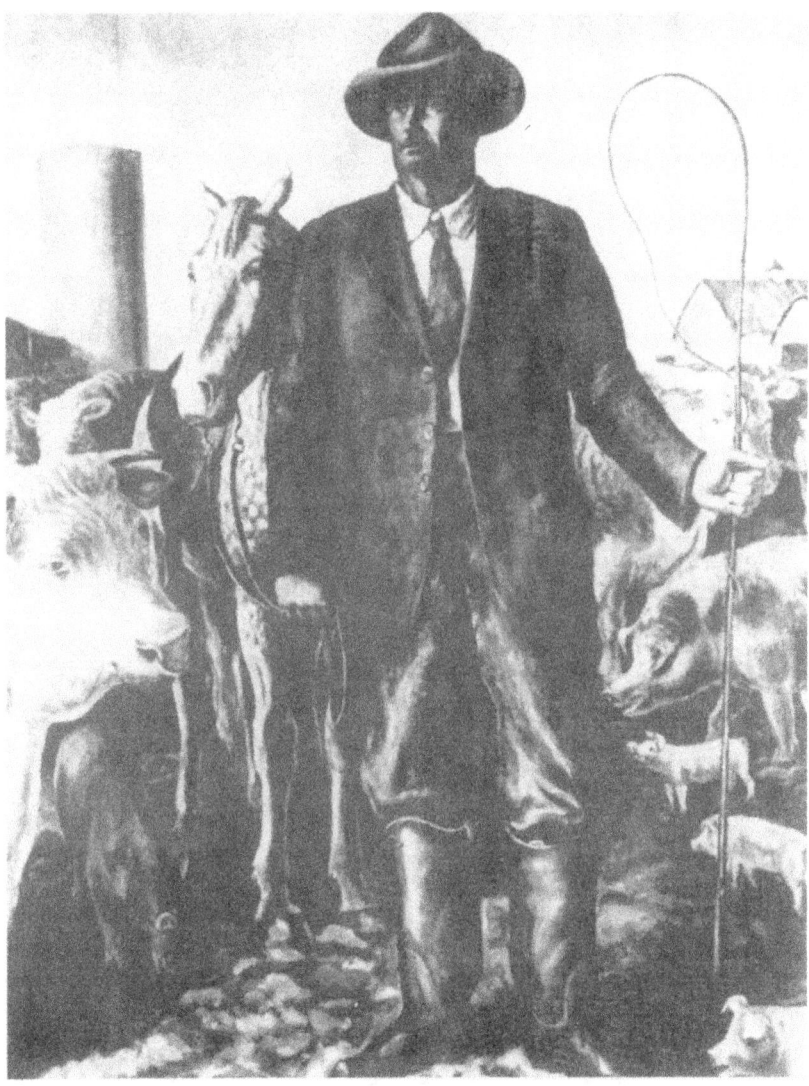

Figure 76. John Steuart Curry. *The Stockman* 1929. Oil on canvas, 52 × 40 in. Whitney Museum of American Art, New York City, 31.161, Purchase. Photograph © 1997 Whitney Museum of American Art. Portrait of the artist's father, Smith Curry.

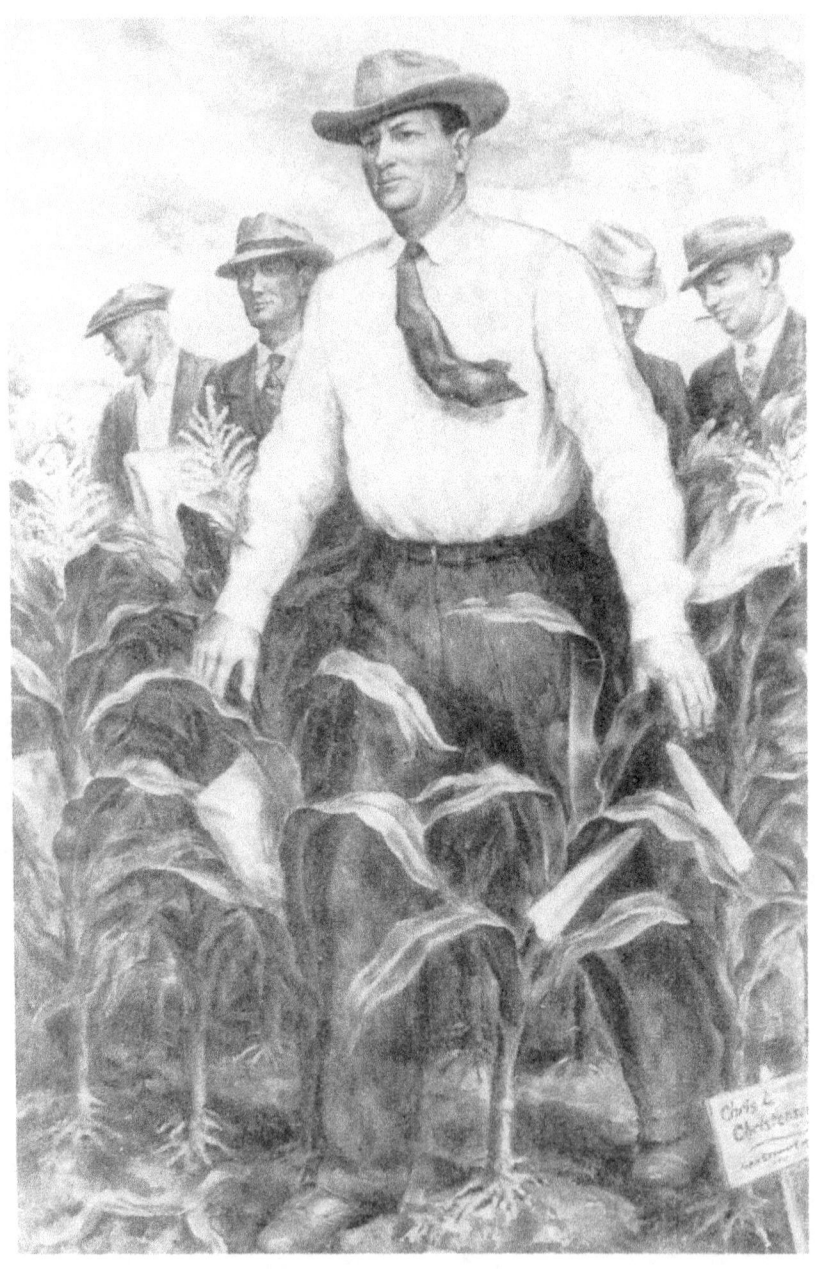

Figure 77. John Steuart Curry. *Chris L. Christensen*. 1941. Oil and tempera on canvas, 70¾ × 47¼ in. College of Agricultural and Life Sciences, University of Wisconsin–Madison, Madison, Wisconsin.

148

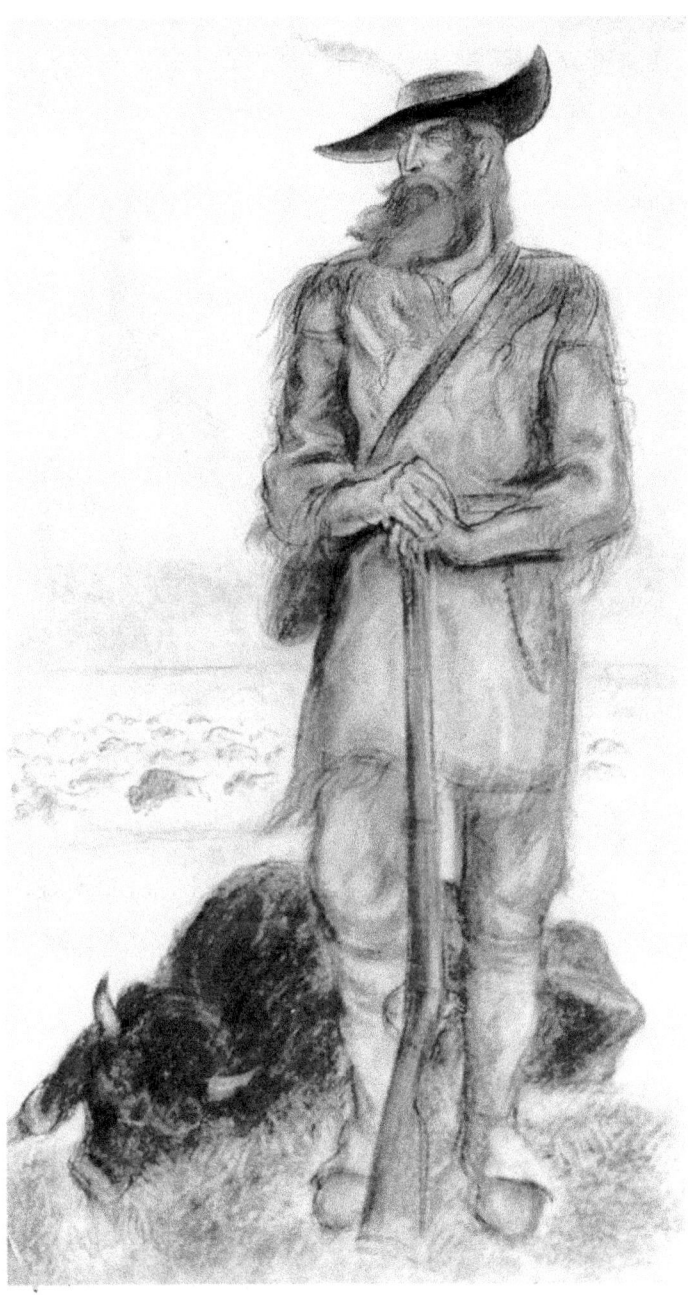

Figure 78. John Steuart Curry. *The Plainsman*, preliminary study for *The Tragic Prelude* mural in the Kansas State Capitol Building, Topeka. 1940. Oil on board, 30¼ × 20 in. Kennedy Galleries, Inc., New York City. Photograph courtesy of Kennedy Galleries, Inc.

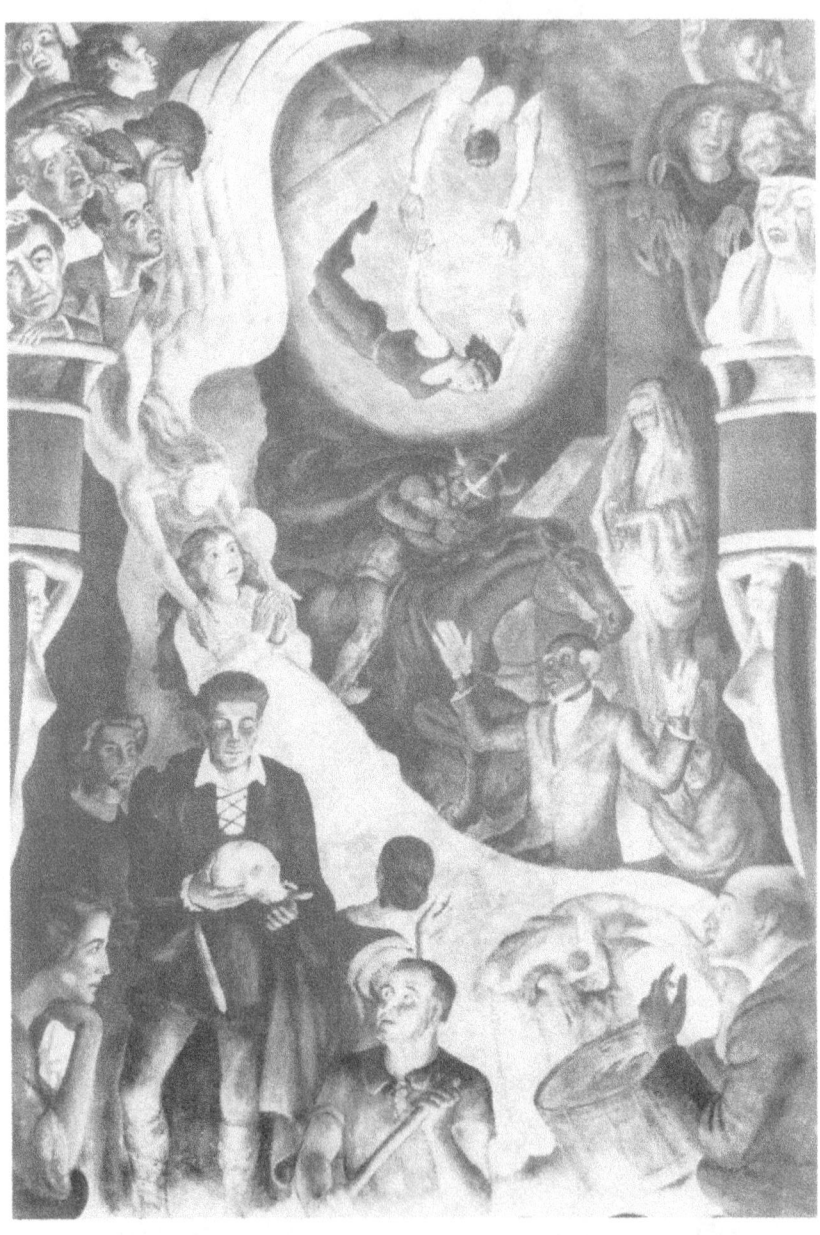

Figure 79. John Steuart Curry. *Tragedy*. 1934. Fresco mural 13 × 8 ft. King's Highway Elementary School Auditorium, Westport, Connecticut.

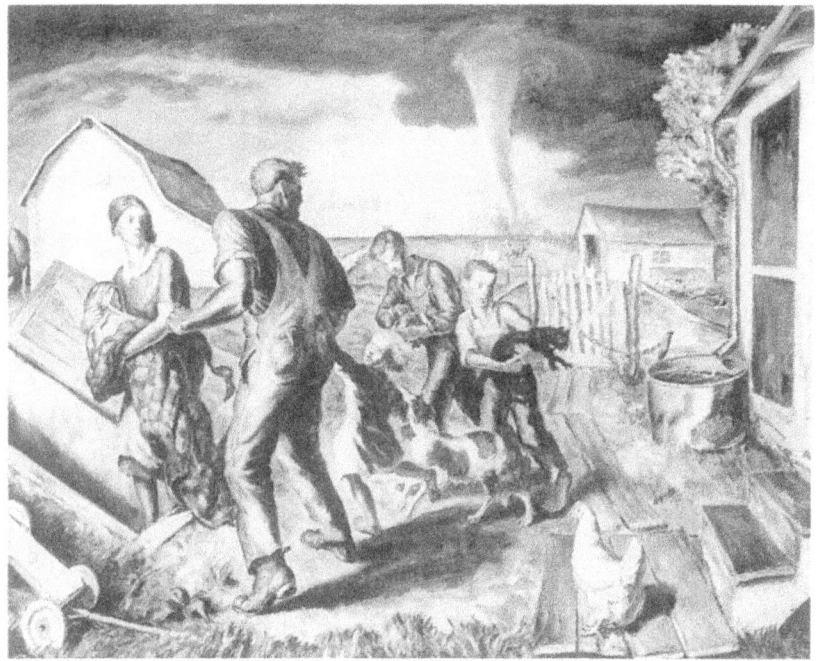

Figure 80. John Steuart Curry. *Tornado Over Kansas*. 1929. Oil on canvas, 46½ × 60⅜ in. Muskegon Museum of Art, Muskegon, Michigan; Hackley Picture Fund.

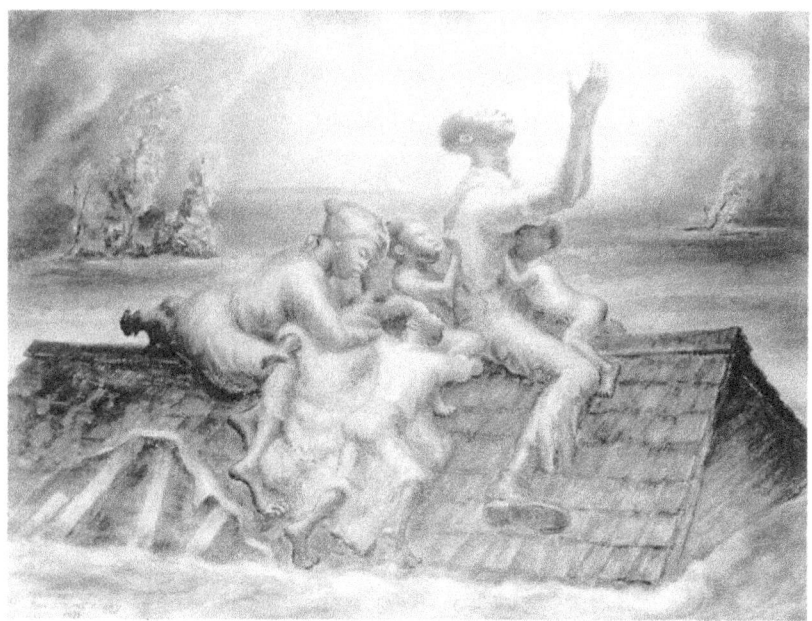

Figure 81. John Steuart Curry. *The Mississippi*. 1935. Oil and tempera on panel, 36 × 47½ in. The Saint Louis Art Museum, St. Louis, Missouri.

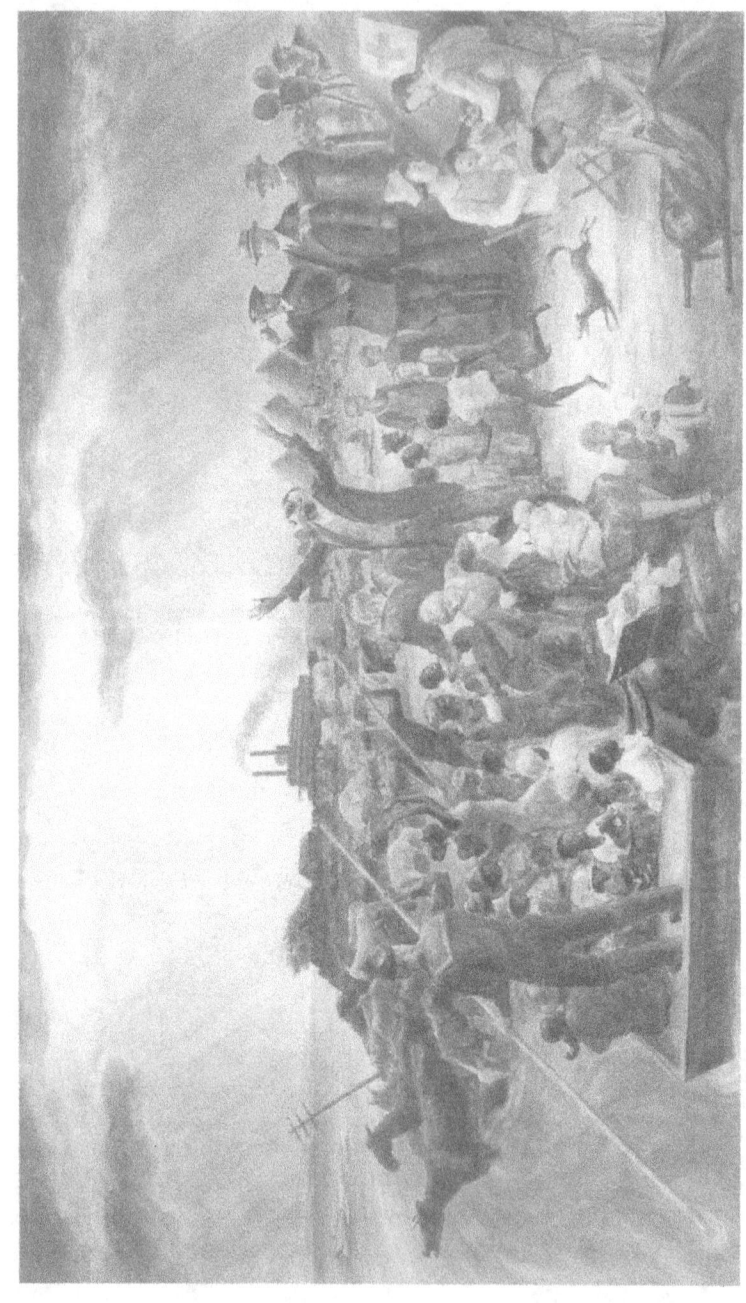

Figure 82. John Steuart Curry. *Hoover and the Flood.* 1940. Oil on canvas, 37½ × 63 in. painted for *Life* magazine, May 6, 1940, pp. 58–59. Kennedy Galleries, Inc., New York City. Photograph courtesy of Kennedy Galleries, Inc.

ceptible to the increasingly popular American stereotype that the historian Glenda Riley has identified as the Sunbonnet Myth:

For the 19th century, the ideal woman was domestic, destined to be a wife and a mother, passive and submissive yet strong and enduring. Moreover, she was the moral guardian of society being tested by the demands of industrialization. Transplant this characterization to the frontier, establish it as a category, and the image of the pioneer woman is born, variously called the Madonna of the Prairies, the Pioneer Mother, or the Sunbonnet Myth.[4]

The myth arose in populist polemics and popular fiction, only to be inflated by romantic historical accounts and public art works. The reformer Mary Lease of Kansas, addressing the National Council of Women in 1891 for the women in the Farmers' Alliance, concluded her speech with the rhetoric of the Sunbonnet Myth:

The women of the East turned their faces towards the boundless, billowy prairies of the West. They accompanied their husbands, sons and brothers; they came with the roses of health on their cheeks; they left home and friends, school and church, and all which makes life dear to you and me, and turned their faces toward the untried West, willing to brave the dangers of pioneer life upon the lonely prairies with all its privations.[5]

Educated eastern women who went West as young wives and mothers became the protagonists of most of the largely autobiographical stories by Mary Hallock Foote, a late nineteenth-century writer, illustrator, and painter.[6] One illustration she drew to accompany her "Picture of the Far West" for *Century Magazine* (1888–89) situated a young homesteading couple outside their rough sod hut.[7] In *The Coming of Winter* (Fig. 83), he scans the sky for wild geese to shoot; she stands beautiful and brave, following his gaze. Having emerged from the dark interior of the doorway flanked by her washboard, tub, and mop, she shields their bundled-up baby in her strong hands.

The conflict between fantasies of a frontier Garden of Eden and the "veracious" facts seems to have eluded earlier twentieth-century writers.[8] Writing during the ratification process for the nineteenth amendment to the Constitution, the novelist-historian Emerson Hough concluded in *The Passing of the Frontier* that the great romance of all America was "the woman in the sunbonnet."[9] Twenty years later, underemphasizing frontier women's independent homesteading, schoolteaching, missionary work, storekeeping, outlawing, and prostitution, Ernest Groves glorified the pioneer woman as undaunted and undivided in her commitment to mothering the progeny of the westward movement.[10] The noble mother could claim the heroic individualism popularly identified with this great drama

153

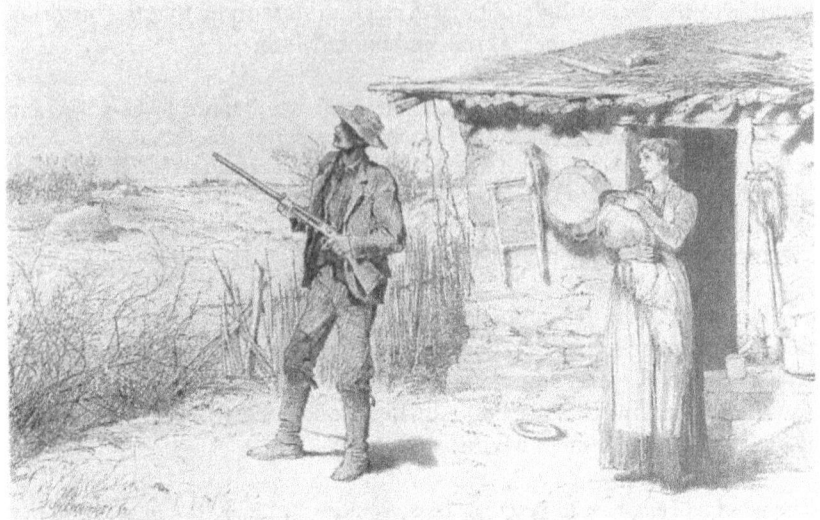

Figure 83. Mary Hallock Foote. *The Coming of Winter*. 1883. Pen and ink illustration for *Century Magazine*, Vol. 37, no. 2 (December 1888), p. 163.

of nineteenth-century American history: "She also felt the atmosphere of freedom with its stress on independence. . . . In teaching her children she emphasized not only the ideal of the self-made man but also of the self-reliant woman." [11]

It was difficult to resist the mythic status of a noble mother, especially when she was depicted as a pioneer. The ideal was embodied in the form of monumental sculpture at the time of Curry's sudden rise to fame. In February 1927, twelve competing sculptors exhibited their models for Oklahoma's Pioneer Woman Monument at the Reinhardt Galleries in New York City. They were displayed in a full page of the *New York Times* Sunday "Rotogravure" section (Fig. 84). Stalwart figures with babies, muskets, and sunbonnets, every one of the proposed mothers peered solemnly toward a distant western horizon. [12] Curry soon conformed to the prevailing characterization of the westering woman as a strong and abiding complement of the frontiersman.

Westward Migration (1936–37, Fig. 85), a Treasury Section mural for the Department of Justice Building in Washington, D.C., features one of his most solemnly monumental women. Sunbonnet blown back, she strides at the side of her handsome and powerful pioneer husband, a blanket-wrapped baby secure in her arms. A barefoot son, a cat, and a hound bitch complete the foreground family group. An array of additional stereotypes suitable for a wagon-train movie provides an immediate backdrop. Two cowboys, sixshooters drawn, ride spooked horses in front of a prairie fire.

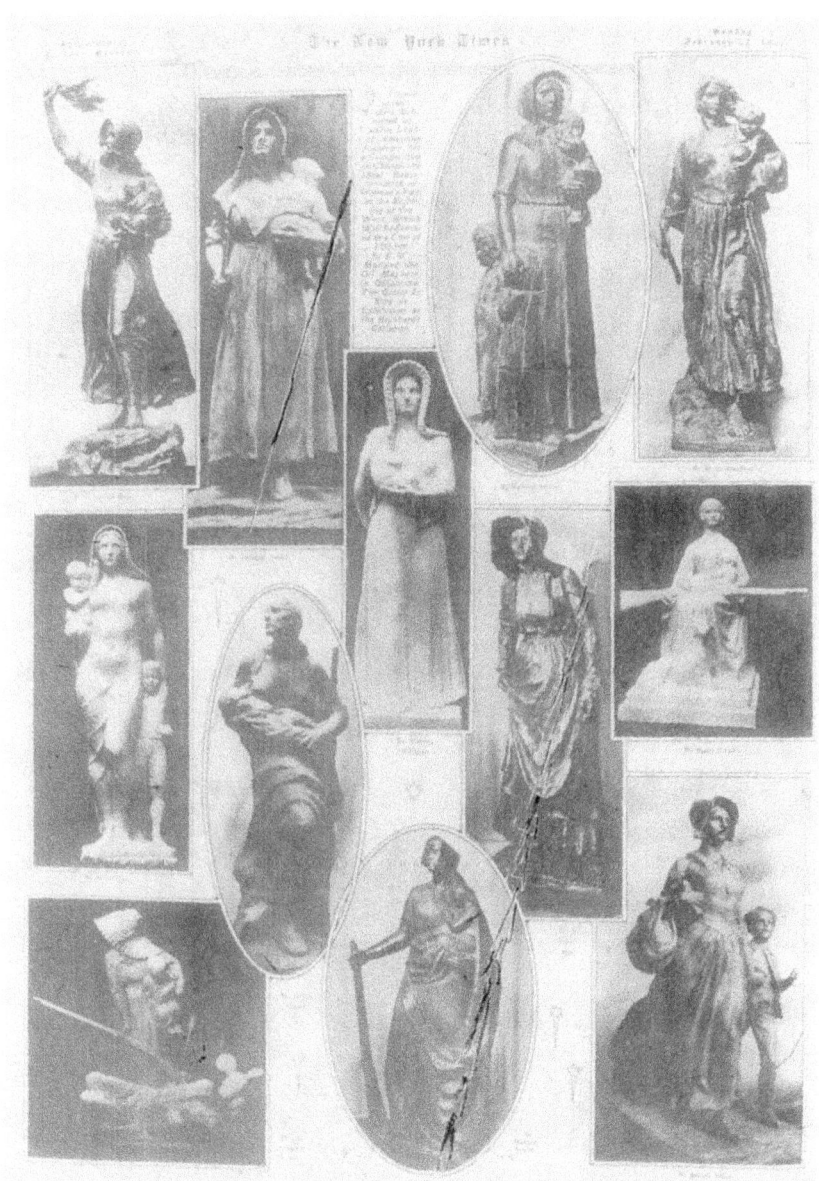

Figure 84. "Competition for a Pioneer Woman Monument for Oklahoma," *New York Times*, Sunday Rotogravure, February 27, 1927.

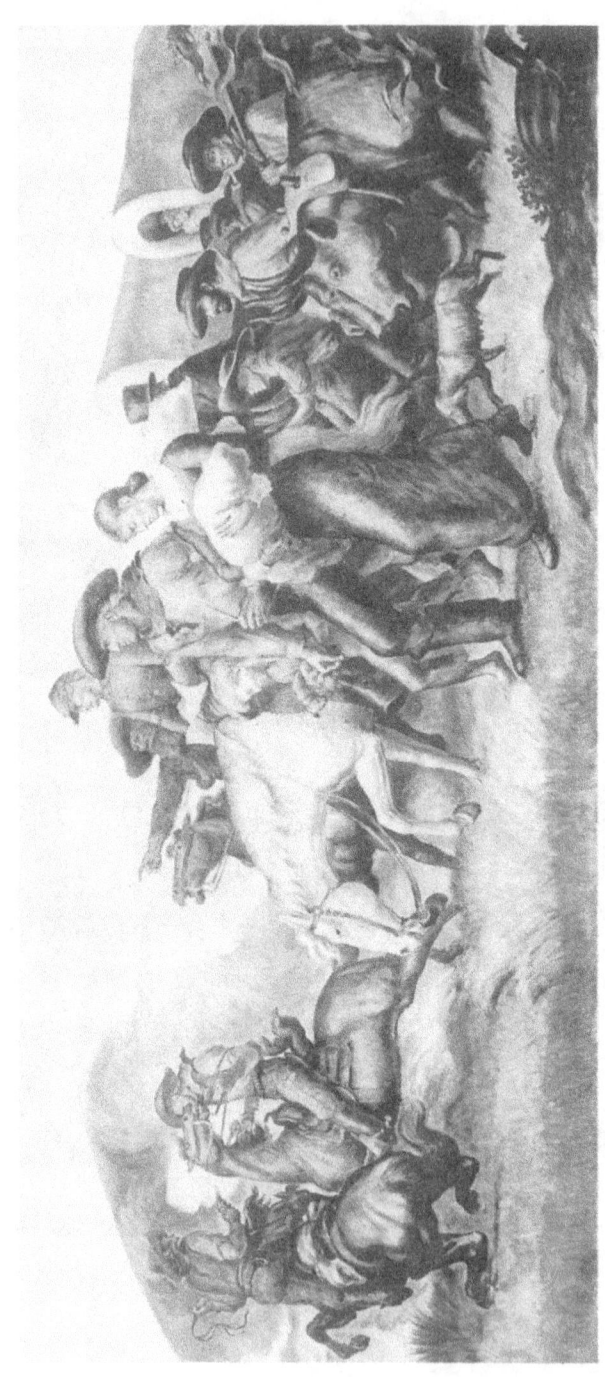

Figure 85. John Steuart Curry. *Westward Migration*. 1936–37. Oil and tempera on canvas, 8 ft. 6 in. × 20 ft. 6 in. Mural in Department of Justice Building, Washington, D.C.

Following them, an old bearded scout, a cavalryman, a top-hatted villain, three anxious youths in broad-brimmed hats, and a yoke of oxen pass by a beautiful stock of corn in full bloom, symbolic of the bountiful life that awaits. A second woman rides obscured in a background covered wagon.

Anxious but looking forward to eventual security, an 1889 pioneer mother, sunbonnet intact, is of greatest importance to the far left foreground of Curry's westward-moving *The Oklahoma Land Rush* (Fig. 86), painted for the Department of the Interior Building in 1938. Perched on a broken-down wagon, she clutches her small son while waving and calling out to her certificate-holding husband, who, astride their rearing horse, is to ride on to claim a new farm site. His hellbent competition includes a cyclist riding a high, "ordinary" bicycle from the 1880s and an overweight, overdressed lady in a rocking chair. She rolls back in an open wagon driven frantically by her balding husband, and, if nothing else, lends comic relief to balance the anxious sincerity of the mother on the ground.

The strain and stress of social change continued to test the strength of Curry's mother figures. In the episodes of nineteeth-century American history that filled several of his larger canvases during the late-thirties economic setback, women struggle for a better life alongside their male companions. Omitted from the Sunbonnet Myth of the Westward Movement, the white majority's stereotype of the maternal black woman, abundant in size, with her head wrapped in a bandana, was identified with the antebellum South. Two such matriarchal figures appear in the University of Wisconsin Law Library mural, *The Freeing of the Slaves* (1936–42, Fig. 20). Their dress, size, and action were perhaps inspired by Hattie McDaniel's Academy Award–winning performance in *Gone with the Wind* (1939). They flank an elongated freeman whose widespread arms and oversized hands turn toward heaven.[13] From the left, riding up front in a cart pulled by a white mule, a third "Mammy" figure, identical to the foremost pair, leads the elders, women, and children from slave cabins in a storm-filled background.

Devastating weather and historical transformations are the stuff of adventure stories. Much less dramatic were the rugged realities of daily life endured by pioneer men, women, and children. Popular memoirs, novels, and films tell of covered wagons endlessly attacked by savage Indians and rescued at the last minute by the U.S. Cavalry. Of deeper human significance were the individual anxieties, strain, tedium, and isolation of homesteading. Sitting in front of a sod house with her helpful little daughter, a striped cat, and the chickens, an impeccable frontier mother placidly peels potatoes in *The Homestead* (Fig. 87), Curry's 1938 mural for the Department of the Interior Building. She patiently waits to be fenced in by her Civil War veteran husband, still wearing his képi, and their three older

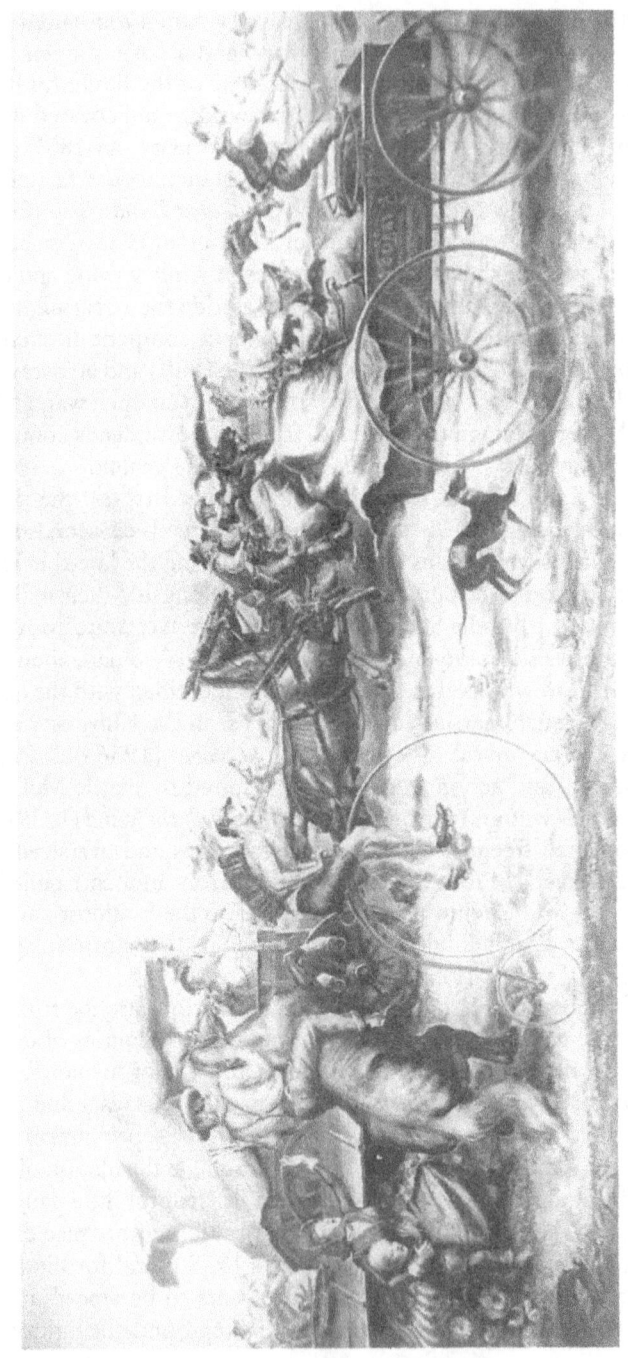

Figure 86. John Steuart Curry. *The Oklahoma Land Rush.* 1938. Oil and tempera on canvas, 9 ft. 2 in. × 19 ft. 8 in. Mural in Department of the Interior Building, Washington, D.C.

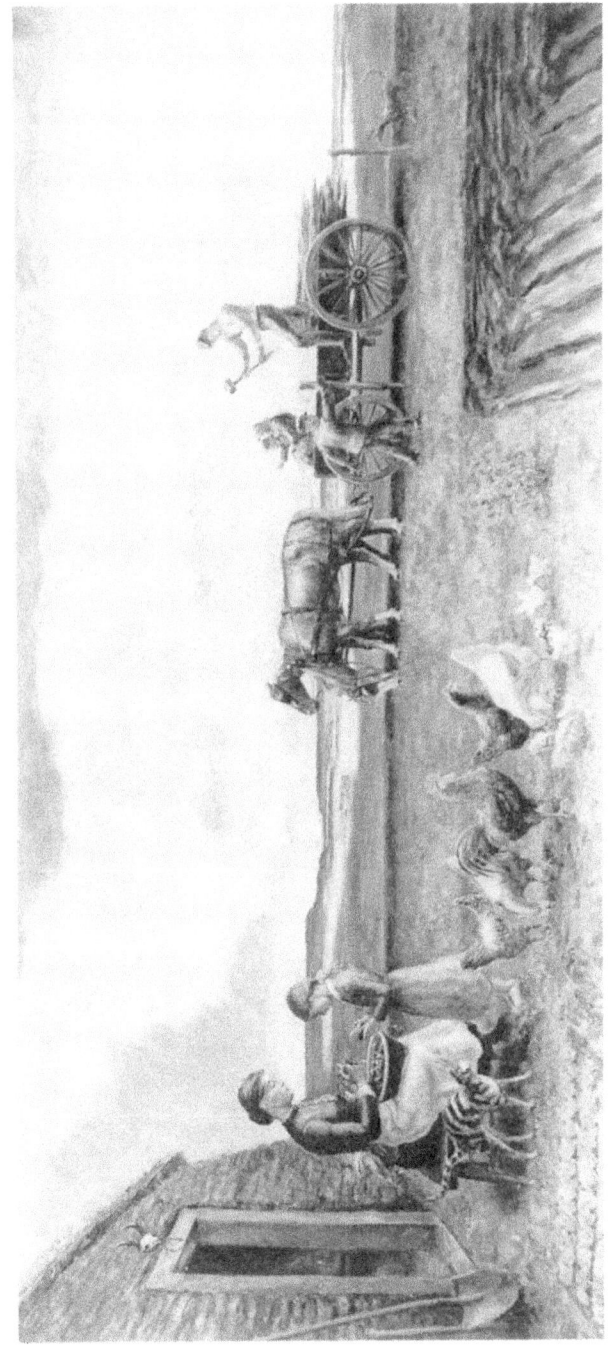

Figure 87. John Steuart Curry. *The Homestead*. 1937–38. Oil and tempera on canvas, 9 ft. 2 in. × 19 ft. 8 in. Mural in Department of the Interior Building, Washington, D.C.

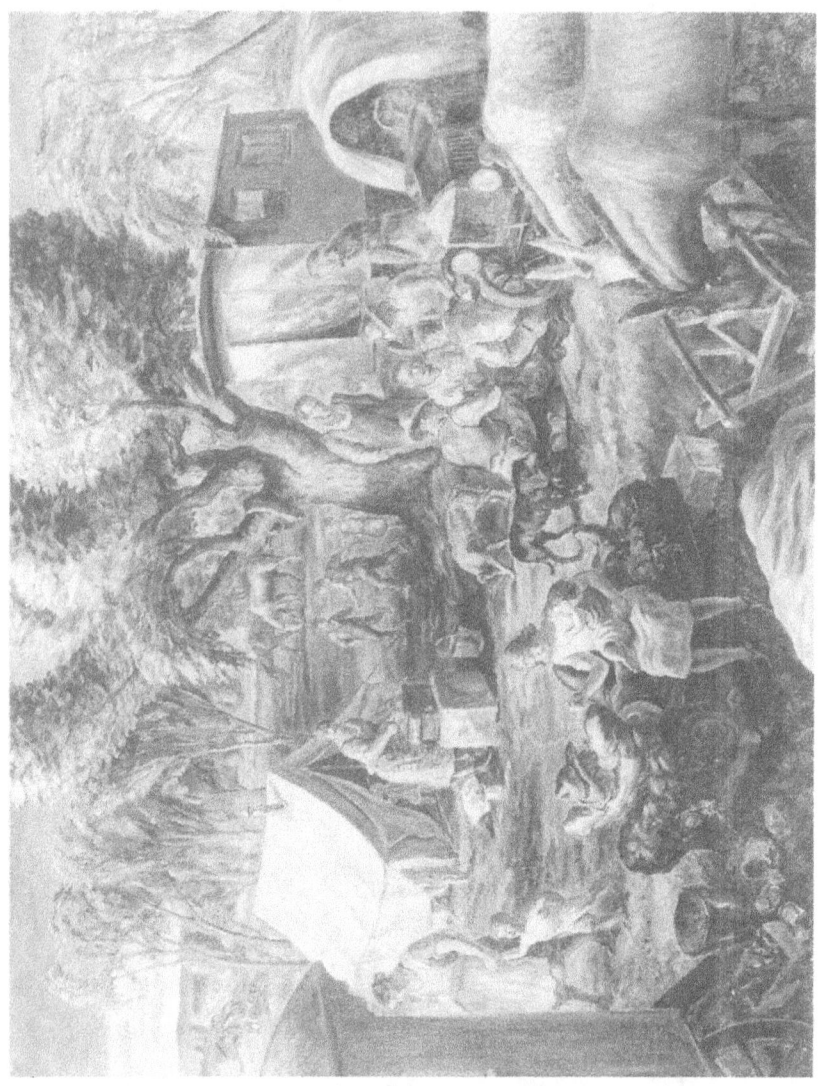

Figure 88. John Steuart Curry. *Roadmenders' Camp*, 1929. Oil on canvas, 48⅛ × 52 in. Sheldon Memorial Art Gallery, University of Nebraska–Lincoln, Lincoln, Nebraska, H-164; F. M. Hall Collection.

offspring as the sun bursts forth from beneath a border of clouds and illuminates a broad river in the distant background.

Written accounts attest to the suffering and season-by-season, day-in-day-out labor involved in establishing a prairie farm, the lonely years of hard work and setbacks out on the plains. Childbearing and -rearing; cooking, cleaning, and mending; tending stock and garden; nursing the ill and injured back to health or into death—all of these household chores bore down upon the frontier wife and mother. Caroline Quiner Ingalls, the mother of Laura Ingalls Wilder, willingly did the "woman's work" to support her husband's pioneering ventures in Wisconsin, Minnesota, South Dakota, and Kansas. While apparently blessed with an exceptionally compassionate mate, her labors throughout their "erratic migration westward" were from all accounts typical. As paraphrased by Kathryn Adam, the creator and co-author of the "Little House" books accurately recorded her mother's arduous life on the prairie:

Ma grew and preserved all her own vegetables; made her own butter, cheese, brown sugar, sausage, and lard; sewed all her own and her children's clothes; knitted mittens, socks and mufflers; made rag dolls; wove straw hats; cooked the daily meals over campfires, in fireplaces, or on wood burning stoves; kept the house clean whether the floor was dirt, puncheon logs, or wooden boards; and raised four daughters, one of whom was handicapped. . . . Beyond "woman's work" Ma at one time or another in her pioneer career put out prairie fires, scared off wolves, placated hostile Indians and helped build a log cabin.[14]

Hamlin Garland, in contrast to Wilder, reacted with guilt when he witnessed "woman's work" upon his first travels as a mature adult through the farmland of the Great Plains:

I no longer looked upon these toiling women with the thoughtless eyes of youth. I began to understand that my own mother had trod a similar slavish round with never a full day of leisure, with scarcely an hour of escape from the tugging hands of children and the need of mending and washing clothes. I recall her as she passed from the churn to the stove, from the stove to the bedchamber, and from the bedchamber back to the kitchen, day after day, year after year, rising at daylight or before, and going to her bed only after the evening dishes were washed and the stockings and clothing mended for the night.[15]

In two major paintings Curry emphasized the extreme hardships of life on the land, migratory or marginal. Both focus on the poverty of contemporaneous rural women and their children. Rural depression forces overworked mothers in *Roadmenders' Camp* (Fig. 88), painted in the same year as *Tornado Over Kansas*, to cope with primitive conditions like those of their pioneer ancestors. Though exhausted by a long day of cooking and

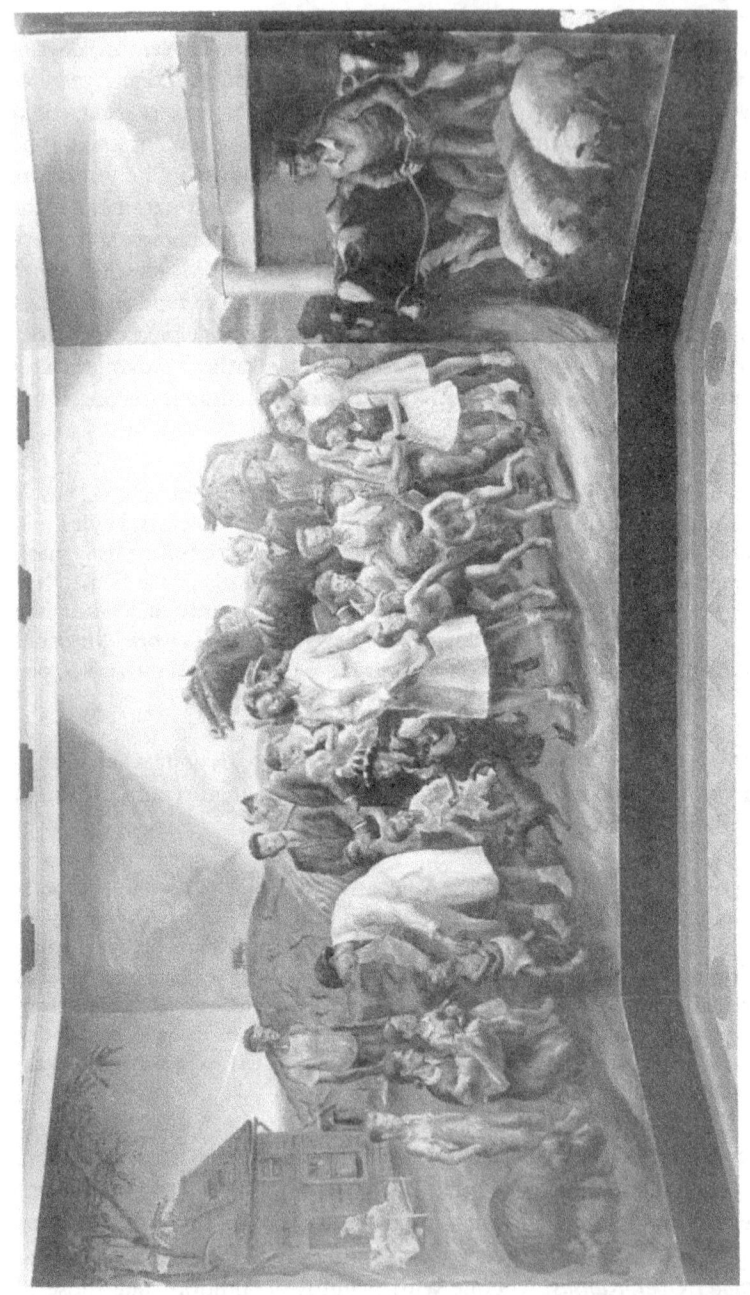

Figure 89. John Steuart Curry. *Social Benefits of Biochemical Research*. 1941. Oil and tempera on canvas, 9 ft. × 14 ft. 4 in. Mural in old Biochemistry Building, University of Wisconsin–Madison, Madison, Wisconsin.

looking after the children, they continue to work into the night while the men idle away their off hours. In the foreground a "nagging" wife, holding a child in her lap, appeals to her husband, who stretches out with his hands behind his head, puffing away on his pipe.

Much worse off, an undernourished, poverty-stricken farm family receives scientific relief in *Social Benefits of Biochemical Research* (1941, Fig. 89), a mural in the hallway of the Biochemistry Building at the University of Wisconsin in Madison. Two robust female lab workers in white, accompanied by faculty researchers, a dozen healthy children, and two draught horses, move toward a gaunt, hollow-cheeked mother brought to her knees by the sudden attention. She is flanked by her starving offspring and shares the focal point with a bony sow. Her emaciated husband stands behind her; in the background, a deathbed, a brokendown house, and an eroded hillside contrast to the big red barn, well-fed milk cows, woolly sheep, and onlooking attendant on the opposite side of the mural. The conditions on the left painfully resemble those of the impoverished Alabama tenant farmers in James Agee's and Walker Evans's *Let Us Now Praise Famous Men* (1939).

Curry did not conform closely enough to the traditional trappings of the Sunbonnet Myth to suit the Kansas public. This failure provoked harsh criticism of his famous Kansas State Capitol murals. The farm mother in *Kansas Pastoral* (Fig. 90) poses with her children and chickens in front of the house as a pendant to her hog-tending husband in front of the barn. The apron is entirely proper, but according to irate letters, wires, and telephone calls, it should have been worn over a long skirt rather than the knee-length housedress of 1940.[16] Lengthen her hemline and give her back her mother's bonnet, and the noble image of the myth would be reinstated. Short of that status, she nonetheless stands as a symbol of survival, a successor to the *Tornado*-driven mother of the fateful year 1929. Tugging at her apron, a barefoot daughter waits to carry on as the faithful hen at her side tends to its chicks.

In sharp contrast to the overt sexual attraction asserted by much of Benton's female imagery, several of Curry's socially significant pictures employ an innocent, girl-woman type with little trace of lasciviousness. Though possibly derived from Pollyanna movies of the teens and early twenties, his girl-woman assumed a role of critical commentary. He directed her purity against insidious encroachments upon individual rights and well-being. *The Medicine Man* (1931, Fig. 91), one of the most ambiguous of his pictorial statements, emphasizes an image of vulnerability under threat. A portly quack in a swallow-tailed professor suit holds up a bottle of a nostrum called "Aqua Vita." He assumes a spread-eagle pose, ultimately shared by Curry's crazed John Brown, as further indication of life-threatening hubris. Flanked by three background Indian figures, asso-

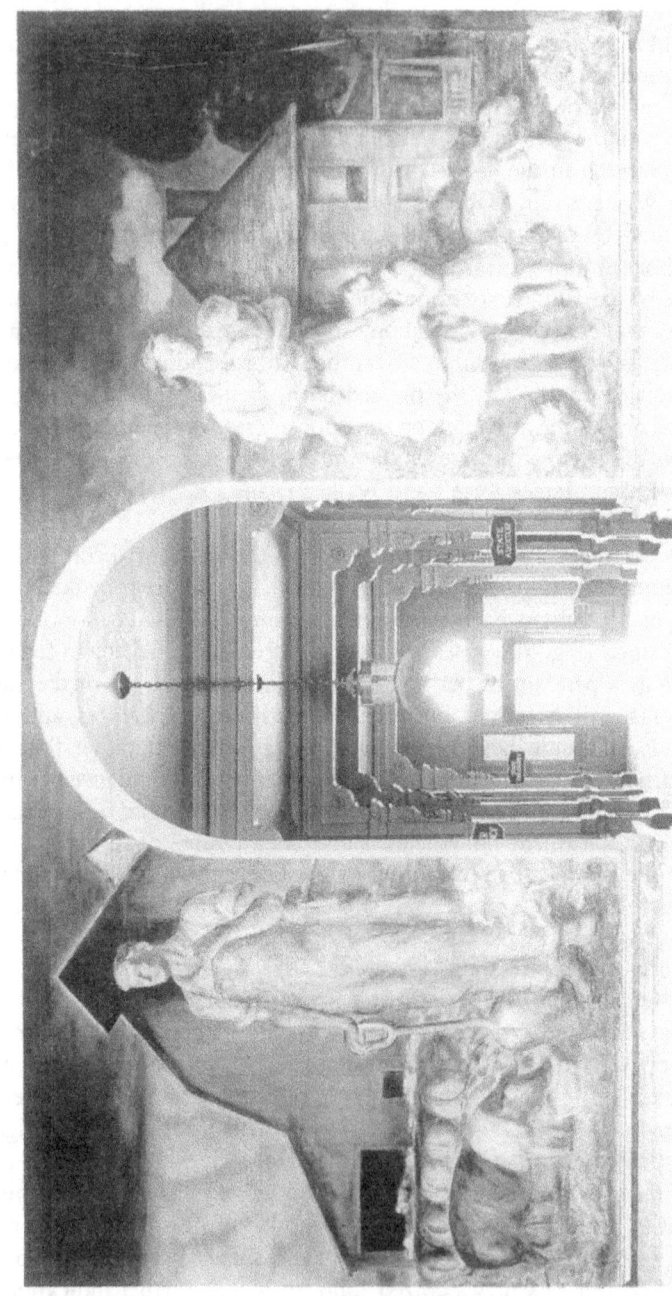

Figure 90. John Steuart Curry. *Kansas Pastoral*. 1937–42. Oil and tempera on canvas, 11 ft. 6 in. × 10 ft. Kansas State Capitol Building, Topeka, Kansas.

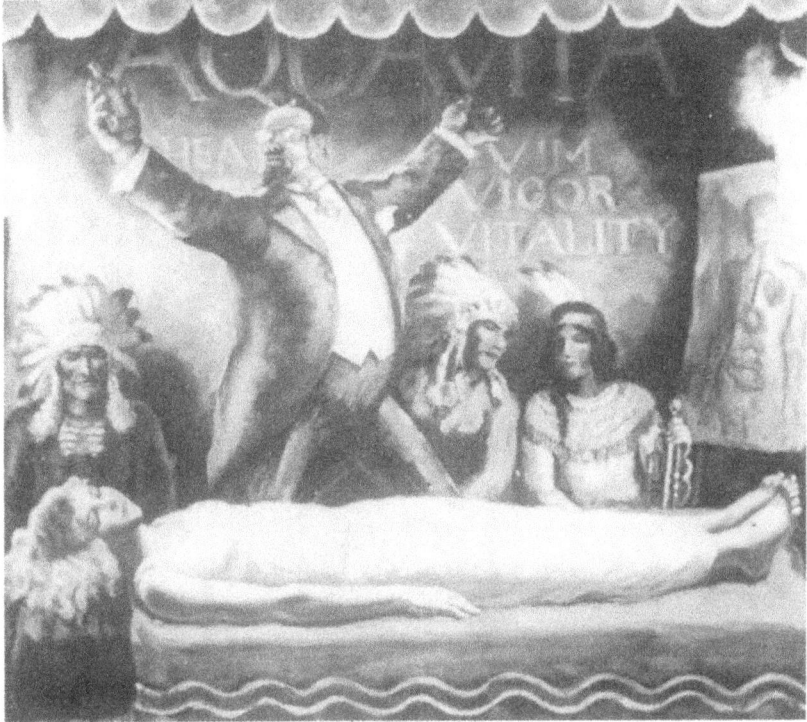

Figure 91. John Steuart Curry. *The Medicine Man.* 1931. Oil on canvas, 36 × 40 in. Private Collection.

ciated with natural cures, the "Doctor" stares up at the medicine with a masklike Mephistophelean face. A barefoot, blond maiden, virtually float-ing in the foreground on a red blanket with serpentine trim and blue pillow, appears to sleep. Stretched out on display in a white gown, she awaits her healing as part of the sideshow act. Or, in a larger beauty-and-the-beast context, the legendary princess of fairytale fame lies unconscious, totally at the mercy of the barking monster.

Three slightly earlier paintings, *Baptism in Kansas, The Gospel Train,* and *Prayer for Grace,* show serious concern for the female initiates of char-ismatic folk religion. In contrast to Benton's salacious descriptions of girls under the spell of salvation, Curry viewed them as helpless victims at the mercy of their elders. An ashen-faced old man in *Baptism in Kansas* (1928, Fig. 92) grasps the beautiful, white-robed, golden-haired young woman in the Germanic tradition of Death and a Maiden.[17] From the extreme left, outside the circle of hymn-singing worshippers, an old woman in black looks severely toward the center as if in charge of the congregation, her

165

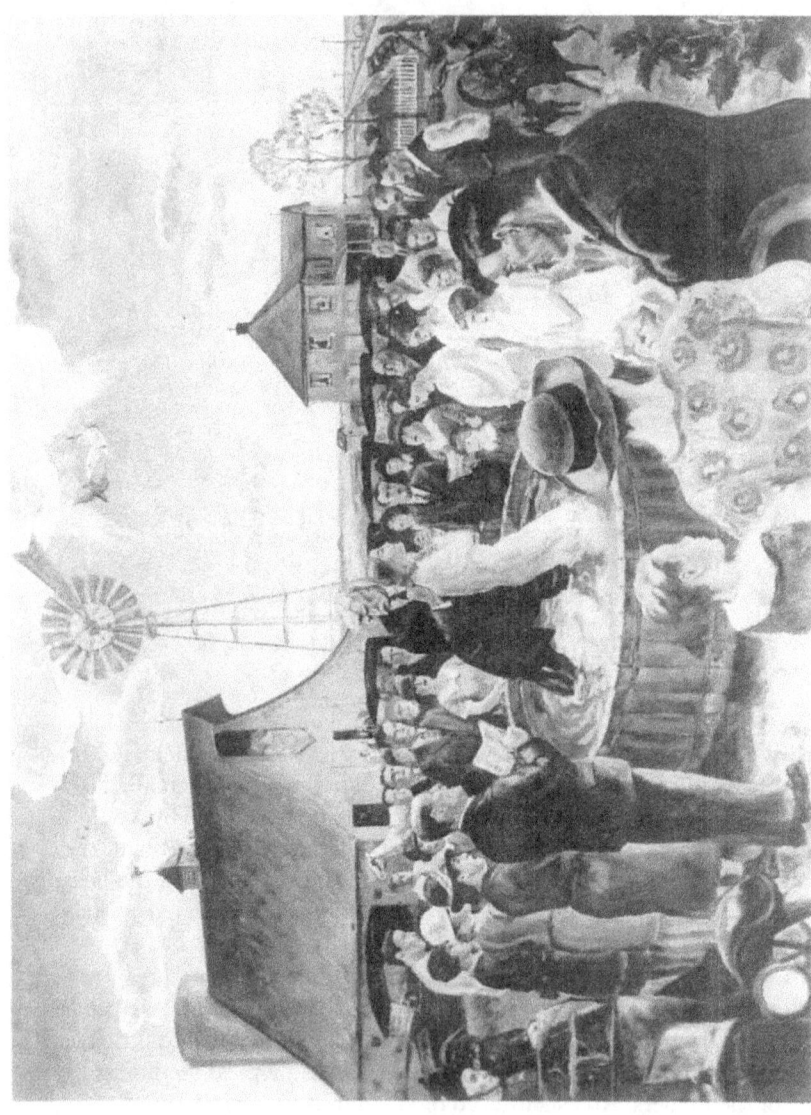

Figure 92. John Steuart Curry. *Baptism in Kansas*. 1928. Oil on canvas, 40 × 50 in. Whitney Museum of American Art, New York City, 31.159, Gift of Gertrude Vanderbilt Whitney. Photograph © 1997 Whitney Museum of American Art.

hand on the steering wheel of an open car in which she sits. The third major point of the figural arrangement coincides with the foreground father figure, who, in sharing the artist's position of outside observer, regards either the moral matriarch or the elderly preacher with suspicion. Laurence Schmeckebier saw this scene as conceived and executed "with sincere reverence and understanding of one who had lived it,"[18] an innocuous Regionalist interpretation. Edward Alden Jewell, of the *New York Times,* was rather more astute, but still slightly off target, when he read the painting as "a *satire* on religious fanaticism."[19] Rather, Curry's depictions of pentecostal practices, as summed up by the historian Robert Gambone, were "meant to offer a critical reflection on fundamentalist religion."[20]

The girl-woman, at first Regionalist in association and in the end a non-Regionalist device for social criticism, allows us to estimate Curry's growth as an independent artist. In *The Gospel Train* (Fig. 93) and *Prayer for Grace* (Fig. 94), blond innocence is scaled down to portray ageless little girls. The first of these closely related works of 1929 focuses on two yellow-haired offspring of a spiritually spaced-out mother, who helplessly reaches out for them as her eyes roll heavenward. The matronly grandmother, dancing in born-again ecstacy with the manipulated youngsters, relates as a large central form to the two foremost men, firmly seated left and right. As elders in charge, they rivet their attention on the proceedings; one holds his hand high in a gesture of command. In the lower right corner sit two grim-faced women staring into the inner circle; the nearest, a mother, appears so intent on her clapping that she is unaware of her small son pleading for attention.

The sequential picture, *Prayer for Grace,* retains only one little girl, painted with bright pink and yellow in the midst of the low-key greens, purples, blues, and browns of the kneeling adults brought down by repentance. Silently perched on the corner of a bench with her hands folded in her lap, she conforms in miniature to the eternal child-women popularized by the pioneer film director D. W. Griffith. His stable of doll-like, nymphet stars, Blanche Sweet, Mary Pickford, Lillian and Dorothy Gish, and Mae Marsh, acted out his fantasy from the early teens to the early twenties.[21] Like the Gish sisters in *Orphans of the Storm* (1922), Curry's ageless images of innocence serve as foils of critical contrast to the oppressive action with which they are encircled.

While Hollywood, approximately ten years later, transformed the blonde into a glamour-girl Siren,[22] the blonde girl-women in two of Curry's major and hardly Regionalist paintings stand up to hatred and violent death. They reverse the innocent maiden's traditional submission to mortality. In *Justice Defeating Mob Violence* (1936–37, Fig. 28) a Treasury Section mural for the Justice Department Building in Washington, D.C., the upper left corner contains two women and a little girl behind a black man holding a torch. The most prominent woman, young, blond, and glamor-

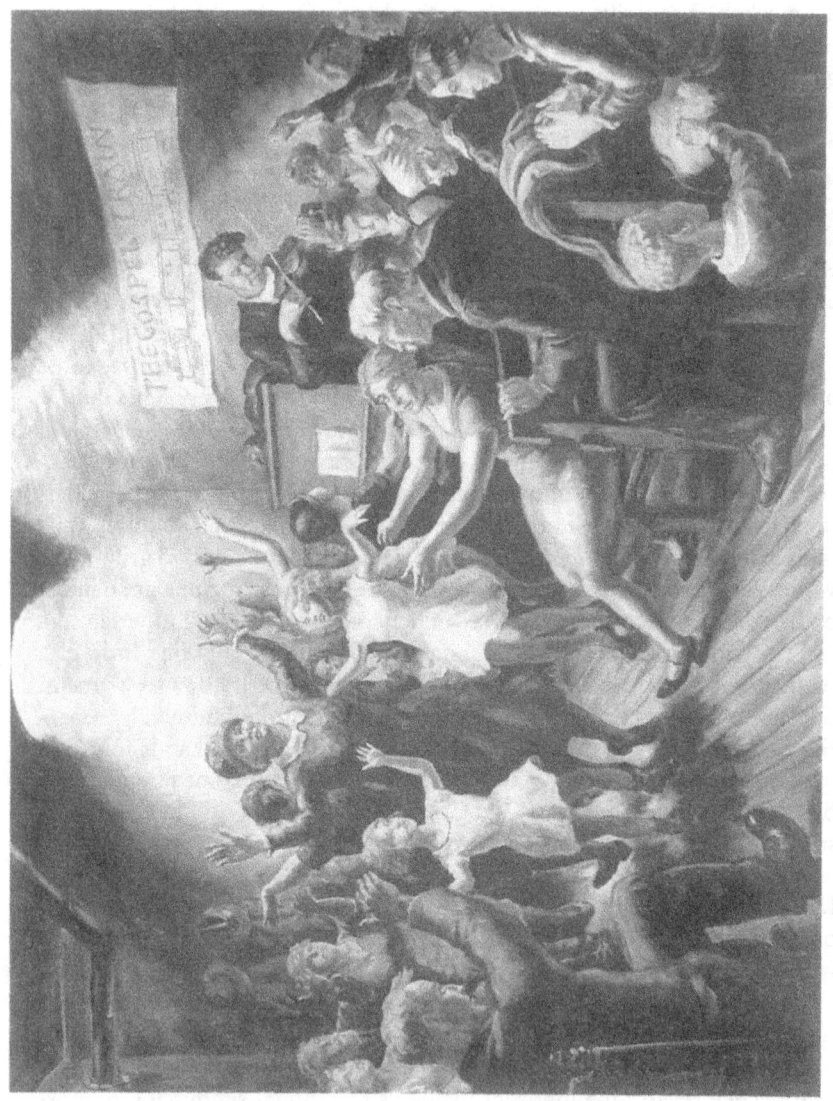

Figure 93. John Steuart Curry. *The Gospel Train.* 1929. Oil on canvas, 40 × 52 in. Joe and Emily Lowe Art Gallery, Syracuse University, Syracuse, New York, 1967.1; courtesy of the Syracuse University Art Collection.

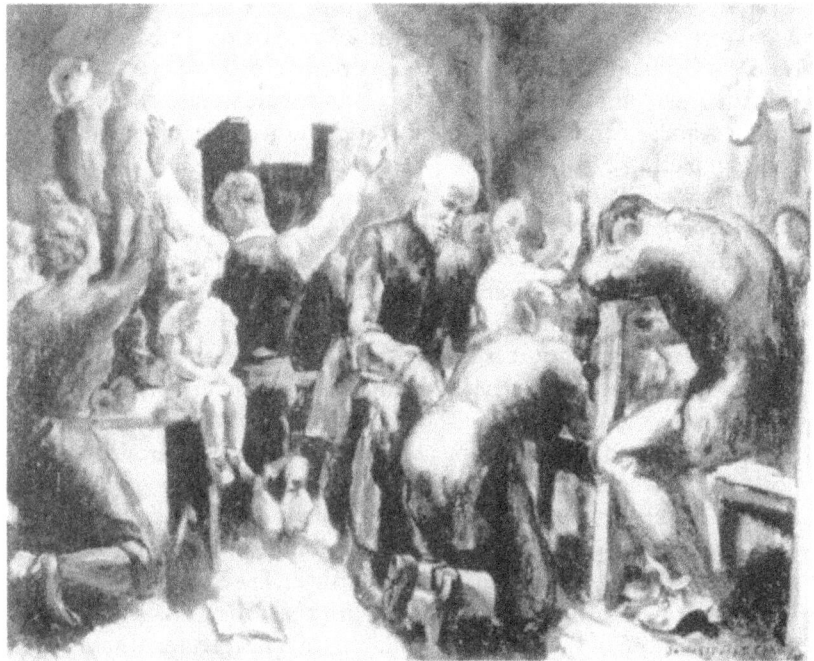

Figure 94. John Steuart Curry. *Prayer for Grace.* 1929. Oil on canvas, 20 × 26 in. Private collection.

ous, appeals with a wave of her left hand to the robed high-court judge. In response he stays the death-led mob before the courthouse steps with his outstretched right hand. In 1939, as the United States approached World War II, Curry centered *Parade to War* (Fig. 29) on an anonymous white-clad young woman, a bow of innocence in her blond hair. Flanked by two running little boys, she embraces a skull-faced soldier marching away with his fellow death's-head infantrymen in the midst of festive patriotism. Her message is emphasized through the mourning mother in black who bows her head in the lower left corner. In contrast, the oblivious middle-class Mom and Dad rush and smile and snap a camera next to a docile motorcycle cop. In this painting Curry elevated his secondary woman image to its highest ideological level: as a sign of his commitment to a waning isolationism. He aimed his updated version of the traditional Death and a Maiden against major engagement in military action abroad.[23]

In extending social commentary to the point of particularized protest, Curry engaged in overt modernist negation to a greater extent than Wood and Benton did in any single work. His noble frontier farm mother, in compliance with the Sunbonnet Myth, projected an image of survival to

169

a Depression-plagued public in dire need of her example. His innocent, blond girl-woman, while generically out of date by the 1930s, abandoned her early Gishian passivity to attract attention to forces of evil endangering individual will and freedom. In that role this increasingly obscure stereotype, a popular banality of the silent screen, turned into a pointed, critical image in paint.

As Marlene Park and Gerald Markowitz thoroughly illustrate in their books *New Deal for Art* and *Democratic Vistas*,[24] narrative and allegorical murals for the two major New Deal art programs abound with the visionary farmlands of agrarian myth and the fabled frontier. Somehow, through wishful thinking and alienated longing, both themes had to survive the overpowering forces of industrialization and urbanization. However, twentieth-century American art in general could not avoid answering to the latter. A gradual relinquishing of community identification in favor of vast commercial consolidation anticipated the eventual programming of post–World War II America into a highly standardized Television Land.

As participants in an art movement professed to be rural and protective of local characteristics, Wood, Benton, and Curry engaged in a rearguard feint against unavoidable social change. They played at a "Revolt Against the City." Accordingly, one might expect their images of women, along with those of their men and children, to repeat regional stereotypes. But this was not the case. In character with their other infractions against Regionalist principles, the "triumvirate" appropriated a broad variety of classified American womanhood: the guardian matron, the sex object of the "new morality," the noble mother, and the innocent girl-woman. Their specific imaging within these classifications might refer critically to local situations or go well beyond the bounds of any territorial claims to address conditions of universal concern or even at times sound an alarm of vital protest. In Part III comparative methods of stylistic analysis demonstrate how three celebrated East Coast modernists were actually more conservative, indeed more nationalistic, in their attachment to specific places than were their exact contemporaries, Wood, Benton, and Curry.

PART III

Modernist Regionalism— Regionalist Modernism

Not a picture of a flower is sought—that can be left to the botanist—but rather an irregular pattern of lines and spaces, something far beyond the mere drawing of a flower from nature.

Arthur W. Dow, *Composition*

8

Grant Wood's Affair
with Abstract Art

Wood's interest in modern ways of composing a picture originated in the Arts and Crafts movement's emphasis on ornamental patterning. He became familiar with this aspect of design in his late teens through a correspondence course offered by the art educator Ernest Batchelder in Gustav Stickley's *Craftsman Magazine.* This initial exposure led him to another American source of modernism, Arthur Wesley Dow, whose manual *Composition: A Series of Exercises in Art Structure for the Use of Students and Teachers* was to set the pace for American art education for decades. Although not as thoroughly influenced as his contemporaries Georgia O'Keeffe and Arthur Dove, Wood exercised certain Dowian principles of modernism in a number of tree-filled landscapes during the late teens. Approximately ten years later his growing modernist tendencies closely matched the concepts of "pictorial seeing" promoted by Leo Stein in his counter-Cubist *A-B-C of Aesthetics* (1927). By the thirties Wood's major stylistic transformation coincided with Art Deco adaptations of aerodynamics, as witnessed in the streamlined contours of such fantasy farmscapes as the recently resurrected *Plowing* of 1936 (Fig. 95). The degree of abstraction in this drawing came closer to that of the first-generation American modernists than the polemics of Regionalism would dare to acknowledge.

Less preoccupied with literal depictions of a particular place than generally alleged, the three leading midwestern Regionalists mulled over the relationships of their individual styles of painting to modern movements of abstract art. Even Curry admired the drawing abilities of Matisse and Picasso, though he could never abandon his conservative loyalty to subject matter true to "American life, its spirit and its actualities." As for nonfigurative abstraction, he declared it obsolete by the mid-thirties: "At this

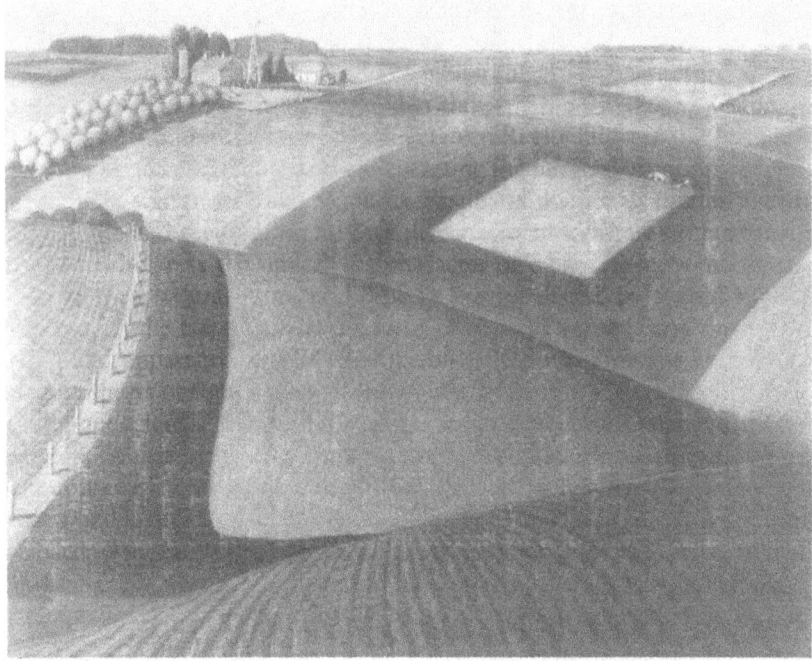

Figure 95. Grant Wood. *Plowing*. 1936. Charcoal, crayon, chalk, and pencil on paper, 23½ × 29½ in. Private Collection. © Estate of Grant Wood/Licensed by VAGA, New York, NY.

time paintings of a purely decorative nature have little appeal. . . . I myself have had no struggle for or with a subject matter. Likewise I have not been worried by the fear that my art form would or would not fit the prevalent esthetic style."[1]

While the "triumvirate" of Regionalism uniformly reprimanded American modernists for annihilating the human figure, at least two of them succumbed to the growing emphasis on reductive abstraction in conceiving and carrying out a picture. As the urban realists John Sloan and George Bellows had discovered, the avant-garde was persuasive. And, in common with the Alfred Stieglitz alliance of abstract painters, Wood agreed that "Paris-School" modernism had "added too many powerful tools to the kit of the artist to be forgotten."[2] Benton explained his inability to resist the influence of recent modernism in a broad art historical pronouncement: "The whole modern movement has been an exploration of the past. We have relearned that design is the important element in painting."[3] In spite of his deep dissatisfaction with his youthful color-Cubist experiments based on the Synchromism of his friend Stanton Macdonald-Wright (Fig. 96) and his disdain for nonfigurative painting in general, Benton's mid-1920s series of

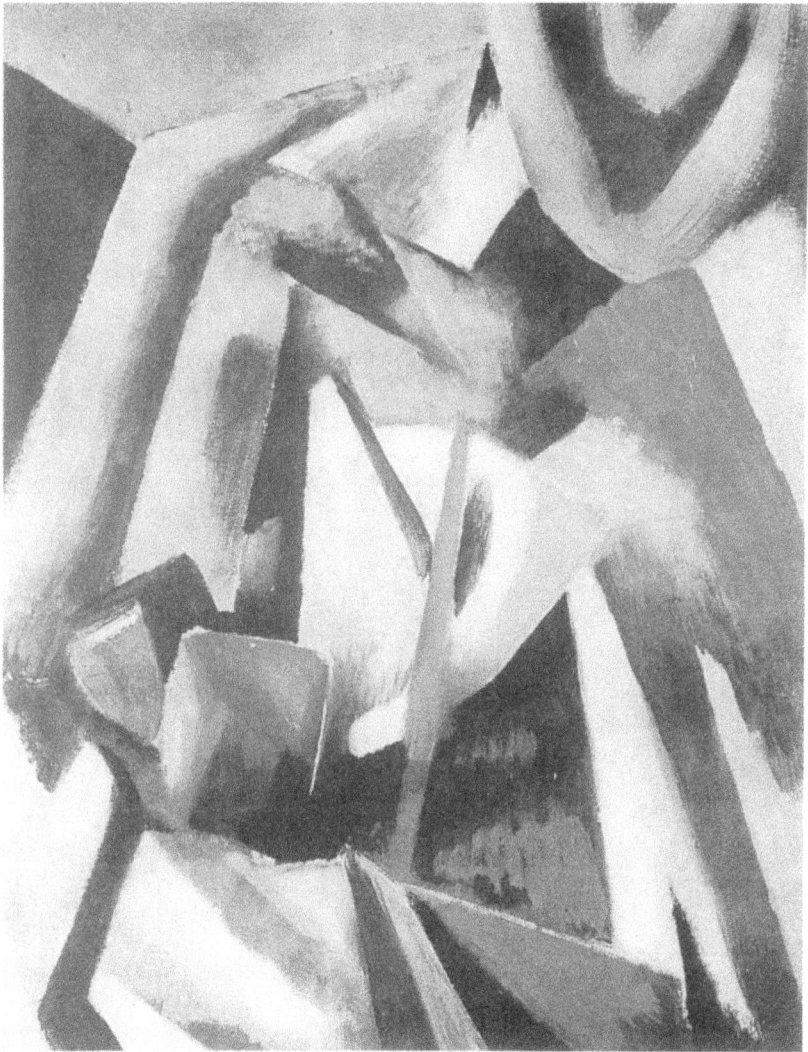

Figure 96. Thomas Hart Benton. *Constructivist Still Life*. 1917. Oil on paper, 17½ × 13⅝ in. Columbus Museum of Art, Columbus, Ohio, 63.006; gift of Carl A. Magnuson. © T. H. Benton and R. P. Benton Testamentary Trusts/Licensed by VAGA, New York, NY.

articles for *Arts Magazine* advocated reliance on abstraction for "synthetically" devising compositions. "Form and the Subject," written in 1924, and his five-part series, "Mechanics of Form Organization in Painting" (1926–27), not only held that the basis for a work of art existed initially in the abstract but also hypothesized that an artist's singular familiarity with a sub-

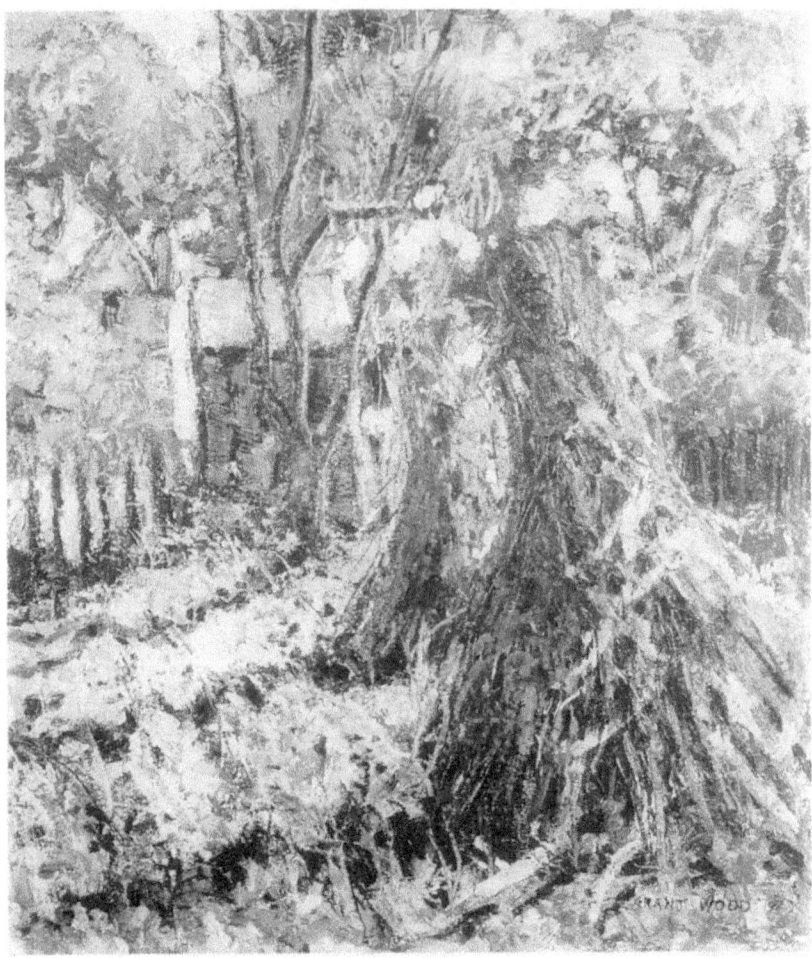

Figure 97. Grant Wood. *Cornshocks*. 1928. Oil on composition board, 15 × 13 in. Private collection. © Estate of Grant Wood/Licensed by VAGA, New York, NY.

ject as "historical material, if adequately represented, would cause the form itself to change."[4] Without embracing Gauguin's mystical visions, Benton visualized a synthesis of cultural meanings and pictorial configurations.

Although Wood was also growing dissatisfied with his early paintings by the time Benton published his articles, it could not have been a Cubist connection that bothered him. Quite the contrary, it was the "picturesqueness" of his "impressionistic" style that made him uncomfortable (Fig. 97). At one point he even experimented with painting a nonfigurative expressionist abstraction to the accompaniment of a phonograph recording of modern romantic music.[5] When that effort failed, he created a series of floral still lifes during the late 1920s in which he began to solve problems of design he had avoided for ten years by use of a painterly surface. Then, by the early 1930s, a precisely linear stylization distinguished his make-believe Iowa landscapes from anything he had done before. Although *Stone City, Iowa* was based on a direct study of a place with which he was thoroughly acquainted, he turned this village and its river valley site into a fantasy of curving contours, ornamental trees, and brightly patterned surfaces (see Figs. 2, 95). Wood considered the "decorative adventures" of his commonplace rural surroundings, their inherent elements of abstraction, as the true origin of the most lasting quality in his work.[6]

Approaching Wood's career in search of abstractionist tendencies, one soon detects the control of decoratively patterned surfaces as a central goal that guided his efforts toward a "twentieth-century" style. In addition to his open eye for early modernist means of pictorial composition, he was attracted to early Renaissance paintings for their clear sense of design. This combination of interests indicates that the importance to Wood of learning basic processes, and not a mere attachment to the life of a region, contributed to his "anticolonial" stance against simply copying currently fashionable European subject matter and styles. Of greatest importance to the eventual independence of his aesthetic ideology, he shared an inclination among first-generation American modernists to study and absorb methods of composition from more immediate sources of art training originating in the United States.

In the wake of imported Modernism, ostensibly on the wane by 1930, Wood claimed that a definite revival of interest in American subjects was taking place throughout the country. While this was to be applauded, artists would need to distinguish themselves as inventive individuals and reject any return to outworn, nineteenth-century academic techniques. A powerful tendency of the revival, according to Wood, would be toward a "literary feeling," the "story telling picture" being the "logical reaction from the abstraction of the modernists." As he hastened to point out, therein lay its greatest danger. The general public would continue to demand illustrations that it could understand without "mental exertion," leading us back to the likes of such nineteenth-century favorites as *A Yard of Puppies* and *The Spirit of '76*. To avoid this reactionary extreme, Wood proposed the establishment of a decorative convention that would hold anecdotal details in check. With other progressive American painters such as John Sloan, he observed this positive limitation in the paintings of fifteenth-century Italian, Flemish, and German masters:

They are decorations first and story telling pictures afterwards, and the story is in no wise weakened by the decorative qualities. The story of American life of this period can be told in a very realistic manner, employing sympathy, humor, irony or caustic criticism at the will of the painter, and yet have decorative qualities that will make it class, not as an illustration, but as a work of fine art with the possibilities of living through the ages — if the decorative side is finely considered.[7]

In the months following the double triumph of *Stone City, Iowa* and *American Gothic,* Wood promoted his current style of painting as representing the "new movement" and compared its compositional inventions to the advent of Mission furniture in his early youth. He enthusiastically applauded anti-Victorian principles of simplified design. But, he added,

The mission period was only a clearing away period for better things to come. . . . A generation later we find art going through the same phases, Modernism instead of Mission. The clearing away period, with its simplification to the point of crudity, is showing signs of decline, and we are already looking forward to the newer, I hope, better things to come.[8]

A key consideration of what is modern in a twentieth-century painting is its surface clarity, or, more specifically, its flat-patterned abstractness, regardless of subject matter or lack thereof. In the nomenclature of leading American art educators during the first decades of the twentieth century, pictorial abstraction was equated with decorativeness. In *Craftsman Magazine,* Wood, still in high school, found his first up-to-date account of these concepts: a series of articles by the California art educator Ernest A. Batchelder, whose correspondence course in design Wood also completed. As if that were not enough, on graduation night in June 1910 he traveled by train to Minneapolis to enroll in a summer course Batchelder taught as a visiting instructor at the School of Design and Handicraft.[9]

In this course, following the chapters of his book, *The Principles of Design,* Batchelder used his own drawings and various historical, mostly Asian, examples to define, demonstrate, and illustrate "Elementary Line," "Rhythm," "Balance," and "Harmony." These were to correspond with "Tone," "Measure" (size), and "Shape" (Fig. 98).[10] Applicable to either "Ornamental" designs or "Pictorial" compositions, Batchelder meant these principles to clarify and control the interaction of line and mass, proceeding from the simple to the complex. Like the Harvard art educator Denman W. Ross, with whom he had studied in 1901, Batchelder disavowed illusionistic adherence to natural form and borrowed his teacher's basic distinctions between "Representation" and "Design."[11] Representation, the recording of observed facts, was not intended to serve any decorative purpose. "Pure Design," on the other hand, amounted to "the arrangement of lines or masses in an orderly way for sake of their decorative value."[12] "Design in Representation" occurs when the element of representation dominates, but at the same time the arrangement of lines recognizes the value of the deco-

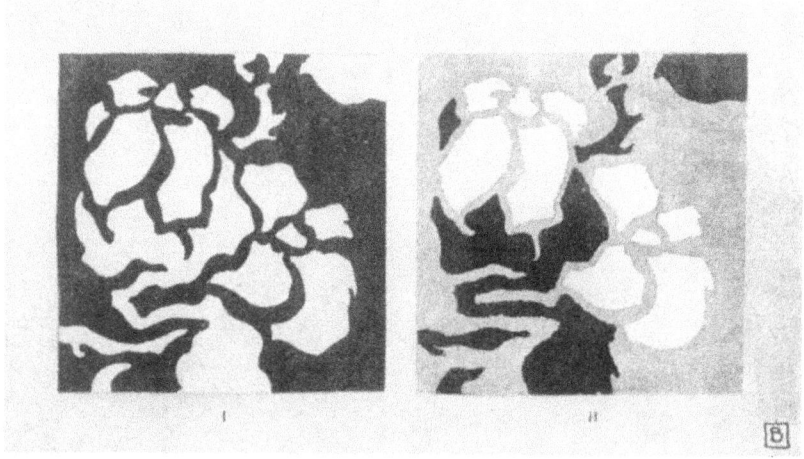

Figure 98. Illustration from Ernest A. Batchelder's *The Principles of Design* (Chicago: Inland Printer, 1904).

rative. "Representation in Design," on the other hand, permits design to receive first consideration and relegates representation to secondary status. Resemblance to some natural feature could very well remain but might be so abstract in compositional function that immediate identification would be difficult.[13]

A glance at examples of Wood's three-dimensional metalwork suggests that Batchelder's decorative design principles became second nature to him. The whimsical *Lilies of the Alley* (Fig. 99) thrives on a constantly changing interaction of lines and masses made up of twisted-wire stems and found-object flower blossoms. A gear or a wood clothespin loses its practical identity and performs as an abstraction of nature, free from literal translation. His symmetrical wrought-iron fire screen ornament (Fig. 100), though more conventional in its craftsmanship and design components, underplays its function in three and a half square feet of line, shape, and moderately descriptive masses. That a candle might sit at its top is of little consequence to the decorative value of its "Design in Representation" or "Representation in Design."

In line of succession, it is clear that Batchelder's basic frame of reference, and in turn Wood's, may be traced through Denman W. Ross to the Fenollosa-Dow system of art education. Ross met Arthur W. Dow in Boston in 1898, and they traveled to Venice together, painted side-by-side, and exchanged views on art.[14] Under the spell of Ernest F. Fenollosa, curator of Japanese Collections at the Museum of Fine Arts, Boston, both Ross and Dow believed that East Asian art, particularly Japanese *Ukiyo-e* painting and printmaking, encompassed "primary" or "abstract" art principles. To

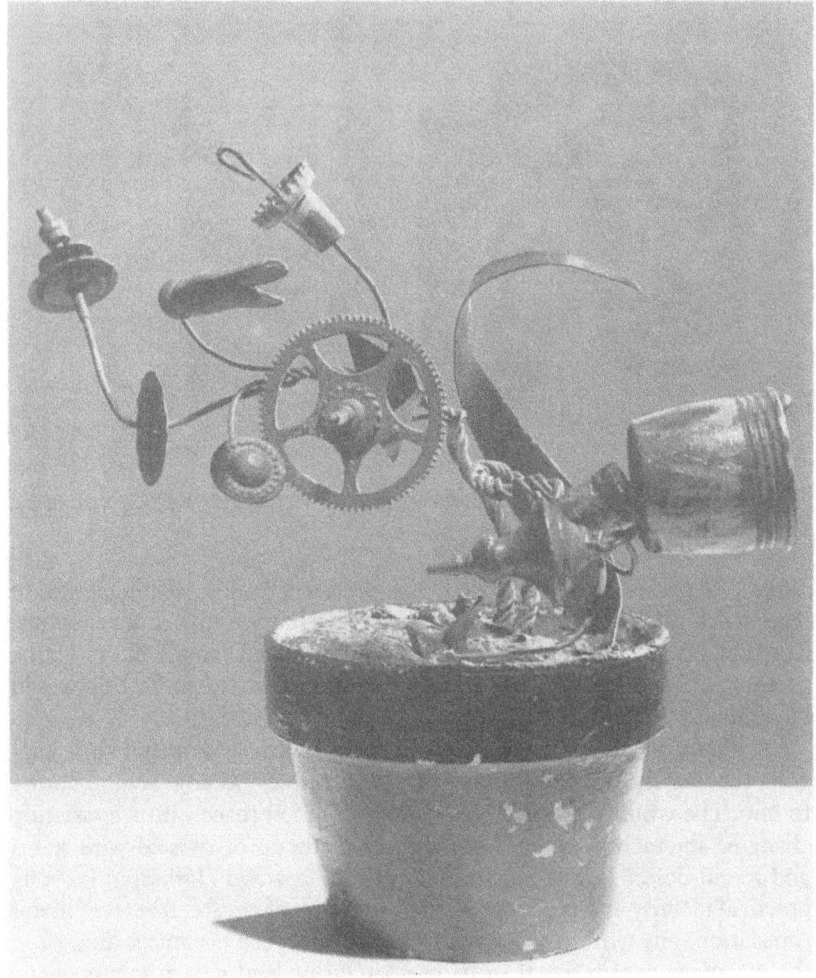

Figure 99. Grant Wood. *Lilies of the Alley.* c. 1922–25. Mixed media, 12 × 12 × 6½ in. Cedar Rapids Museum of Art, Cedar Rapids, Iowa; gift of Happy Young and John B. Turner II. © Estate of Grant Wood/Licensed by VAGA, New York, NY.

them, imagination implied an exact, sharply focused singularity, a "funda-mental unity of line, mass and color." [15]

Composition, Dow's manual of art exercises for students and teach-ers, aimed at "a better method of teaching than the prevailing nature-copying." [16] Its success may be measured by its longevity: first published in 1899 and revised and enlarged in 1913, it was published by Double-day in more than twenty editions until the early 1940s. In it Dow orga-

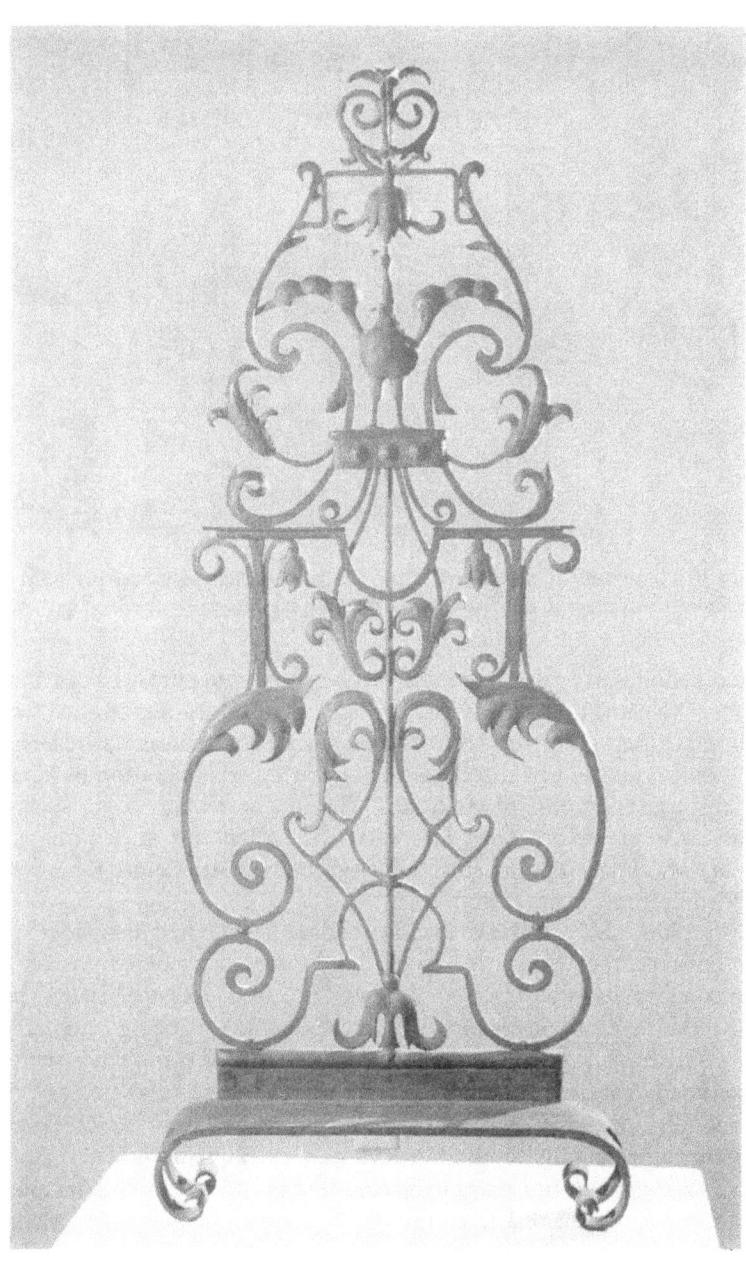

Figure 100. Grant Wood. *Fire Screen Ornament*. c. 1924. Wrought iron, 50¼ × 21¼ × 4½ in. Cedar Rapids Museum of Art, Cedar Rapids, Iowa; gift of John T. Hamilton III © Estate of Grant Wood/Licensed by VAGA, New York, NY.

Figure 101. Illustration from Arthur W. Dow, *Composition: A Series of Exercises in Art Structure for the Use of Students and Teachers* (Garden City, New York: Doubleday-Page, 1913)

nized Fenollosan principles of abstract harmony and pure art as a trinity of "Line," "*Notan*" (a Japanese term for light and dark patterns), and "Color" (Fig. 101). Regretting the divorce of decorative and representative elements in Western art, he had discovered their continued integration in Japanese art through the prints of Hokusai: "The Japanese know of no such divisions as Representative and Decorative; they conceive of painting as the art of two dimensions; an art in which roundness and nature-imitation are subordinate to the flat relations."[17]

In 1891, the year Dow met Fenollosa, he adopted Fenollosa's central concept, the Whistlerian belief that beauty in art relied primarily on formal elements of abstraction. Because "its essence is pure beauty," music provided the most perfect model for the fine arts, it being essentially an art of abstract, synthetic arrangements of form. In compliance with this often-made parallel, "space-art" might aspire to and be valued as "visual music."[18] Line, *notan*, and color, indispensable to "all forms of space-art, whether representative or decorative, architectural, sculptural or pictorial," were to be applied and integrated according to "a few simple principles."[19] Dow was confident that from this easily grasped, democratized aesthetic, "a powerful, distinctly American school" could arise that would be responsive to the history and character of the country.[20] No more obvious forerunner and source of inspiration could be found for the fundamental ideals, if not the respective practices, of Wood, Benton, and Curry.

Dow explained the progression of line, *notan,* and color as interdependent units of a hierarchical order. Line would always be the initial determinant of composition and the measure of ultimate success or failure: "all kind of line harmony, beauty of contour, proportion of spaces, relations of size—all drawing whether representative or decorative."[21] The second step of the learning process, *notan,* the distribution of values, achieves a balanced, harmonious order. Distinct from rendered effects of light and shadow, it is instead "a placing together of masses of dark and light, synthetically related."[22] Whether based on two or many tones, the beauty associated with *notan* necessarily implies abstract, pictorial space: "We do not wish to be misunderstood as advocating the entire omission of shadows, or of modelling . . . but the flat relations are of first importance; in them must lie the art of painting."[23] On this central point hinges modernist abstraction, including that of Wood. Regardless of color intensities, he drew and painted compositions emphasizing relationships of value rather than those of hue. The clustered lights and darks of *Floral Still Life with Terracotta Pot and Blue-green Vase* (Fig. 102) create a "beautiful arrangement" that loosens left and right into a "decorative" surface pattern of leaves and shadows in response to the geometrically patterned table cloth and the rectangle in the upper-right corner. Modulated ochres and touches of red provide chromatic contrasts to the painting's turquoise tonality.

In *Mixed Bouquet in White Vase* (Fig. 103), *Delphiniums in White Vase* (Fig. 104), and *Zinnias* (Fig. 105), robustly rendered pottery containers anchor the compositions. In these paintings, the generous proportions of the vase or crock, placed on a tabletop or a shelf against a wall or, in the case of *Zinnias,* cropped at the bottom, provide a solid contrast to the energetically impastoed flower, stem, and leaf forms bursting beyond the upper and outer edges of the picture plane. Sharply contrasted hues and values flatten the illusion of tangible blossoms. The immediate "field" of painterly shadows within the bouquets, or of larger cast shadows and illuminated areas of wall, refuses to remain behind the flower "figures." It too claims the picture surface as a complex of pronounced shapes in the abstract. Thus, Wood's floral paintings evoke the basic dynamic of modern pictorial art in their "push-pull" tensions as solid forms and flat shapes vie to share the vital zone of attention between picture plane and picture surface.

Beyond naming color as the third of the structural elements, cautioning the student to coordinate it with *notan,* and citing a few historical examples of its best use, Dow had little to say on the subject in the 1899 edition of his manual. In fact, from the start he signaled his intent to treat only line and *notan.*[24] But both his intervening *Theory and Practice of Teaching Art,* a teacher's handbook published in 1908, and the 1913 edition of *Composition,* whose publication coincided with Wood's decision to become a

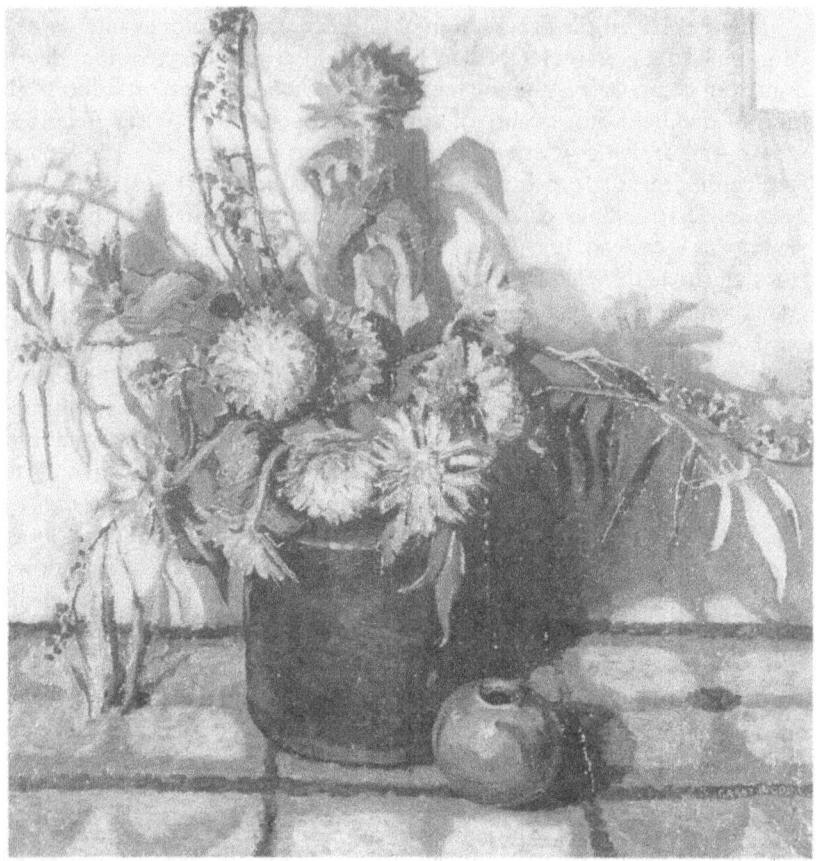

Figure 102. Grant Wood. *Floral Still Life with Terracotta Pot and Blue-green Vase.* c. 1927. Oil on composition board, 21½ × 21½ in. Private collection. © Estate of Grant Wood/Licensed by VAGA, New York, NY.

painter, devote an entire section to color. As Dow frankly admitted, however, color remained "baffling, its finer harmonies, like those of music, can be grasped by the appreciation only, not by reasoning or analysis." [25]

Likewise, basic composition, as ironic as it may seem, received no systematic coverage in Dow's manual until the expanded version of 1913. [26] To begin the art of picture making, an understanding of "Subordination" and "Rhythmic Repetition" would suffice; the refinements of "Symmetry," "Opposition," and "Transition" could follow. In the exercise section of "Line Composition part VII—Landscape Arrangement," the subject-matter suggestions read as if they had been dictated to Wood: "A street where there is variety in the size of buildings and trees," or "ranges of

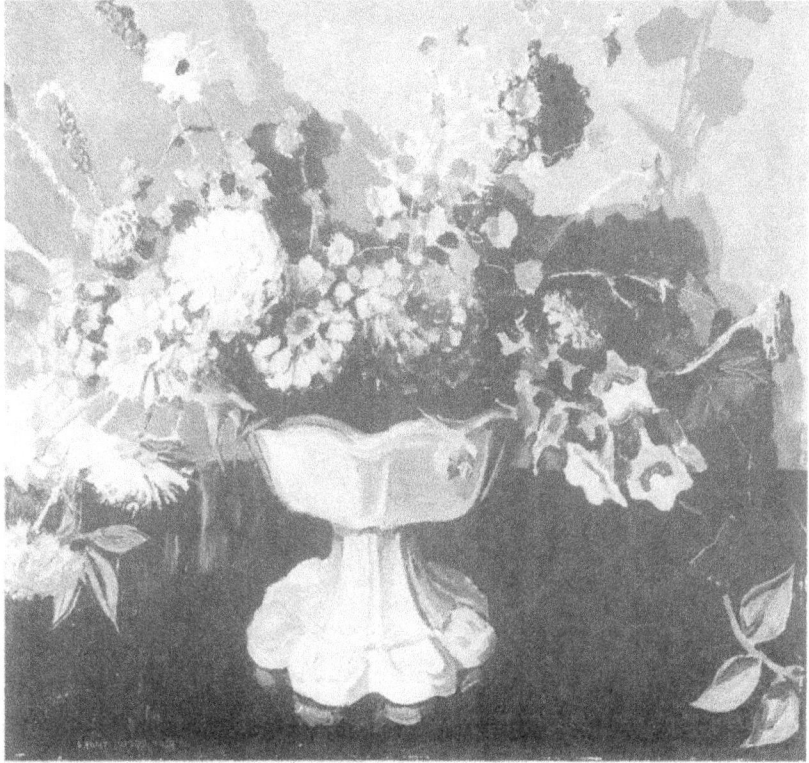

Figure 103. Grant Wood. *Mixed Bouquet in White Vase*. 1929. Oil on masonite, 20 × 22 in. Private collection. © Estate of Grant Wood/Licensed by VAGA, New York, NY.

hills, spires and pinnacles, clumps of large and small trees, clusters of hay-stacks" (see Fig. 2). Dow also prescribed form reduction in the service of a decorative scheme of images: "Take any landscape that has some good elements in it, reduce it to a few main lines and strive to present it in the most beautiful way." [27] It would seem that this is precisely what Wood was trying to accomplish in his 1919 paintings, *Fall Landscape* and *Feeding Time* (Figs. 106–107). In each, the main lines of silhouetted tree limbs bend and bow to create light, positive shapes thick in paint. Their decorative abstractness is matched by the shapes of four pigs, over which is scratched a surface pattern of vertical and horizontal lines.

If such advice were not enough to inspire the fledgling painter, this same section of *Composition* compares the linear interplay of land and tree forms to that of a familiar woven fabric: "Looking out from a grove we have trees as vertical straight lines, cutting horizontal lines, or nearly so. Leaving small forms out of account we have in the main lines an ar-

185

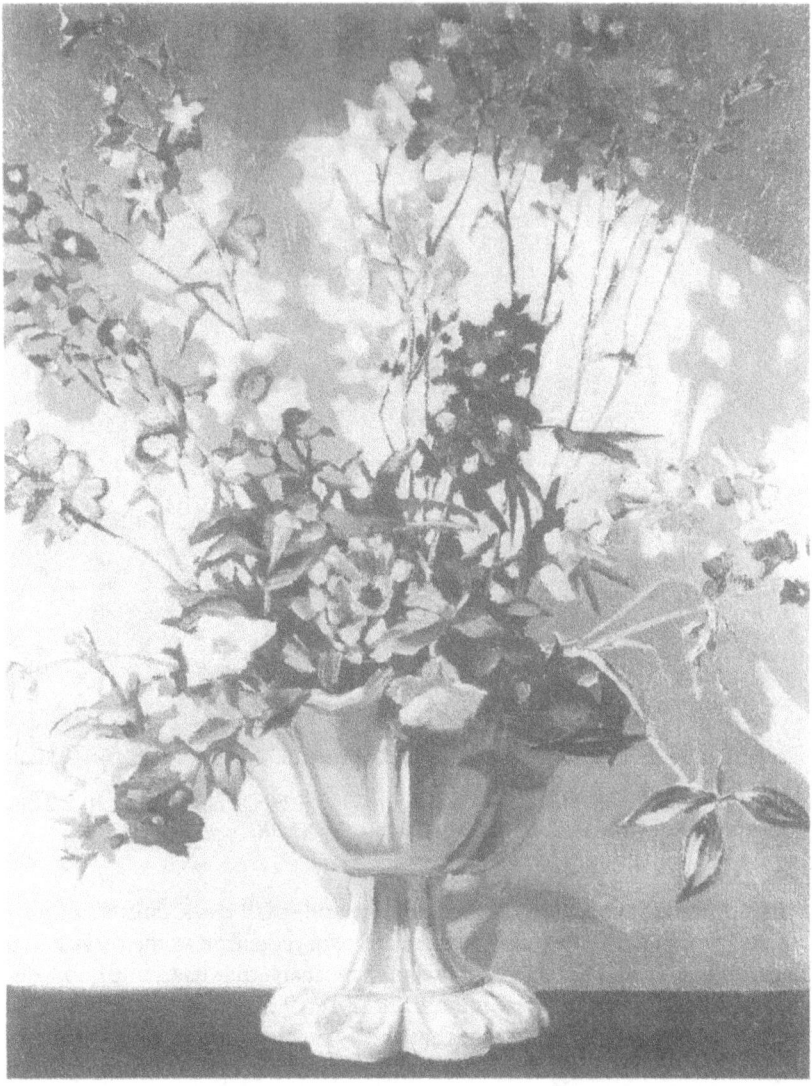

Figure 104. Grant Wood. *Delphiniums in White Vase*. 1929. Oil on canvas, 24 × 18¼ in. Private Collection. © Estate of Grant Wood/Licensed by VAGA, New York, NY.

rangement of rectangular spaces much like gingham and other simple patterns."[28] Such an analogy, in keeping with Wood's taste for the commonplace, strengthens the assumption that he developed his means of pictorial composition under Dow's pervasive influence, even if it was received indirectly through Batchelder. Regardless of its original source, his adherence

186

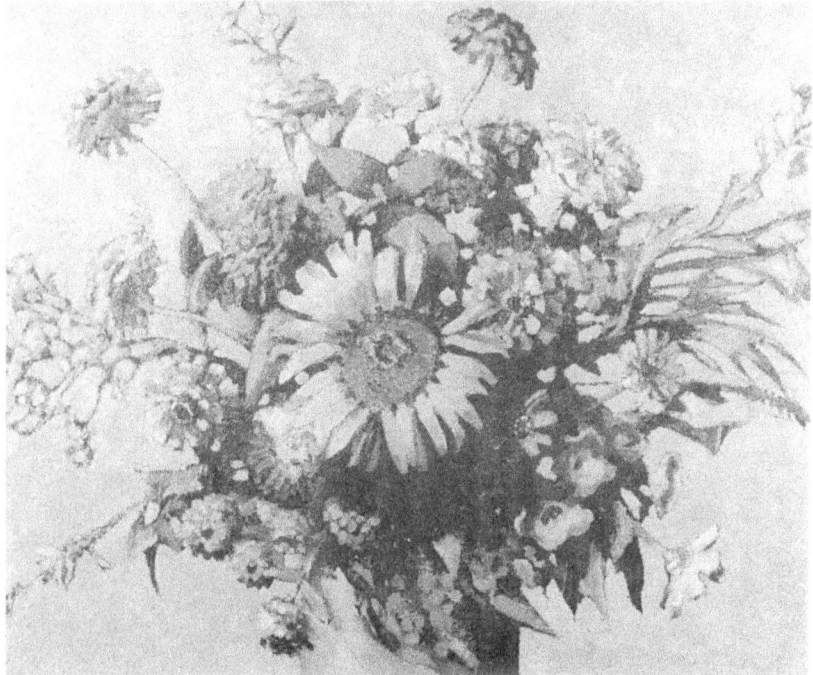

Figure 105. Grant Wood. *Zinnias*. 1930. Oil on composition board, 24 × 30 in. Private collection. © Estate of Grant Wood/Licensed by VAGA, New York, NY.

to reductive abstraction affiliated him with the first generation of American modernists.

Dow counted among his students and proponents several painters, photographers, and critics who were to be identified with the American vanguard during the first quarter of the twentieth century.[29] Photographer Gertrude Kaesebier, a colleague at Pratt Institute in Brooklyn, was among the first photographers affiliated with the Photo-Secession Gallery, as was Alvin Langdon Coburn, who enrolled in Dow's summer class at Ipswich, Massachusetts, in 1903. Pamela Coleman Smith, the first American painter to be exhibited by Stieglitz at 291 (in January 1907), had attended Dow's classes at Pratt between 1893 and 1899. The painter Max Weber, who studied with Dow at Pratt as *Composition* was first coming into print, taught his mentor's principles at the State Normal School in Duluth, Minnesota. After two years as head of its Department of Drawing and Manual Training, he left the school in 1905 to study in Paris, an undertaking for which, he would claim, Dow had prepared him. Once abroad, however, Weber strayed from the anti-imitation principles of *Composition* by appropriating avant-garde styles. After discovering Cézanne and enrolling in a painting

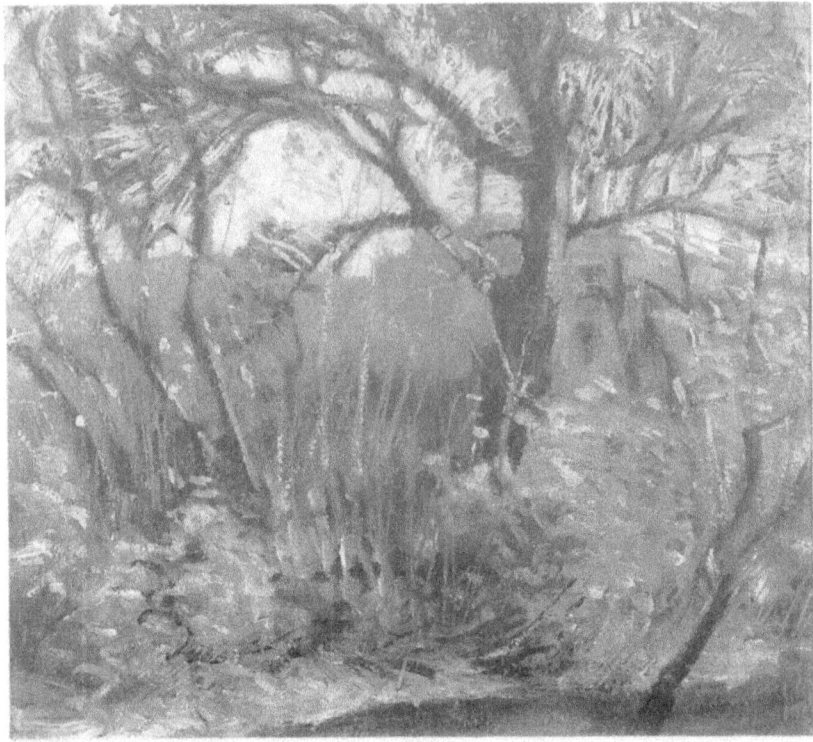

Figure 106. Grant Wood. *Fall Landscape*. c. 1919. Oil on composition board, 13 × 15 in. Private collection. © Estate of Grant Wood/Licensed by VAGA, New York, NY.

course offered by Matisse, he attached himself to Picasso and the Futurists. Their combined influence qualified his derivative paintings for Regionalist attacks against the "colonial spirit" of stylistic dependence on Europe.[30]

Georgia O'Keeffe learned of the Fenollosa-Dow system at the University of Virginia in the summer of 1912, when she took a drawing class from Dow's disciple Alon Bement. She studied under the master teacher himself at Columbia University's Teachers College in 1914–15 and during the spring term in 1916. O'Keeffe credited Dow with strengthening her powers of pictorial composition, especially in her experiments with abstracting flowers and leaves into a rectangular format (Fig. 108).[31] As demonstrated by the illustrations throughout *Composition* and *Theory and Practice of Teaching Art*, success in composing such subject matter characteristically involved asymmetry and, often, a closeup view of the image partially cut off at the edges (see Fig. 102). Subsequent to her initial nonobjective abstractions of the late teens, it was through this process of object-oriented configuration, shared with photographers Paul Strand and Imogen Cun-

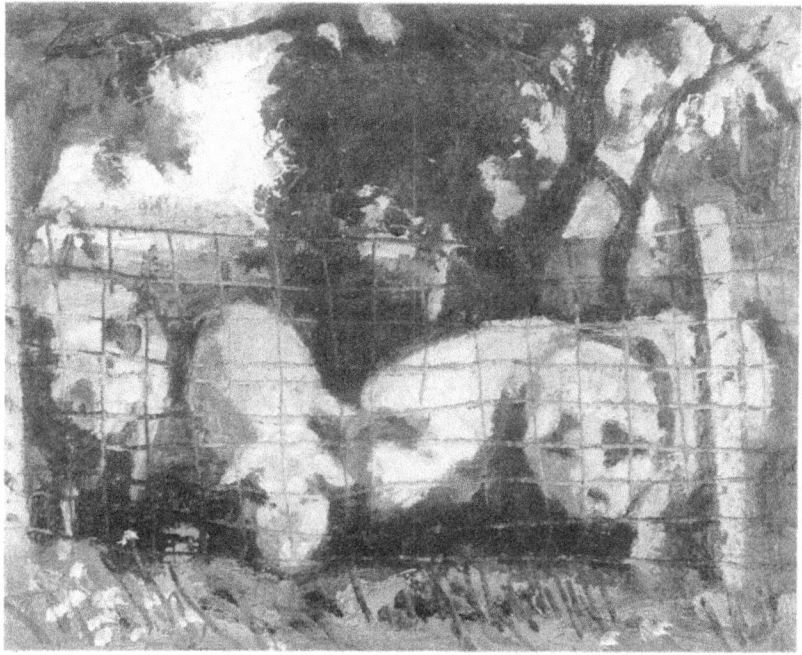

Figure 107. Grant Wood. *Feeding Time.* c. 1919. Oil on composition board, 6½ × 8½ in. Private collection. © Estate of Grant Wood/Licensed by VAGA, New York, NY.

ningham, that O'Keeffe achieved her most monumental single-flower abstractions.

Visual lessons in *Composition* also correspond to Arthur G. Dove's highly personal, abstract style of painting, which was fully developed at the very beginning of his career (Fig. 109). That Dow provided more of a stimulus to this rapid development than did the 1911 Picasso exhibition at 291 is indicated by the distinctly decorative abstraction of Dove's oils and pastels as early as 1912. In a statement to the Chicago art collector Arthur Jerome Eddy for his book *Cubists and Post-Impressionism* (1914) — a statement reiterated to Samuel Kootz for his *Modern American Painters* sixteen years later — Dove maintained that "all good art" is guided by a few fundamental principles of form and composition in the abstract, and that he, as Wood later did, had abandoned "more disorderly methods of impressionism." [32] In tune with Dow, Dove developed a trio of basic precepts to guide his creative instincts toward a pictorial process that was abstract in spirit and substance. Though he was never a colorist in the manner of Sonia and Robert Delauney's Orphism or its American version, Synchromism, he allowed color, the most problematic element for Dow, a prominent role. In union with form and line, a triad of hues, plus black and white, originated

189

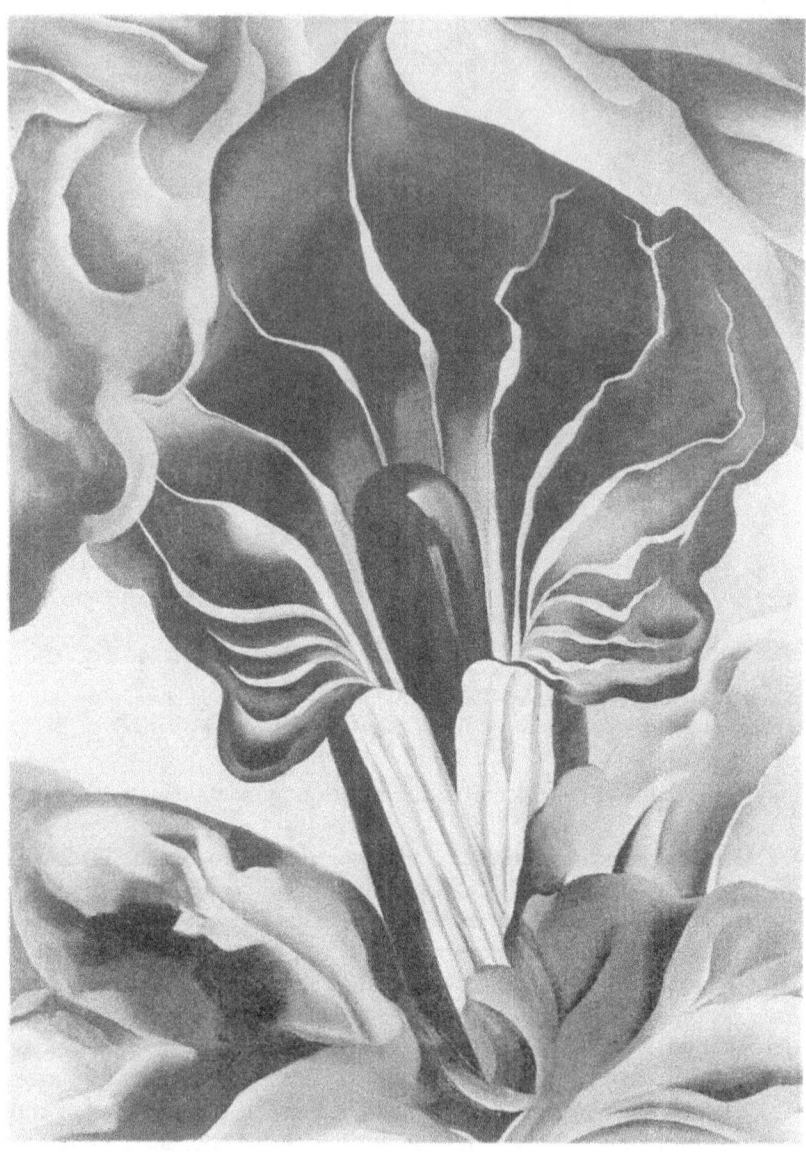

Figure 108. Georgia O'Keeffe. *Jack-in-the-Pulpit, No. 2.* 1930. Oil on canvas, 40 × 30 in. Private collection.

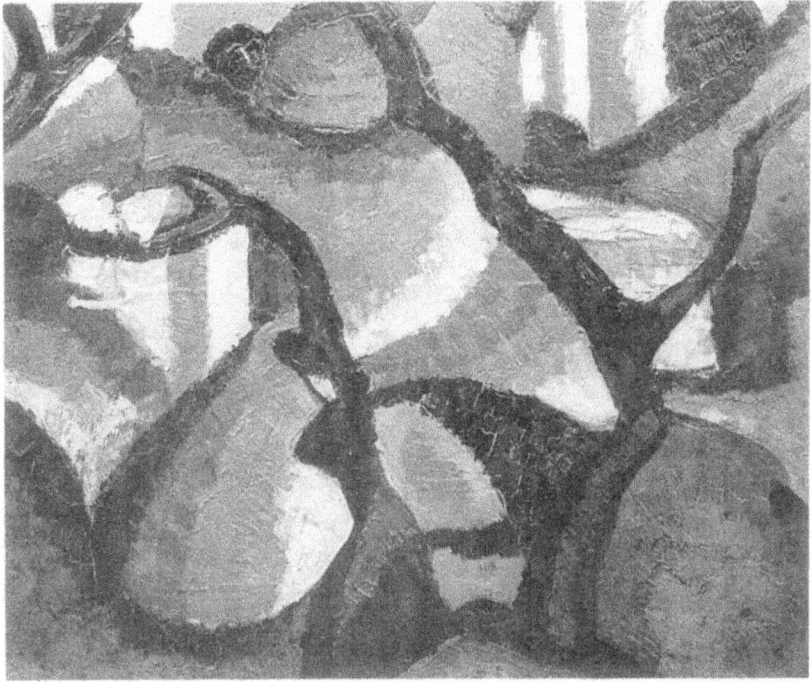

Figure 109. Arthur Dove. *Abstraction No. 3.* 1910. Oil on composition board, 9 × 12 in. Private collection.

with "the condition of light," an aura that Dove contemplated as unique to any object from which his paintings evolved.[33] Material possession of limbs, foliage, shadows, and surfaces, of all volumes and masses, would thereby diminish at a level of nonobjective abstraction higher than that of either Wood's *Cock's-Combs* (Fig. 110) or O'Keeffe's *Jack-in-the-Pulpit, No. 2* (see Fig. 108). But, to his credit, Wood's most abstractive moments advanced Dowian means of expression beyond the narrow limits of conventional anecdotal realism, as when the shapes of shadows combine with those of cockscomb stems and flared leaves to create a dynamically patterned design at the expense of a faceless Madonna and child.

As may be judged by frequent references to Dow in Stieglitz's art periodical *Camera Work* and by the adoption of Dow's terminology and aesthetic standards by the prominent art critic/historians Charles Caffin and Sadakichi Hartmann, he seems to have contributed significantly to the progress of art criticism, advancing it from purely descriptive accounts to formal analysis. This American-spawned modernist sensibility was not lost on Leo Stein, who was indebted to Bernard Berenson for his early appreciation of Cézanne. Stein's later bias against the Synthetic Cubist works

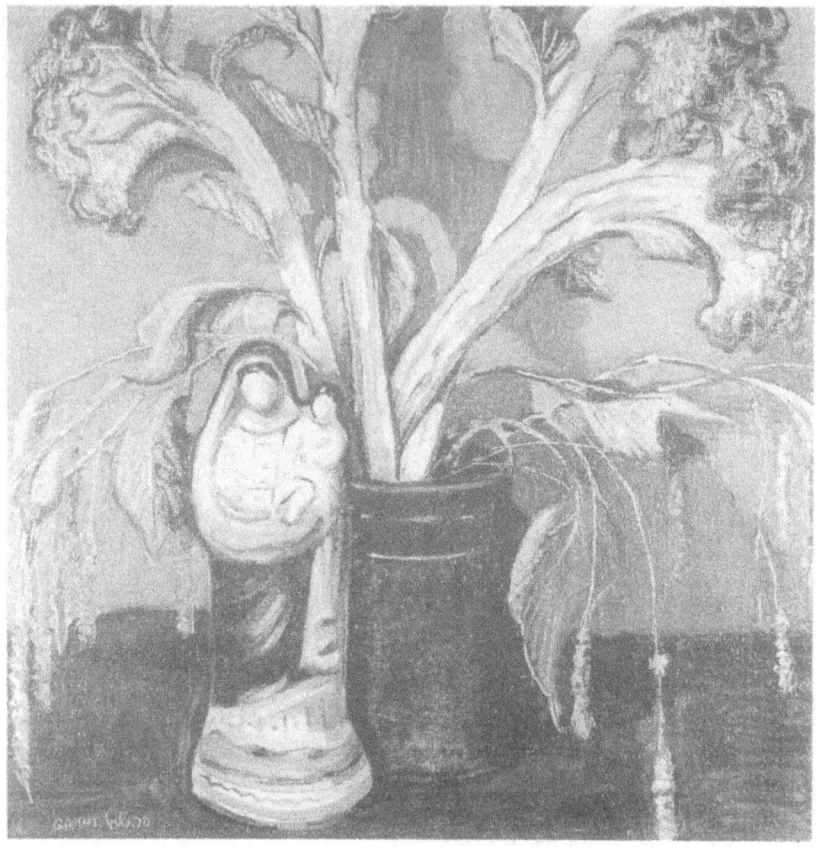

Figure 110. Grant Wood. *Cock's-Combs*. c. 1927–28. Oil on canvas, 21½ × 21¼ in. Private Collection. © Estate of Grant Wood/Licensed by VAGA, New York, NY.

of Picasso and the ornate figurations of Matisse emerged as his ideas and vocabulary of "pictorial seeing" acquired an increasing resemblance to the Fenollosa-Dow instructions on abstraction.

In time for the major changes of Wood's final development, Stein's *A-B-C of Aesthetics* appeared in 1927, the year Wood began his floral still-life series. Stein saw a good picture as "something that one looks into, but . . . keeps out of." [34] Whether an interior or exterior, its subject matter must constitute "a composed abstraction," with some degree of distortion imposed upon "inventorial things." [35] Petals, leaves, and stems, for example, must unite across the surface as active components of a work. Whereas success in flat composition was quite common, a true painting, as opposed to an anecdotal illustration or stenciled pattern, must also be rhythmically arranged into a cohesive spatial order. The key to everything else is the

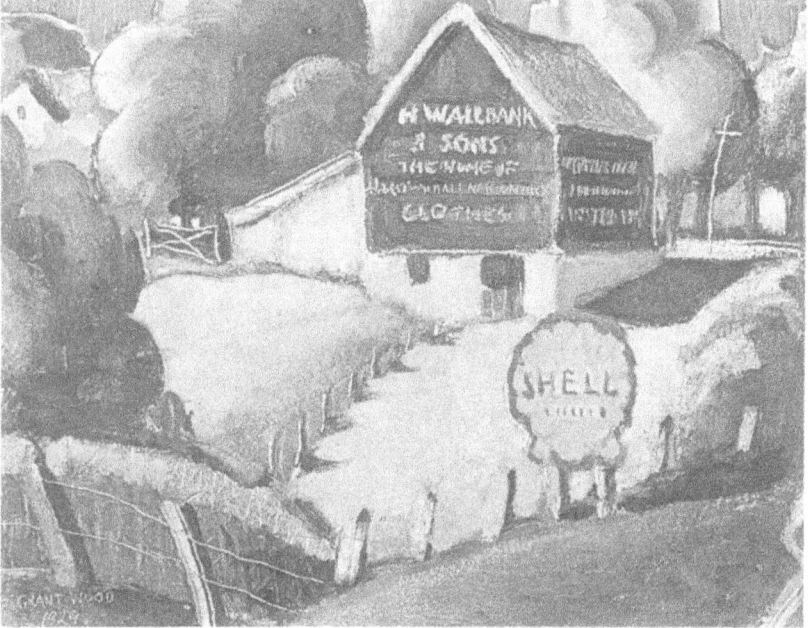

Figure 111. Grant Wood. *Black Barn*. 1929. Oil on composition board, 9½ × 13 in. Private Collection. © Estate of Grant Wood/Licensed by VAGA, New York, NY.

"compositional relation of depth to the flat plane of the picture's surface."[36] Diagonal (that is, perspective) planes should reciprocate with transverse planes, "like the successive layers of scenery on the stage":[37]

A picture could, in fact, be conceived as made up of transverse planes like successive layers of theater scenery, in which the object would be to emphasize the intervals, rather than, as in naturalistic stage scenery, to blend and so obscure them. These transverse planes are the means for creating a series of intervals and therefore for producing rhythmic movement in the deep dimension of the picture.[38]

Complementing the stage analogy to his mature style of painting, Wood occasionally designed sets for the Cedar Rapids community theater in the late twenties and early thirties. It was during those years that he created his most fanciful farmscapes, perfect illustrations of Stein's most instructive phrases. The rhythmically related intervals of Wood's breakthrough painting of 1929, *Black Barn* (Fig. 111), followed by those of his oil study for *Stone City, Iowa* (see Fig. 2), maintain a continuous back-and-forth movement, what Stein calls a "rhythmic throwback to the frontal plane."[39] While Picasso and Braque shunned mere surface decoration, they, in Stein's

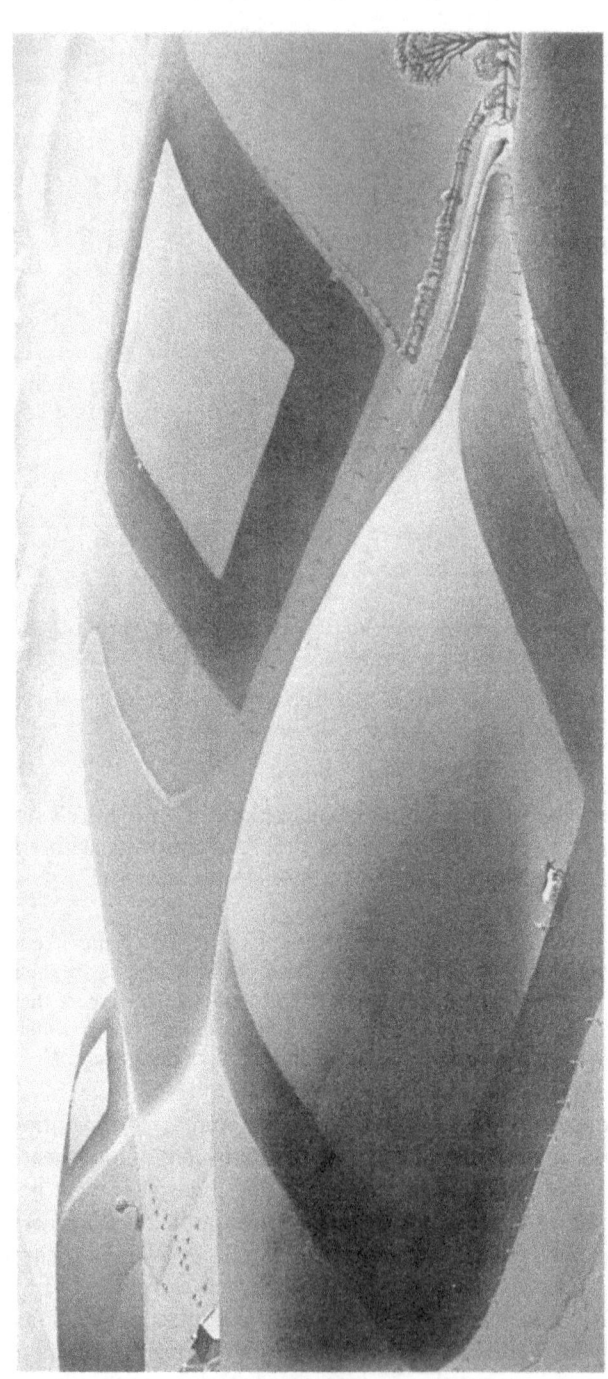

Figure 112. Grant Wood. *Spring Turning*. 1936. Oil on masonite panel, 18¼ × 40¼ in. Reynolda House, Museum of American Art, Winston-Salem, North Carolina; gift of Barbara B. Millhouse. © Estate of Grant Wood/Licensed by VAGA, New York, NY.

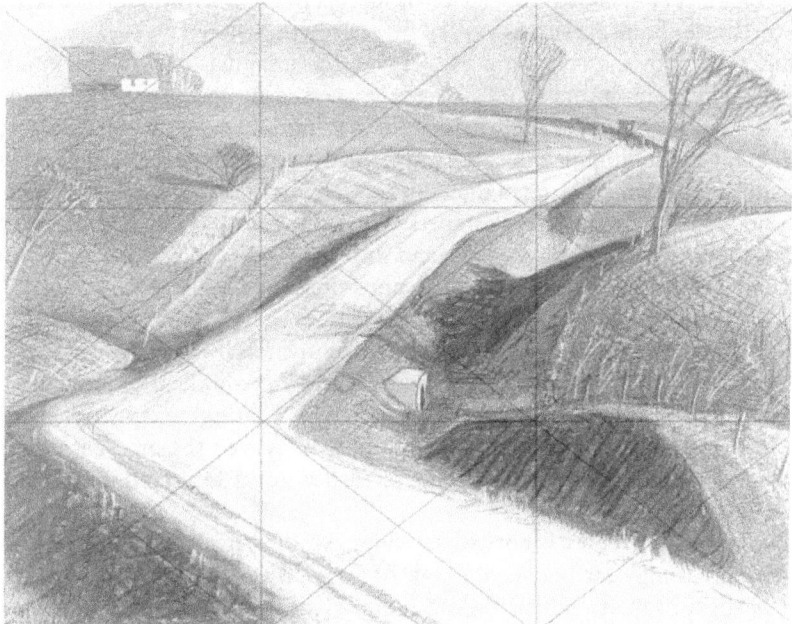

Figure 113. Grant Wood. *March.* 1940. Charcoal and chalk on paper, 18 × 23 in. Private Collection. © Estate of Grant Wood/Licensed by VAGA, New York, NY.

opinion, never effectively controlled the relationship of forms in recessive space: "The departure from design on a flat surface leads to all these difficulties of design in depth, which the modern artists have tried to solve." [40]

Stein also stressed a trait that Batchelder discussed as good "curve sense." Wood eventually applied it in such later landscapes as his great, green stretch of a painting, *Spring Turning* (Fig. 112) and in the rather vertiginous drawing of the same year, *Plowing* (see Fig. 95). In their wide-open expanses of space, the broad surfaces of undulating, earth-mother groundswells acquire decorative patches of warm brown soil at the hands of the plowmen. The painter, with the lasting encouragement of his foremost teacher and the theoretical approval of a contemporary critic, amplified and manipulated visual information that to him might have seemed too familiar. Surrounding "hill country becomes transformed," abstracted beyond the picturesque:

The lines are made to serve in a definite way instead of rolling accidentally. By moving the pictorial planes backward or forward, masses are flattened or developed at will. The plasticity of natural materials is in fact almost infinite, if only one has learned to mould them. [41]

195

Batchelder stressed the "curve of force," or, to borrow John Ruskin's term, the "infinite curve," as expressive of growth, a sign of fecund vitality.[42] If motivated by the "play impulse," a vigorous imagination would rekindle the legendary innocence and pleasure witnessed in "primitive" work and in the work of medieval craftsmen.[43] Romantic historicism aside, it was arguably a play impulse that activated the dynamic curve sense of Wood's major pictures and hastened them into the streamlined period of Art Deco. In line with the industrial designers who by the mid-1930s had modeled the modern automobile, airplane, and ship using aerodynamic calculations, Wood superimposed streamlined compositions over his system of "thirds," an intricate grid pattern of precisely drafted verticals and horizontals intersected with diagonals (Fig. 113).[44] Now motivated by a mechanistic aesthetic that annulled the commonplace, Wood's methodical process minimized the "applied ornaments" of local color. Through exaggerations of man-made angles and rounded topography, it stylized the inherent nature of even the most desolate segments of eastern Iowa farmland into an appealing abstraction.

Regionalist identity notwithstanding, Wood's mature paintings, few and increasingly far between, speak of their process and design as a crucial aspect of their content and meaning. Their independence of invention characterizes the modernism of his generation of American painters. For the majority of the Stieglitz circle of artists, as in the works of Dove and O'Keeffe, form and subject matter were fortunately not strictly derived from the most immediate source of modern painting: the Cubism of Picasso and Braque.

This free spirit may also be seen in the nonfigurative realism of three other major modernists. Charles Demuth, Charles Sheeler, and Marsden Hartley followed the advice of their mutual friend, the doctor-poet William Carlos Williams, and became a triumvirate of American place painting more regionally oriented than the three Regionalists themselves. The next three chapters concentrate on this stylistic revelation.

9

Charles Demuth's Affair
With Lancaster, Pa.

Throughout their decade of ascent and decline, the midwestern Regionalists were advised by the poet-turned-critic Thomas Craven to paint the
things they knew best: the common reality of their particular place and
time, the daily existence of the people with whom they grew up. Wood and
Benton, as leading publicists of the movement, said that this was what they
wanted to do, and claimed to be doing it. In fact, however, much of their
painting dwells on far-reaching legends and myths, personal fantasies, and
caricature. Their silent partner, Curry, came closest to doing what Craven
advocated. He painted, especially at the beginning of his career in Westport, Connecticut, moments on a Kansas farm (Fig. 114). But, as we have
seen, he too abandoned such personal memories for historical melodrama,
social criticism, and sporadic political protest (see Figs. 28–29). In short,
not one of the three midwestern Regionalists, no matter what he might de-
claim, concentrated for long on local realities. As a group, they did not
conform to the regional genre tradition of their American predecessors,
William Mount, George Bingham, Charles Russell, and John Sloan.

First-generation American modernists, in keeping with inaccurate, too
often sensational, publicity about what avant-garde artists were doing in
Paris, were not expected to depict the specifics of their surroundings.[1]
Yet the three closest painter friends of William Carlos Williams—Charles
Demuth, Charles Sheeler, and Marsden Hartley—while averse to traditional figurative realism, did indeed incline toward continuous place identification in their paintings of intensely observed things. In ironic contrast to the sum and substance of Wood, Benton, and Curry's diverse
efforts, the Williams trio were ultimately attached to a few basic themes of
tangible identification: hometown mills and warehouses, heavy industrial
complexes, or the rugged scenery of Maine. This attachment places them

197

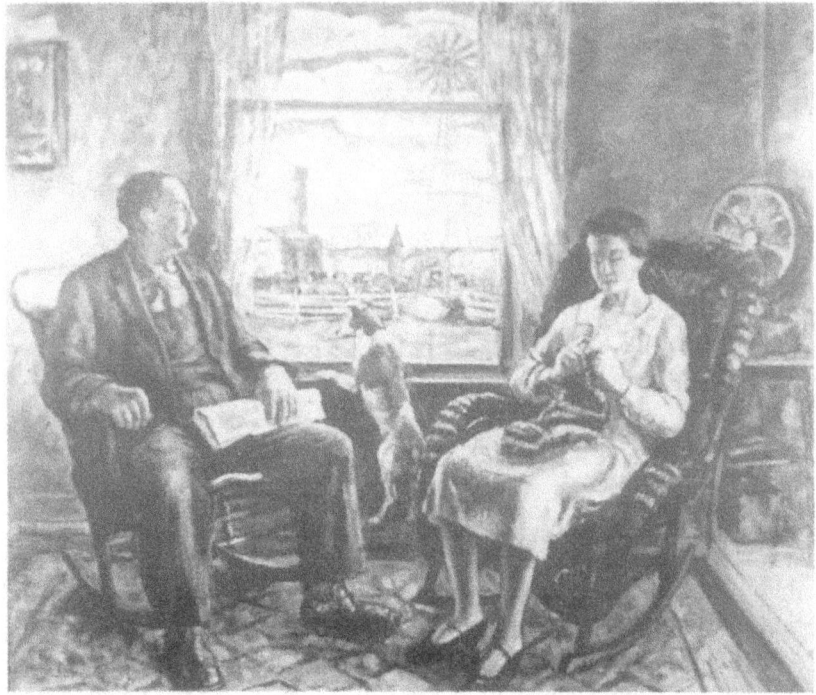

Figure 114. John Steuart Curry. *Portrait: My Mother and Father*. 1929. Oil on canvas, 30 × 36 in. D. Wigmore Fine Art, Inc., New York, N.Y. Courtesy of D. Wigmore Fine Art, Inc. New York, N.Y.

in solid accord with any generic definition of regionalism as localization. Individual perceptions of localized facts, free from any vested interest in promoting the ideology of an art movement vis-à-vis the art market, also distinguished them from the midwestern Regionalists' competitive drive to be hailed as the nation's laureate painters.

According to Williams, poems and paintings (whatever their subject matter) were to be precise thing-machines reflective of the materialistic culture of the United States. As a national way of art, they were to be, for better or worse, efficient re-enactments of a new high-speed life: "rapid-transit" moments of what the cultural historian Cecelia Tichi characterizes as "the poetics of the gear-and-girder world."[2] Demuth painted immaculate pictures of the factories and warehouses of his hometown, Lancaster, Pennsylvania. As he had done to its early American church towers, he tended to dematerialize industrial structures through translucent surface faceting that diminished the objectivist immediacy Williams sought (see Figs. 123, 126). Still, the high stacks, smoke, vents, and wall signs, local landmarks of industry and commerce, are what one tends to remember about his pictures, as the linear refinements of their modernist compositions fade from view.

Sheeler surpassed Demuth in complying with Williams's wishes. His photograph-paintings of craftwork and carpentry in Bucks County, Pennsylvania, or of the new industrial complex at River Rouge, Michigan, the Ford Motor plant, remained purely focused on the objects at hand (see Fig. 132). Hartley, seemingly oblivious of the machine age, culminated his career by returning to Maine to picture its rocks, trees, logs, streams, and highest mountain (see Figs. 145–147). His thick impasto bothered Williams, who thought it distracted from the otherwise clear perception of native material.

Resistance to European-derived eclecticism through individualized indigenousness preoccupied the Williams trio as much as it did the midwestern "triumvirate." It did so, however, without the defensiveness or remorse that Benton appeared to suffer for previous Cubist-generated traits. After Stieglitz compared some of his paintings unfavorably with works by O'Keeffe, Benton refused to revisit the galleries of the patron-dealer. He may consequently have lost sight of abstract paintings subsequent to 1919. His later attacks on nonfigurative painting by Americans seem anachronistic, apparently aimed at early, somewhat more eclectic phases from 1910 to 1917, when Benton himself, according to his own account, was "zigzagging" as an Impressionist, Neo-Impressionist, Cézannist, Synchromist, and Constructivist.[3] Even when they committed stylistic appropriation from Cubism, Demuth, Sheeler, and Hartley subordinated it to a given subject matter with a special-place meaning. Personal choices of imagery eliminated stylistic clichés, such as the guitars and harlequins belonging to the Cubism of Picasso and Braque.

It was precisely this emphasis on independence that the three diverse painters shared with their poet friend. Williams too struggled to liberate his works from predetermined directives of style. He wished in particular to disassociate his poetry from the highly intellectual, persistently metaphoric Imagism practiced by its originator and short-termed impresario, Ezra Pound, and his compatriots Hilda Doolittle and Amy Lowell. Williams's quest for immediate clarity of form and content through the elimination of the nonessential carried him to a high level of "objectivism."[4] By the early thirties he was questioning Cubist-Futurist devices of simultaneity. Already in the mid-teens he had become attracted to Marcel Duchamp's Dada "ready-mades," which inspired him to focus on "no ideas but in things." This principle must have entered the discussions of the small, Duchamp-centered circle of avant-garde artists and writers in which Williams participated at the New York apartment of the patron Walter Arensberg.[5]

Retention of solid facts alone distinguished major works by Williams

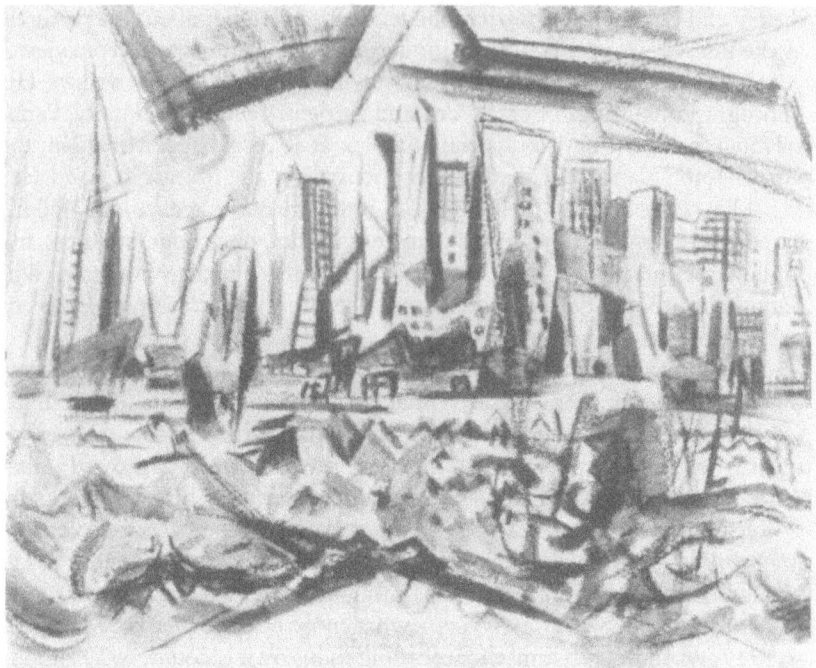

Figure 115. John Marin. *Lower Manhattan from the River, No. 2.* 1921. Watercolor. Collection of John Marin, Jr.

and his three painter friends from the greatly diminished object matter of other prominent, locale-oriented modernists in the United States. Generated by the dynamism of his original visual vocabulary, John Marin's responses to Maine and Manhattan speak of flux and vitality, whether natural or urban (Fig. 115). Joseph Stella went from Coney Island to the Brooklyn Bridge, dissolving both into mystical abstractions via Futurism (Fig. 116). Arthur Dove dematerialized tangible "extractions" from nature into contemplative abstractions (Fig. 117). Georgia O'Keeffe's closeup magnifications of flowers and leaves, pelvic bones, crosses, and crevices isolate these objects into dissociated abstract forms (Fig. 118). And Stuart Davis's brightly patterned, interlocking planes, jazzed up with ornamental calligraphy, vibrate to the beat of syncopated, big-city tempos (Fig. 119).

Efforts by Demuth, Sheeler, and Hartley to maintain aesthetic distance from subject matter, even when it contained deep personal associations, paralleled Williams's concisely composed poetry. Unable to abstain altogether from subjective reactions, however, they revealed their attachments to tangible realities of particular places much more regularly than

200

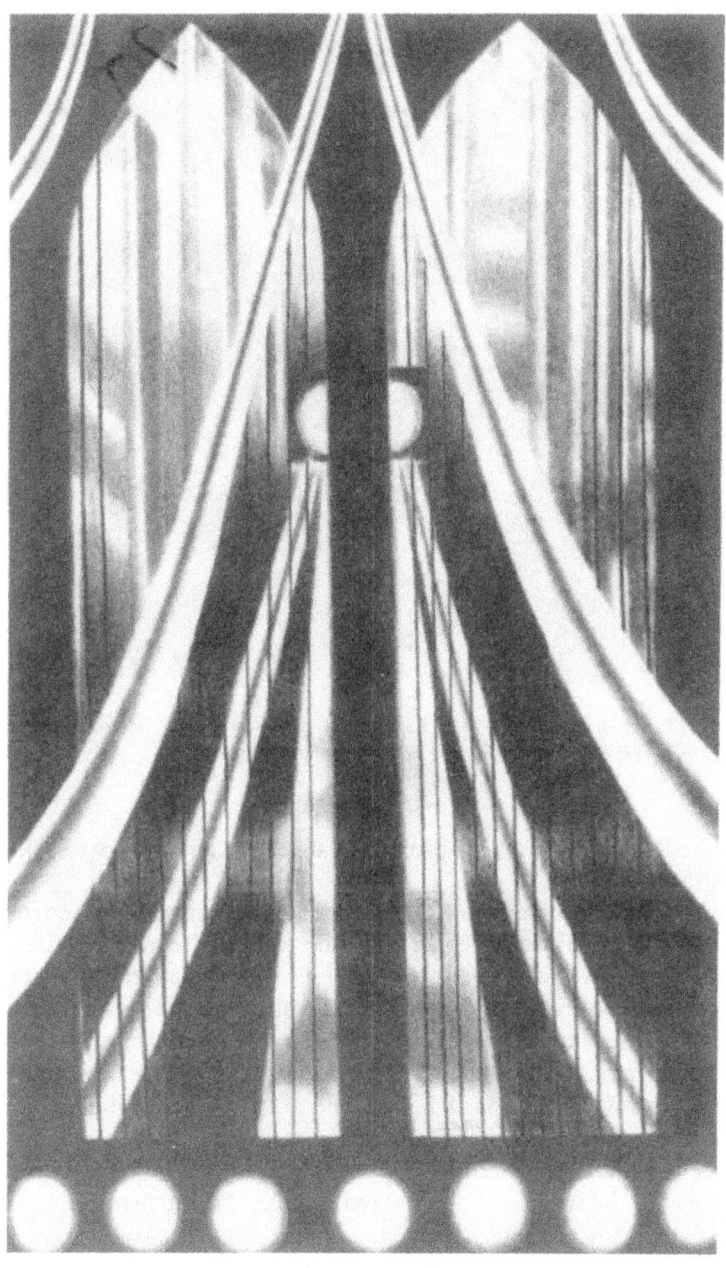

Figure 116. Joseph Stella. *Bridge*. c. 1936. Oil on canvas, 55½ × 35½ in. Fine Arts Museums of San Francisco, San Francisco, California; Work Projects Administration Allocation.

201

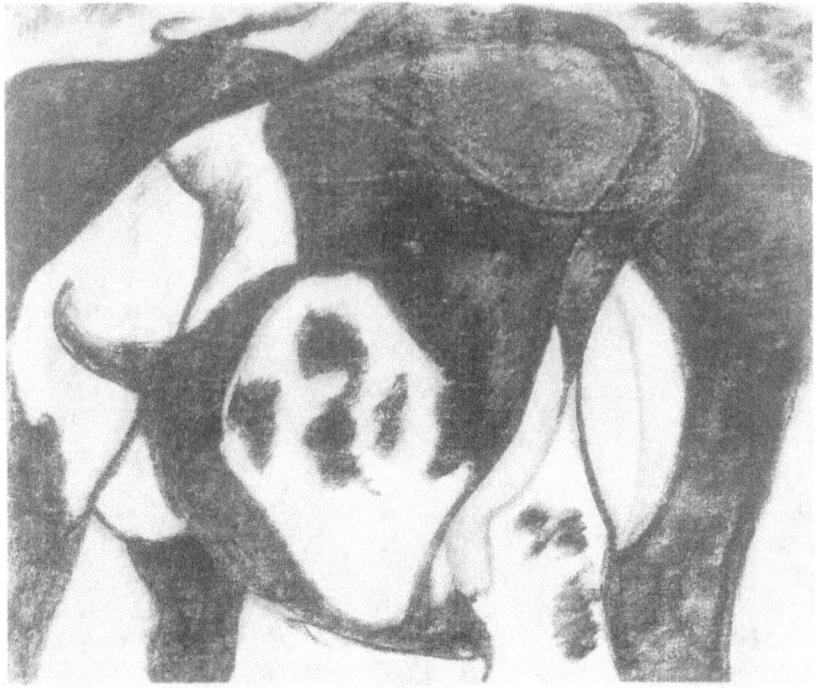

Figure 117. Arthur Dove. *Cow*. 1911. Pastel on linen, 17¾ × 21½ in. Metropolitan Museum of Art, New York City, 49.70.72; Alfred Stieglitz Collection.

did the Regionalists, whose pictorial wanderings outdistanced back-home identification.

Given his push for objective detachment, Williams understandably suffered moments of doubt concerning the form and content of Demuth's major works. Regardless of their indelible object matter, they fluctuated too much between fashionable abstraction and personal sentiments, underlined by commentary titles. Though the honored subject and recipient of the most famous of Demuth's "poster portraits," *I Saw the Figure 5 in Gold (Homage to William Carlos Williams)* (Fig. 120), Williams maintained that its composition would have been more successful if its forms had been better stabilized. Specifically, the title figure should have been made to merge with the surface of its solid red center.[6] His criticism indicates Williams's uneasiness about having an animated, Futurist-style succession of 5's flying out of the picture plane at an accelerated, rather melodramatic, rate. After all, the momentary visual intensity, the "direct experience of the perceived moment" captured by the spontaneously written poem "The

202

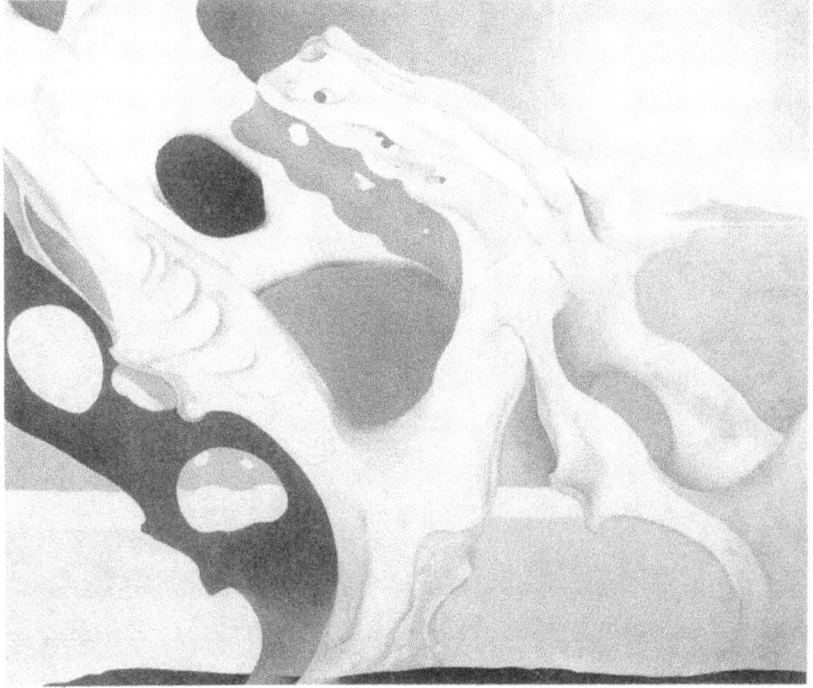

Figure 118. Georgia O'Keeffe. *Pelvis with Shadows and the Moon.* 1943. Oil on canvas, 40 × 48¾ in. Frank Lloyd Wright Foundation, Scottsdale, Arizona.

Great Figure," had imprinted the gold figure 5 on his memory as the fire engine flashed by at the end of the street.[7] His earlier discomfort with Demuth's 1920 tempera, *Machinery (For W. Carlos W.)* (Fig. 121), as analogous to a woman suggests that the painter tended to go too far for the poet-doctor's taste in creating "stylized symbols" instead of focusing exclusively on solid facts that speak for themselves.[8]

Even Demuth's most explicit pictures of favorite local buildings risked compromising the "thingness" Williams advocated. Whether portraying neighborhood church towers (Fig. 122) or interpreting nearby factories, water towers, or grain elevators, his major compositions entail precisely ruled syncopations of delicate, translucent faceting, having little to do with the tangible objects involved. At times this surface technique gives the impression of refracted shafts of light, but more often it results in an ambiguity of pictorial space that, alternating from deep to shallow, pays small heed to the picture plane. With no simultaneity of views involved, this prismatic effect tends to disrupt and dislocate given particulars into

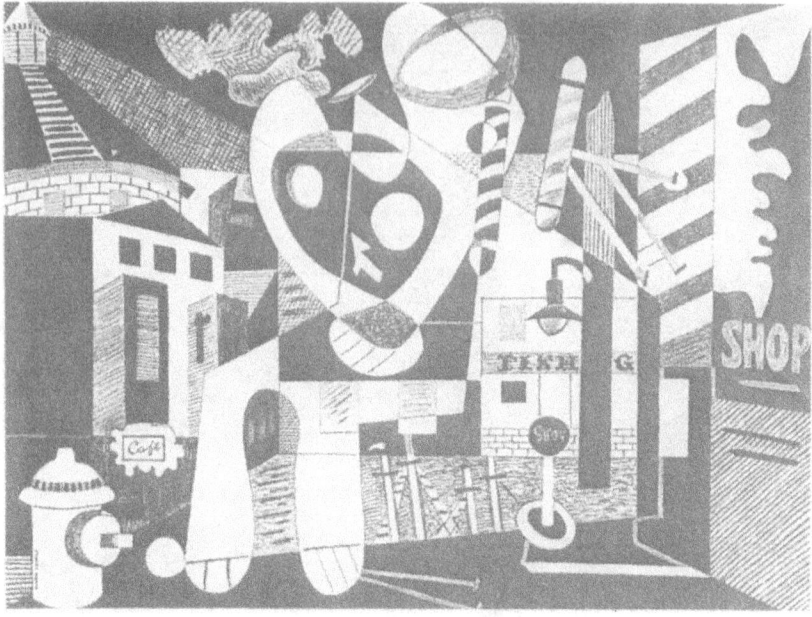

Figure 119. Stuart Davis. *Barber Shop Chord*. 1931. Lithograph, 14 × 19 in. Private collection.
© Estate of Stuart Davis/Licensed by VAGA, New York, NY

a suspended plurality. As the mechanically engineered compositions and streamlined stylizations in Grant Wood's fantasy farmscapes (see Fig. 95) contradict his misgivings about the beneficial nature of modern mechanization, the straight-edge lines that overlie Demuth's renderings of industrial object matter might, in a subtle but overt fashion, indicate his apprehension toward machines. Nevertheless, while not a Sheeler, Demuth was attracted to the geometric power of local large factory forms and appreciated the "ready-made" beauty of their functional accessories.

The moderate position toward industry conveyed in Demuth's paintings resembles the mediating stance of Lewis Mumford in a debate that flourished during the twenties. Antiscience, anti-industrial New Humanism was represented by the critics Irving Babbitt and Paul Elmer More; and proscience, promachinery New Mechanism was represented by the historian Charles Beard and the philosopher John Dewey.[9] While he hated skyscrapers as "mere exercises in technique, having little to do with the human arts of seeing, feeling and living,"[10] Mumford looked to machine-made implements and purely utilitarian structures as possible perpetrators of a new aesthetic sensitivity charged with utopian potential. In "Machinery and the Modern Style" (1921), he was willing to give machines the benefit of his doubt.

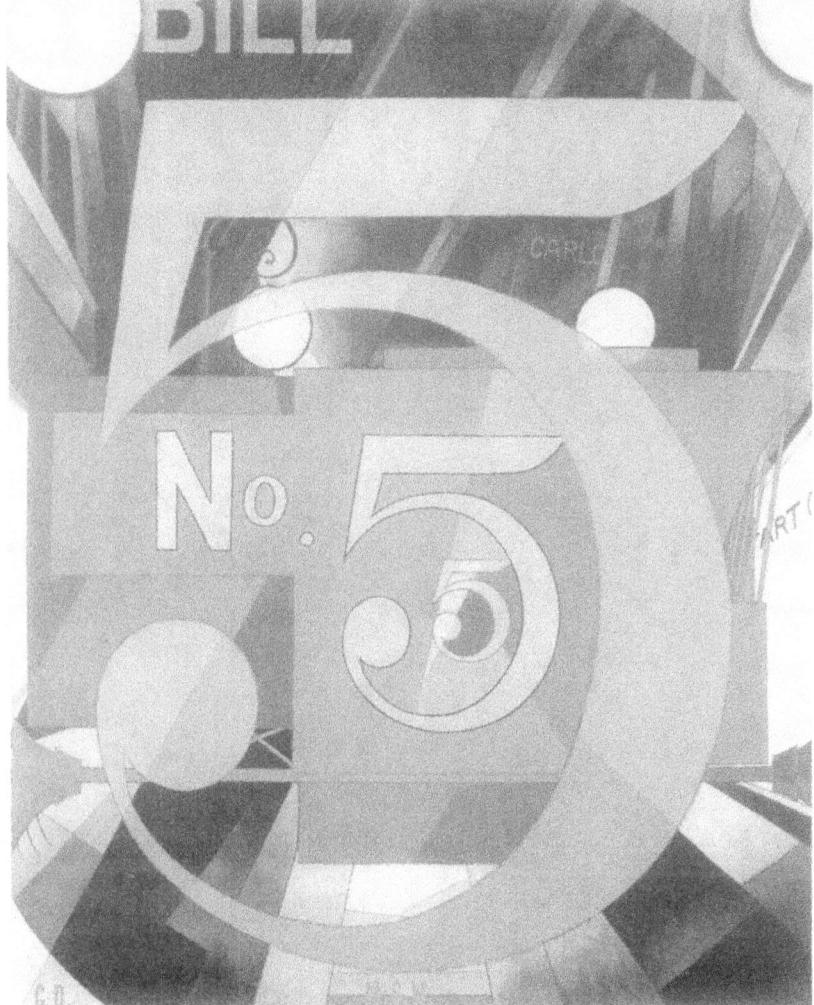

Figure 120. Charles Demuth. *I Saw the Figure 5 in Gold (Homage to William Carlos Williams)*. 1928. Oil on board, 35½ × 30 in. Metropolitan Museum of Art, New York City, 49.59.1; Alfred Stieglitz Collection.

We have yet to see what human fulfillments the machine may bring about when we finally come to grips with it. We must neither allow ourselves to be overridden by a crude and boisterous utilitarianism nor turn a repugnant ineffectual face completely away from the instrument which promises to liberate the community.[11]

Avoiding Main Street sentimentality in his paintings of hometown landmarks, Demuth could not refrain from sly comment, or from what

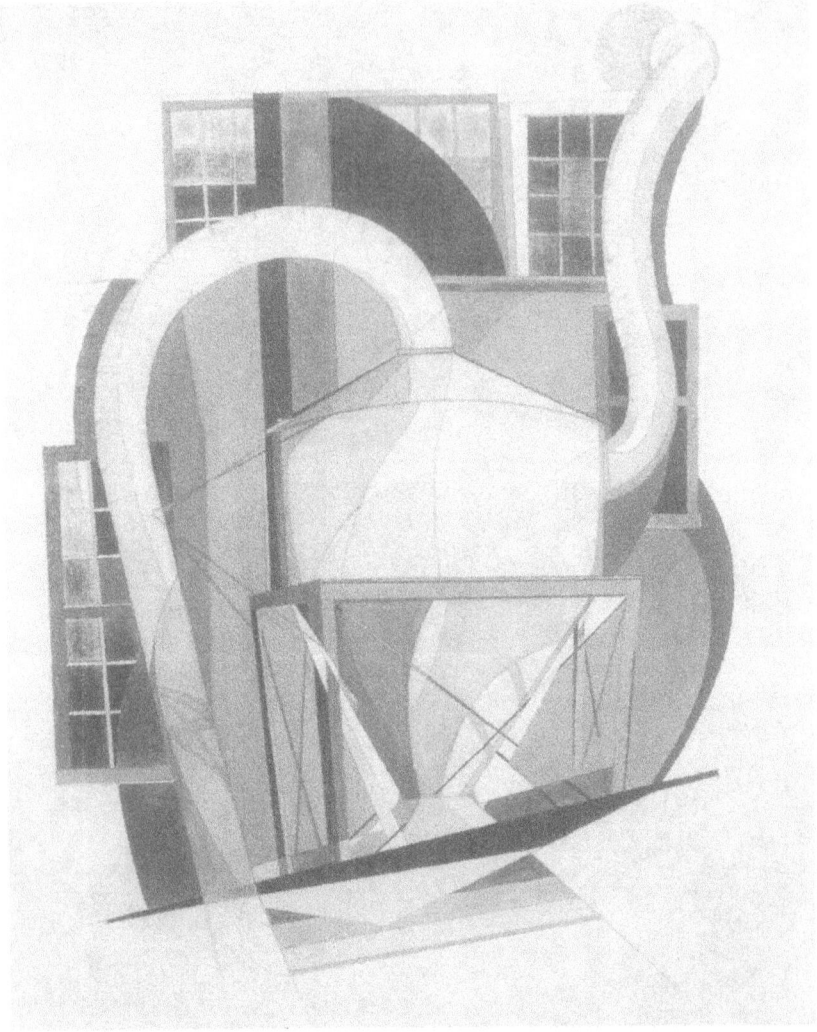

Figure 121. Charles Demuth. *Machinery (For W. Carlos W.)*. 1920. Tempera and pencil on board, 24 × 19⅞ in. Metropolitan Museum of Art, New York City, 49.59.2; Alfred Stieglitz Collection.

Wood advocated as "editorializing." He enlivened his renditions of Lancaster buildings with enigmatically ironic titles that tempered the *Ding an sich* immediacy that Williams deemed appropriate for a new American art. Yet, while speaking in jest about a machine-ridden society geared to business, Demuth did not set out to expose its ugly effects on the way people live. In his 1920 tempera *End of the Parade, Coatesville, Pa.* (Fig. 123),

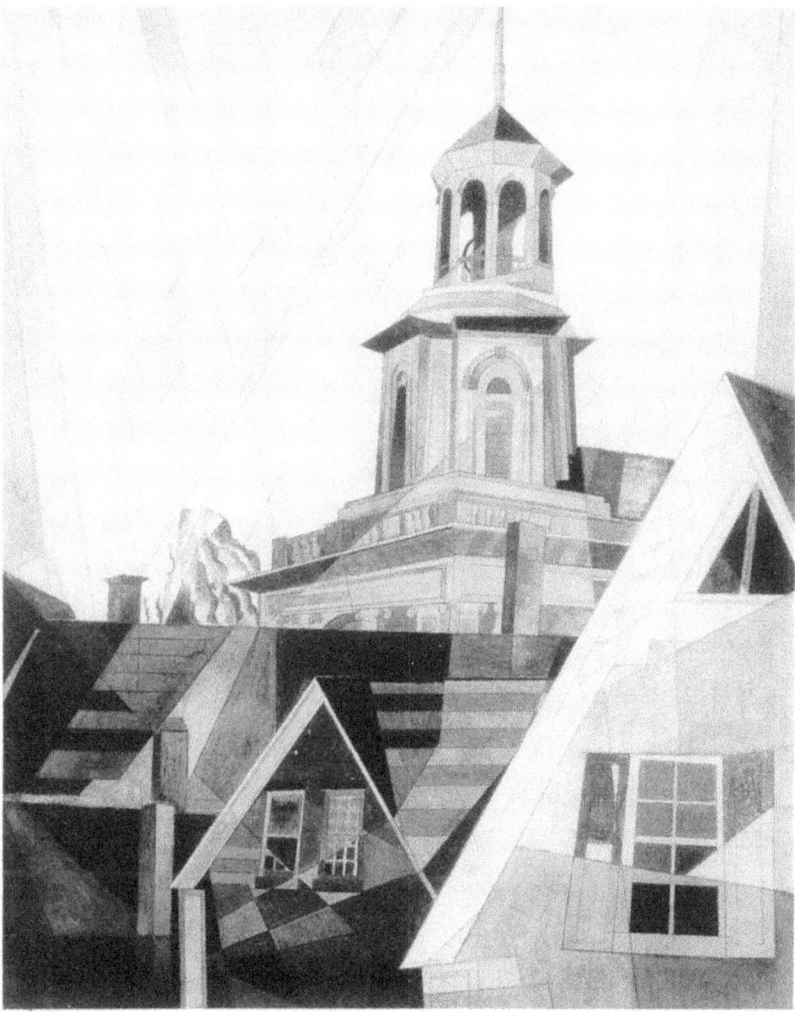

Figure 122. Charles Demuth. *After Sir Christopher Wren.*1920. Watercolor, gouache, and pencil on board, 24 × 20 in. Metropolitan Museum of Art, New York City, 1984.433.156; bequest of Scofield Thayer.

drawn just down the road from Lancaster and purchased within weeks by Williams from the Daniel Gallery in Manhattan, or in the less localized *Incense of a New Church* (Fig. 124) of a year later, Demuth rendered utilitarian forms into attractive pictorial shapes and introduced a paradoxical appeal to softly modulated smudge and stylized smoke. Braiding steelmill fumes into decorative "incense" delivered a whimsical comment with, perhaps inadvertently, a critical edge. The blessed stench of industry filling the

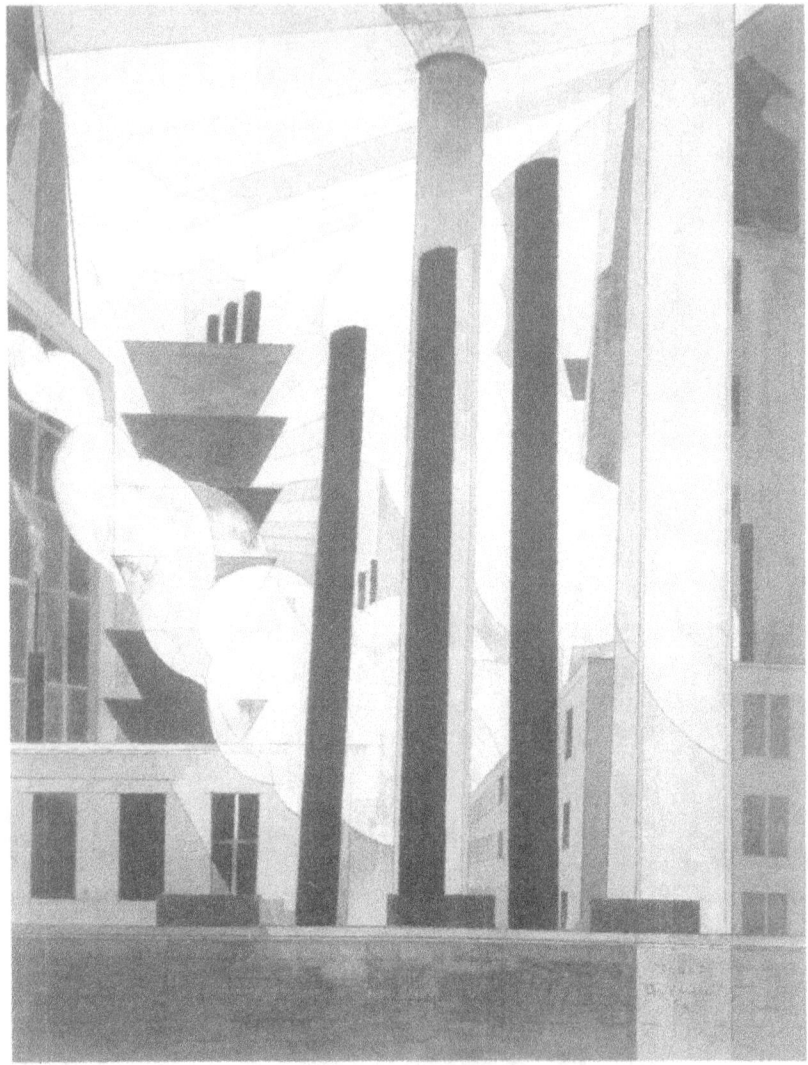

Figure 123. Charles Demuth. *End of the Parade, Coatesville, Pa.* 1920. Tempera and pencil on board, 19⅞ × 15¾ in. Curtis Galleries, Minneapolis, Minnesota.

air and polluting the atmosphere, however, denoted full-powered profits, and Demuth, the heir to a longstanding family business, does not seem to have had anything against that. Inscribing the factory windows of *Business* (Fig. 125) with digits and days of the week transformed them into a chart or calendar that parodies the mechanical efficiency of corporate management and its administrative computations.[12]

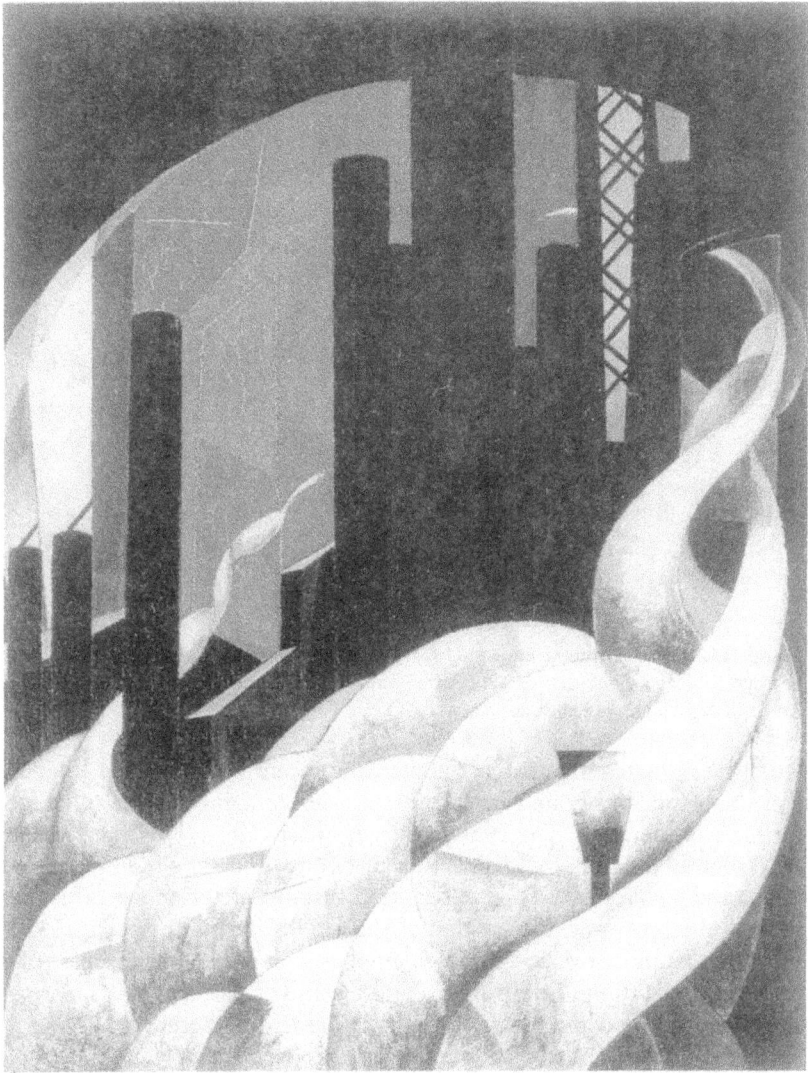

Figure 124. Charles Demuth. *Incense of a New Church*. 1921. Oil on canvas, 26 × 20⅛ in. Columbus Museum of Art, Columbus, Ohio, 31.135; gift of Ferdinand Howald.

Interspersed with watercolors of fruits and flowers and poster portraits, Demuth's most provocative oil paintings of Lancaster subjects continued to bear ironic titles that serve as clues to content. He doubtless intended a metaphoric meaning for his best-known and most enigmatic painting, *My Egypt* of 1927 (Fig. 126). Since a solution to its verbal-versus-visual riddle

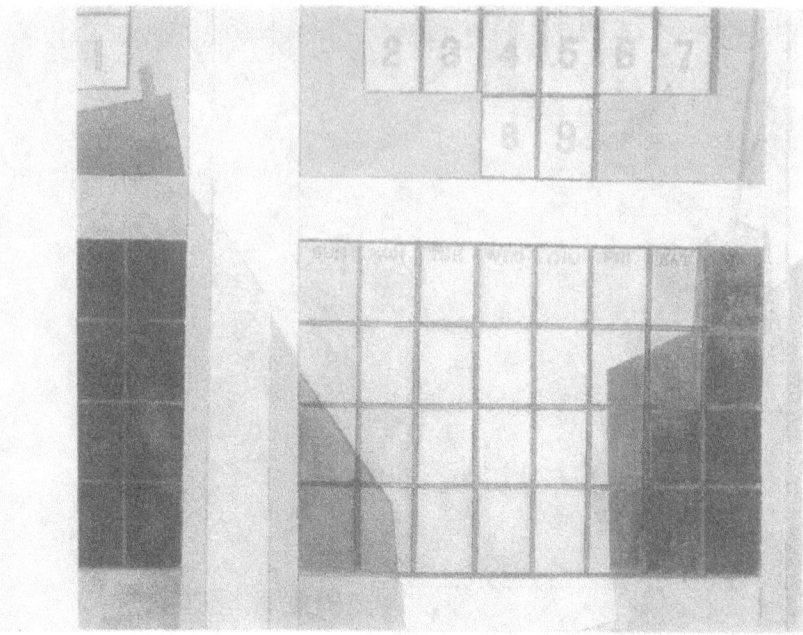

Figure 125. Charles Demuth. *Business*. 1921. Oil on canvas, 20 × 24½ in. Art Institute of Chicago, Chicago, Illinois, 1949.529; Alfred Stieglitz Collection. Photograph © 1996 The Art Institute of Chicago. All rights reserved.

is evasive,[13] its tangible subject matter, the recently constructed John W. Eshelman and Sons grain elevator in Lancaster, remains the prevailing factor for consideration. The straight-edged, quasi-Cubist, "ray line" veneer only slightly disrupts the delineation of twin cylinders, windows, funnel vents, and smokestack. Their description sustains attention even if it fails to be as discrete or detailed as that of Sheeler's *Upper Deck* (see Fig. 133).

Apart from its exotic title, such emphasis on the solid substance of a new industrial thing, firmly attached to a sense of place, came as close as Demuth possibly could to complying with the central dictum of Williams's aesthetic ideology. In the random prose of his *Spring and All* (1923), dedicated to Demuth, Williams as poet-essayist sounded momentarily like Walt Whitman. He ordered that art be "freed from the handcuffs of 'art.'"[14] When creating "a work of the imagination," the artist "does exactly what every eye must do with life, fix the particular with the universality of his own personality."[15] In *In the American Grain* (1925), he insisted that the American artist must escape from a Puritan fear and denial of the tactile world. Better yet, by concentrating on the particulars of objective reality that surround him, he will "become awake to his own locality."[16]

Mumford, in "Beauty and the Industrial Beast" (1923), once again

210

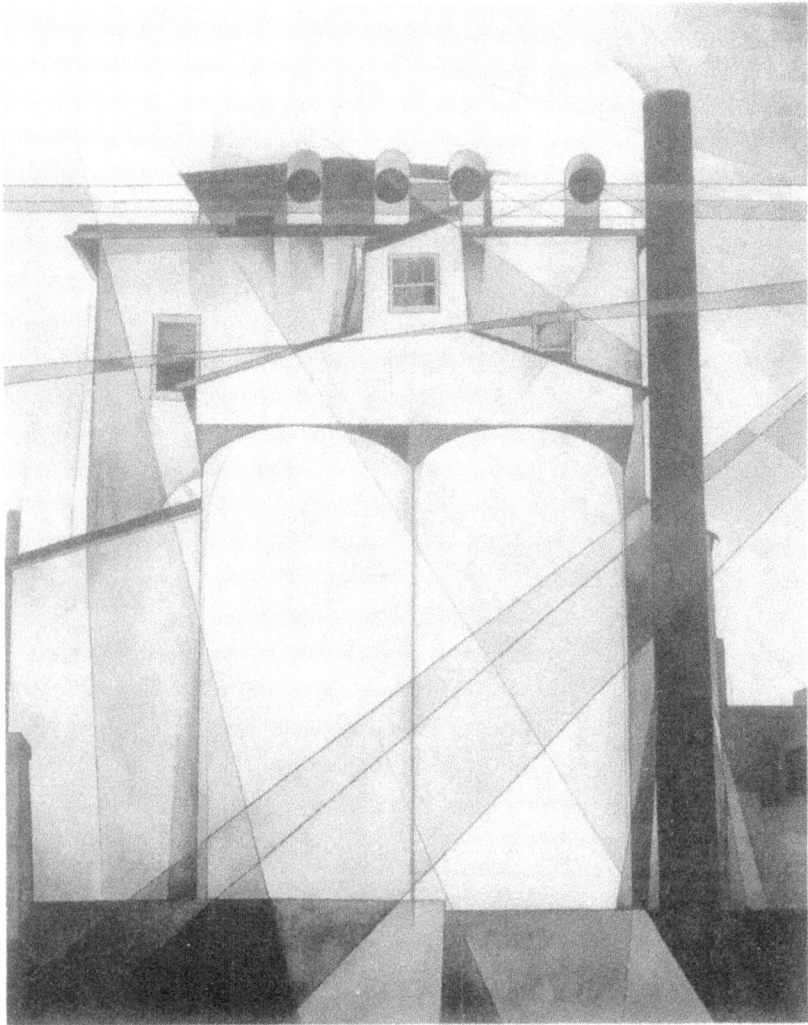

Figure 126. Charles Demuth. *My Egypt.* 1927. Oil on composition board, 35¾ × 30 in. Whitney Museum of American Art, New York City, 31.172, purchased with Funds from Gertrude Vanderbilt Whitney. Photograph © 1997 Whitney Museum of American Art.

looked at industrial structures as monuments of modern American culture. Alluding to a recent book from Berlin that featured photographs of American grain elevators, automobiles, and office buildings as "machine art,"[17] he praised the "peculiar felicities" of mechanically motivated designs and anticipated Demuth's commemoration of an indigenous monument in *My Egypt.* Independent of antiquity or academic sources, engineered into exis-

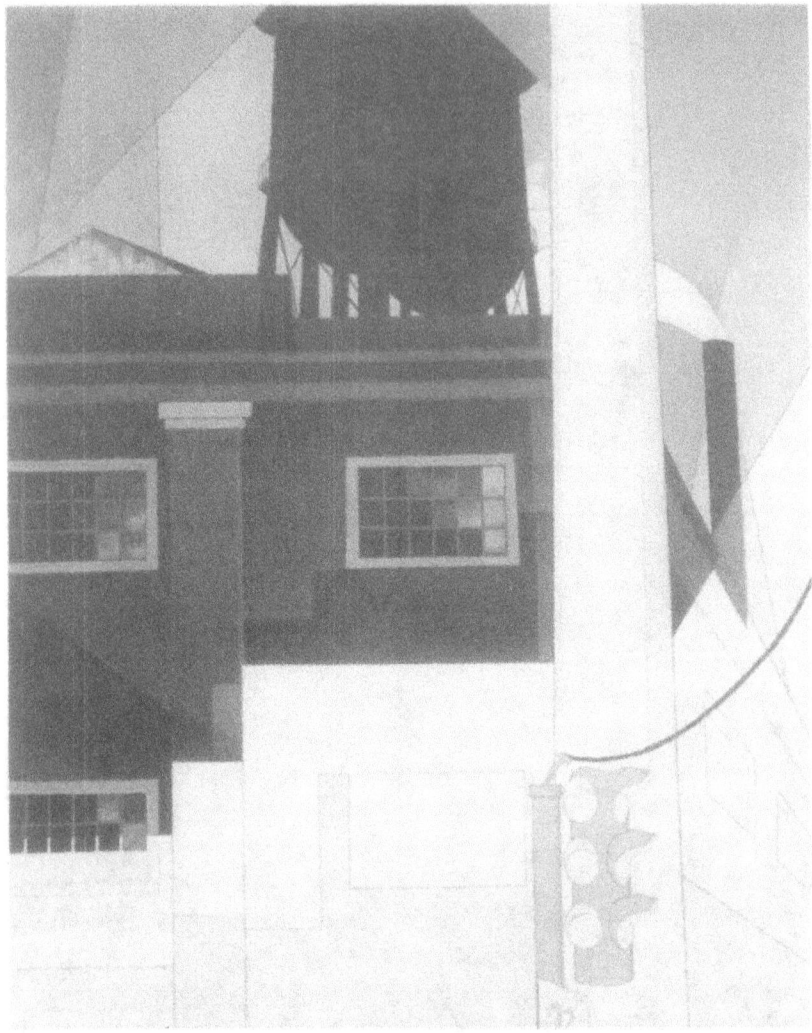

Figure 127. Charles Demuth. . . . *And the Home of the Brave*. 1931. Oil on board, 30 × 24 in. Art Institute of Chicago, Chicago, Illinois, 1948.650; gift of Georgia O'Keeffe. Photograph © 1996 The Art Institute of Chicago. All rights reserved.

tence as a utilitarian piece of equipment, the elevator attained an admirable status free of eclecticism: "Who doubts a great part of the success of these new buildings is due to the fact that the designer did not attempt to model his grain elevator after an Egyptian temple, his garage after a Louis XV stable, or his automobile after a Trojan war-chariot." [18]

Eight years later, the music and art critic Paul Rosenfeld reviewed a

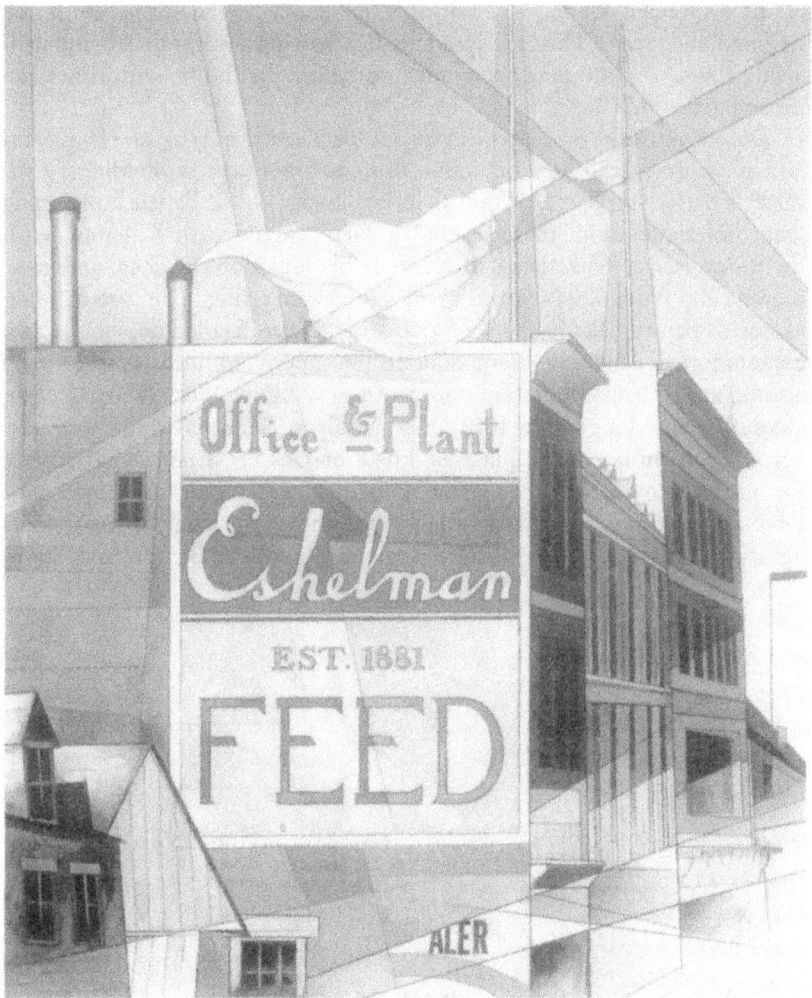

Figure 128. Charles Demuth. *Buildings, Lancaster*. 1930. Oil on board, 24 × 20 in. Whitney Museum of American Art, New York City, 58.63, gift of an anonymous donor. Photograph © 1997 Whitney Museum of American Art.

group of recent Demuth paintings. As if attempting to align the artist with Williams's increased emphasis on objectivism as a "functional aesthetic" for a machine-minded United States, Rosenfeld ignored the paintings' decorative overlays as well as their potentially metaphoric undertones. Responding enthusiastically to such works as . . . *And the Home of the Brave* (Fig. 127) and *Buildings, Lancaster* (Fig. 128), he stressed their "objective reality," their "fidelity to the object," and their "chance harmonies

213

of the American scene. . . . For all their delicacy, the forms are tense, stripped and steely. They are spontaneous creations, not induced and artificial things. . . . And they bring one into relation with life, with American life in particular." [19]

Demuth's use of word-play in his titles ended with *After All* (1933), his last oil painting and final depiction of hometown factory buildings. Lancaster's native son lent a certain skeptical humor to the debate concerning "machine civilization" that was not completely in line with Williams's wish for no-nonsense objectivism. Reserved for depictions of local industry, present and palpable, his ironic asides are exactly that. They are as often as not so private that they no more distract from detailed depictions of a contemporary American scene than do the superficial linear overlays they accompany. In this progression of paintings spanning more than a decade, Demuth created a genuine form of regionalism. Modernist, nonfigurative accounts of things in the place he knew best assert a persistently direct form of personal realism. By virtue of their subject matter they have a contemporary national relevance much more immediate than the mythically agrarian themes of the midwestern Regionalists, Wood, Benton, and Curry.

10

Charles Sheeler's Love of
a New Industrial Region

The William Carlos Williams trio of modernist realism, Demuth, Sheeler, and Hartley, varied considerably in their choices of subject matter and means of expression, as good, self-assertive modernists should. Nevertheless, each consistently identified with an American place, and together they recounted the nation's rapid alteration from wilderness to industrial worldliness. They had little if any regard for a fleeting agrarian moment—an American pastoral interlude, if you will. Their binary condensation of an enormous historical development defined the regions of what Williams, as their mentor, called the true "American grain."

Exactitude sums up Charles Sheeler's art: the broad planes of a barn, mill, skyscraper, or factory, clearly divided into components of bright illumination and dark shadow shapes, precisely contoured handicraft objects and highly detailed descriptions of industrial machinery. He sighted, framed, and claimed his places through a compound camera lens and printed, drew, or painted them in a nonnarrative order. Once he focused on and exposed a site within his region of interest, he preserved it intact from negative to finished product. In contrast to Demuth's somewhat erratic surface faceting, Sheeler's photo-determined, mechanically controlled approach to Shaker furniture or to the brand new Ford Motor factory was one of restraint. As he explained his "no comment" approach: "My things do not go out of the boundaries of the actual. Theoretically a blast furnace by someone else might symbolize a madman. But mine would always have to do with a blast furnace."[1]

While he may become personally attached to things that attract him, the artist tends to erase himself "in taking inventory," according to Leo Stein. On the other hand, the endless moment of concentrated description, the ongoing effort to particularize human craft and productivity into nonfigurative abstractions, caused Sheeler to identify with a specific locale, whether it be Bucks County, Pennsylvania, or River Rouge, Michigan. The northeastern United States was the place to be for a collector of highly refined country-made furniture and a lover of machines. Here he could record the accelerated change that they represented, from a transitory agrarian commune to an urban immensity. It was the brief span of this head-spinning historical experience that measured Sheeler's sense of place, quite in agreement with Williams's restrained view of what the true art of America should embrace.

Not many months after moving from Bucks County to New York City in 1919, Sheeler collaborated on a small film project that turned a weed patch of architecture into a cinematic montage. His partner in creating the six-minute reel *Mannahatta* was Paul Strand, whose 1917 photograph *Wheel Organization* (Fig. 129) was considered by Van Deren Coke to be the first closeup of modern machinery dedicated to its formal beauty.[2] The project gave Sheeler the photographer-painter valuable experience in composing a clutter of visual material into a cohesive succession of distinct frames. While involved in the editing process, Sheeler printed a series of still shots, some taken from a bird's-eye view, that articulate the dynamic interaction of Manhattan buildings, especially their constantly changing contrasts of light and shadow (Fig. 130). He transcribed selected frames onto several oil paintings, allowing masses and spaces to further consolidate as surface patterns (Fig. 131). Pictorial refinements of windows, ledges, smokestacks, and the like retain their identity as the most vividly impressive forms of the premier modern city, unmistakably New York.

Concurrently during the early twenties, Williams, in his efforts to subdue subjective metaphors, had begun to structure "small machines made out of words."[3] His verses built on commonplace situations, actions, emotions, and objects. With no emphasis on associative meaning, let alone premeditated symbolism, he gazed at birds, leaves, grass, girls, flowers, eyeglasses, a fire truck, and a rain-glazed red wheelbarrow. Possibly under the spell of Duchamp's Dada, these things functioned as his verbal "readymades": aspects of day-by-day existence with which to "connect" aesthetically. Originating in perceptive observation out of his windows, from his car, or on a walk, his pictorial poetry provided genuine affirmations of too often trivialized subjects. Williams scholar William Marling clarified the process: "As close as possible to the point of their perception, he translates his visual impressions into words and lines. . . . he writes of discrete objects and solid colors whenever possible. His nouns are simple and visual, his adjectives strong, and his prepositions serve to locate objects visually."[4]

In 1927 Sheeler too became "all eyes" in the middle of an industrial "city": the new Ford Motor plant in River Rouge, Michigan. Commissioned by the Fords to photograph its complex of functional components,

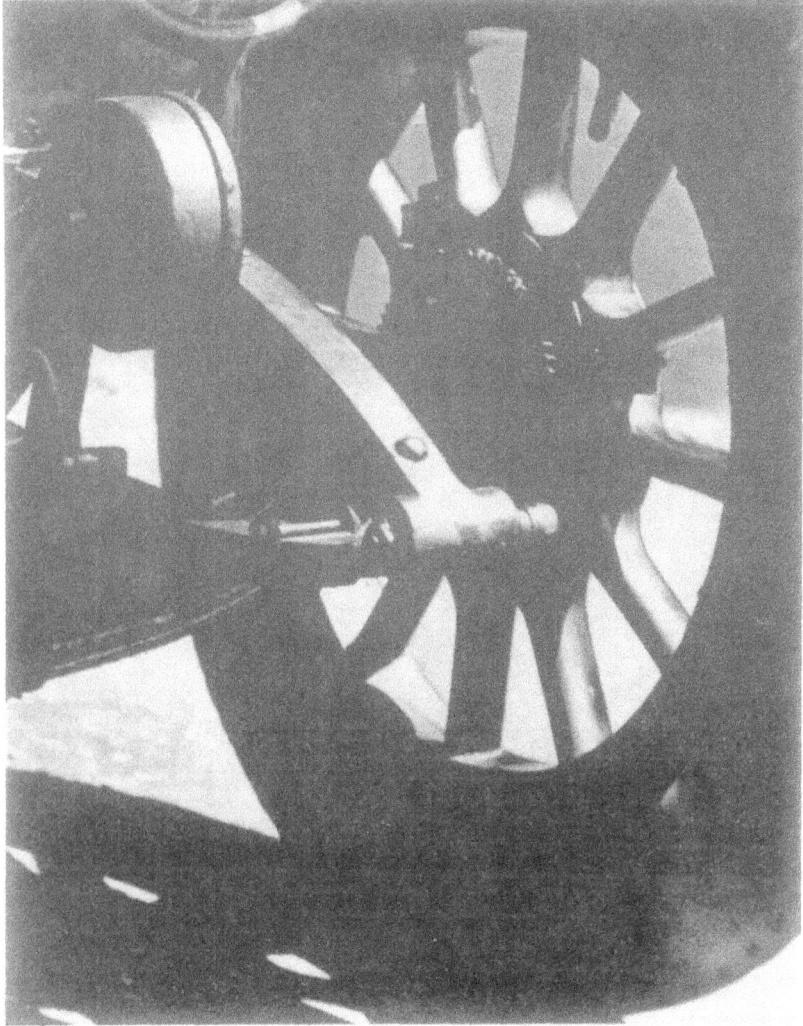

Figure 129. Paul Strand. *Wheel Organization*. 1917. Palladium print, 12¹¹⁄₁₆ × 10 in. Private collection.

he shot such structures as a stamping press, slag buggy, funnels, and the power house (Fig. 132), delivering thirty-two pictures from the many he developed and printed. Constance Rourke, the artist's equally well-known wife, described his approach and process:

He spent six weeks at the plant, clambering about the wharves and factory bridges, moving from one point of vantage to another for angles of view, taking no photo-

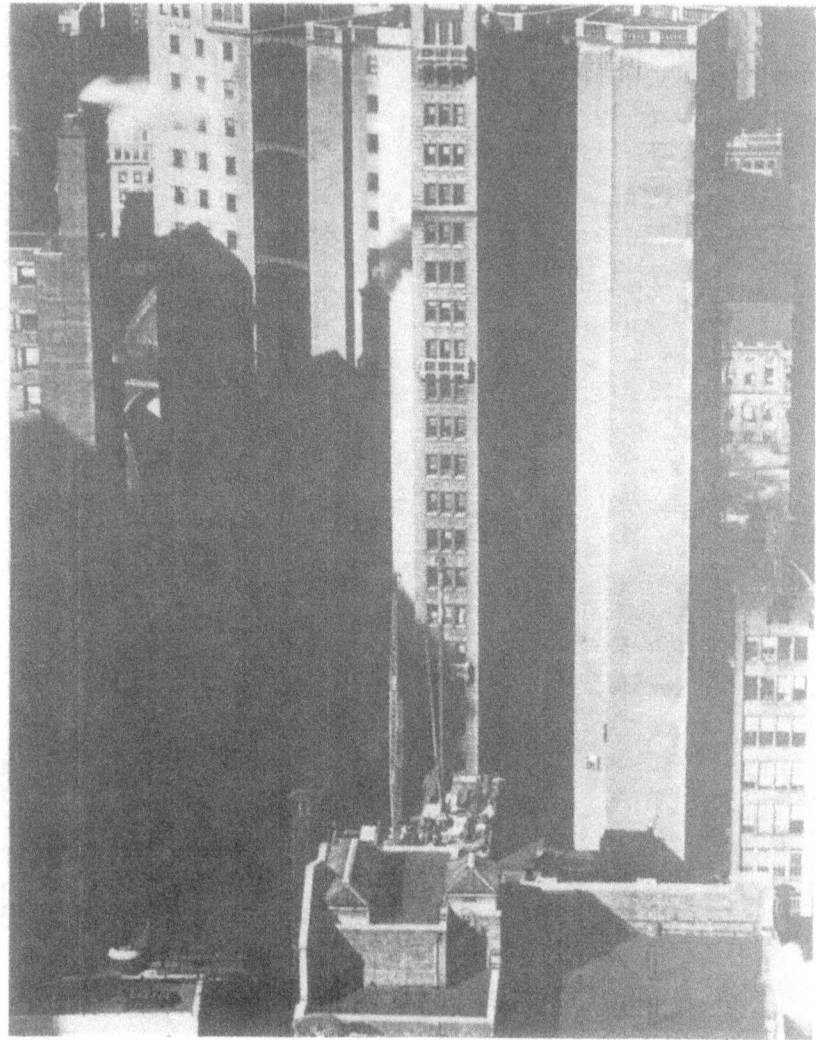

Figure 130. Charles Sheeler. *New York*. 1920. Gelatin silver print, 9 11/16 × 7 3/4 in. Private collection.

graphs until the character of these structures had become a possession for the eye, until he had approximated that saturation in form which he might have experienced more casually over a longer period.[5]

It is no wonder that Sheeler saw eye-to-eye with Williams on what American art had to be. "It was a bond," declared Williams. "We both had become aware of a fresh currency in expression, and as we talked we found

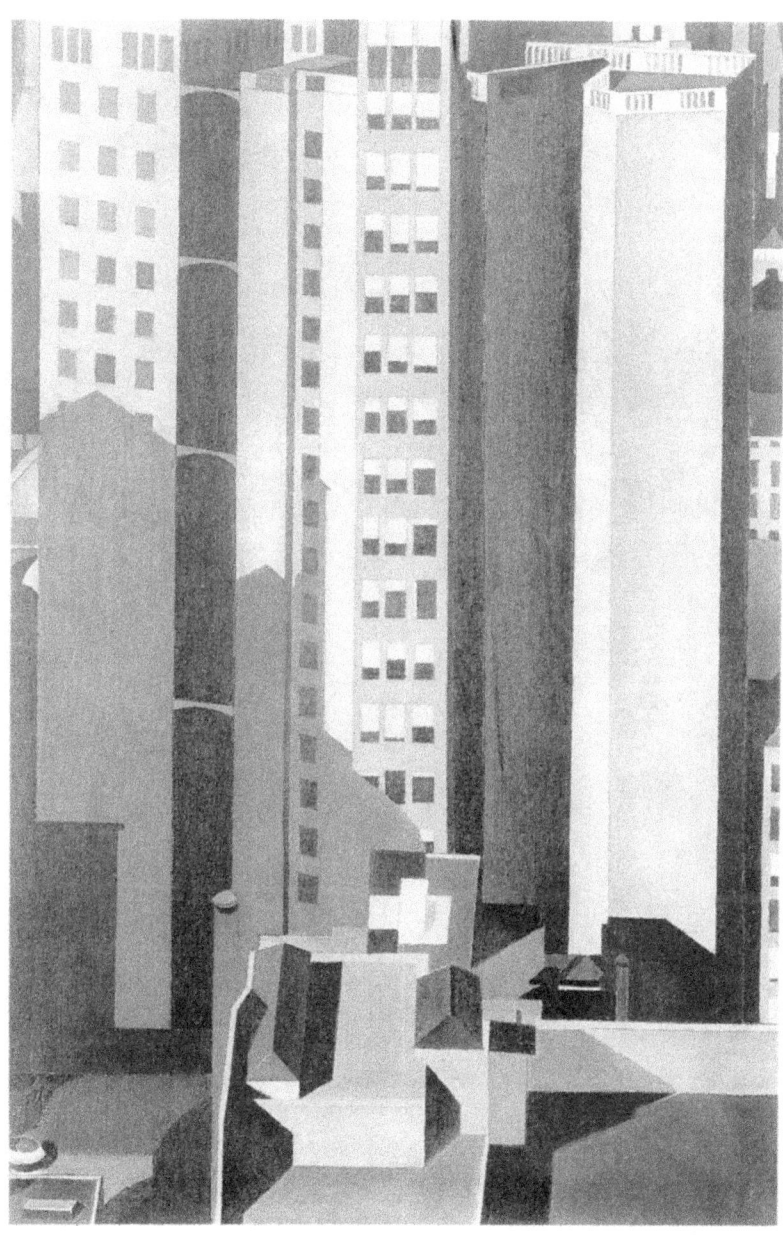

Figure 131. Charles Sheeler. *Skyscrapers*. 1922. Oil on canvas, 20 × 13 in. The Phillips Collection, Washington, D.C., acquired 1926.

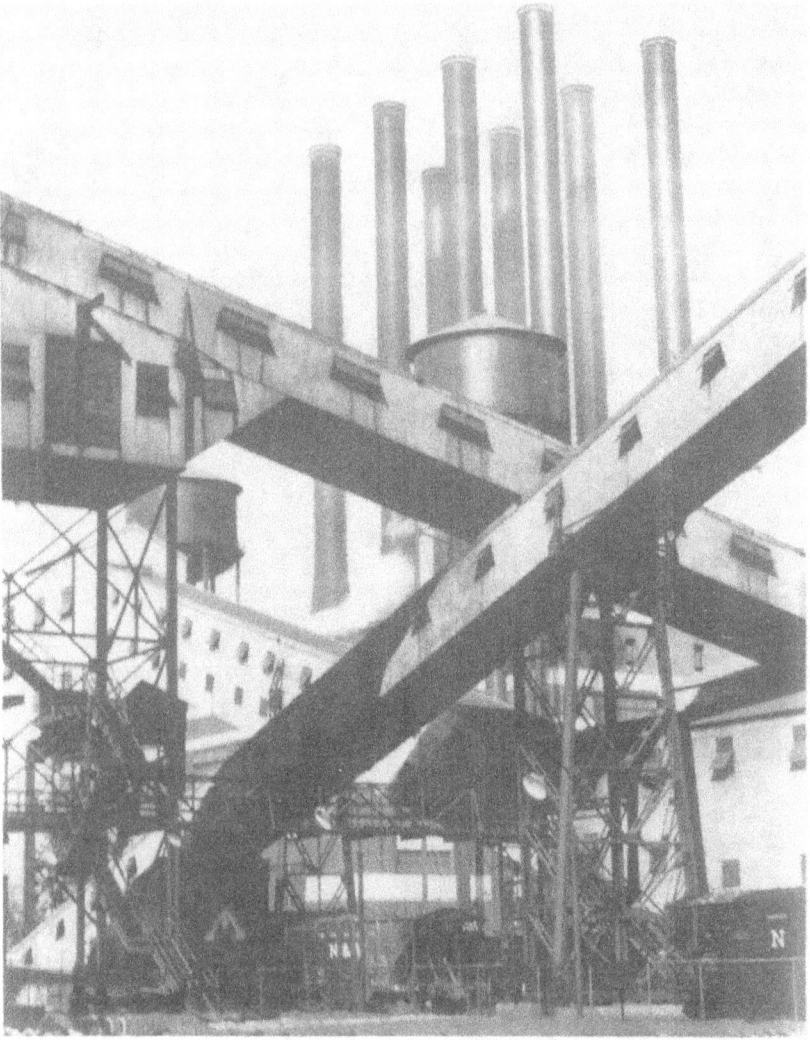

Figure 132. Charles Sheeler. *Ford River Rouge Plant*. 1927. Gelatin silver print, 9¼ × 7⁷⁄₁₆ in. Private collection.

that we both meant to lead a life which meant direct association and communication with immediate things."[6]

Sheeler was not alone in endorsing the aesthetics of Machine Age America as evoked by such sites as River Rouge. The possibility had occurred to a variety of artists in the United States and abroad, including Francis Picabia, Fernand Léger, and the architects Charles Le Corbusier and Erich Mendelsohn. The latter in particular became entranced by the cylindrical concrete grain elevators originating in Minneapolis at the turn of the century.[7] The poet Hart Crane, having completed his Brooklyn Bridge masterpiece *The Bridge,* wrote that the machine contains as much poetry as the pastoral. It would "act creatively" when, "like the unconscious nervous responses of our bodies, its connotations emanate from within — forming as spontaneous a terminology of poetic reference as the bucolic world of pasture, plow and barn."[8] Unknowingly, Crane hit upon a central dichotomy in the pictorial referents of Wood and Benton.

Traditional means of classical landscape composition would serve Sheeler all too well in two major factoryscapes derived from River Rouge photographs (see Figs. 134–135). His 1929 painting *Upper Deck,* however, closed in on a pair of electric generators (Fig. 133). Surrounded by conduits, cables, and braces, they protrude from matching ventilators and are breathed upon by two funnels, with mouths "black, like pistol shots."[9] Beautifully engineered and precisely installed, these sun-soaked objects caught and held Sheeler's light-metered attention much more than did the Northern Gothic paintings of the Madonna he would admire in German museums a month or so later. *Upper Deck,* he said, was what he had "been getting ready for." As a picture it "incorporated the structural design implied in abstraction" and as such could be "presented in a wholly realistic manner."[10] A "mental image" took form before the actual work began, and "the accumulation," despite aesthetic objectification, did take on "a personal identity."[11]

Significantly, Sheeler was unable to share Henry Adams's love for Notre Dame of Chartres or, in turn, his fear of the dynamo. Although Sheeler photographed the great Gothic cathedral in 1929 on this last trip abroad, he closed a dialogue concerning the experience by confessing: "It seems to be a persistent necessity for me to feel a sense of derivation from the country in which I live and work."[12] His thoroughgoing enthusiasm for *Upper Deck* suggests that its beautifully engineered mechanical forms signified the United States to him as had the urinal to Duchamp ten years earlier.

In *American Landscape* of 1930 (Fig. 134) and its immediate successor, *Classic Landscape* of 1931 (Fig. 135), national identity corresponded to American Scene art, suddenly fashionable that season. In contrast to Benton's pre-Crash *Boomtown* (Fig. 136), with its acutely high eye level, animated caricatures, toy cars, cardboard buildings, and discharge of black smoke, both of Sheeler's industrial scenes reverted to a traditional style of landscape painting originating in the seventeenth century. Claudian devices of a dark-into-light progression from foreground to middle ground combine with the classical convention of placid water or, in the case of the 1931 painting, resort to sunlit sand as an area of visual repose. Repoussoirs in the form of trees or hills give way to a heavy steel mechanism designed to unload Great Lake ships or are replaced by a pile of coal. Railroad tracks

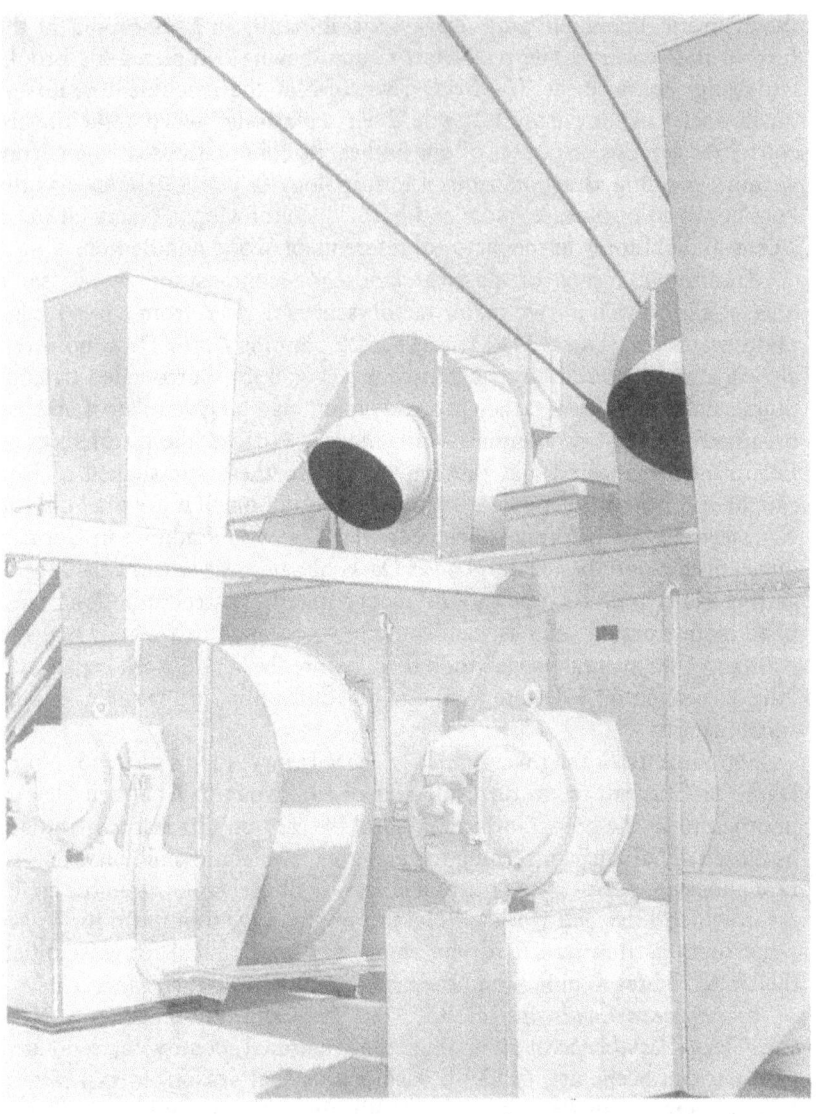

Figure 133. Charles Sheeler. *Upper Deck*. 1929. Oil on canvas 28¾ × 21¾ in. Courtesy of the Fogg Art Museum, Harvard University Art Museums, Cambridge, Massachusetts, 1933.97; Louise E. Bettens Fund.

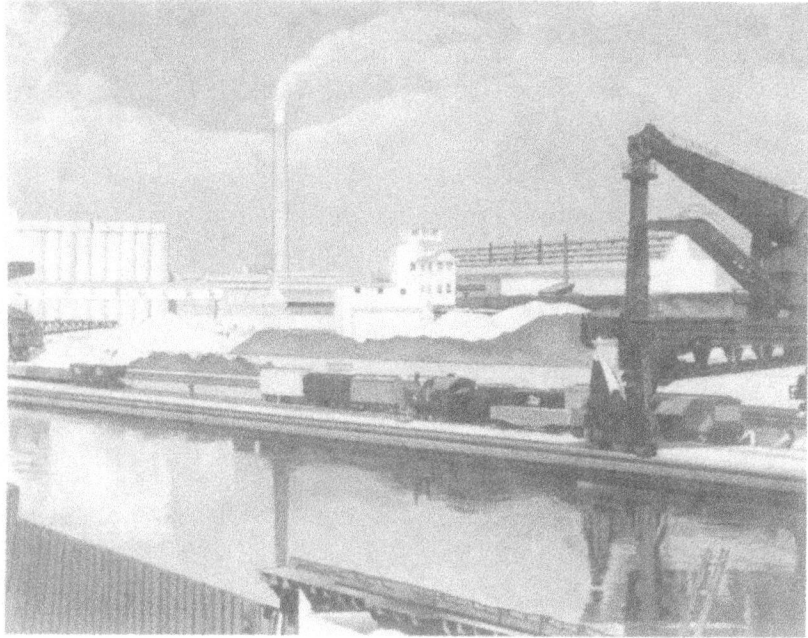

Figure 134. Charles Sheeler. *American Landscape*. 1930. Oil on canvas, 24 × 31 in. Museum of Modern Art, New York City; gift of Abby Aldrich Rockefeller, 1934.

and a freight train inscribed "Ford" lead diagonally to the temples of a new age, as precise in their linear drawing as the cross-ties and ladder rungs of the foreground. A high stack punctuates the smoke-laden sky in each painting. With conventional staffage of figures forbidden, a solitary railroad man, reduced to approximately one-fiftieth the height of the canvas, provides a judiciously placed accent mark to the left of the major vertical in *American Landscape*.

While Rourke labeled Sheeler's linear techniques "classical," [13] others have assigned specific pastoral attributes to his two most reproduced industrial images. This notion relates primarily to the absence of "picturesque" grime, grease, rust, and pollution in all of his paintings. No matter how far away or how focused and detailed, fastidiously rendered components, cleared of corrosion, share the innocence of an Arcadian middle landscape, eternally clean and pure. They reflect the pipe dream of America as a heavenly place, free of flaws. As the cultural historian Leo Marx saw it, Sheeler's *American Landscape* expressed "pastoral hope" in the face of massive industrialization. [14]

American and classic "landscapes," sanctified by their conservative style and blessed by arcadian/agrarian analogies, would undoubtedly please

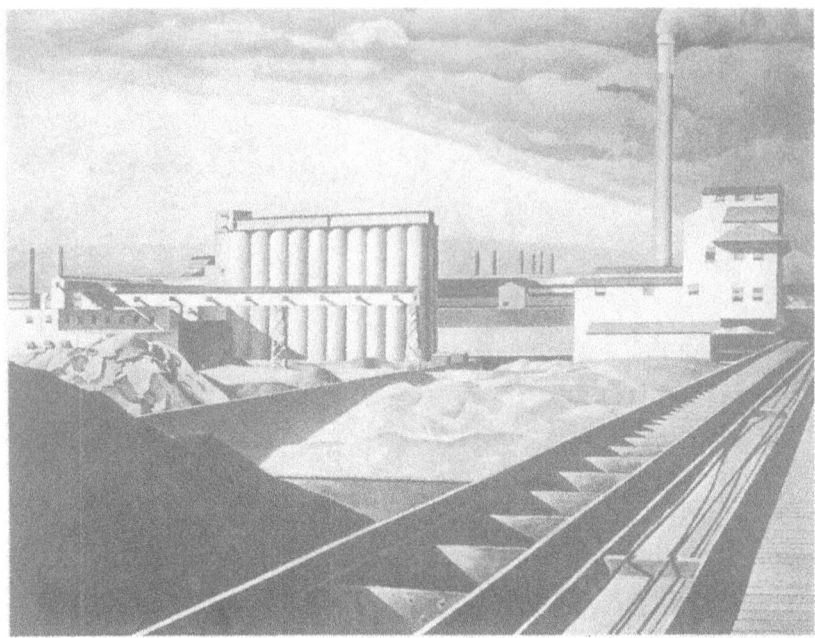

Figure 135. Charles Sheeler. *Classic Landscape*. 1931. Oil on canvas, 25 × 32¼ in. Collection of Mr. and Mrs. Barney A. Ebsworth Foundation.

the industrialist patron. But they may have momentarily loosened the bond Williams sensed between his way of looking and seeing and Sheeler's. This possibility may be gauged by the manner in which Williams's concise "Classic Scene" departed from the painting upon which it was ostensibly based.[15] While the poet visualized "a powerhouse / in the shape of / a red brick chair / 90 feet high," the two buildings and smokestack that Sheeler photographed and painted for *Classic Landscape* simply repeat those in its immediate predecessor, *American Landscape*. Though viewed from a different angle and shorter distance than in the earlier painting, neither building is a powerhouse and neither supports two stacks "in the shape of a red brick chair." The clustered stacks in the distant background of the *Classic Landscape* may be those of the powerhouse at the River Rouge plant.[16] Furthermore, an "area of squalid shacks" under the "command" of the "red brick chair," as imagined by the poverty-alert doctor, would never find a place in the work of the photographer-painter. Depression or not, Sheeler could never, he himself said, "indulge in social comment" by including such an allusion.[17] There was no more allowance in his idealized region of industry for the depiction of human distress than there was for the machine in Wood's fantasy farmscapes.

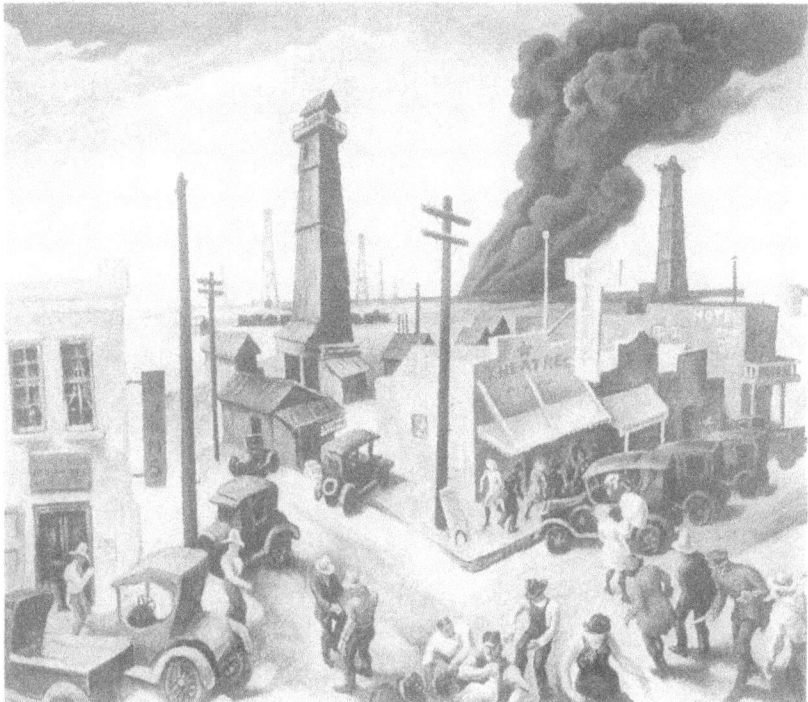

Figure 136. Thomas Hart Benton. *Boomtown.* c. 1927–28. Oil on canvas, 46⅛ × 54¼ in. Memorial Art Gallery of the University of Rochester, Rochester, New York, 51.1; Marion Stratton Gould Fund. © T. H. Benton and R. P. Benton Testamentary Trusts/Licensed by VAGA, New York, NY.

Williams's ideal of "direct association and communication with immediate things," as epitomized in *Upper Deck,* inevitably reappears in Sheeler's work. From his file of photographs, a strong sense of place-connected thingness surfaced in two "interior" paintings of unrelated subject matter. First came *American Interior* of 1934 (Fig. 137), an intimate overhead depiction of a room in the artist's house: a self-portrait of possessions, as it were, and a declaration of national pride. Its composition flattens out as two tabletops angle at each other from opposite corners of the frame. Hand-made scatter rugs and a bedcover push their varied patterns to the picture surface. Then a ladder-back Shaker chair, partially in shadow, casts its own shadow beyond that of the larger table and asserts itself as the most memorable of the objects.

Two years later, the comforts of home are succeeded by *City Interior* (Fig. 138), the most intricate and regionally based picture Sheeler ever created. Its main street of shining tracks, far removed from that of Sinclair

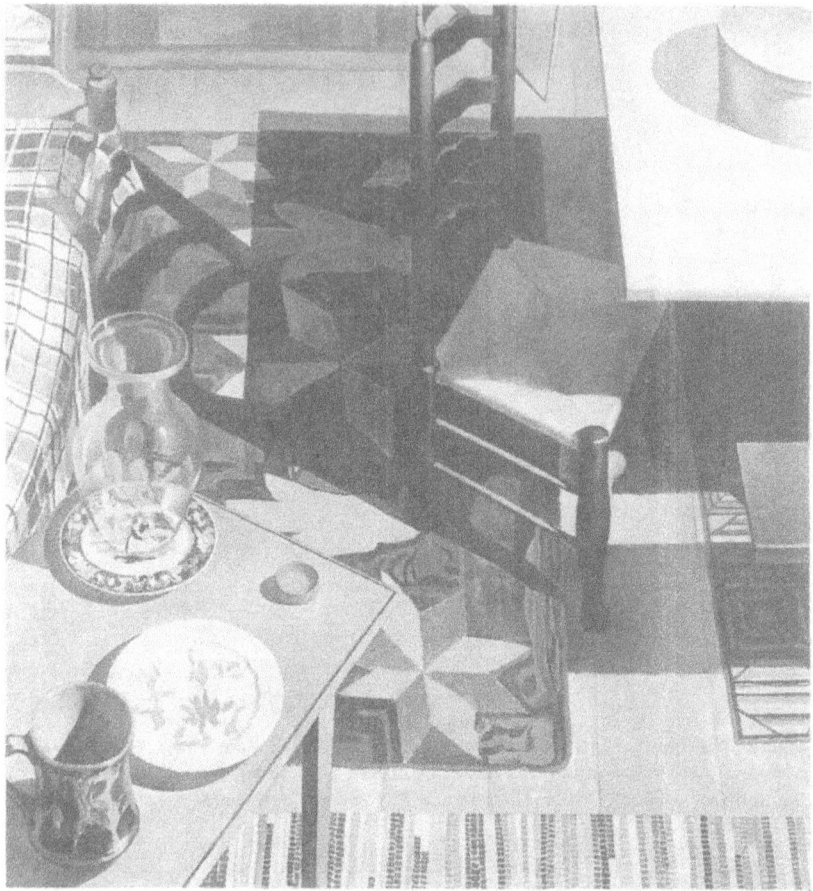

Figure 137. Charles Sheeler. *American Interior*. 1934. Oil on canvas, 32½ × 30 in. Yale University Art Gallery, New Haven, Connecticut; Gift of Mrs. Paul Moore.

Lewis's Gopher Prairie, offsets the primary sentiment of Wood's *Revolt Against the City*. In line with what Williams considered the most obvious and appropriate thrust for American art, it recedes through the heart of the River Rouge Ford factory-city, past seven worker-pedestrians. Reduced to minor anecdotes, they are unable to compete with the immensity of it all. In contrast to Benton's figure-jammed compositions, the amazing complexity of engineered forms, overhead and all around, monumentalizes human presence in an impersonal manner at the expense of picturesque portrayals. As severe as it might seem, this is the true city center of consumer-related mass production, of the car culture. At the time, it represented the greatest environmental alteration in history, and it had all happened in less than

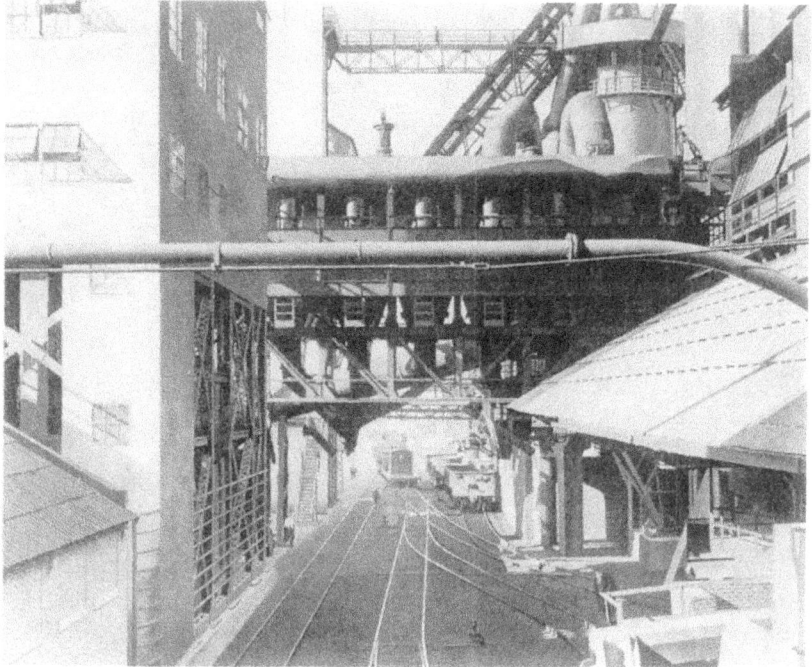

Figure 138. Charles Sheeler. *City Interior*. 1935. Aqueous adhesive and oil on composition board, 22 × 27 in. Worcester Art Museum, Worcester, Massachusetts, 1937.3; Elizabeth M. Sawyer Fund, in memory of Jonathan and Elizabeth M. Sawyer.

thirty years. The modern region was here, and small-town America would eventually become an intersection or be bypassed altogether.

In the thirties, Sheeler's sharp-contrast photographs, conté crayon drawings, and oil paintings turned interchangeably to craft objects, the framing and joining of basic carpentry, and industrial forms of steel. A Williamsburg kitchen with its copper and cast-iron utensils (Fig. 139), an enclosed wooden spiral staircase, and a silo directly preceded *Rolling Power* of 1939 (Fig. 140), Sheeler's much admired rendering of a soon-to-be-obsolete steam locomotive, as seen close-up below the boiler. At a glance, the right two-thirds of the painting appears to be an exact, photo-realist duplication of the photograph *Drive Wheels* (Fig. 141). But further examination increases appreciation of the painting as a subtly altered abstraction of primarily moving parts, plus fasteners and hydraulic tubing. The romantic folklore of particular trains, so loved by Benton, gives way to a universal statement of mechanical locomotion. Once again, by emphasizing contrasts of light and shadow in place of painterly modulations, which in this case could have described the oil and grease recorded by the camera,

227

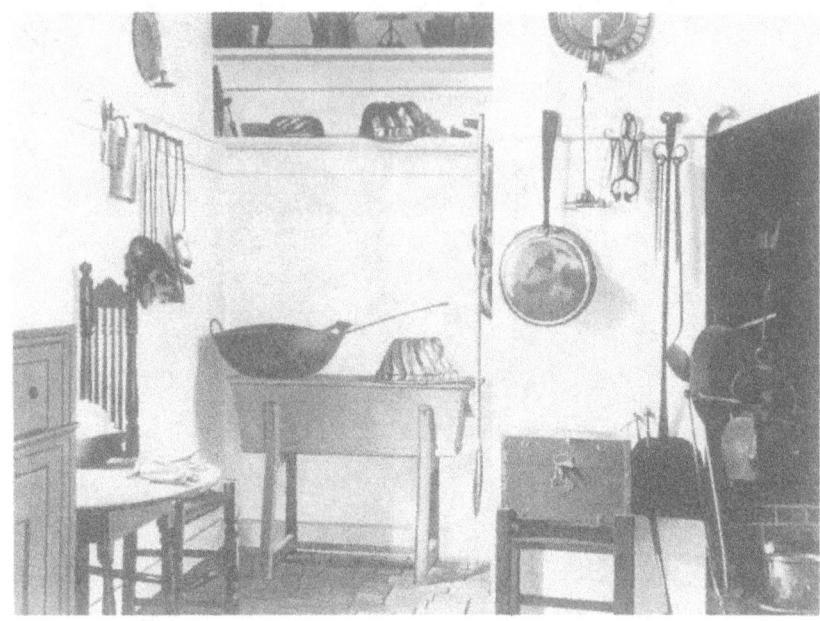

Figure 139. Charles Sheeler. *Kitchen, Williamsburg.* 1937. Oil on panel, 10 × 14 in. Private collection.

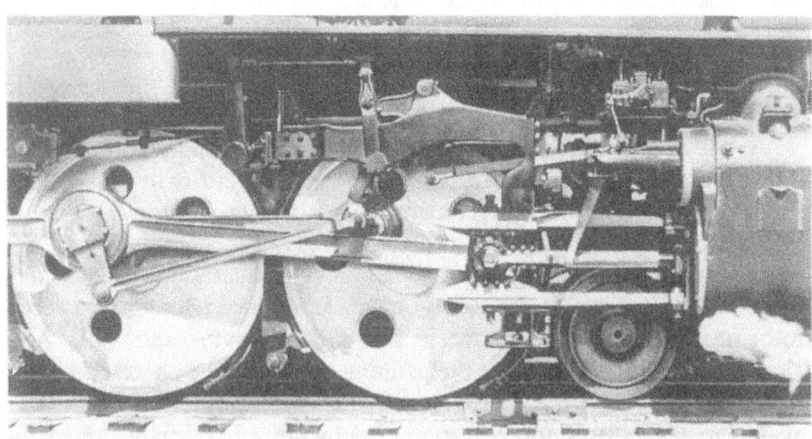

Figure 140. Charles Sheeler. *Rolling Power.* 1939. Oil on canvas, 15 × 30 in. Smith College Museum of Art, Northampton, Massachusetts; Drayton Hillyer Fund, 1940.

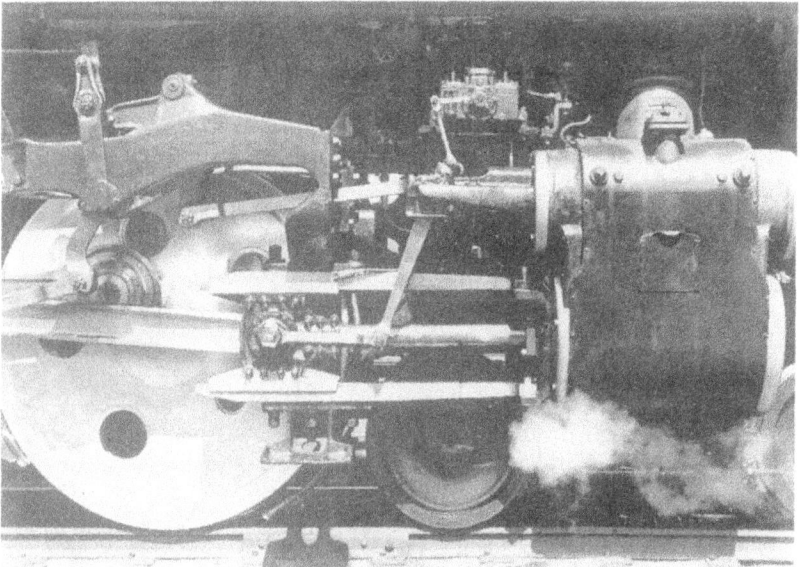

Figure 141. Charles Sheeler. *Drive Wheels*. 1939. Gelatin silver print, 6⅝ × 9⅝ in. Smith College Museum of Art, Northampton, Massachusetts; Gift of Mrs. Holger Cahill (Dorothy C. Miller '25).

Sheeler avoided random realty. Through a rhythmic correlation of fixed lines and shapes, he emphasized essential mechanized forms. Coincidental contours, determined strictly by form and function, participate as unifying elements of the picture. The one variable within this configuration of constants, the steam emitted by the pistons, was rearranged and reshaped so it would not distract from the total account of solid facts. Once cornered, it accented the driving energy of the subject as a whole.

In 1939 Sheeler wrote that he tried to start each work with "a complete conception of the picture established . . . much as the architect completes his plans before the work of bringing the house into existence begins." [18] Similarly, Williams noted that his early poems "lacked structural necessity" and that over the years he had worked "to remedy this fault by fusing with each image a form in its own right." [19] Their common stress on clearly envisioned compositions coincided with the concept of objectivism formulated by Williams in the early thirties. Accordingly, as its words present a direct sensation of tangible things, the poem, "an intense expression of the poet's perceptions," achieves authenticity and metaphor-free autonomy through the inherent requirements of its subject matter.[20] This drive toward objectivity is most convincing in Williams's short poems:

229

BETWEEN WALLS

the back wings
of the
hospital where
nothing
will grow lie
cinders
in which shine
the broken
pieces of a green
bottle

THE ATTIC WHICH IS DESIRE

the unused tent
of
bare beams
beyond which
directly wait
the night
and day—
Here
from the street
by
```
*   *   *
*   S   *
*   O   *
*   D   *
*   A   *
*   *   *
```
ringed with
running lights
the darkened
pane
exactly
down the center
is
transfixed

Elevated or reduced to a status of equal validity, objects in familiar places of his daily existence attracted and held the artist's attention. They entered the highly crafted structure of a poem both verbally and visually, immune from intentional comment. Sounding increasingly like a Williams disciple, Sheeler spoke as a strict abstract realist:

Painting for me has been a continuous objective pursuit. The pictures I produce are attempts to put down the inherent beauty of the subject with as little personal inter-

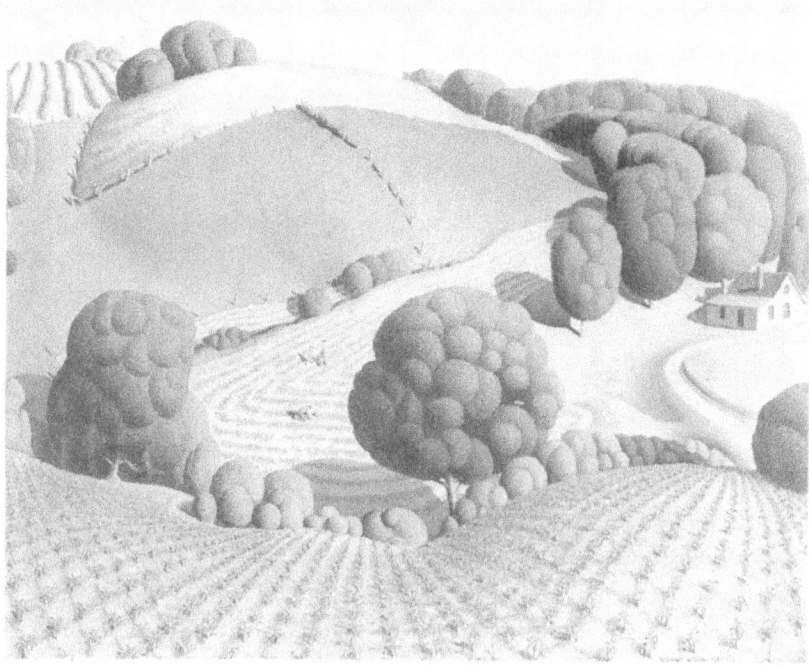

Figure 142. Grant Wood. *Young Corn.* 1931. Oil on masonite panel, 23½ × 29⅞ in. Commissioned by Cedar Rapids Community Schools; memorial to Linnie Schloeman, Wilson School; exhibited at Cedar Rapids Museum of Arts, Cedar Rapids, Iowa. © Estate of Grant Wood/Licensed by VAGA, New York, NY.

ference as possible, spoken in a language in general use rather than an exotic one. Having no theories I respond to those things which give me a pleasurable reaction, in themselves and their relation to other things, and I attempt to set them down in a visual design.[21]

As precisely crafted responses to rapidly multiplying mechanical regions, Sheeler's major pictures throughout the thirties demonstrate, cleansed and purified, an intimate affection for the unfolding industrial scene of the United States. Within this vast development, which Wood and Curry ignored as much as possible (Figs. 142–143) and Benton liked to mimic through outpourings of black smoke and animated steam engines (see Fig. 3), Sheeler located his place as an American artist and defined it securely. "Place is the only universal" proclaimed Williams, writing of the artist late in their juxtaposed careers:

Charles Sheeler has lived in a mechanical age. To deny that was to lose your life. That, the artist early recognized. In the world which immediately surrounded him

231

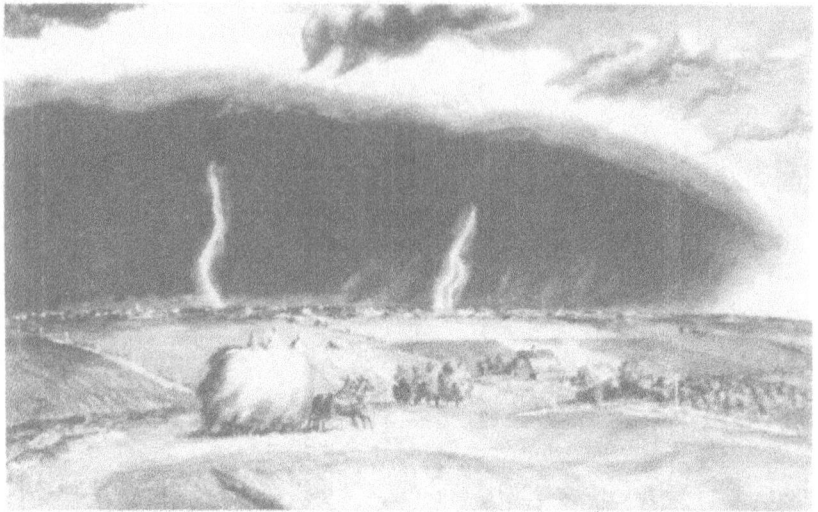

Figure 143. John Steuart Curry. *The Line Storm*. 1934. Oil and tempera on panel, 30⁹⁄₁₆ × 48¾ in. Babcock Galleries, New York City.

it was more apparent than anywhere else on earth. What was he to do about it? He accepted it as the source of material for his compositions.

Sheeler made a clean sweep of it. The man found himself impressed by the contours of the machine; he was not impressed by the romantic aspects of what the machine represents but the machine itself.[22]

The constitution of Sheeler's paintings between the two world wars, as diagnosed by the good doctor, was marked by the peculiarly American character of the things it fed upon. Declaring their independence from European stylistic sources, his photo-based works alternate between rural America's most refined craftsmanship and the new nation's preeminence in modern industry. When one asks where Sheeler lived, the answer in his art refers to no city or state but to a Shaker chair and table, at which he may very well have contemplated his next pictorial excursion into the advanced machine age. Unlike Demuth's skeptical attitude toward industrialization and in contrast to the obvious divergencies displayed in such pictures as Wood's *Death on the Ridge Road* (Fig. 18), Benton's *Boomtown* (Fig. 136), and Curry's *The Farm Is a Battleground, Too* (Fig. 35), Sheeler's obsessively rendered idealizations of the industrial locale celebrated America's growing claim on it. He felt as much at home in doing a factoryscape as American landscape painters a century earlier must have felt in meticulously describing the nation's vanishing wilderness.

11

Marsden Hartley's Return as a Nativist

Machine-alert expressions of modern America, whether achieved through boldly asserted photo-facts transmitted to canvas or through angular trans-lucencies across the picture plane, were of little relevance to the art of William Carlos Williams' third painter friend, Marsden Hartley. Though he wandered far and wide, Hartley began and ended in Maine, eventually abstracting subject matter from its landscape into thickly painted, highly tactile compositions. Cézanne may have been emotionally detached from the landmarks of Aix-en-Provence, but Hartley yearned for personal iden-tification with a particular place. His migratory pursuit of such a connec-tion represents a peculiarly American paradox.

Following an intense avant-garde period in Berlin at the beginning of World War I, Hartley moved from season to season, painting in Ber-muda, the Southwest, Mexico, southern France, Germany, and Nova Sco-tia.[1] After more than twenty years, he finally rediscovered his roots, as his patron-dealer Alfred Stieglitz encouraged him to do and as Williams in *In the American Grain,* advised all American artists to do. Hartley resettled in the state of his birth, where he endeavored to sustain a nativist mode for the remainder of his life. By this time, the late thirties, Benton and Curry had returned after many years on the East Coast to the Mississippi Basin. They, however, even more than the Iowa-residing Wood, continued their cosmopolitan and modern diversification.

In *Adventures in the Arts* (1921), Hartley espoused a regionalist attitude about what the American artist should paint and then, ironically, departed once again for Europe. He would remain there for almost nine years, apart from two brief visits to New York in 1924 and 1928. At exactly the same time that Benton resumed painting people and places on Martha's Vine-yard, Hartley stressed the need to cease emulating European art of any kind

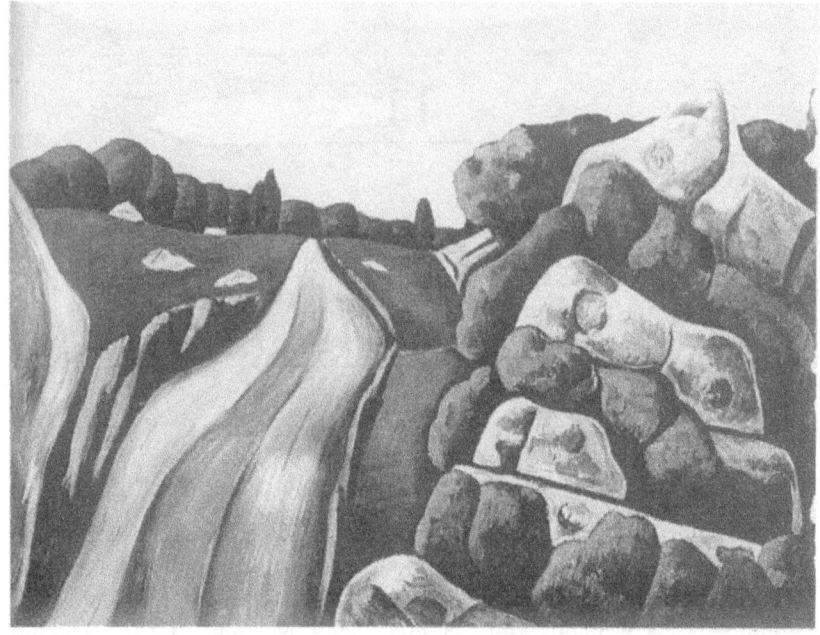

Figure 144. Marsden Hartley. *Summer Outward Bound, Dogtown.* 1931. Oil on board, 18 × 24 in. Private collection.

and to seek "artistic destinies on home soil." The "real art of America" will be that of "imaginative artists" working as "indigenous creators." [2]

Over a decade later he apparently decided to benefit from the current rise of Regionalism. His 1932 exhibition at the Downtown Gallery was entitled *Pictures of New England by a New Englander.*[3] For the brief catalogue he went so far as to write a poem, "Return of the Native," with no apologies to the recently deceased Thomas Hardy. The paintings in the exhibition, produced a year earlier, were the first of three series to depict Dogtown, a rock-strewn moraine on Cape Ann, near Gloucester, Massachusetts (Fig. 144). They still revealed signs of a Cézannesque phase that Hartley had launched in Aix-en-Provence in 1926 with several paintings of Mont Sainte-Victoire. Intervening seasons in Mexico and the Bavarian Alps saw the stylizations of Cézanne's structural devices dwindle. Hartley summered on the Nova Scotia coast in 1936, and by the time he returned to Maine the following year, those devices had yielded to forms inspired by Albert Ryder, whose paintings served as the most obvious nineteenth-century American prototypes for modern nature abstractions (Fig. 145).

Featuring forms natural to Maine, many works of Hartley's final years manifest a self-conscious commitment to a particular place and therefore

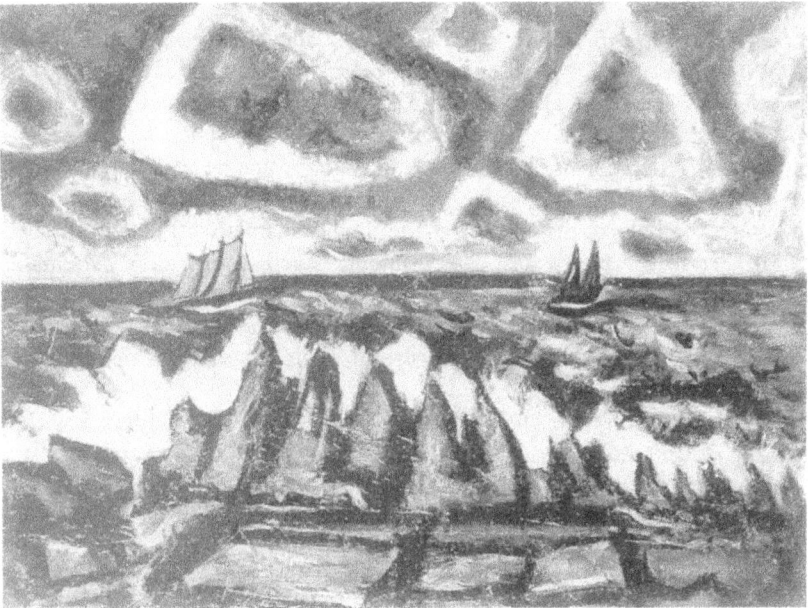

Figure 145. Marsden Hartley. *Northern Seascape, Off the Banks.* 1936. Oil on cardboard, 18³⁄₁₆ × 24 in. Milwaukee Art Museum, Milwaukee, Wisconsin; bequest of Max E. Friedman.

seem bent on answering a criticism by Paul Rosenfeld. Writing in the mid-twenties, the critic admired Hartley's sensitivity "to the identity of the spot in which he finds himself," including "frenzied Berlin of the early months of the war."[4] However, he felt that Hartley suffered a weakness common among American artists: a failure to immerse himself sufficiently in his material, a withdrawal from objective reality into intellectual fancies. "He has not been able to lose himself in his 'object.' "[5] A long absence from the place that had nourished him divested him of a sense of oneness with the earth. To regain it, "Hartley will have to go back to Maine."[6]

Preceding Rosenfeld's essay by several seasons, Hartley's *Adventures* had included identical thoughts on the matter. They too equated the substance of "localized sensibility" with the loss of oneself in a given object, "whether it be mountain or apple or human."[7] His eventual retirement "down East to Maine," as he later explained to the dealer-critic Samuel Kootz, provided him "the only relief from a present hyper-intellectualism and fear of the objective world."[8] These were tendencies that also disturbed Williams as symptomatic of Puritan-bred America.

A full fifteen years after Hartley first emphasized the necessity of creating the "real art of America" on home soil, and only two years before he

declared himself "the Painter from Maine" in "On the Subject of Nativeness — A Tribute to Maine,"[9] Wood published his Regionalist manifesto,
Revolt Against the City. Its sentiments of personal identification with a region, one's native locale in particular, correspond to Hartley's rhetoric.
Hartley, however, attributed a creative sense of nativeness to intuition, a
"purity of vision for life itself,"[10] while Wood urged a reasoned process of
regional interpretation. Though painting in bib-overalls as the ex-farmboy,
he, with the help of his editors, made Regionalism sound like an intellectual exercise, if not a scientific experiment: "Each section has a personality
of its own, in physiography, industry, psychology. Thinking painters and
writers who have passed their formative years in these regions will, by care-
taking analysis, work out and interpret in their productions these varying
personalities."[11]

Regardless of their differences in approach, both painters basically
echoed Iowa's most prominent literary figure of the nineteenth century.
The relentless realist Hamlin Garland, lecturing at the Chicago World's
Fair in 1893, two years after the publication of his *Main-Travelled Roads,*
anticipated their regionalist polemics practically to a word: "Every novel-
ist should draw his inspiration from the soil, should write of nothing but
the country he was bred in and the people most familiar to him."[12]

Whereas Hartley was ultimately consistent, Wood, as we have seen,
did not abide by his own pronouncements. Direct contact with the "native
materials" of his homeland became increasingly tenuous in his satires on
American legends, his caricatured stereotypes, or his fantasy farmscapes. In
updated versions of the mythic middle landscape of ancient Arcadian origin, his make-believe Iowa paradoxically exhibits no signs of the industrial
technology invading the countryside. For fear of losing an all-time agrarian
appearance to agricultural progress, he undermined modernization by cen-
soring the machine and the dynamo. On the other hand, he extended a
pastoral ideal into the "great green garden" of America's midland through
mechanical means of design and abstract generalizations. In *Spring Turning* of 1936 (see Fig. 112), tiny figures of faraway farmers, manning rapidly
disappearing hand plows and teams of horses, inch along the streamlined
surfaces of a sleek, wide-angle farmscape as time-warped anachronisms.

In the meantime, Hartley's painterly depictions of the coast and woods
in Maine did stick to concrete facts, including the lumbering industry. As
he had stated, they are "attached to the life of it as exemplified in the vividness of the moment" (Fig. 146).[13] In referring to his aesthetic sensitivity as
a youth, Hartley emphasized, in the manner of Williams, his preoccupation
with the "being of things": "Things in themselves engrossed me more than
the problem of experience. I was satisfied with the effect of things upon
my senses, and cared nothing for their deeper values."[14]

During his final ailing but highly motivated years, the landscape of

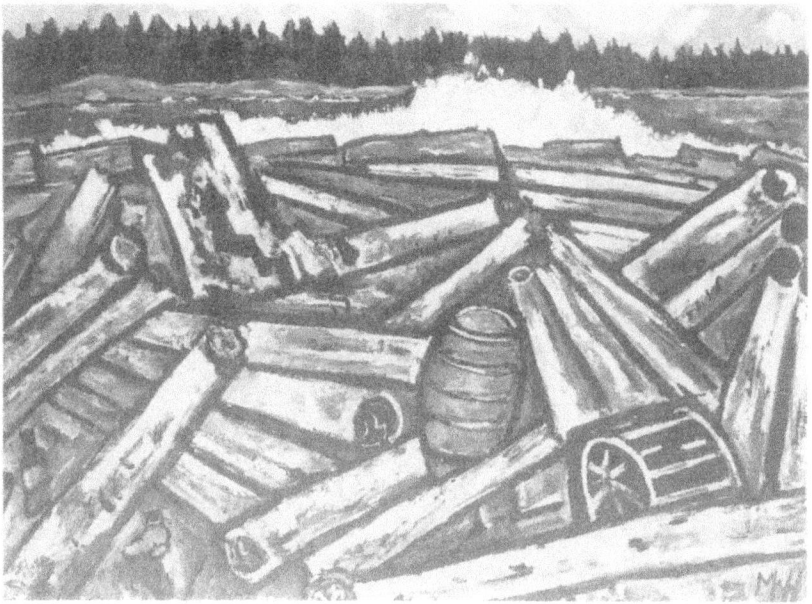

Figure 146. Marsden Hartley. *Log Jam, Penobscot Bay*. 1940–1941. Oil on masonite, 30 1/16 × 40 15/16 in. The Detroit Institute of Arts, Detroit, Michigan, 44.5; gift of Robert H. Tannahill. Photograph © 1997 The Detroit Institute of Arts.

Maine continued to preoccupy Hartley. After a "sacred pilgrimage" to its base in 1939, Mount Katahdin engrossed him above all else (Fig. 147). He set out to do eighty paintings of the state's largest mountain, as he believed Hiroshige had done for Japan's "Fujiyama." By painting it from a single vantage point, with none of the melodrama of Curry's storm-ridden memories of Kansas, Hartley sought to isolate what he sensed as the essential peculiarity of the mountain. In order to implant his vivid perception in the viewer's memory, he eliminated details that would detract from the purity of the initial visual moment he had experienced. Through this subtractive process, he captured its character much more intensely, he claimed, than Cézanne had that of Mont Sainte-Victoire: "And each time I do it I feel I am nearer the truth, even more so than if I were trying to copy nature from the thing itself." [15]

Such an extensive, serial identification with a singular landscape monument of local fame could hardly be equaled in Hartley's rare portrayals of people. A stay in a Nova Scotia fisherman's household during 1935 and 1936 inspired his first figure abstractions. In retrospective response to the drowning of two adult sons, the central example of his Mason family paintings, *The Lost Felice* of 1939 (Fig. 148), offered an elegiac tribute to the

237

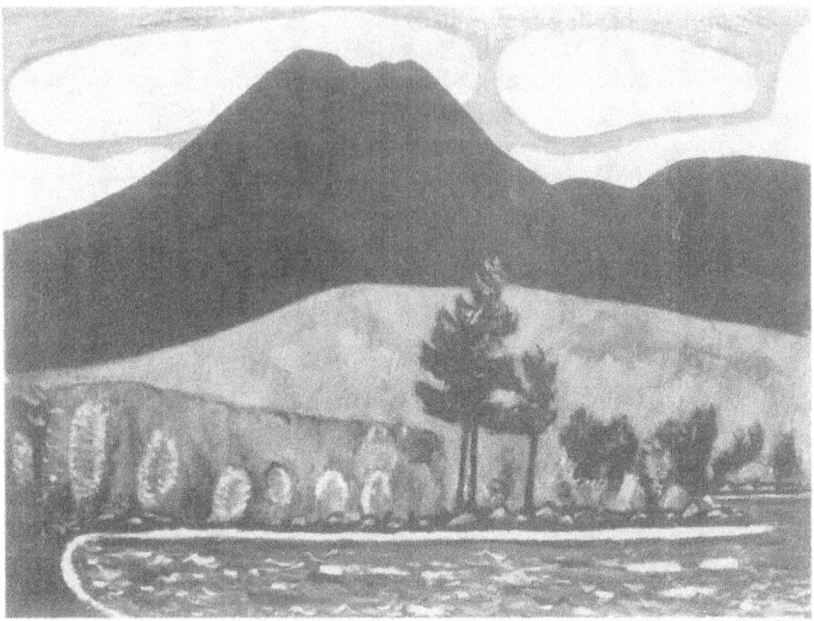

Figure 147. Marsden Hartley. *Mount Katahdin, Autumn No. 2.* 1939–40. Oil on canvas, 30 × 40½ in. Metropolitan Museum of Art, New York City, 1992.24.3; Edith and Milton Lowenthal Collection, bequest of Edith Abrahamson Lowenthal, 1991.

strength of their "giantesque" sister. She appears as a cold white vision, flanked by her fisherman brothers, who recede into a black background.[16] His ability to override any emotional attachment and abstract them into impersonal, masklike images may well have resulted from his basic attitude that human beings "have the same propensities as all other objects in nature."[17]

Objectification of a family's tragic loss distinguishes Hartley's figure of Felice from the iconic farmer of Wood's *Sultry Night* of 1937 (Fig. 149). Wood's controversial male bather could more easily be transformed into a universal symbol than could Hartley's expressionistic responses to a tragic event. A culminating portrayal of agrarian plenitude, Wood's American Adam, cooling off and cleansing himself at the edge of his broad field, stood for a promised life of self-sufficiency denied to Depression- and drought-ridden farm families. As an emblem of a natural life on the land, preciously rendered on a lithographic stone for urban distribution by the Associated American Artists in New York City, the full-frontal male nude barely related to the hard-pressed people of rural Iowa. Characteristic of Wood's "Regionalist" imagery, its bold sophistication eluded those it allegedly represented.

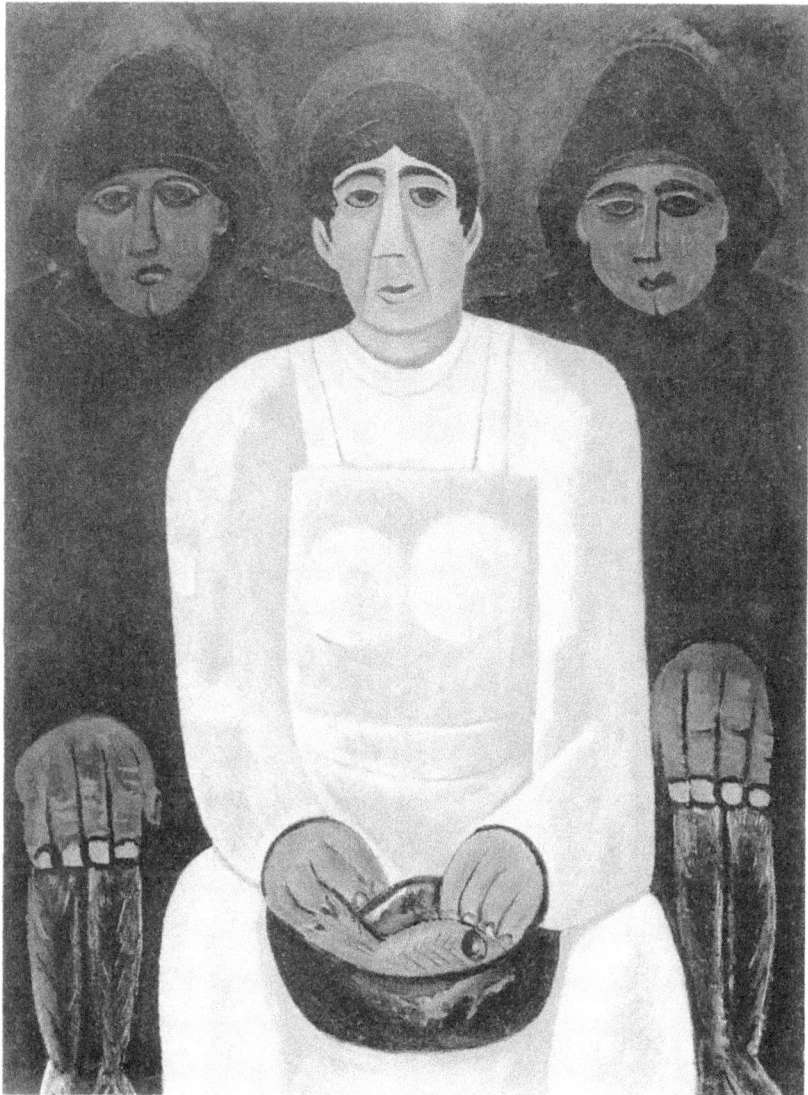

Figure 148. Marsden Hartley. *The Lost Felice*. 1939. Oil on canvas, 40 × 30 in. Los Angeles County Museum of Art; Mr. and Mrs. William Preston Harrison Collection.

Wood's highly refined, fantasy farm world would doubtless have been rejected by Rosenfeld as a typical American escape into "the far unseen," exposing an inability to "breast the moment quite nakedly."[18] The "restless maladjustment" that the immigrant critic construed as a preponderant characteristic of the American mind would, in his opinion, continue to

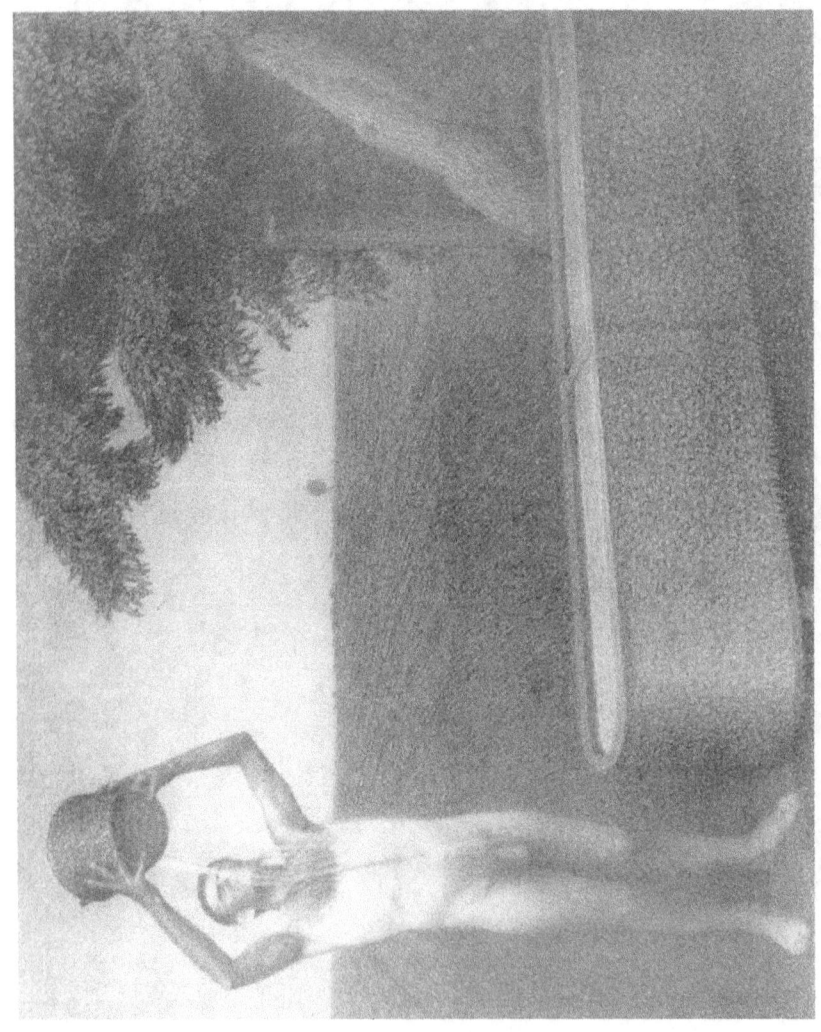

Figure 149. Grant Wood. *Sultry Night*.1937. Lithograph, 9⅝ × 12¼ in. Private collection. © Estate of Grant Wood/Licensed by VAGA, New York, NY.

"fancy" works of art with too many "perfections." [19] Experimental abstraction, as in works by Dove and O'Keeffe during the teens, provided a remedy for this malady. From a much more simplistic point of view, Thomas Craven, the nationalistic drummer of the Regionalist camp, ordered Wood to "paint a naked statement of the Iowa terrain" with no "frills or fantasy." [20] In effect he meant to rescue a leader of Regionalism from overly imaginative Modernism by advising him to turn around and follow the universally popular path of anecdotal realism.

Wood suffered this scolding from an ultraconservative critic in June 1937. That very month Williams wrote to Stieglitz expressing reservations about Hartley's recent paintings. He had just visited Stieglitz's gallery, "An American Place," where he saw the third Dogtown landscape series and several Nova Scotia paintings done during the previous year. By his strict criteria of objectivity and conciseness of form in relation to place identity, he found them lacking. Warning against straying from actuality into sentimental exaggeration, which in Hartley's case meant heavily impasted, generalized distortion, Williams sermonized:

He might better let his wit go into discovery, into showing what there *is* . . . rather than in overloading them with emotion which, in a sense, makes them sentimental. A painter needs to be more of a scientist. We exaggerate our own importance, and all exaggeration—unless more accurately aimed—is questionable practice.[21]

Thus, both men were simultaneously indicted for distortional responses to nature—Wood, an introverted artist who used his rural locale as a point of departure into an imaginary land of eternal bliss, and Hartley, a prodigal intent on identifying with the solid substance of his native state after years of absence. Yet, Craven's and Williams's overlapping complaints might have been more appropriately directed against Benton. At their most extravagant, his melodramas overwhelmed the sense of locale he claimed to cherish. When pitted against Sheeler's photography-paintings of machines and factories, the meandering narratives and entertaining anecdotes of Benton's murals and larger panel paintings betray an unmistakable Wanderlust. They record little if any "scientific discovery" of what is special about a place, even if the loquacious artist considered himself a realist engaged in "the drama of *things as they are*." [22] In developing his central theme of restlessness and maladjustment as an American affliction, Rosenfeld could have convincingly illustrated it with a montage of Benton pictures: "There always has to be frenetic movement: stupendous skyscrapers, motor-racings, families on wheels, lightning changes, rebuilding, tearing down, putting up, refurnishing, moving, blasting, enlarging, spreading, bursting." [23]

For Benton, acceleration toward total mechanization unfolded in a

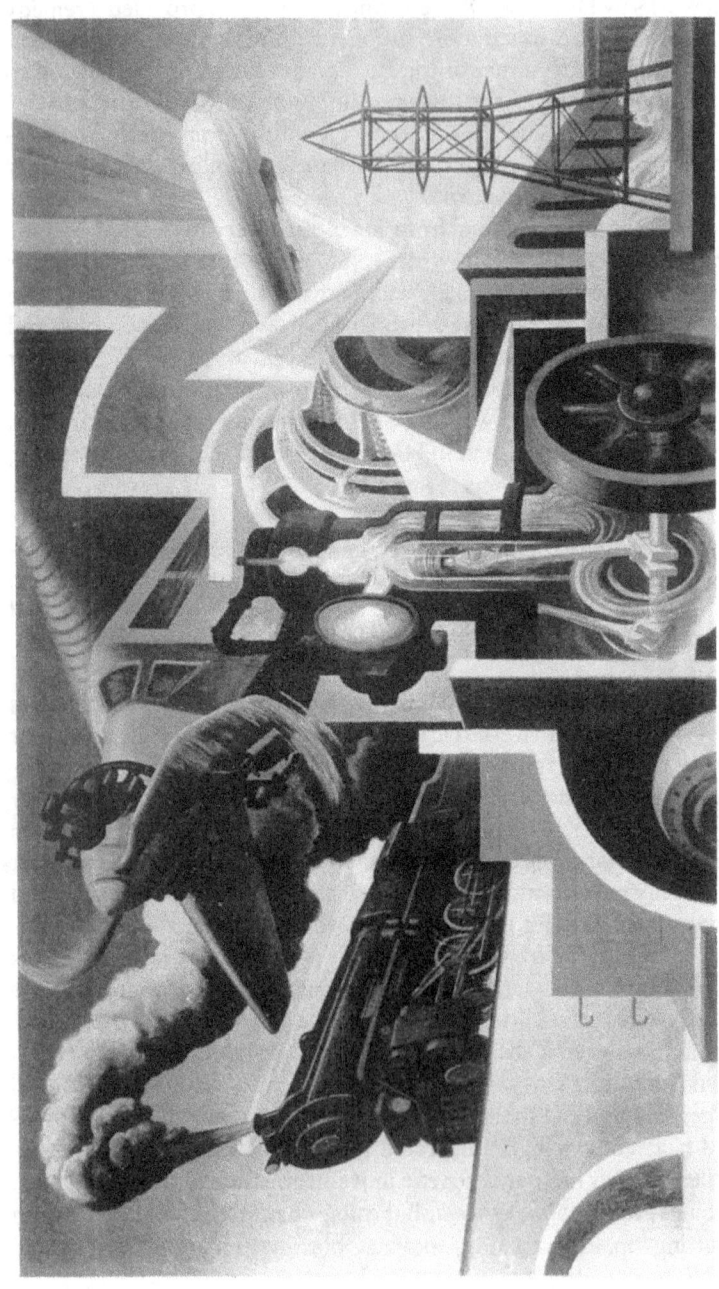

Figure 150. Thomas Hart Benton. *Instruments of Power*. 1930. Distemper and egg tempera on gessoed linen with oil glaze, 92 × 160 in. Mural for New School for Social Research, New York City; Collection, The Equitable Life Assurance Society of the U.S. Copyright © The Equitable Life Assurance Society of the U.S., T. H. Benton and R. P. Benton Testamentary Trusts/Licensed by VAGA, New York, NY.

242

complicated construction of mechanical energy. His *Instruments of Power* of 1930–1931 (Fig. 150) combines cutaway views and segmented details to exalt the internal-combustion engine and the dynamo, whose fusion emits a steam locomotive, an aeroplane, and a zeppelin. No textural distinctions impede their "flow" as compositional devices. According to his art theory, form evolves as a "function" of the subject matter, guided by the artist's will, which is imposed upon raw experience. Constructive elements of line, color, and plane never derive directly or spontaneously from actual objects but arise from a conscious analytic act. The artist, Benton claimed, constructs "this new thing" with no parallels in physical reality. Thus, in spite of his diatribes against French Modernism, Benton liked to think of his compositions as abstract ensembles.[24]

As is now widely recognized, none of the leading first-generation modernists in the United States were utterly dependent on European avant-garde sources. Such a cause-and-effect relationship would have denied them the native sensibility that Williams considered "the first prerequisite for creation." As for subject and content, his three object-oriented painter friends consistently sought a substantial sense of place identifiable as American, through individualized concentration on particular things. While Demuth lingered over factories, warehouses, and a grain elevator in his own backyard, Sheeler alternated between a love for the Shaker-craft interiors in which he lived and a fascination for the complexities of mechanized object matter residing in modern American industry. Hartley simply went home to what came naturally in Maine. Each in his own way proved to be as confirmed a regionalist as the self-certified midwestern Regionalists—if not more so. With no interest in forming a movement or promoting themselves as the true American artists sworn to oppose alien intrusion, they chose the subject matter immediately at hand: tangible realities directly described. In this manner, the major paintings of their respective mature styles automatically localized an art of national identity with firmer focus than do those of their more erratic counterparts in the Midwest.

More escapist, Wood's good-humored, mythic visions offered respite from both the rugged and the mechanized actualities of rural life. Curry left the realities of his boyhood Kansas far behind and conjured up more sublime and legendary remembrances. Meanwhile, Benton raced through wherever with a full head of steam. So stand the basic divisions between a trio of abstract realists and the "triumvirate" of Regionalism. The former wished to be at home with straightforward things: looking, seeing, and touching. The latter tended to wander about, often into a world of make-believe. Deviations in abstract form, subject matter, and content from their assignment as *the* indigenous American art movement of the Depression decade prove them to be modern independents.

243

Conclusion

The avant-garde of twentieth-century painting is identified with movements —Cubism, Orphism, Futurism, Expressionism, Dada, and Surrealism— whereas Modernism, as Ihab Hassan observed, is enacted by individual talents, and predicated on the invention of personal styles.[1] Independence of composition and subject matter was unquestionably shared by Wood, Benton, and Curry. In opposition to the deterministic world of nineteenth-century positivism, their overall pluralism was one of fluctuating sensations and recollections. Their reality was that of ongoing experiences, and while they were receptive to change, to the new, they were apprehensive of modernization, and in particular urbanization. They negated the city in the name of Regionalism. They were entirely capable of criticizing attitudes and behavior, especially those inherited from Victorian tastes and values. They indulged in mimicry, satire, caricature, social criticism, and protest at the expense of tradition and past. In so doing they demonstrated an anti-academic, democratic union of high and low art, detachment from place and time, and, in the case of Wood and Benton, machine-aesthetic formalism. Myth they exploited as a structuring device, a means of integration, an ultimate goal of Modernism.

In writing about Regionalism, critics consistently took its rhetoric at face value and insisted that its leaders literally record local, particularly rural, realities in their pictures. This demand for "direct realism" continued to confront the "triumvirate." They were repeatedly scolded for not having accurately depicted their assigned Middle Border region and its inhabitants. Most reviewers of Regionalist works considered any emphasis on abstract form in place of detailed object matter or any indulgence in personal fantasies (such as Wood's make-believe farmscapes and Benton's melodramatic meanderings) excursions into forbidden territory. Universal realities of human nature, especially the less seemly ones, were also out of bounds. Wood's *Daughters of Revolution* (Fig. 24), Curry's *Tragic Prelude* (Fig. 19), and Benton's *Politics and Agriculture* mural (Fig. 21) convey

244

critical opinions hardly in keeping with regional boosterism or unabashed nationalism. When critics failed to recognize the social negation in their art, a convoluted progression of misinterpretation culminated in trumped-up charges of fascism.

As documentation of contextual conflict, the artists' most diversified subject matter, their representations of women, are of provocative cultural interest. In signaling the changing status of the modern woman, Wood, Benton, and Curry reached their furthest points beyond the immediate, tangible realities ascribed as proper subject matter to Regionalism. They in fact transgressed any fixed art historical label in their woman imagery. It left traditional academic forms of allegorization behind, the first requirement of modern independence.

However personally motivated, their appropriations of nineteenth- and twentieth-century stereotypes register the erratic evolution of the New Woman out of the traditional strictures of True Womanhood. Within this extensive sociopolitical frame of reference, their representations of mythic frontierswomen, guardian matrons, sex-objects, or glamour symbols emerged. Curry turned from a nineteenth-century convention of womanhood, as applied to the legendary westward migration, to a contemporary "girl-woman" to whom he assigned his most crucial social causes. Benton objectified women as sensual "girls" in tune with a current "new morality." Wood's favored type, his ever-alert guardian matron, does her best to keep watch on the morality of America at large, in addition to tending plants, produce, poultry, or children. His ingrained affection for this embodiment of maternal duty underlies his winsome parodies of community matriarchs, no matter how much they might annoy him at times. So stands the dominant one in *American Gothic*, "a Virtuous Woman, the Bond of Domestic Union."[2] In command, she continues to peer over her husband's shoulder as he stares blankly at a quizzical world that rightly assigns the co-dependent pair meanings far removed from Regionalist borders.

Popular definitions of Regionalism originated in the rhetoric of its artists and in the writings of both approving and disapproving critics. For instance, Regionalism was supposed to be dead set against Modernism, derived from the "School of Paris," that is, from Picasso and Braque styles of Cubism, the colorist Orphism of Robert and Sonia Delauney, Matisse, or Italian Futurism. In this view East Coast abstractionists such as Max Weber and John Marin were mere "colonial" followers of the Europeans. Coinciding with the beginnings of Regionalism at the end of the 1920s and with the advent of the "American Scene," realist painters launched an all-out campaign to drive Modernism from American shores. Yet both Benton and Wood consorted with the enemy by experimenting with abstract painting, and they continued to incorporate the composition lessons they had learned into their mature works. Benton's source of inspiration, Stanton

Macdonald-Wright and Morgan Russell's Synchromism, belonged to the modernist mainstream of color Cubism. Wood's stemmed from the teachings of Arthur Wesley Dow, the premier twentieth-century American art educator, whose method of pictorial abstraction provided an alternative to the Cézanne-Cubist persuasion. To a lesser extent, Curry accommodated his illustrational style to a modern system of color emphasis: Hardesty Maratta's system of triadically determined simultaneous contrasts, so exciting to Robert Henri, George Bellows, and John Sloan as they did their best to progress stylistically. Of greater significance to Curry as an independent were his daring themes of sublime nature and social realist protest against sexism, racism, and war.

In view of their openness to contemporary tendencies of expression and the diverse subject matter to which they applied them, we can see an ironic contrast between the modern realism of Wood, Benton, and Curry and that of three easterners, Demuth, Sheeler, and Hartley. Under the influence of their friend and mentor William Carlos Williams, the latter group maintained a much more consistent attachment to their respective locales than did the three midwesterners. This inverse relationship between the two trios—or counter-deconstruction, if you will—strengthens the claim of modern independence for all six American artists.

Recognition of Modernism as something more than stylistic categorization, to see it as a state of creative self-assertion, inventiveness, personal fancy, political arousal, eccentricity, or neurosis, refreshingly complicates one's view of any twentieth-century art movement. By evaluating the critical writing on Wood, Benton, and Curry vis-à-vis their major works of art, I wish to demonstrate that their association with Regionalism was not as unitary or simple as it has been commonly portrayed. By suggesting ways in which the three cosmopolitan artists participated in Modernism, and the ways in which their modernist contemporaries, Demuth, Sheeler, and Hartley, had commonalities with Regionalism, I propose a reorientation and, if I may be so bold, a new synthesis within the complex, multifarious content of American painting belonging to their generation.

Notes
Index

Notes

INTRODUCTION

1. Daniel Bell, "Modernism Mummified," in *Modernist Culture in America,* edited by Daniel Joseph Singal (Belmont, Calif.: Wadsworth, 1991), 159-60.

2. Malcolm Bradbury and John Fletcher, "The Introverted Novel," in *Modernism, 1890-1930,* edited by Malcolm Bradbury and James McFarlane (New York: Penguin, 1976), 19.

3. Bell, "Modernism Mummified," 163.

4. Daniel Bell, "Beyond Modernism, Beyond Self," in *The Winding Passage: Essays and Sociological Journeys, 1960-1980* (Cambridge, Mass.: Abt Books, 1980), 278.

CHAPTER I. "DIRECT REALISM" VERSUS MODERN ABSTRACTIONS

1. For a detailed account of Curry's sudden success, see M. Sue Kendall, *Rethinking Regionalism: John Steuart Curry and the Kansas Mural Controversy* (Washington, D.C.: Smithsonian Institution, 1986), 22-24.

2. Lewis Mumford, *The City in History, Its Origins, Its Transformations, and Its Prospects* (New York: Harcourt, Brace, and World, 1961), 447.

3. Of the three, Benton was the foremost theorist regarding the significance of abstraction. His extensive instructions on the subject appear in "Mechanics of Form Organization in Painting," *Arts* 10-11 (1926-27), a series of five essays.

4. Marlene Park and Gerald E. Markowitz, *Democratic Vistas: Post Offices and Public Art in the New Deal* (Philadelphia: Temple University Press, 1984), 138-39.

5. Edward Alden Jewell, "In the Realm of Art: Controversy and Exhibitions, Issues in the Debate Between Leading Exponents of 'Abstract' And 'Nationalist' Tendencies—Mr. Benton's Recent Painting," *New York Times,* April 7, 1935.

6. Ibid.

7. Wallace Spenser Baldinger, "Formal Change in Recent American Painting," *Art Bulletin* 19 (December 1937), 590.

8. Both Bulliet and Williams are quoted at length in "Sculptor Wins First Prize at Chicago's Annual Exhibition," *Art Digest* 5 (November 1, 1930), 5-6.

9. Edward Alden Jewell, "Benton Depicts America Aggressively for the Whitney Museum," *Art Digest* 7 (December 15, 1932), 5.

10. Henry McBride, "Thomas Benton's Murals at the Whitney Museum," *New York Sun* (December 10, 1932), quoted in full in Henry McBride, *The Flow of Art: Essays and Criticisms of Henry McBride* (New York: Atheneum Publishers, 1975), 295-97.

11. Paul Rosenfeld, "Ex-Reading Room," *New Republic* 74 (April 12, 1933), 245-56.

12. Mumford, *The City in History*, 416.

13. Throughout her *Benton, Pollock, and the Politics of Modernism: From Regionalism to Abstract Expressionism* (Chicago: University of Chicago Press, 1991), Erika Doss sees Mumford and Benton in complete political accord with regard to restoring "organic" communities of "producerism" in the United States (see p. 120). She advised the author, however, that the Rosenfeld and Mumford critiques of the Whitney Museum Library murals were not based on taste or differing aesthetic points of view but were "driven by their political differences and personality conflicts with Benton." Mumford definitely assumed overtly political positions within the vast scope of his analytic writings that hinge on his disillusionment with industrial capitalism and its concentration of wealth and power in ever larger, impersonal corporations. Benton shared this basic fear and expressed it in his attraction to the people as vital subjects and free forms. Rosenfeld's sophisticated, basically stylistic art criticism includes generalities about cultural matters that may be interpreted as indications of power and class conflicts but contains little if any of the ideological or partisan fire fanned by either Mumford or Benton.

14. Lewis Mumford, "The Three Bentons," *New Yorker* 20 (April 20, 1935), 48, 50, 53.

15. "Benton in Indiana," *Art Digest* 7 (March 1, 1933), 20. For more about the relationship of Benton's drawings to the form and content of his murals, see Karal Ann Marling, *Tom Benton and His Drawings* (Columbia: University of Missouri Press, 1985).

16. Thomas Craven, "American Month in the Galleries," *Arts* 11 (March 1927), 151.

17. Thomas Craven, "American Painters: The Snob Spirit," *Scribner's Magazine* 91 (February 1932), 81-86.

18. Thomas Craven, "Politics and the Painting Business," *American Mercury* 27 (December 1932), 463-72. Much of the original article is quoted in "Vitriol for Murals," *Art Digest* 6 (December 15, 1932), 6.

19. Thomas Craven, *Modern Art* (New York: Simon and Schuster, 1934), 338-39.

20. Ibid., 313. It is in this same paragraph—in its first sentence as a matter of fact—that Craven refers to Alfred Stieglitz as "a Hoboken Jew without knowledge of, or interest in, the historical American background . . . hardly equipped for the leadership of a genuine American expression" (p. 312).

21. Ibid., 336-37.

22. Ibid., 238.

23. Frank Jewett Mather, *New York Herald Tribune* review of Thomas Craven's *Modern Art*, as quoted in *Art Digest* 9 (June 1, 1934), 29.

24. See Wayne W. Parrish, "American Art Scrapes Off French Veneer," *Literary Digest* 30 (June 1934), 22, 35.

25. Edward Alden Jewell, "In the Realm of Art: Quickenings, Visions That Stir the Mural Pulse," *New York Times*, May 27, 1934.

26. Ibid. The remainder of the article is primarily a lengthy letter from Grant Wood describing plans and projects for a newly formed mural-painting group at the University of Iowa.

27. Allen Jackson, "U.S. Scene," *Time* 24 (December 24, 1934), 24–27.

28. Stuart Davis, "The New York American Scene in Art," *Art Front* 1 (February 1935), 6.

29. Ruth Pickering, "Thomas Hart Benton on His Way Back to Missouri," *Arts and Decoration* 42 (February 1935), 15. That he did recognize a human capacity for dignity and heroism regardless of race may be witnessed in his portrait of Ben Nichols, 1941, and in his *Negro Soldier,* 1942, illustrated in Henry Adams, *Thomas Hart Benton: An American Original* (New York: Knopf, 1989), 297, 316. For further defense of Benton's basically mawkish caricaturing, see Doss, *Benton, Pollock, and the Politics of Modernism,* 116–24.

30. Erika Doss, "The Year of Peril: Thomas Hart Benton and World War II," in *Thomas Hart Benton, Artist, Writer and Intellectual,* edited by R. Douglas Hurt and Mary K. Dains (Columbia: State Historical Society of Missouri, 1989), 37–43. In reference to Robert Henri and his circle, critic and painter Guy Pène du Bois, sounding like Benton, wrote of its idealistic republican spirit. "With two or three exceptions they were republicans, singing the song of the plain man and his family." At one time, "we were a real republic: every man as good as his neighbor." But now all we have is "a kind of reminiscence of something which was good while we had it but which now, alas, was gone." Guy Pène du Bois, "Art by the Way: The Passing of Republican Painting," *International Studio* 75 (September 1922), 535–36.

31. Davis, "New York American Scene," 6.

32. Stephen Alexander, "White Haired Boy of the Crisis," *New Masses* 15 (June 1935), 28.

33. See Wood's manifesto *Revolt Against the City,* Whirling World Series, no. 1 (Iowa City: Clio, 1935), 30–35.

34. Lewis Mumford, "The Art Galleries: A Group of Americans," *New Yorker,* May 4, 1935, p. 28. Constance Rourke reversed Mumford's opinion of the relative merits of Wood's major subjects. She saw him at his best in "some of his more casual decorations" or in "direct satire," which she also termed "portraiture of the type" coming out of folk humor. Constance Rourke, "American Art: A Possible Future," *American Magazine of Art* 28 (July 1935), 397.

35. Mumford, "Art Galleries," 31–32.

36. Lewis Mumford, "The Art Galleries: In Capitulation," *New Yorker,* June 1, 1935, p. 57.

37. James Johnson Sweeney, "Grant Wood," *New Republic* 83 (May 29, 1935), 76–77. In a somewhat less wordy fashion and more appropriately, Ralph Pearson registered the same complaint against the paintings of Curry. Pearson "mourned the lack of 'visual music' which would have made these paintings breathe with that other kind of life which the moderns call the plastique (or design) of the picture." Ralph M. Pearson, "The Artist's Point of View, John Steuart Curry and the American School of Painting," *Forum* 97 (February 1937), 113.

38. Quoted in "Modern Museum Opens Show Despite Ignorance of U.S. Mar-

tinets," *Art Digest* 10 (March 15, 1936), 10. That abstract art was alive and well was indicated not only in this exhibition but in the comprehensive exhibition of examples by American artists held by the Whitney Museum a season earlier. Oil paintings, watercolors, and drawings were on exhibit as "Abstract Painting in America" from the middle of February through March 22, 1935. Works by Arthur G. Dove, John Marin, Max Weber, Marguerite Zorach, Marsden Hartley, Charles Sheeler, Stuart Davis, and others were meant to present an overview of the modernist movement in the United States.

CHAPTER 2. "DIRECT REALISM" VERSUS MIMETIC FANTASIES

1. The other two jurors were Edward Bruce, wealthy landscape painter and director of the Treasury Department Section of New Deal Mural Projects, and Henry G. Keller, a prominent painter in Cleveland and the early teacher of Charles Burchfield. Quoted in "Critics at Loggerheads Over Merit of Chicago Artists Show," *Art Digest* 9 (February 15, 1935), 6.

2. This dual plan was a central part of the new Agricultural Adjustment Act passed by Congress on February 16, 1938, one of the last major enactments of the "Second New Deal."

3. Peter Roffman and Jim Purdy, *The Hollywood Social Problem Film: Madness, Despair and Politics from the Depression to the Fifties* (Bloomington: Indiana University Press, 1981), chap. 8, "Rural Problems," 121–35.

4. Ibid., 134. Months after World War II ended, a musical version of *State Fair* appeared with Rodgers and Hammerstein's only film score, including the hit songs "Grand Night for Singing" and "It Might as Well Be Spring." If that were not enough, still another musical version followed in 1962 in which the country-bumpkin dad played by Tom Ewell kisses his prize pig.

5. Ibid., 132.

6. Ralph M. Pearson, "Renaissance in American Art," *Forum* 93 (September 1935), 202–4.

7. In 1921 Wood invited an audience to join him on a trip to the Imagination Isles while unveiling a landscape scroll that he had guided a class of ninth-grade boys in creating for the school cafeteria. The introduction turned into a lecture as he warned of the damage an all-too-comfortable materialism does to "our imagination machinery." Quoted in James M. Dennis, *Grant Wood: A Study in American Art and Culture*, 2d ed. (Columbia: University of Missouri Press, 1986), 100. The two-page typescript of this talk is in the Archives of American Art, Smithsonian Institution, Washington, D.C., a gift of Nan Wood Graham.

8. Lincoln Kirstein, "An Iowa Memling," *Art Front* 1 (July 1935), 6.

9. Ibid., 8.

10. Thomas Craven, "Grant Wood," *Scribner's Magazine* 101 (June 1937), 21. It is strange that both Mumford and Craven allude to Wood's "portraiture" as his best work, considering how few portraits he painted. Without specifically referring to them, they must have had in mind such allegorical likenesses as *Woman with Plant* (1929), *American Gothic* (1930), and *Victorian Survival* (1931).

11. Craven, "Grant Wood," 21.

12. Thomas Craven, "John Steuart Curry," *Scribner's Magazine* 103 (January 1938), 41.

13. Ibid., 96.

14. Thomas Craven, ed., "The Line Storm," in *A Treasury of Art Masterpieces: From the Renaissance to the Present Day* (New York: 1939), 582.

15. "Grant Wood: Brilliant Painter of the Mid-Western Scene," *London Studio* 15 (February 1938), 88.

16. Ibid., 91.

17. Grant Wood, "John Steuart Curry and the Midwest," *Demcourier*, 11, no. 2 (1941), 2–4.

18. Laurence E. Schmeckebier, *John Steuart Curry's Pageant of America* (New York: American Artists Group, 1943), 345.

19. Malcolm Vaughan, "Up from Missouri," *North American Review* 245 (1938), 87–88.

20. Ibid., 91.

21. Ibid., 88.

22. Ibid., 90.

23. Ibid., 92. For a discussion of Benton's Missouri Capitol Building House Lounge murals within the context of liberal republicanism and its mythic adjunct "producerism," ideological bases inherited from his namesake great-uncle and his father, see Erika Doss, *Benton, Pollock, and the Politics of Modernism: From Regionalism to Abstract Expressionism* (Chicago: University of Chicago Press, 1991), 126–31.

24. Benton's letter to the visitors is reproduced in Henry Adams, *Thomas Hart Benton: An American Original* (New York: Knopf, 1989), 256–58.

25. Meyer Schapiro, "Populist Realism," *Partisan Review* 4, no. 2 (1938), 55.

26. Doss, *Benton, Pollock and the Politics of Modernism*, 264–72. Also see Douglas Hyland, "Benton's Images of American Labor," in *Benton's Bentons*, edited by Elizabeth Broun, Douglas Hyland, and Marilyn Stokstad (Lawrence: Spencer Museum of Art, University of Kansas, 1980), 23–31. Hyland reemphasizes the importance of Dr. John Weischel and his short-lived, pre–World War I "People's Art Guild" in New York for Benton's compassionate and celebratory images of industrial workers.

27. In her descriptions of the New School murals ("Thomas Hart Benton and Progressive Liberalism: An Interpretation of the New School Murals"), the historian Emily Braun maintains that "the proletariat is the only segment of society represented in the mural" and tends to overinterpret Benton's identification with the working man as an implied Marxist criticism of capitalism. Emily Braun and Thomas Branchick, *Thomas Hart Benton: The America Today Murals* (Williamstown, Mass.: Williams College Museum of Art, 1985).

Henry Adams supports this view by pointing out Benton's friendly acquaintance with Mike Gold, founder of the Communist Party U.S.A., and his friendship with soon-to-be-disenchanted leftists Max Eastman, Sidney Hook, and Caroline Pratt, one of the women portrayed in the "City Activities with Dance Hall" panel. He also refers to Benton's illustrations for Leo Huberman's *We, the People* (New York: Harper & Bros., 1932), a popular history of American working people and their ongoing struggles to organize labor unions. Adams, *Thomas Hart Benton*, 168–71.

28. See Andrew Bergman, *We're in the Money: Depression America and Its Films* (New York: New York University Press, 1971), chap. 10, "Frank Capra and Screwball Comedy, 1931–1941," 132–49.

29. Schapiro, "Populist Realism," 56.

30. Ibid., 57.

31. *Common Sense*, September 1937, p. 21.

32. Milton Brown, "From Salon to Saloon," *Parnassus* 13 (March 1941), 193.

33. Ibid., 194.

34. Ibid.

35. Ibid., 193.

36. Lawrence Alloway, "The Recovery of Regionalism: John Steuart Curry," *Art in America* 64 (July–August 1976), 70–73.

37. Ibid., 72.

38. Ibid., 73.

39. Hilton Kramer, "The Return of the Nativist," *New Criterion* 2 (October 1983), 63.

40. Ibid., 61.

41. Ibid.

CHAPTER 3. NATIONALISM!

1. David Harvey, *The Condition of Postmodernity* (Oxford and New York: Blackwell, 1989), 273.

2. Dorothy Grafly, *Public Ledger* (Philadelphia), as quoted in "Carnegie Uproar," *Art Digest* 6, no. 3 (November 1931), 6.

3. Edward Alden Jewell, "Toga Virilis: The Coming of Age of American Art," *Parnassus* 4, no. 4 (April 1932), 1.

4. Ironically, this rebellion against European art continued to motivate the anti-American Scene abstractionists of the New York School in the forties and fifties. Concurrent with the rapid demise of Regionalism, Abstract Expressionism successfully reversed the direction of trans-Atlantic influence, causing the rise of New York and the fall of Paris as the art center of the Western world. No longer would the United States remain a debtor nation in the international art trade, let alone a colony. For a detailed account of this transformation in relation to the politics of a hot and cold war, especially as perceived by the critic Clement Greenberg, see Serge Guilbaut, *How New York Stole the Idea of Modern Art* (Chicago: University of Chicago, 1985).

5. The other judges were Hardinge Scholle, director of the Museum of the City of New York, Francis Taylor, director of the Worcester Museum, and Herbert Tschudy of the Brooklyn Museum. *New York Times*, February 24, 1932. The affirmative won 3–1. Apparently one of the judges abstained or was absent.

6. "The Debate," *Art Digest* 6 (March 15, 1932), 15, 21–22.

7. "The Debate," *Art Digest* 6 (April 1, 1932), 15–16, 21, 28–29.

8. Thomas Hart Benton, "Some Revolutionary Speeches Heard at Federation Conclave: Benton's Onslaught," *Art Digest* 7 (July 1, 1933), 6.

9. Erika Doss, *Benton, Pollock, and the Politics of Modernism: From Regionalism to Abstract Expressism* (Chicago: University of Chicago Press, 1991), 96.

10. Benton, "Some Revolutionary Speeches," 6.

11. "Mid-West Is Producing an Indigenous Art," *Art Digest* 7 (September 1, 1933), 10. Art historian and curator Henry Adams perhaps went overboard in crediting Walker with inventing, devising, and creating the Regionalist movement. The movement was well underway by late 1933, with all its rhetoric fairly well in place thanks to Thomas Craven, Benton, and Wood. Furthermore, to say that "Regionalism" was the creation of Walker alone ignores the "American Scene"'s earlier emphasis on the need for American artists to break away from European Modernism and paint immediate, tangible, realities on their own. Adams properly underlines the boost that Walker gave to the leading midwestern edge of Regionalism, continued a year later by *Time* for its Christmas 1934 issue. Henry Adams, *Thomas Hart Benton: An American Original* (New York: Knopf, 1989), 217–20.

12. Hazel Crow Ewell, "Regional Art," *Christian Science Monitor,* June 19, 1935, pp. 8–9.

13. Henry Adams, without citing any documentary evidence, states that *Revolt Against the City* (Iowa City: Clio, 1935) was "ghostwritten" by Frank Luther Mott, a well-known journalism professor and scholar at the University of Iowa. According to Adams, as publisher-editor of four pamphlets called the "Whirling World Series," Mott "spliced together statements Wood had made in lectures and interviews" to create the first of these pamphlets to be released. Adams, *Thomas Hart Benton,* 244. Wanda Corn also doubts Wood's authorship because the essay contains so many literary references and is more antiurban than she thinks Wood was. Corn, *Grant Wood: The Regionalist Vision* (New Haven: Yale University Press, 1983), 153 n. 85.

Publication of *Revolt Against the City* was underway when Wood hired a young graduate of the university, Park Rinard, to assist him with an autobiography that would never be completed. Rinard, who became Wood's secretary-assistant, informed me that Mott did indeed essentially write *Revolt*. Rinard also agreed that the essay does not accurately reflect Wood's attitude toward the city and the urban culture from which he benefited. Telephone conversation between author and Park Rinard, July 20, 1996.

Any implication that the well-read Wood could not essay his own thoughts, however, would seem inaccurate in light of his earlier writings.

14. Wood, *Revolt,* 15–19.

15. Ibid., 18.

16. Ibid., 22.

17. Ibid.

18. Ibid.

19. Ibid., 28.

20. Ibid., 28–29.

21. Ibid., 29.

22. Ibid., 33–35.

23. Ibid., 40–41.

24. John Steuart Curry, address to Madison, Wisconsin, Art Association, January 19, 1937, quoted in Laurence Schmeckebier, *John Steuart Curry's Pageant of America* (New York: American Artists Group, 1943), 299.

25. John S. Curry, statement to legislative commission for Kansas State Capitol Murals, quoted by Schmeckebier, *Curry's Pageant*, 321.

26. See M. Sue Kendall, *Rethinking Regionalism: John Steuart Curry and the Kansas Mural Controversy* (Washington, D.C.: Smithsonian Institution Press, 1986), 126-32.

27. Curry, address to students at the University of Wisconsin, 1937, quoted in Schmeckebier, *Curry's Pageant*, 123-24.

28. For a thoroughly researched discussion of Curry's African-American-related paintings of the thirties, see Kendall, *Rethinking Regionalism*, 74-81.

29. "Mysterious Protests Bar 'Lynching Show,' " *Art Digest* 9 (February 15, 1935), 14.

30. *Parnassus* 7 (March 1935), 24.

31. Arthur Schlesinger, Jr., *The Politics of Upheaval* (Boston: Houghton Mifflin, 1960), 436-38.

32. Curry arrived in Madison in time to witness the rise of Philip La Follette's new party, the National Progressives of America and did on-the-spot sketches at its major 1940 rally in the Stock Pavilion on the university campus near his studio. See Schmeckebier, *Curry's Pageant*, 254-57.

33. For a detailed analysis of *Gabriel Over the White House*, see Peter Roffman and Jim Purdy, *The Hollywood Social Problem Film: Madness, Despair and Politics from the Depression to the Fifties* (Bloomington: Indiana University Press, 1981), 68-72. For an evaluative discussion of the Federal Theatre performances of *It Can't Happen Here*, see Barbara Melosh, *Engendering Culture: Manhood and Womanhood in New Deal Public Art and Theater* (Washington, D.C.: Smithsonian Institution Press, 1991), chap. 1, pp. 15-31.

CHAPTER 4. FASCISM?

1. Stephen Alexander, "White Haired Boy of the Crisis," *New Masses* 15 (June 1935), 28.

2. For well-balanced discussions of the Popular Front debates waged by American painters, writers, and critics, especially among those belonging to the American Artists' Congress, see Matthew Baigell and Julia Williams, eds., *Artists Against War and Fascism: Papers of the First American Artists' Congress* (New Brunswick, N.J.: Rutgers University Press, 1986), "The American Artists' Congress: Its Context and History," 3-44; Serge Guilbaut, *How New York Stole the Idea of Modern Art,* chap. 1: "New York, 1935-1941: The De-Marxization of the Intelligentsia," 17-41; and Cecile Whiting, *Antifascism in American Art* (New Haven: Yale University Press, 1989), chap. 2: "The Popular Front Antifascist Crusade," 35-65. Whiting very convincingly demonstrates the supplementation of sectarian, anticapitalist proletarianism, contained in revolutionary illustrations of the early thirties, by antifascist, social-realist paintings of the Popular Front period. Paintings by William Gropper and the prime example of antifascism, Peter Blume's semisurrealist *Eternal City*, allowed for a diversification of thematic and stylistic reactions to the horrors occurring in Europe after 1935.

3. Stuart Davis, "Davis Rejoinder," *Art Digest* 9 (April 1, 1935), 12-13, 26-27.

4. Thomas Hart Benton, "On the American Scene," *Art Front* 1 (April 1935),

3, 8. Here are published the answers Benton submitted to ten questions he had solicited from the editors of *Art Front.*

5. Davis, "Rejoinder," 13.

6. Ibid. For a balanced discussion of the Benton–Davis debate, including the accusations of fascism, antisemitism, and racism aimed at Benton and Thomas Craven, his chief champion, see Erika Doss, *Benton, Pollock, and the Politics of Modernism: From Realism to Abstract Expressionism* (Chicago: University of Chicago Press, 1991), 116–24. Doss rationalizes Benton's more offensive caricatures as popular stereotypes similar to those used by Hollywood to reach, not teach, a broad national audience (p. 123). She also proposes that Benton was accused of bigotry because of his close association with Craven, who is still remembered for his published crack that Alfred Stieglitz was "a Hoboken Jew . . . hardly equipped for the leadership of a genuine American expression." This unfortunate statement is as indicative of prejudice against Stieglitz's taste for modernist painting and his introduction of its premier innovators to New York as it is of prejudice against his ethnicity.

7. Samuel Kootz, *New Frontiers in American Painting* (New York: Hastings House, 1943), 10.

8. Ibid., 11.

9. Ibid., 14.

10. See Hancher's twenty-two page transcript entitled "Notes made in relation to conferences in my office with regard to members of the staff of instruction of the Department of Art," and dated November 25, 1940. That the issues were still alive at the end of the academic year may be seen in a seven-page memorandum from the Office of the President entitled "Conference with Mr. Park Rinard and Mr. Dan Dutcher Held May 7, 1941," Grant Wood Archives, State University of Iowa Library, Iowa City.

11. H. W. Janson, "The International Aspects of Regionalism," *College Art Journal* 2 (May 1943), 110–15.

12. Ibid., 112.

13. Ibid. For an explanation and evaluation of the term *Neue Sachlichkeit* from G. F. Hartlaub, the director of the Mannheim *Kunsthalle,* who coined it in 1924, see Alfred H. Barr, Jr., "Otto Dix," *The Arts* 17 (January 1931), 237. In a letter of July 8, 1929, to Barr, Hartlaub explained that the term and its art related to "the general contemporary feeling in Germany of resignation and cynicism" as well as to an "enthusiasm for the immediate reality." He summed it up as "healthy disillusionment" and felt that after five years of increasing misuse, it was "high time to withdraw it from currency."

14. Janson, "International Aspects," 113.

15. Ibid., 113–14. As to "tempera technique," 99 to 100 percent of Wood's paintings used oil-based pigment, as everyone but Janson seems to have known.

16. Ibid., 114.

17. Ibid., 114–15.

18. Ibid., 113.

19. H. W. Janson, "Benton and Wood, Champions of Regionalism," *Magazine of Art* 39 (May 1946), 184–86, 198–200.

20. Ibid., 184.

21. Ibid.

22. See Guilbaut, *How New York Stole the Idea of Modern Art,* 105-19; also see Milton Brown, "After Three Years," *Magazine of Art* 39 (April 1946), 138-66.

23. Janson, "Champions," 184.

24. Ibid., 185.

25. Grant Wood, *Revolt Against the City* (Iowa City: Clio, 1935), 22.

26. Janson, "Champions," 185.

27. Wood, *Revolt,* 22. Italics are mine.

28. Janson, "Champions," 199.

29. Ibid., 186. If Iowa ever had a painter who was a fascist, possibly a Nazi sympathizer, it would have been the academician Charles A. Cumming, the director of the Cumming School of Art in Des Moines and founder of the University of Iowa's art department. Before he died in 1932 he published two pamphlets on "The White Man's Art" in which he invoked Aryan superiority. Like Hitler's art theorists and historians, he traced the art he approved of back to the ancient Greeks and through the "Nordic branch of the Aryan race." It flourished "until the white race mixed its blood with primitive peoples or till the government fell into the hands of democracy." For more about Cumming and his disapproval of both European modernism and Grant Wood's mature style, see Evan R. Firestone, "Incursions of Modern Art in the Regionalist Heartland," *The Palimpsest* 72 (Fall 1991), 148-60.

30. Janson, "Champions," 186.

31. Ibid.

32. Ibid., 199.

33. Wood, *Revolt,* 8-11.

34. See the exhibition catalogue, *Realismus und Sachlichkeit—Aspekte deutscher Kunst 1919-1933* (Berlin: Deutsche Democratische Republik, 1974).

35. See Berthold Hinz, *Art in the Third Reich* (1974; rev. ed., New York: Pantheon, 1979).

36. George L. Mosse, *The Crisis of German Ideology* (New York: Grosset and Dunlap, 1964), chaps. 6, 9.

37. Ibid., 111-18.

38. George L. Mosse, *Nazi Culture* (New York: Grosset and Dunlap, 1966), "Toward a Total Culture," 135-38; and Hinz, *Art in the Third Reich,* "National Socialist Painting," chap. 5, pp. 77-172.

39. F. A. Kauffmann, as quoted by Hinz, *Art in the Third Reich,* 77-78.

40. Meyer Schapiro, "Populist Realism," *Partisan Review* 4, no. 2 (1938), 53-57.

41. Morris Janowitz, "Black Legions on the March," in *America in Crisis,* edited by Daniel Aaron (New York: Knopf, 1952), 304-25.

42. George L. Mosse, *Confronting the Nation* (Hanover, N.H.: University Press of New England, 1993), chap. 2, "National Self-Representation During the 1930s in Europe and the United States," 33. Mosse earlier stated that regionalism ran counter to nationalism: "Fascism must come in unified countries. America is a regional country, one of more or less coherent ethnic groups which would be almost impossible to unify. As such the United States lacks the first and most elementary prerequisite for fascism, namely an integrated nationalism." George L. Mosse,

Nazism: A Historical and Comparative Analysis of National Socialism, an interview with Michael A. Ledeen (New Brunswick, N.J.: Transaction Books, 1978), 127.

43. Whiting, *Antifascism*, chap. 4, "American Heroes and Invading Barbarians," 99–100.

44. Ibid., 113.

45. Ibid., 131.

46. Kootz, *New Frontiers in American Painting*, 4.

47. Whiting, *Antifascism*, 122.

48. Ibid., 114.

49. Ibid.

50. Ibid., 113.

51. "Interview with Grant Wood," *Cedar Rapids Gazette*, June 29, 1941. The pair of paintings, said Wood, were "inspired by a new appreciation of an America tranquil in a warring world, of democracy free and hopeful, of a country worth preserving."

52. Whiting, *Antifascism*, 113.

53. These drawings belong to a private collection in Cedar Rapids, Iowa. See James M. Dennis, *Grant Wood: A Study in American Art and Culture* 2d ed. (Columbia: University of Missouri Press, 1986), 241, n. 6.

54. Whiting, *Antifascism*, 111.

55. For a thorough analysis of the painting *Parson Weems' Fable*, see Wanda Corn, *Grant Wood: The Regionalist Vision* (New Haven: Yale University Press, 1983), 120–23.

56. Thomas Hart Benton, "Painting and Propaganda Don't Mix," *Saturday Review* 43 (December 24, 1960), 16–17.

CHAPTER 5. GRANT WOOD'S MATRIARCHATE

1. For emphasis on Wood's promotion of Regionalism, see Wanda Corn, *Grant Wood: The Regionalist Vision* (New Haven: Yale University Press, 1983). Part III, "The Regionalist," 35–62, treats him as "the compleat Regionalist," who publicized and disseminated the basic principles of Regionalism through teaching and lecture tours.

2. Barbara Melosh, *Engendering Culture: Manhood and Womanhood in New Deal Public Art and Theater* (Washington, D.C.: Smithsonian Institution Press, 1991), 4.

3. Joyce Carol Oates, "The Woman Before Hillary," a review of *Leading with My Heart*, by Virginia Kelley with James Morgan, *New York Times Book Review*, May 8, 1994, p. 1.

4. Melosh, *Engendering Culture*, 63.

5. Ibid., 4.

6. For examples, descriptions, and discussions of New Deal pictures, easel and mural, see Francis V. O'Connor, ed., *Art for the Millions* (New York: 1973); Matthew Baigell, *The American Scene: American Painting of the 1930s* (New York: 1974); and Karal Ann Marling, "A Note on New Deal Iconography: Futurology and the Historical Myth," *Prospects: An Annual of American Cultural Studies* 4

(1979), 420–40. For an insightful and entertaining region-by-region study of the post office murals sponsored by the Treasury Department Section of Fine Arts, see Marling's *Wall-to-Wall America: A Cultural History of Post-Office Murals in the Great Depression* (Minneapolis: University of Minnesota Press, 1982). Also see Marlene Park and Gerald E. Markowitz, *Democratic Vistas: Post Offices and Public Art in the New Deal* (Philadelphia: Temple University Press, 1984), chap. 5, "Regionalism," 68–111, in which thematic differences in the Section murals from region to region are astutely observed. Melosh's *Engendering Culture* compares and contrasts Treasury Section murals with plays performed under the auspices of the Federal Theatre Project. Her purpose is to analyze the social and political significance of reciprocal male and female roles during the New Deal.

7. See Matthew Baigell with Allen Kaufman, "The Missouri Murals: Another Look at Benton," *Art Journal* 37 (1977), 314–21. This essay points out the obvious class and race conflicts depicted by Benton in his murals for the Missouri State Capitol Building in Jefferson City. It also interprets its references to crime and corruption as consistent with his Populist hatred of self-serving, centralized power of any kind.

8. William H. Chafe, *The American Woman: Her Changing Social, Economic and Political Roles, 1920–1970* (New York: Oxford University Press, 1972), 104–7. See also Ellen Wiley Todd, *The "New Woman" Revised: Painting and Gender Politics on Fourteenth Street* (Berkeley: University of California Press, 1993), 32–34, for discussion of Dorothy Bromley's credo for a moderate New Woman of the post-franchise era who would reconform to the "heterosexual ideal that privileges wifehood, motherhood, and feminine charm over a strong woman-centered community that might threaten the patriarchal order."

9. Mary P. Ryan, *Womanhood in America: From Colonial Times to the Present* (New York: New Viewpoints, 1975), chap. 3, "Mothers of Civilization: The Common Woman, 1830–1860," 139–91.

10. Ruth H. Bloch, "The Rise of the Moral Mother," *Feminist Studies* 2 (1978), 101. A primary source of Bloch's observation could very well have been provided by the Reverend John Abbot, who in 1833 sermonized: "When our land is filled with pious and patriotic mothers, then will it be filled with virtuous and patriotic men. The world's redeeming influences, under the blessing of the Holy Spirit, must come from a mother's lips." John Abbot, *The Mother at Home, or Principles of Maternal Duty* (New York: American Tract Society, 1833).

11. Bloch, "Moral Mother," 116.

12. Anonymous, *Sketches of the History, Disposition, Accomplishments, Employments, Customs and Importance of the Fair Sex* (Philadelphia, 1791), 103–4. Quoted in Bloch, "Moral Mother," 117.

13. William L. O'Neill, *Everyone Was Brave* (New York: Quadrangle, 1969), 34.

14. Ibid.

15. Bloch, "Moral Mother," 115.

16. For a good summary analysis of maternal altruism among middle-class women as practiced devotedly by Jane Addams, see Ryan, *Womanhood in America*, chap. 5, "Workers, Immigrants, Social Housekeepers: Women and the Industrial Machine, 1860–1920," 225–49.

17. Todd, *"New Woman" Revised,* 31–37.

18. Grant Wood, "An Iowa Secret," *Art Digest* 8 (October 1933), 6.

19. See Corn, *Grant Wood,* 129–42, for a discussion of *American Gothic* parodies and a small selection of examples. With regard to the initially intended meaning of the painting, Wood was not alone in his choice of subject matter. In the midst of her most creative and prolific decade, Ruth Suckow classified the Iowa culture that inspired her stories. Leaning on Sinclair Lewis, she acknowledged "the Main Street element of small town hardness, dreariness and tense material ambitions. Still below this, solid and unyielding, is the retired farmer element in the towns; narrow, cautious, steady and thrifty, suspicious of 'culture' but faithful to the churches. . . . And then there are the working farmers, the folk element, and still the very soil and the bed rock of our native culture." Ruth Suckow, "Iowa," *American Mercury* 9 (September 1926), 45.

20. Elizabeth Cady Stanton, "The Matriarchate, or Mother Age," in *Transactions of the National Council of Women of the United States,* edited by Rachel Foster Avery (Philadelphia, 1891), 221–22. In her book *When God Was a Woman* (New York and London: Harcourt, Brace, Jovanovich, 1976) Merlin Stone alludes to *The Woman's Bible,* a compilation of writings in which Stanton and other early feminists challenged the divine right to rule over women vested in men by Judaism, Christianity, and Mohammedanism. Merlin discusses the ancient goddess cultures of the Near and Middle East, whose matriarchal aspects were eliminated by the later male-dominated religions.

21. Stanton, "The Matriarchate," 221–22.

22. Mary Lease, "Women in the Farmers' Alliance," in Avery, *Transactions,* 229.

23. Corn, *Grant Wood,* 80.

24. In concocting this rural versus urban picture, Wood posed Edward Rowen, at the time director of the American Federation of Arts' "Little Gallery" in Cedar Rapids, as the farm woman and his friend Mary Lackersteen, a cousin of Frank Lloyd Wright, as the city woman.

25. The painting is a takeoff on a tintype of Matilda Peet now in the Grant Wood Collection, Davenport Art Gallery, Davenport, Iowa.

26. Karal Ann Marling swears that in comical commemoration of George Washington's two hundredth birthday in 1932 and as a "sight gag" satirizing superpatriotism, the left-hand woman in *Daughters of Revolution* is a takeoff on Gilbert Stuart's "Athenaeum" portrait of the first president (the one on the dollar bill). Karal Ann Marling, *George Washington Slept Here: Colonial Revivals and American Culture, 1876–1986* (Cambridge: Harvard University Press, 1988), 345–46.

27. For a thorough documentation and discussion of Leutze's *Washington Crossing the Delaware* as an inspiration to the Revolution of 1848, see Barbara S. Groseclose, *Emanuel Leutze, 1816–1868: Freedom Is the Only King* (Washington, D.C.: Smithsonian Institution Press, 1976), part 4, pp. 33–47. The original canvas, in an art museum in Bremen, was, ironically, destroyed by an American air raid during World War II.

28. O'Neill, *Everyone,* 229.

29. No documents, primary or secondary, record this event. My source of information was a World War I veteran and Legionnaire in Cedar Rapids, who said

that while the local chapter of the DAR passed no resolution against the Memorial Window, several of its members spoke out against its dedication.

30. "Art in the 1934 Fair," *Chicago Daily News,* June 18, 1934. In Boston, a DAR chapter's censorship committee laughed and applauded when shown a lantern-slide reproduction of the painting. "News from the States," *Saturday Review of Literature* 10 (August 12, 1933), 47.

31. "This War to Give America Art Leadership, Wood Says," *Milwaukee News Sentinel,* January 7, 1940. Wood made this statement to a meeting of the Milwaukee College Club, whose members were primarily female.

32. See G. W. Ferguson, *Signs and Symbols in Christian Art* (New York: Oxford University Press, 1959), 12–37.

33. For a summary of Eleanor Roosevelt's feminist activism, see June Sochen, *Movers and Shakers: American Women Thinkers and Activists, 1900–1970* (New York: Quadrangle/The New York Times, 1973), esp. "Eleanor Roosevelt: A Living Symbol of Feminism," 151–70.

34. Chafe, *American Woman,* 40–44. Also see Susan Ware, *Holding Their Own: American Women in the 1930s* (Boston: Twayne, 1982), chap. 4, "Feminism and Social Reform," 87–115; and Joseph P. Lash, *Eleanor and Franklin* (New York: Signet/American Library, 1971), 512–14.

35. Chafe, *American Woman,* 107–10.

36. Melosh, *Engendering Culture,* 54.

37. Kathryn Stoner Hicks Moody, "Territorial Days in Minnesota," manuscript, Minnesota Historical Society, St. Paul, Minnesota, pp. 10–12.

38. See Walker D. Wyman, *Frontier Woman: The Life of a Woman Homesteader on the Dakota Frontier* (Madison: University of Wisconsin–River Falls Press, 1972).

39. Melosh, *Engendering Culture,* 64.

40. This information was shared by Miss Prescott during a visit at her home in Cedar Rapids in the summer of 1971.

41. For illustrations of these, see James M. Dennis, *Grant Wood: A Study in American Art and Culture* (New York: Viking Press, 1975), 162–65.

CHAPTER 6. TOM BENTON'S "GIRLS" AS REVERBERATIONS OF MODERNIZATION

1. Mary Ryan, *Womanhood in America: From Colonial Times to the Present* (New York: New Viewpoints, 1975), chap. 5, "The Sexy Saleslady: Psychology and Consumption in the Twentieth Century," 257–65. Also see Kathryn Weibel, *Mirror Mirror: Images of Women Reflected in Popular Culture* (New York: Anchor Press, 1977), chap. 4, "Images of Women in Women's Magazines and Magazine Advertising," 135–55; and Stuart Ewen, *Captains of Consciousness: Advertising and the Social Roots of the Consumer Culture* (New York: McGraw-Hill, 1976), chaps. 6–7: "Consumption and the Ideal of the New Woman," 159–76, and "Consumption and Seduction," 177–84.

2. Charlotte Perkins Gilman, "The New Generation of Women," *Current History* 18 (August 1923), 731–37.

3. Ellen Wiley Todd, *The "New Woman" Revised: Painting and Gender Politics on Fourteenth Street* (Berkeley: University of California Press, 1993), 152.

4. Marjorie Rosen, *Popcorn Venus* (New York: Avon Books, 1973), chap. 5, "Delineating the Flapper: Youth Flamed and Beauty Fluttered," 75–97.

5. Ewen, *Captains of Consciousness,* 179.

6. Thomas Hart Benton, *An Artist in America* (New York: Robert M. McBride & Co., 1937), 4. For information about Benton's parents see the narrative account of his early years in Henry Adams, *Thomas Hart Benton* (New York: 1989), chaps. 1–3. As explained in a bibliographic essay, an unpublished third autobiography, "The Intimate Story," personal letters, and interviews with the artist's sister, Mildred, and his daughter, Jessie, served as primary sources.

7. Benton, *Artist in America,* 77.

8. Ibid., 269. For insightful accounts of Benton's early sexual experiences see Adams, *Thomas Hart Benton,* chaps. 1–2, pp. 2–36.

9. Walter Lippmann, *A Preface to Morals* (New York: Macmillan, 1929), 6.

10. See Adams, *Thomas Hart Benton,* 10–19.

11. As quoted in Adams, *Thomas Hart Benton,* 191.

12. For a discussion of the Siren as a successor to the flapper, see Todd, *"New Woman" Revised,* 196–204.

13. Benton, *Artist in America,* 99.

14. Ibid., 171.

15. Josef von Sternberg, *Fun in a Chinese Laundry* (New York: Macmillan, 1965), 120, as quoted in Lucy Fischer, "The Image of Woman as Image: The Optical Politics of *Dames,*" in *Sexual Strategems: The World of Women in Film,* edited by Patricia Erens (New York: Horizon, 1979), part 2, "Films Directed by Men," 45.

16. Fischer, "Image of Woman," 58.

17. The actress Jessica Tandy, who played Blanche in the original theater production of Tennessee Williams's *Streetcar Named Desire,* refused to pose with her co-stars Karl Malden and Marlon Brando in a *tableau vivant* of Benton's painting for *Look* magazine. This was her way of protesting against its obvious emphasis on Stanley's libidinous attraction to his defenseless wife. Adams, *Thomas Hart Benton,* 333.

18. Victor Koshkin-Youritzin ends his "Thomas Hart Benton: 'Bathers' Rediscovered," *Art Magazine* 49 (May–June 1980), 12, with a brief attempt at psychoanalyzing Benton's penchant for "dramatically violent and explicitly sexual paintings" as symptomatic of a little-man complex. His analysis of *The Music Lesson* (1943) within this sensitive frame of reference treads on risky ground, perhaps reading more into a painting than the visual evidence affords and thereby suggesting more about the eye of the beholder than the intent of the artist: see pp. 101–2.

19. For reactions to *Susannah* and *Persephone* see Adams, *Thomas Hart Benton,* 290–93.

20. Betty Friedan, *The Feminine Mystique* (New York: Dell, 1963), 261.

CHAPTER 7. JOHN CURRY'S REACTIVE WOMEN: FROM MYTH TO PROTEST

1. For a discussion of the latter see Ellen Wiley Todd, *The "New Woman" Revised: Painting and Gender Politics on Fourteenth Street* (Berkeley: University of California Press, 1993), chap. 1, "The 'New Woman' Revised," 1–38.

2. See James M. Dennis and Kathleen M. Daniels, "A Modern American Purgatory, Isabel Bishop's *Dante and Virgil in Union Square, 1932*," in *Between Heaven and Hell: Union Square in the 1930s* (Wilkes Barre: Sordoni Art Gallery, Wilkes University, Pennsylvania, 1996), 4–20.

3. Reproduced in color in the May 6, 1940, issue of *Life* magazine, this painting was commissioned to commemorate President Hoover as the organizer of relief during the 1927 Mississippi River flood. In his descriptive analysis of the composition, Laurence Schmeckebier ignored the foremost mother group and saw the ex-president flanked by two other statuesque officials as the "stabilizing hub" of the composition. Laurence E. Schmeckebier, *John Steuart Curry's Pageant of America* (New York: American Artists Group, 1943), 269.

4. Glenda Riley, "Images of the Frontier Woman: Iowa as a Case Study," *Western Historical Quarterly* 2 (1977), 192. The mythic image of the frontier woman obviously comprises the four virtues of piety, purity, domesticity, and submissiveness defined by Barbara Welter as components of the nineteenth-century "Cult of True Womanhood." Barbara Welter, "The Cult of True Womanhood: 1820–1860," *American Quarterly* 18 (Summer 1966), 151–74. Riley later investigated the erroneous stereotyping of frontier women's experiences in her "Women of the West," *Journal of American Culture* 3 (Summer 1980), 311–29, and *Frontierswomen: The Iowa Experience* (Ames: Iowa State University Press, 1981). Still later she published a comprehensive study of the varied roles of women on the frontier, distinguishing the earlier settlements on the Midwest prairies from those on the trans-Mississippi plains. Glenda Riley, *The Female Frontier: A Comparative View of Women on the Prairie and the Plains* (Lawrence: University Press of Kansas, 1988). For the varieties of strenuous work performed by women throughout the West, see esp. chap. 3, "Home and Hearth on the Prairie," 42–76, and chap. 4, "Home and Hearth on the Plains," 76–102.

5. Mary E. Lease, "Women in the Farmers' Alliance," in *Transactions of the National Council of Women of the United States,* edited by Rachel Foster Avery (Philadelphia, 1891), 216. Lease earned notoriety by exhorting: "What you farmers need is to raise less corn and more hell!"

6. See Mary Hallock Foote, *A Victorian Gentlewoman in the Far West* (San Marino, Calif.: Huntington Library, 1972).

7. Mary Hallock Foote, "The Coming of Winter," *Century Magazine* 37 (1888), 163.

8. The Cultural historian Annette Kolodny came to a somewhat different conclusion: Annette Kolodny, *The Land Before Her: Fantasy and Experience of the American Frontiers, 1630-1860* (Chapel Hill: University of North Carolina Press, 1984). See especially chap. 6, "Margaret Fuller: Recovering Our Mother's Garden," 112–31; chap. 7, "The Literary Legacy of Caroline Kirkland: Emigrants' Guide to a Failed Eden," 131–60; and chap. 8, "The Domestic Fantasy Goes West," 161–77. This book is Kolodny's sequel to *The Lay of the Land* (Chapel Hill: University of North Carolina Press, 1975), in which she traces men's erotic fantasies of possessing and transforming the virgin American landscape.

9. Emerson Hough, *The Passing of the Frontier* (New Haven: Yale University Press, 1921), 93.

10. Ernest Groves, *The American Woman: Images and Realities* (New York,

1942). For a pictorial survey of the occupations of frontier women, see *The Women,* text by Joan Swallow Reiter, vol. 23 in the Time-Life series *The Old West* (New York, 1978).

11. Groves, *American Woman,* 92.

12. *New York Times,* Sunday Rotogravure, February 27, 1927.

13. It seems that every major black male figure painted by Curry is depicted with his arms stretched out and his hands raised high in a pleading stance. See also *The Fugitive* (1933-1940), oil and tempera on canvas, illustrated in M. Sue Kendall, *Rethinking Regionalism: John Steuart Curry and the Kansas Mural Controversy* (Washington, D.C.: Smithsonian Institution Press, 1986), 80. The central figure of *The Freeing of the Slaves,* originally intended for a mural in the Department of Justice Building, in Washington, D.C., was criticized and rejected for its racist "hallelujah" pose by the Commission of Fine Arts in 1936. After becoming artist-in-residence at the University of Wisconsin, Curry became a close friend of Lloyd K. Garrison, dean of the law school and great-grandson of the abolitionist William Lloyd Garrison. Dean Garrison wanted the work as a mural in the new law library and found a donor, Robert Uihlein, head of the leading Milwaukee brewing family, to pay for it. Ibid., 74-77.

14. Kathryn Adam, "Laura, Ma, Mary, Carrie, and Grace: Western Women as Portrayed by Laura Ingalls Wilder," in *The Women's West,* edited by Susan Armitage and Elizabeth Jameson (Norman: University of Oklahoma Press, 1987), 101.

Also see Sandra L. Myres, *Westering Women and the Frontier Experience 1800-1915* (Albuquerque: University of New Mexico Press, 1982), chap. 6, "New Home —Who'll Follow? Women and Frontier Homemaking," 141-66, emphasizes that "the frontier, like the trail, tended to blur sex roles." She cites several examples of women and girls doing a great amount of field work and actually assuming the entire burden of farming when husbands were ill, absent, or deceased.

15. Hamlin Garland, *A Son of the Middle Border* (New York: Macmillan, 1917), 310. In spite of Garland's sympathy for overworked farm women, his conservative conceptions of the woman's sphere remained unchanged up to his death in 1940. Women, he advised his two artistic daughters, should marry and stay at home. See Roger E. Carp, "Hamlin Garland and the Cult of True Womanhood," in *Women, Women Writers, and the West,* edited by L. L. Lee and Merril Lewis (Troy, N.Y.: Whitson, 1979), 83-99.

16. Calder M. Pickett, "John Steuart Curry and the Topeka Murals Controversy," *Kansas Quarterly* 2 (1970), 38. For the idea that the contemporary apparel of Curry's Kansas Madonna was of central significance to a theme of modernity and prosperity in *Kansas Pastoral,* see the excellent analysis of this mural and the unpainted Rotunda panels as sociological studies in Kendall, *Rethinking Regionalism,* 104-12.

17. For the Death and a Maiden theme into the twentieth century, see Friedrich W. Kasten, "Gründerzeit, Kaiserreich und Weimarer Republik—Totentanzdarstellungen zwischen 1871 und 1933," in *Thema Totentanz, Kontinuität und Wandel einer Bildidee vom Mittelalter bis Heute* (Mannheim: Mannheimer Kunstverein, 1986), particularly "Junge Frau und Tod" and "Werden und Vergehen," 86-96.

18. Schmeckebier, *Curry's Pageant,* 52.

19. *New York Times,* November 4, 1928. Italics are mine.

20. Robert L. Gambone, *Art and Popular Religion in Evangelical America, 1915–1940* (Knoxville: University of Tennessee Press, 1989), 194. For a detailed description of *Baptism in Kansas* and a quotation from a 1942 letter in which Curry identifies the farmyard of the painting as that of a Kansas neighbor, Will McBride, in the twenties, see 191–94. Gambone identifies the event as a Campbellite immersion ceremony and discusses Curry's revolt against his family's Scottish Covenanter background. In support of the possibility that Curry was at least skeptical about the "holy roller" customs of Pentecostals, such as the Campbellites in his hometown of Winchester, Kansas, see Kendall's discussion of his family's conservative Presbyterian religion in *Rethinking Regionalism, 92–94.*

21. Marjorie Rosen, *Popcorn Venus* (New York: Avon Books, 1973), chap. 3, "Mary's Curls, Griffith's Girls, Eternal Girl-children, Sugar 'n' Slurps," 34–58.

22. See Todd, *"New Woman" Revised, 196–202.*

23. Another isolationist protest was *The Return of Private Davis from the Argonne,* completed in 1940. He had started it in 1928 in memory of a high school friend whose flag-draped coffin was returned from France to be buried in a rural graveyard out on the Kansas plains. For Curry's Wisconsin-based isolationism in the light of Roosevelt's foreign policies after 1937, see Kendall, *Rethinking Regionalism,* 83–85. For further war-related Death and a Maiden examples, see Kasten, "Der I. Weltkrieg als Thema im Totentanz," in *Thema Totentanz, 167–92.*

24. Marlene Park and Gerald E. Markowitz, *The New Deal for Art: The Government Art Projects of the 1930s with Examples from New York City and State* (Hamilton, N.Y.: Gallery Association of New York State, 1977), and *Democratic Vistas: Post Offices and Public Art in the New Deal* (Philadelphia: Temple University Press, 1984).

CHAPTER 8. GRANT WOOD'S AFFAIR WITH ABSTRACT ART

1. John Steuart Curry, public address sponsored by the Art Association of Madison, Wisconsin, on his assumption of the position of artist-in-residence at the University of Wisconsin, 1937. The full address appears in Laurence E. Schmeckebier, *John Steuart Curry's Pageant of America* (New York: American Artists Group, 1943), 240–99.

2. "Grant Wood Explains Why He Prefers to Remain in Middle West in Talk at Kansas City," *Cedar Rapids Sunday Gazette and Republican,* March 22, 1931.

3. As quoted in Ruth Pickering, "Thomas Hart Benton on His Way Back to Missouri," *Arts and Decoration* 42 (February 1935), 20.

4. Benton also commented on his methods of this period in a later article in *Creative Art* magazine. Thomas Hart Benton, "My American Epic in Paint," *Creative Art* 3 (December 1928), xxxi–xxxvi. Matthew Baigell published the earliest art historical accounts of Benton's development of figurative abstraction in theory and practice. See Matthew Baigell, *Thomas Hart Benton* (New York: Harry N. Abrams, 1975). In addition to his monograph on Benton, see Matthew Baigell, "Thomas Hart Benton in the 1920s," *Art Journal* 4 (Summer 1970), 422–29. The emergence of Benton's "Mechanics of Form" out of his Stanton Macdonald-Wright Synchromist period ten years earlier is discussed in Victor Koshkin-Youritzin, "Thomas Hart Benton: 'Bathers' Rediscovered," *Art Magazine* 49 (May 1980), 98–

102. For evaluations of Benton's proabstraction leanings, see Gail Levin, "Thomas Hart Benton: Synchromism and Abstract Art," *Arts* 4 (December 1981), 144–48, and Hilton Kramer, "Benton: The Radical Modernist," *New York Times,* January 10, 1982.

5. In the fall of 1922 or the spring of 1923, Grant Wood is reported to have exhibited a totally nonfigurative abstract painting at the Cedar Rapids Art Association. He called it *Song of India.* Allegedly, it consisted of swirls of oil paint in contrasting colors that he applied to burlap while playing Rimsky-Korsakov's composition on a Victrola. Interview with Mrs. Marvin Cone, Cedar Rapids, Iowa, April 13, 1981. H. W. Janson dismissed this interlude in Wood's career as "a brief and uncomfortable attempt at abstraction following his first visit to Paris." H. W. Janson, "Benton and Wood, Champions of Regionalism," *Magazine of Art* 39 (May 1946), 198.

6. "Grant Wood Helps Young Artists Develop Technique," *Daily Iowan,* November 3, 1935.

7. "Grant Wood Explains," *Cedar Rapids Sunday Gazette and Republican,* March 22, 1931.

8. Ibid.

9. As recalled by Wood's late sister, Nan Wood Graham, and brother, Frank Wood, during interviews with the author.

10. Ernest A. Batchelder, *The Principles of Design* (Chicago: Inland Printer, 1904), 8–10.

11. In the preface to his *Principles of Design,* Batchelder forthrightly acknowledged Ross's influence. Although a much less intellectual systematization of design than that published by Ross in his *Theory of Pure Design: Harmony, Balance, Rhythm* (1907), Batchelder's *Principles of Design* includes certain concepts and terminology that apparently originated with his teacher.

12. Batchelder, *Principles of Design,* 4.

13. Ibid., 5–6.

14. Marianne Martin, "Some American Contributions to Early 20th Century Abstraction," *Arts Magazine* 10 (June 1980), 158–65.

15. Ernest Fenollosa, *Imagination in Art* (Boston: Boston Art Students Association, 1894), 7, as quoted in Martin, "Some American Contributions," 159.

16. Arthur W. Dow, *Composition: A Series of Exersises in Art Structure for the Use of Students and Teachers* (Garden City, N.Y.: Doubleday, Page, 1899), 5. (A revised edition was published in 1913.)

17. Ibid., 60.

18. Ibid., 5.

19. Arthur W. Dow, *Theory and Practice of Teaching Art* (New York: Columbia University Press, 1908), 4.

20. As quoted in Frederick C. Moffatt, *Arthur Wesley Dow* (Washington, D.C.: Smithsonian Institution Press, 1977), 50.

21. Dow, *Theory and Practice of Teaching Art,* 5.

22. Dow, *Composition* (1899), 37.

23. Ibid., 52.

24. Ibid., 15.

25. Dow, *Composition* (1913), 100.

26. Moffatt, *Arthur Wesley Dow*, 63. Dow, however, is thought to have established his compositional principles by 1892.

27. Dow, *Composition* (1913), 47.

28. Dow, *Composition* (1899), 25.

29. Moffatt, *Arthur Wesley Dow*, 95. In addition to being an instructor at Pratt Institute, he held summer classes at Ipswich, Massachusetts, and, beginning in 1903, served for many years as the director of the Department of Fine Arts at Teachers College, Columbia University.

30. Lawrence W. Chisolm, *Fenollosa: The Far East and American Culture* (New Haven: Yale University Press, 1963), 237.

31. Jack Cowart, Juan Hamilton, and Sarah Greenough, eds., *Georgia O'Keeffe: Art and Letters* (Washington, D.C.: National Gallery of Art, 1987), 275, n. 3. For a consideration of Dow's influence on O'Keeffe see Katherine Kuh, *The Artist's Voice* (New York: Harper and Row, 1962), and Sandra Fillin Yeh, "Innovative Moderns: Arthur G. Dove and Georgia O'Keeffe," *Arts Magazine* 56 (June 1982), 68–72.

32. Quoted in Samuel Kootz, *Modern American Painters* (New York: Brewer and Warren, 1930), 37. For the best treatment to date of Dove's awareness and assimilation of Dow's teachings, see Arlette Klaric, *Arthur G. Dove's Abstract Style of 1912: Dimensions of the Decorative and Bergsonian Realities* (Ph.D. diss., University of Wisconsin-Madison, 1984).

33. Kootz, *Modern American Painters*, 37.

34. Leo Stein, *A-B-C of Aesthetics* (New York: Boni and Liveright, 1927), 156.

35. Ibid., 118–28.

36. Ibid.

37. Ibid., 163.

38. Ibid., 169.

39. Ibid., 166.

40. Ibid., 171.

41. Ibid., 176–77.

42. Batchelder, *Principles of Design*, 34, fig. 15.

43. Ibid.

44. By dividing each edge into thirds and criss-crossing diagonals from point to point through the intersections of nine equal oblongs, Wood contrived an easily learned system vaguely comparable to the plane geometry of determining a "golden section," popularized as "dynamic symmetry" by the art educator Jay Hambidge. In an interview early in 1984, the noted African American sculptor and printmaker Elizabeth Catlett, an M.F.A. student under Wood at the University of Iowa, described the system: "He made us work step by step; he separated the whole thing. First we got an idea, and we did a drawing, a line drawing. Then we did dynamic symmetry, which he taught us. You divide up the space, and you use a lot of lines, straight lines and diagonal lines. And you project your drawing over that, so that it changes very slightly, but it fits onto one of the lines which you've made. So then, instead of just an ordinary drawing, you got a dynamic drawing, with slight distortions. But the distortions strengthened the drawing." Elizabeth Catlett, interview with Clifton Johnson, Amistad Research Center, Tulane University, New Orleans, January 5, 1984.

1. In chapters 2 and 4 of her survey *American Art Since 1900* (New York: Praeger, 1968), Barbara Rose adroitly alternated between two grounds for dismissing the leading first-generation American modernists: the necessity of Cubist-Futurist precedence and self-expression. With regard to self-expression, she essentially ignored the relevance of place or locale to the subject matter or to its particular treatment in their paintings.

2. Cecelia Tichi, *Shifting Gears: Technology, Literature, Culture in Modernist America* (Chapel Hill: University of North Carolina Press, 1987), chap. 5, "Machines Made of Words," 240–52.

3. See Thomas Hart Benton, *An American Art: A Professional and Technical Autobiography* (Lawrence: University Press of Kansas, 1969), 43–45.

4. Cecelia Tichi places Williams's development of his "machines made of words" in the context of Taylorism, the efficiency movement started and promoted by the engineer Frederick W. Taylor. She goes so far as to say that Taylorism "let Williams redefine the poet and the poem as designer and design." Tichi, *Shifting Gears*, 262.

5. For evaluative discussions of Williams's early interest in the experiments of contemporaneous painters see Bram Dijkstra, *The Hieroglyphics of a New Speech: Cubism, Stieglitz, and the Early Poetry of William Carlos Williams* (Princeton: Princeton University Press, 1969); William Marling, *William Carlos Williams and the Painters, 1909–1923* (Athens: Ohio University Press, 1982), esp. chaps. 5–10, pp. 83–196; and Christopher McGowan, *William Carlos Williams' Early Poetry: The Visual Arts Background* (Ann Arbor: UMI Research Press, 1984). For more specific discussions of the importance of Duchamp to Williams, see Dickran Tashjian, *William Carlos Williams and the American Scene 1920–1940* (New York: Whitney Museum of American Art, 1978), 56–63, and Henry M. Sayre, "Ready-mades and Other Measures: The Poetics of Marcel Duchamp and William Carlos Williams," *Journal of Modern Literature* 8, no. 1 (1980), 3–22.

6. William Carlos Williams, *Selected Letters of William Carlos Williams*, edited by John C. Thirlwall (New York: McDowell, Obolensky, 1957), 97–98.

7. William Carlos Williams, *The Autobiography* (New York: Random House, 1951), 172. In her catalogue essay for the 1987–88 Charles Demuth exhibition originating at the Whitney Museum, Barbara Haskell quoted Williams with regard to the discrepancy between the origin of the poem and the design of the painting. She explains that Williams eliminated "narrative sequence" in writing his poem in order to achieve the instantaneity of the experience. Each line was conceived as an "object." She does not include Williams's specific suggestions for how the painting might have been corrected to conform with the poem. Barbara Haskell, *Charles Demuth* (New York: H. N. Abrams, 1987), 183–85. For a more detailed account and discussion of Williams's complaints and corrections, including a May 1928 letter to Demuth, see Tashjian, *Williams and the American Scene*, 71–72.

8. According to Tashjian, *Williams and the American Scene*, 68, Williams was still perturbed by Demuth's *Machinery* twenty-four years later when he wrote that it remained guilty of "faking the psychologic appearance of the machine, making perhaps a 'woman' of it, so that it appears to be what it is not." William Carlos Williams, "Postscript by a Poet," *Art in America* 42 (October 1921), 215.

9. Charles Beard opened an essay entitled "Toward Civilization": "The battle over the meaning and course of machine civilization grows apace, with resounding blows along the whole front. What appeared to be a few years ago a tempest in a teapot, a quarrel among mere 'literary persons,' has become a topic of major interest among hard-headed men of affairs. . . . No theme . . . engages more attention." *Saturday Review of Literature* 6 (April 6, 1930), 894.

10. Lewis Mumford, *Sticks and Stones* (New York: Boni and Liveright, 1924), 81.

11. Lewis Mumford, "Machinery and the Modern Style," *New Republic* 27 (August 3, 1921), 263–65.

12. S. Lane Faison, "Fact and Art in Charles Demuth," *Magazine of Art* 43 (April 1950), 128, for some undetectable reason discusses this painting as a "literary" and "lesser" work.

13. Wolfgang Born, *American Landscape Painting* (New Haven: Yale University Press, 1948), 207, viewed the painting and its title simplistically as an analogy between the "collective structure of Egyptian society and the mass civilization of America." Faison, "Fact and Art," saw the architecture of *My Egypt* as monumental and serene, comparable to the "grandeur of Karnak," no less. Emily Farnham, *Charles Demuth, Behind a Laughing Mask* (Norman: University of Oklahoma Press, 1971), simply referred to the painting in passing, categorizing its title as "witty," its elevators as "monumental" and its composition as "hieratic." Karal Ann Marling, "*My Egypt*: The Irony of the American Dream," *Winterthur Portfolio* 15 (Spring 1980), 25–40, has provided the most extensive and substantial interpretation of *My Egypt* to date. She evaluates the "literature" on the painting, reviews its Dada-Duchamp connections as well as its relationship to Williams, and suggests that its pyramidal form, though evasive, might amount to an elegiac memorial to the diabetic artist himself. As a "self-sufficient barrier between the observer and the landscape," the grain elevator, according to Marling's most ambitious hypothesis, becomes a tragic "American place marker" beyond which lay "the mythic yonder," the great green garden of the frontier dream into which a materialistic, mechanistic civilization had obstructed deliverance (see pp. 36–39). Similar in its sense of tragedy, Barbara Haskell's quite plausible explanation for the title relates the artist's "captivity" in Lancaster to the Hebrew bondage in Egypt. Therefore the building as barrier became "my Egypt" to Demuth. Haskell, *Demuth*, 194–95.

14. William Carlos Williams, *Spring and All* (Dijon: Contact Editions, 1923), 19.

15. Ibid., 27.

16. William Carlos Williams, *Selected Essays* (New York: New Directions, 1969), 28.

17. This book may very well have been the German architect Erich Mendelsohn's *Amerika: Bilderbuch eines Architekten* (Berlin: R. Mosse, 1926), published in Berlin upon his return from a camera-in-hand tour of the United States.

18. Lewis Mumford, "Beauty and the Industrial Beast," *New Republic* 35 (June 6, 1923), 38.

19. Paul Rosenfeld, "Art: Charles Demuth," *The Nation* (October 7, 1931), 371–73.

CHAPTER IO. CHARLES SHEELER'S LOVE OF A NEW INDUSTRIAL REGION

1. As quoted in Frederick S. Wight, "Charles Sheeler," *Art in America* 52 (October 1954), 190-92.

2. Archives of American Art, Smithsonian Institution, Washington, D.C., Sheeler papers, Nsh-1, frame 66. For a concise discussion of the *Mannahatta* project and the significance of Strand's photography to the photography and paintings of Sheeler, see Karen Tsujimoto, *Images of America: Precisionist Painting and Modern Photography,* San Francisco Museum of Modern Art catalogue (Seattle: University of Washington Press, 1982), 77-80, 93-96.

3. William Carlos Williams, *Selected Essays* (New York: New Directions, 1969), 256.

4. William Marling, *William Carlos Williams and the Painters, 1909-1923* (Athens: Ohio University Press, 1982), 109.

5. Constance Rourke, *Charles Sheeler, Artist in the American Tradition* (New York: Harcourt, Brace, and Co., 1938), 124.

6. Ibid., as quoted on pp. 49-50.

7. Erich Mendelsohn, *Amerika: Bilderbuch eines Architekten* (Berlin: R. Mosse, 1926).

8. Quoted in reprint of Hart Crane's 1929 essay, "Modern Poetry," in *The Collected Poems of Hart Crane* (New York: 1946), 177-78.

9. Quoted in Rourke, *Charles Sheeler,* 143.

10. Quoted ibid., 143. See Rourke's typically inspiring description of *Upper Deck,* 143-45.

11. Quoted in Abigail Booth, "Catalogue of the Exhibition and Biographical Notes," in *Charles Sheeler* (Washington, D.C.: Smithsonian Institution Press, 1968), 18.

12. Quoted in Rourke, *Charles Sheeler,* 130.

13. Ibid., 188-93.

14. Leo Marx, *The Machine in the Garden: Technology and the Pastoral Ideal in America* (New York: Oxford University Press, 1964), 355-56. Marx also interprets *American Landscape* as "the machine's incursion into the garden." Martin J. Friedman, *The Precisionist View in American Art* (Minneapolis: Walker Art Center, 1960), 36, refers to Sheeler's *Classical Landscape* as "modern Arcadia." See also Hilton Kramer, "Charles Sheeler: American Pastoral," *Art Forum* 7 (January 1969), 36-39.

15. The discrepancies between the poem and the painting are pondered in the context of Precisionism, a pictorial style of industrial America, by Dickran Tashjian, *William Carlos Williams and the American Scene 1920-1940* (New York: Whitney Museum of American Art, 1978), 84-85, and by Peter Schmidt, "Some Versions of Modernist Pastoral: Williams and the Precisionists," *Contemporary Literature* 21 (Summer 1980), 393.

16. The powerhouse of the Ford River Rouge plant has eight stacks. See Tsujimoto, *Images of America,* plates 39-40 both 1927 photographs by Sheeler.

17. Quoted in Wight, "Charles Sheeler," 199. Peter Schmidt quite rightly observed that Williams had a tendency to slip into "the half-ironic attitude toward industry" that Demuth exhibited in his Lancaster depictions and titles. He also notes that Williams had a more acute sense of the gap between the neo-pastoral

ideals of the so-called Precisionists and American reality. Schmidt, "Williams and the Precisionists," 400. As a doctor of the poor in Paterson, New Jersey, Williams could hardly help revealing his compassion for their estrangement, even in his most concise poems, theories of Objectivism notwithstanding.

18. Charles Sheeler, "A Brief Note on the Exhibition," in *Charles Sheeler: Paintings, Drawings, Photographs,* exhibition catalogue (New York: Museum of Modern Art, 1939), 11.

19. Quoted in James Guimond, *The Art of William Carlos Williams* (Urbana: University of Illinois Press, 1968), 101.

20. Williams, *Selected Essays,* 257.

21. Charles Sheeler, "The Black Book" (a bound notebook), quoted in "Writings of Charles Sheeler," in *Charles Sheeler* (Smithsonian Institution catalogue), 95.

22. William Carlos Williams, "Introduction," in *Sheeler: Retrospective Exhibition* (Los Angeles: Art Galleries, University of California, 1954), n.p.

CHAPTER II. MARSDEN HARTLEY'S RETURN AS A NATIVIST

1. For a sense of this itinerant quest see Barbara Haskell, *Marsden Hartley* (New York: Whitney Museum of American Art, 1980).

2. Marsden Hartley, *Adventures in the Arts* (New York: Boni and Liveright, 1921), 57.

3. See Haskell, *Marsden Hartley,* 111.

4. Paul Rosenfeld, *Port of New York* (New York: Harcourt, Brace, and Co., 1924), 91–92.

5. Ibid., 93.

6. Ibid., 99.

7. Hartley, *Adventures,* 30, 60.

8. Quoted in Gorham Munson, "Homage to Marsden Hartley," *Arts* 35 (February 1961), 38.

9. This essay appears in *Marsden Hartley: Exhibition of Recent Paintings* (New York: An American Place, 1936), 1–5.

10. Hartley, *Adventures,* 47.

11. Grant Wood, *Revolt Against the City,* Whirling World Series, no. 1 (Iowa City: Clio, 1935), 39.

12. Quoted in Clarence Andrews, *Literary History of Iowa* (Iowa City: University of Iowa Press, 1972), 48.

13. Hartley, *Adventures,* 8.

14. Ibid., 6.

15. Quoted in Haskell, *Marsden Hartley,* 118, from a letter from Hartley to Carl Sprinhorn, October 23, 1942, Archives of American Art, Smithsonian Institution, Washington, D.C.

16. For an excellent consideration of Hartley's experiences in Nova Scotia and their effect on his painting, poetry, and prose, see *Marsden Hartley and Nova Scotia,* edited by Gerald Ferguson with essays by Ronald Paulson and Gail R. Scott (Halifax, Nova Scotia: Mount Saint Vincent University Art Gallery, 1987). Of particular significance to understanding the importance of the Mason family to Hartley, this catalogue includes letters Hartley wrote to Adelaide Kuntz in 1935 and 1936, jour-

nal entries he wrote while in Nova Scotia, his fictionalized account of living with the Mason family, *Cleophas and His Own, a North Atlantic Tragedy,* and Gail Scott's explanation of this account, "Cleophas and His Own, The Making of a Narrative."

17. Hartley, *Adventures,* 6.

18. Quoted in Bram Dijkstra, *The Hieroglyphics of a New Speech: Cubism, Stieglitz, and the Early Poetry of William Carlos Williams* (Princeton: Princeton University Press, 1969), 118, from Rosenfeld, "American Painting," *The Dial* 71 (December 1921), 670.

19. Rosenfeld, *Port,* 9.

20. Thomas Craven, "Grant Wood," *Scribner's Magazine* 101 (June 1937), 22.

21. William Carlos Williams, *Selected Letters of William Carlos Williams,* edited by John C. Thirwall (New York: McDowell, Obolensky, 1957), letter dated June 27, 1937, p. 170.

22. Thomas Hart Benton, *An Artist in America* (New York: Robert M. McBride & Co., 1937), 268. Italics are mine.

23. Rosenfeld, *Port,* 9.

24. Thomas Hart Benton, "Mechanics of Form Organization in Painting," *Arts* 11, no. 1 (January 1927), 43-44. For a concise summary of all five articles that ran under this title from November 1926 to March 1927, see Henry Adams, *Thomas Hart Benton: An American Original* (New York: Knopf, 1989), 114-17.

CONCLUSION

1. Ihab Hassan, *The Dismemberment of Orpheus* (New York: Oxford University Press, 1971), 267.

2. William Lyman, *A Virtuous Woman: The Bond of Domestic Union* (New London, 1802).

Index

276

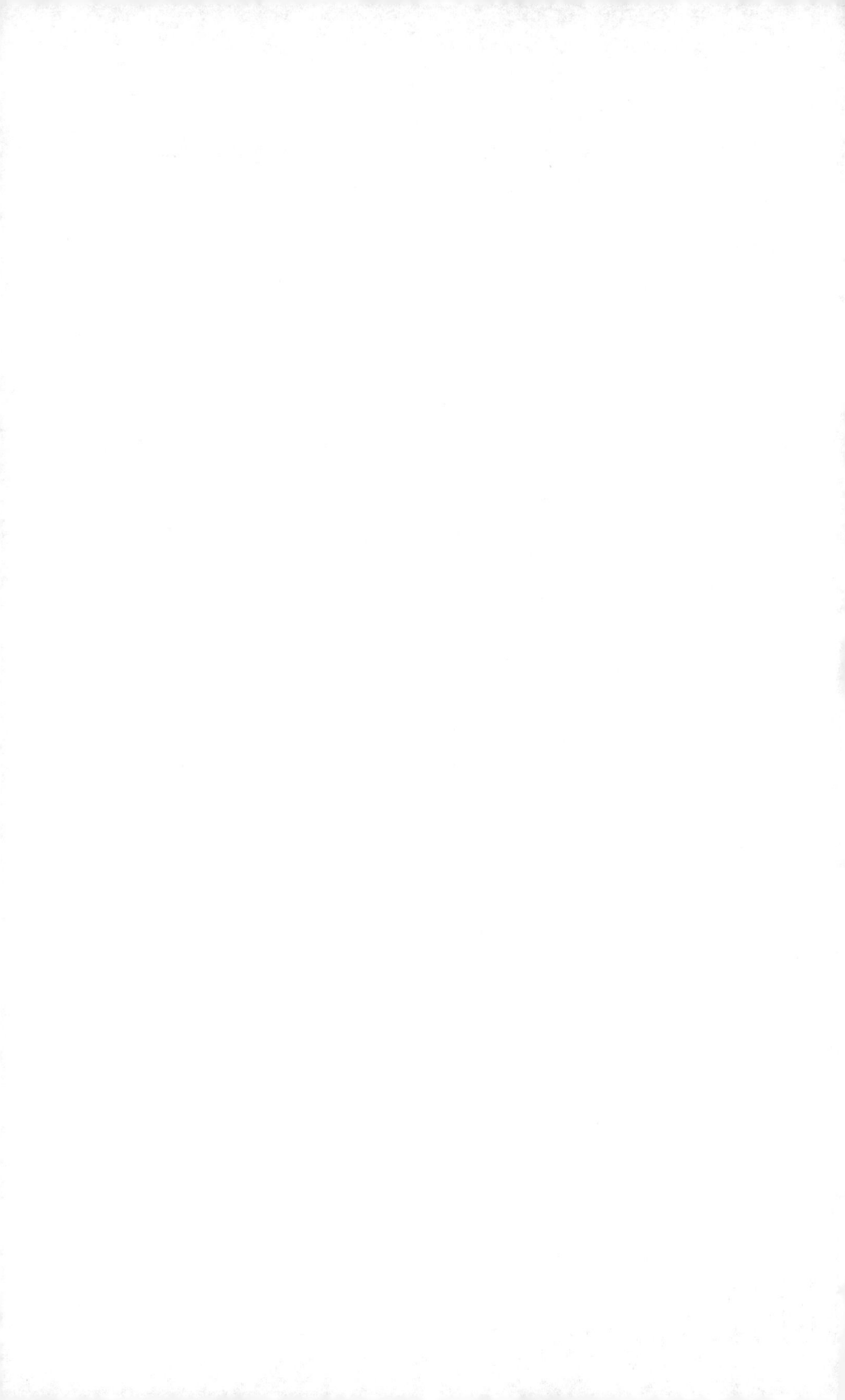